REMEMBERING HISTORY AND HONORING CULTURE

Statues, Monuments, and Memorials on Hawai‘i, Kaua‘i, Maui and Moloka‘i

Cheryl D. Soon, Ph.D.

Mutual Publishing

Front cover photos: Queen Kamakahelei at Kamakahelei School in Puhi, Kaua'i; Father Damien at St. Maria Lanakila Church in Lahaina, Maui; Sugar Planters Immigrant Memorial in Kōloa, Kaua'i; Lawai'i at Na 'Āina Kai Botanical Garden & Sculpture Park in Kīlauea, Kaua'i.

Back cover photos: Queen Ka'ahumanu at Ka'ahumanu Shopping Center in Kahului, Maui; Monument to the Hawaiian Cowboy in Waimea Town, Hawai'i; One of the 88 shrines at Lawai International Center, Kaua'i.

ISBN-13: 978-1-949307-61-0
Library of Congress Control Number: 2023952540

Design by Jane Gillespie
First Printing, April 2024

Mutual Publishing, LLC
1215 Center Street, Suite 210
Honolulu, Hawai'i 96816
Ph: (808) 732-1709
Fax: (808) 734-4094
email: info@mutualpublishing.com
www.mutualpublishing.com

Printed in South Korea

CONTENTS

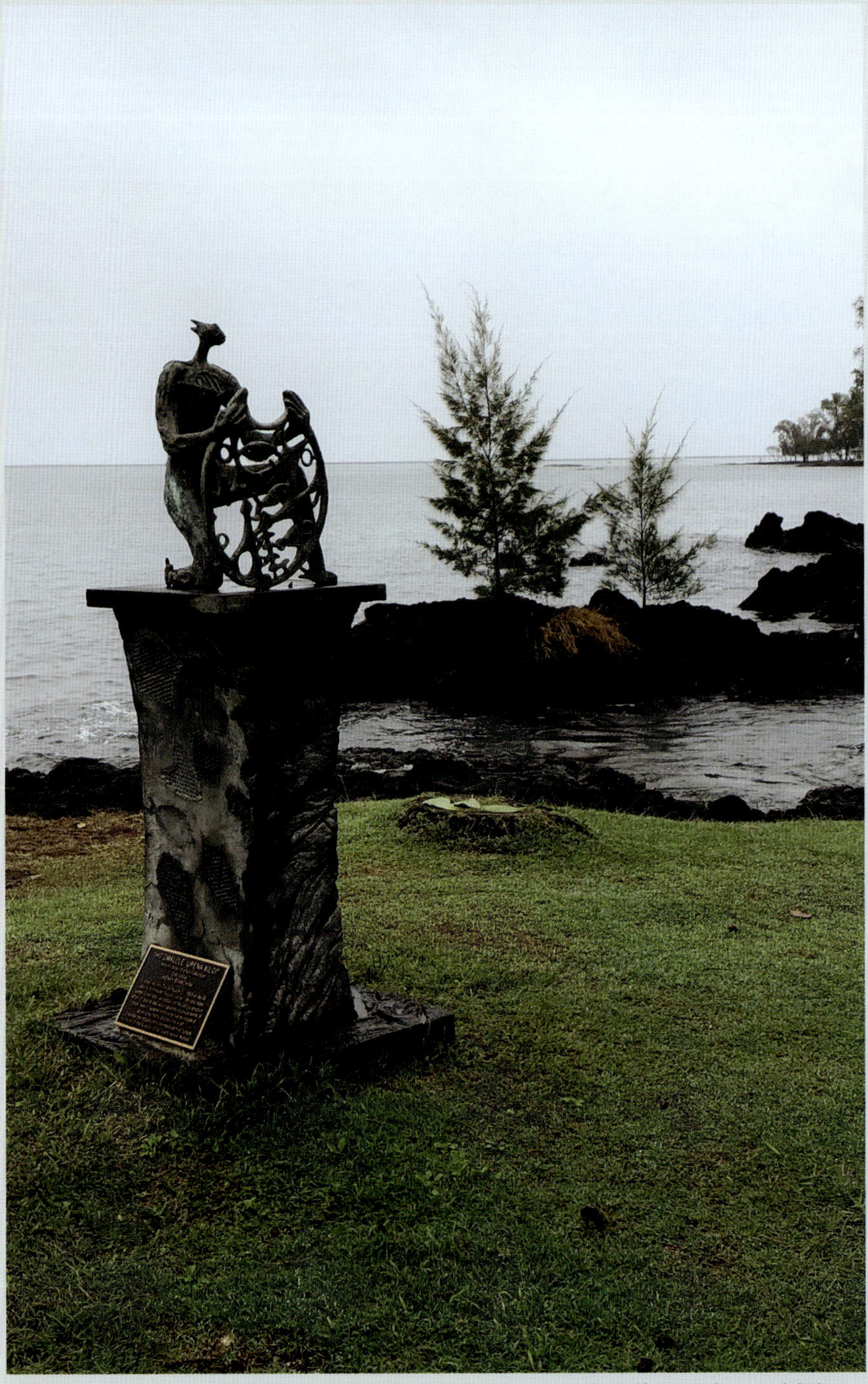

Hawai'i's beauty presents infinite possibilities for integrating man-made artifacts and memorials in mountain or ocean settings as well as gardens and parks. Here, a sculpture honors net fishermen along Hilo Bay. Artist Henry Bianchini. Photo by Cheryl Soon

PREFACE

On Tuesday, August 8, 2023, Hawai'i news stations repeatedly aired "Breaking News" regarding a brush fire on Maui's west side that had reignited, swept by gale force winds, and eventually reached historic Lahaina Town. By dawn, the historic town, its landmarks, homes, churches, boat harbor, and storefronts were in ashes. The losses were staggering. Impacts to families and the community will last generations. The town, once the center of government for the Hawaiian Kingdom, designated a National Historic Landmark in 1962, and home of the oldest Banyan tree in the US, was no longer.

Among the lost or damaged were at least four statues highlighted in this book, along with the churches, temples, schools, and museums that hosted them. This was a somber reminder of the importance, even urgency, of remembering and honoring our heritage.

This book was already getting ready for publication when the fires did their damage. The book was pulled back and updated to reflect the loss and tragedy. In some instances, the pictures taken for this book were possibly the last recorded photos in their original state. Their stories become a tribute to those who cared, who lost, who will rebuild.

Sense of place is a term commonly used in architecture and planning to connote people's attachment to a physical environment. It is a feeling developed through shared experiences and cultural events that help bond people to a particular location.

For the past twenty-plus years, I have had the honor and privilege of regularly traveling to Hawai'i, Kaua'i, and Maui islands in my profession as a city planning consultant. I am grateful to the lifelong friends I made there. They exposed me to their sense of place, communities, unique island's character, and to the wahi pana, sacred places, of their 'āina.

This book is my gift to them as repayment for their friendship, generosity, and aloha. My intention has been to research and document the statues, busts, and memorials that help contribute to their sense of place. I have tried my best, with their expert assistance, to describe the special persons who populated that island and the events that took place throughout its history as expressed in statues and monuments, as well as some of the experiences shared between islands.

The work of showing multiple perspectives is a bit like asking a group of blind men to describe the same elephant. Each man will say something different, depending on whether they approach the trunk, ears, tail or feet. So too will an event appear differently based on where one stands. A battle bears a different perspective from the winner and loser. The stories of Kamehameha, Ka'ahumanu, Saint Damien, or an immigrant group are described differently on Kaua'i, Maui, Hawai'i, or O'ahu according to what he/she did on that island. And the marker(s) and their plaque(s) can vary dramatically as a result.

In Japan, there are markers called tsunami stones, giant tablets on the coastline, that are both memorials to the victims and warnings to descendants not to build their homes past a certain point. These monuments date back to 1896, when two tsunamis killed twenty-two thousand people. The Japanese believe that it takes three generations to forget. Those who experience a trauma pass it along to their children and their grandchildren, but then the memory fades.

To the survivor of a tragedy, that is unthinkable—living through something terrible often creates a strong need to convey the lessons you have learned. Since nothing can replace what you have lost, the only way to extract meaning from that experience is to ensure no one else goes through what you did. Like the tsunami markers at home, after the Japanese came to Hawai'i, they placed wooden obelisk markers to show where fishermen died in rough ocean currents and statues of Jizo in especially dangerous areas to warn others to avoid a similar fate. Although the custom has waned, wooden *jizu* are still found in several shoreline areas. (Clark, *Guardians of the Sea*, 2007).

The importance of remembering and honoring applies to many parts of the experience, but people carry a similar desire to remember things. Installing a tangible instrument of that remembrance offers them a symbolic way to do so. Statues of heroes and beloved persons represent some of the most obvious examples of this type of symbolism. Their lives and achievements are honored and remembered by their descendants and future generations. "We Shall Never Forget" is a common refrain. Busts are similar, although smaller in scale. Sometimes the marker of a person being remembered is simpler, placing a bronze plaque on a stone. The most visible non-statuary markers come in the form of stone memorials, such as monuments and markers that symbolize ideals and values. Examples include memorial bells, eternal flames, and clock towers.

Exploring statues and monuments and the stories behind them creates a unique lens and an exciting way to appreciate Hawai'i. The research for this book was very much a quest, an extensive search for the markers of history in Hawai'i placed by humans throughout the years and the history surrounding them. This book tells the stories behind the subjects represented, the person or people who decided to put them there and why, the artists' efforts and interpretations, and stories of celebration of those symbols. During one of the writers' classes I took at Kaua'i Writer's Conference, Joshua Mohr, a talented writing instructor there, taught students to, "Write the book you want to read." That is what this book is—a collection of stories that have captivated me about the various statues and memorials in Hawai'i and what they say about the islands' cultures.

This book is based on research, site visits, interviews with artists and sponsors, and reviews by local experts. As a professional city planner, and due to my personal interest in place-making, I am blessed with a natural curiosity when it comes to man-made forms and landmarks. Wherever I travel in the world, I indulge that curiosity by seeking out major monuments and statues, and then set out to explore their backgrounds. Unique stories emerge, but, so too, do common themes for remembering and honoring.

My first book, *Reflections in Stone and Bronze* (Mutual, 2022), explored over sixty statues on O'ahu, some related statues beyond O'ahu, and even nationally. The task felt incomplete, however, and a deeper look at the statues on the islands of Hawai'i, Kaua'i, and Maui seemed both important and needed. As the research developed, it became clear that monuments and memorials should be included, along with statues, to properly cover the subject of remembering and honoring the heritages in these island places.

I have incorporated some positive feedback offered by readers of my first book into this volume. One of the most important things I have learned is how much people feel ownership towards these markers and how pleased they were to see them included and recognized in book form. This book has become another way of remembering and honoring important people, events, and cultures.

Another addition, based on reader feedback, is the inclusion of location maps. These maps, one for each of the major populated islands, were beautifully designed by Carah Kadota. The island maps include the flowers and colors assigned to each island. On Hawai'i Island, the color red and 'ōhi'a lehua blossoms are used. For Kaua'i Island, it is purple and the mokihana berry. For Maui, it is pink and the lokelani rose. For Moloka'i, green and kukui nut are used, and for Lāna'i it is orange and the kauna'oa plant.

Why Have Historical Figure Statues?

This is a frequently asked question, and the response is multifaceted. First, statues of historical figures are, in a sense, teachers of history. The figures, along with the base and identifying plaques, mark and memorialize someone's interpretation of what has taken place in the past. The sponsors want to go beyond that third generation.

Second, statues and markers humanize history, giving it a three-dimensional aspect. We can touch them and relate to them in size and bulk. This distinguishes them from books, pictures, or paintings, which are two-dimensional and lack the fullness that one can derive from visiting a physical representation.

Third, statues are often used as centerpieces in public spaces and civic place-making. They are intentional in design and form gathering places, allowing people to linger and reflect or to just pass by to consider another day. They are sites for anniversary celebrations and more. Statues help unite us in a common history and often in pride.

Statues go on to create new histories: The stories of those who helped to make the statue come to reality are shared and spread; as are those who visit and perhaps leave a lei or stone to show their respect.

This glowing assessment of why statues are used to represent historical figures must be tempered with the fact that some subjects and statues are offensive to certain people who may seek to change (or in their view, correct) the story, interpretation, or context of the statues. Others may seek their removal. Protests are a new layer of history.

Book Organization

This book is organized into two parts. The first part covers the statues, busts, and memorials of historical persons located on Hawai'i, Kaua'i, and Maui. For statues and busts, the narrative details the piece name and subject, who commissioned it, the year, and the artist. Full-page, color photos show the look of the statue in its setting to provide the sense of place. Also covered are bronze plaques mounted on large stones meant to honor a particular individual. This style of memorial became especially popular in the first half of the twentieth century in Hawai'i.

Chapter One provides a historical look at Hawai'i in the nineteenth and twentieth centuries, focusing on the histories surrounding those who are the subjects of the statues. It details the subject's origins and the circumstances of their arrival in the Hawaiian Islands. Chapters Two through Four are devoted to the statues and busts on Hawai'i, Kaua'i and Maui respectively. Chapter Two (Hawai'i Island) contains lengthier sections about Kamehameha I; about paniolo culture; and Buddhist statues of Shinran Shonin. While pieces for these appear in sections devoted to other islands, they are first introduced and receive the most attention in this initial chapter where they are introduced. Chapter Four (Maui) contains a lengthier section on Saints Damien and Cope.

The terms "monument," "memorial," and "marker" are sometimes used interchangeably. But whenever appropriate in the book, I use "memorial" to denote a person being honored, "monument" for an event or theme, and "marker" when referring to a place.

Part II is devoted to monuments. This theme is organized with chapters on Monuments to Peace, Honoring the Dead, and Ethnic and Heritage Monuments. The three thematic chapters are sorted by island and grouped to show similarities and comparisons. Chapter Eight describes places where statues are a key element in presenting collections and landscapes. The collections explored include Kepaniwai Park and Heritage Garden in Wailuku, Maui; Hindu Monastery of Kapa'a, Kaua'i; Na 'Āina Kai Botanical Gardens & Sculpture Park in Kilauea, Kaua'i; and three sets of replicas of "88 shrines" in Lāwa'i, Kaua'i; Waimea, Kaua'i; and Pa'auilo, Hawai'i

Chapter Nine is devoted to a commentary called "Reflections." In this chapter, I review what I have discovered during my research and draw together the themes detailed in the book.

The concluding Chapter Ten provides information about the statue artists/makers and includes brief biographies of each. Getting to know such interesting people and learning about their work in their own words was one of the most joyful parts of writing this book. I appreciate their willingness to share key insights about their work.

Use of Hawaiian Words

J. Hau'oli Lorenzo-Elarco reviewed the copy of the draft manuscript and offered suggestions. The spelling of place names follows the conventions of *Place Names of Hawai'i* and the *Hawaiian Dictionary.* 'Okina and kahakō are used to assist with pronunciation. Place names and personal names follow accepted norms of pronunciation. For example, Lahaina and Maui are more commonly used today than the older versions with 'okina. The traditional spelling of Maunakea and Maunaloa are used as single words versus two words. If an organization, publication, or base plate does not use diacritics, this book does not add them.

The back of the book includes a Glossary of Hawaiian Terms.

Gratitude

I have lived in Hawai'i for forty-seven years, and my half-Hawaiian husband, Ray Soon, has been my companion through each step in the book creation process. Ray deserves extra credit for taking the majority of the photos presented, except where noted.

I wish to thank several of the island photographers who contributed their work: Christian R. Cook, Andrew Graham, Aubrey Hurd, Lucas Kashtan, Travis Ota, Mikiala Pescara, Paul Senano, Rebecca Soon, David Tarnas, Jan TenBruggencate, and Sarah Yamanaka.

I appreciate all those who invited us in to share their collections: the Kaua'i Museum, Na 'Āina Kai, the Himalayan Academy, Lawai International Center, many Catholic Churches and Buddhist Missions, Dr. Billy and Pat Bergin, the Returned Peace Corps Volunteers of Hawai'i, Miki'ala Pescaia of National Parks Service, and so many others. I appreciate the time they spent to explain the intricacies in different cultures, to Billy Bergin about paniolo culture, to Rev. Kazunori Takahashi about the differences between Buddhist sects, and many others.

Because I am non-Hawaiian, I try to remain humble and cautious when describing the history, culture, and events of this multilayered society. Out of respect, I have asked other knowledgeable persons in the community to review stories and entries. I am grateful to my beta readers: Andi Simpson of Los Gatos, California; John Clark of Honolulu, Jan TenBruggencate of Kaua'i, and Hans Santiago of Hawai'i island for reviewing key sections within their expertise. All errors are my own. I also want to thank Jo-Anna Herkes for her help in gathering permissions on Hawai'i Island, and Rebecca Soon for her help organizing photos. Finally, I am grateful to Bennett Hymer and Jane Gillespie at Mutual Publishing for all their support over the past two years.

I am grateful to live in this beautiful place called Hawai'i.

"...the loveliest fleet of islands that lies anchored in any ocean"

— Samuel Clemens, aka Mark Twain

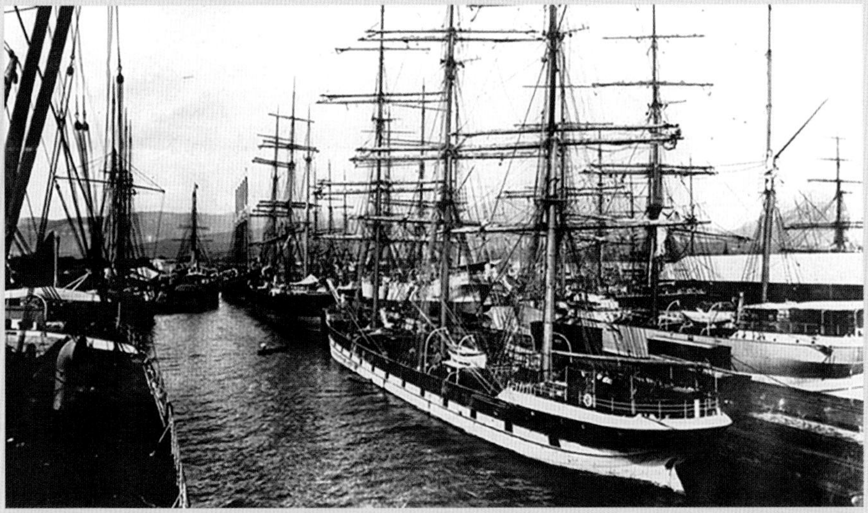

These clipper ships in Honolulu Harbor are typical of those used by Portuguese from Madeira and the Azores. All immigrant groups sailed to Hawai'i, not always on such lovely vessels.

CHAPTER ONE

ORIGINS AND ARRIVALS

A people without knowledge of their past history, origin, and culture is like a tree without roots.

—Marcus Garvey

The statues and monuments found on the islands of Hawai'i, Kaua'i, and Maui are three-dimensional illustrations that represent an intriguing time in Hawai'i's history. Most of these statues' subjects lived during the nineteenth and early twentieth centuries, an era when Hawaiian governance transformed from separate territories run by chiefs who fought each other in continuous war to a single kingdom united under one king. By the end of the nineteenth century, this system was overthrown by merchant interests who wanted affiliation with the United States so they could enjoy favorable trade and freedom from tariffs. Hawaiian society and economy changed quickly in this period.

Because many who will read this book have limited exposure to Hawaiian history, this chapter provides brief explanations for arrivals, where people came from, why they came to Hawai'i, and for those who stayed, what their impact was. There are other sources where such information can be found, but this book only explains the stories behind major players who became the subjects of statues or memorials. The book identifies who sponsored those pieces and what those sponsors wanted to be remembered, honored, or respected.

As is customary, the narration starts with an origin story, how this place came to be. This look is both at the origin of the islands as lands within the Pacific Ocean and the origins and arrivals of human inhabitants and their resulting footprint on the islands.

Every culture has a unique way of telling its origin history. For centuries, the Hawaiian origin story, called the Kumulipo, has been memorized, chanted, and passed down. The full Kumulipo is a sacred chant which includes the genealogy of the royalty who dwelled in the islands.

According to Kamehameha Schools, the Kumulipo has 2,102 lines and takes over three hours to complete. It was not recorded until the nineteenth century. Queen Liliʻuokalani prepared her translation in 1897 while she was under house arrest at ʻIolani Palace; her version was later published. Martha Warren Beckwith's 1951 translation is considered one of the standard written versions.

The Hawaiian origin creation story begins with utter darkness connected to invisible intelligence. The darkness is called Papahānaumoku (Papa), the mother of gods, earth, and the underworld. Wākea is the sky father who provides creative light. These opposites are different, yet equal. Together they bear a daughter, Hoʻohokukalani.

Wākea and Hoʻohokukalani in turn had a stillborn child. From the place of the child's burial grew a daughter, the kalo (taro) plant, providing sustenance for mankind. A second child, Hāloa, becomes the first man on earth, a high-ranking chief, and ancestor to all Hawaiian people.

Using a geologic lens, the Hawaiian archipelago originated deep in the Pacific Ocean and took over seventy million years to form. It started with an underwater volcano spewing lava towards the surface. The Pacific Plate slowly moves over this "hot spot" in a northwest direction forming multiple land masses. Some of these eroded and became atolls or coral reefs. According to Grigg (*In the Beginning: Archipelago: The Origin and Discovery of the Hawaiian*, Island Heritage Publishing, 2012), Kauaʻi and Niʻihau formed fifty million years ago, followed by Oʻahu, Molokaʻi, Maui, Lānaʻi, Kahoʻolawe, and the largest (and newest) island, Hawaiʻi. The hot spot is currently forming a new seamount named Kamaʻehuakanaloa, once known as Lōʻihi, twenty miles off the coast of Hawaiʻi. While Kamaʻehuakanaloa is still three thousand feet underwater, it may eventually become a new island. Years of rain and erosion form the mountains and valleys that are seen today. Understandably, the resulting ʻāina (land) differs from island to island, with Kauaʻi having the most pronounced peaks.

Plants and creatures made long passages to this land mass, blown by the winds and sea currents. The first animals were likely birds that carried seeds on their bodies and in their beaks. They settled onto the land, which, for centuries, was home to species found nowhere else on earth. Hawai'i has the world's greatest number of extinct and endangered species.

The origin story for humans, as told above, starts with Hāloa. The taro plant is the origin and relative of humans. The first people began to arrive by double-hulled canoes as early as 400 C.E. They traveled using stars, birds, and currents for navigation over a distance of more than two thousand miles from the Marquesas, proving that they were skilled navigators. Habitation of Hawai'i seems to have been deliberate, as the Polynesian travelers brought provisions to help sustain them in new places. Multiple crossings between Hawai'i and their homelands likely took place. Once on land, they fished in the sea, hunted in the upper reaches, and planted in the lower reaches. By the fifteenth century, the islands were densely settled. Around this time the voyages ended.

Eight of the land masses were large enough to be permanently settled by the voyagers. Due to their relative isolation, each island maintains its own distinct identity and diversity, both ecologically and within the parameters of human experience. Each island maintained its own political hierarchy of chiefs, ali'i, and other rulers. For decades, intra-island fighting over land and resources raged. Whenever a chief died, his title and land holdings became up for grabs, settled most often by bloody battle. By the sixteenth century, the chiefs began to capture nearby islands, with control often going back and forth among relatives and allies.

This was mostly resolved when Kamehameha united all the islands under a single Kingdom of Hawai'i in 1810. While he never conquered Kaua'i by battle, Kamehameha negotiated with Kaua'i Chief Kaumuali'i, to become part of the kingdom, in return for Kaumuali'i having the lifetime role of vassal and political ruler of Kaua'i.

It is incorrect to ascribe this entirely to Kamehameha. In fact, many historians attribute the success as shared with the intellect and skills of his wife, Ka'ahumanu. She was a trusted advisor and companion in both battle and in meetings with rivals and foreigners. Upon Kamehameha's death, Ka'ahumanu became the kuhina nui, or prime minister, during the rule of his two sons. This period lasted for several decades.

The balance of power, however tenuous, was altered with a new arrival: British Captain James Cook in 1778. Cook originated from England, and his early career spent tracking Newfoundland's coastline gained the attention of the Admiralty and the Royal Society. They sponsored his three scientific voyages to the Pacific. Cook, in turn, named Hawai'i the Sandwich Islands for one of his financial sponsors, John Montagu, the fourth Earl of Sandwich.

The first voyage (1768-1771) on the ship *Endeavor* took him to Australia and New Zealand. This mission was to observe the "Transit of Venus" while in Tahiti. Venus' position was considered key to understanding the scale of the universe. But Venus crosses the sun only once every 120 years; if it were missed, the next opportunity would be in 1874, or in modern times, 2004. Cook's second voyage (1772-1775) aboard the ships *Resolution* and *Adventure,* took him to the Antarctic in search of a new continent. During the return of the second voyage, Cook went to Tahiti, New Zealand, and several other islands of the Pacific, awarding him his exposure to the Polynesians.

Cook's third voyage (1776-1780) was on the *Resolution* and the *Discovery*, with an assignment to find a northwest passage across the North American continent (no such passage existed then due to ice, but does today). Cook was a cartographer and explorer by profession, charting maps of the islands and logging detailed journals, descriptions, and illustrations of the flora, fauna, and people.

It is useful to consider Cook's arrival from the perspective of Indigenous persons. It must have been quite a surprise for the Hawaiians when, one morning, two ships appeared out of nowhere, bearing creatures with the palest skin imaginable. Goodhue (*Queen Kaahumanu of Hawaii*, McFarland & Co. Publishers, 2022) likens this to awakening one morning and having a flying saucer land in your backyard. Little space people start emerging, then disappear just as quickly. Showing their stature, bravery, and curiosity, Kamehameha, Ka'ahumanu, Kahekili and others in Kaua'i and Hawai'i (Cook never moored at Maui for lack of a suitable harbor) warmly welcomed the newcomers and showered them with gifts, a show of their royal stature and generosity. Some of these gifts can still be seen at museums around the world.

The third voyage did not end well. Cultural misunderstandings and a dispute over a stolen boat brought the death of Cook and four of his shipmates. The remaining crew left the harbor with a parting bombardment by cannon, killing over a dozen Hawaiians. But Cook's death did not end the visits by foreign ships; in fact it may have brought attention to the isolated islands, enticing others to travel there. Cook was one of the first white men to come to Hawai'i, and his arrival forced the archipelago into the modern world. Hawai'i's long history of isolation had ended.

After Cook's logs were published, Hawai'i became a favorite port of call for traders. They came from China, Boston, and other locales around the world. The ship visits continued to undermine the practice of local customs and kapu, or forbidden things. Major ports in Honolulu, Lahaina, and Hilo became accustomed to providing supplies to ships for the next leg of their sea journeys. An industry to provision whalers (who came long distances from New England) thrived for forty years between 1819 and 1859. At its height around 1845, over seven hundred whaling ships arrived in Hawai'i. This only ended when petroleum oil wells replaced the need for whale oil for lamps and other uses.

The appearance of Cook and his crew brought other surprises. The most unfortunate was disease. Within a few years, Hawaiians began dying from gonorrhea and syphilis. It was observed that the ship crew and their guests did not follow the Hawaiian kapu. This changed when they were on the ships, with no ill effect. But it undermined confidence in continuing the kapu throughout the islands, including with Ka'ahumanu, who had tired of the restrictions placed on her.

When their husband Kamehameha died in 1819, Ka'ahumanu and Kamehameha's sacred wife, Keōpūolani, conspired to end the 'ai kapu which restricted women from eating with men, or from eating certain foods such as bananas, pork, and certain fish. All these things, the women had done on the ships (rationalizing that the kapu applied only on land, not sea). Next, Ka'ahumanu attacked the religious practices of chiefs, heiau (temples), and idols, ordering the heiau and idols destroyed. These changes were transformative and left the Hawaiian society without a fixed religion, order of authority, or moral code.

This void was soon filled by the arrival of a new group, the Calvinist missionaries of the American Board of Commissioners for Foreign Missions based in Boston. They were urged and inspired to do so by Native Hawaiian Henry ʻŌpūkahaʻia who, after his parents were killed, had been brought by a ship master to live in New Haven, Connecticut. There he became Christian and was anxious to spread the religion back home.

The missionary group came from towns in New England, were trained and ordained at a Mission Church in Cornwall, Connecticut, and in some cases hastily married to qualify for the mission. The first group was led by Hiram Bingham, Asa Thurston, and their wives. After a grueling 164-day-long, eighteen-thousand-mile trip around Cape Horn on the *Thaddeus*, they arrived first at Kawaihae and then in Kailua-Kona on April 4, 1820.

Their objective was to convert the Hawaiian people to their faith. To accomplish their mission, they created a written Hawaiian language based on phonetics and encouraged literacy in hopes that the people would read the Bible and embrace Christianity. The printing press they brought with them (which can still be seen at Mission House Museum on O'ahu) greatly enhanced their attempts to improve the indigenous people's literacy. Seeing pamphlets in their own language motivated the Hawaiians toward learning. All this was done with the approval of the ruling regent, Kaʻahumanu.

Over a forty-year period (1820-1863) about 180 Protestant missionary men and women arrived to serve as teachers, doctors, and farmers at eighteen stations on Hawaiʻi, Kauaʻi, Maui, Oʻahu, and Molokaʻi. Missionaries from other religions followed which had an equally great long-term impact.

Catholic Don Francisco de Paulo Marin arrived in 1793 or 1794 and baptized nearly 300, including several chiefs. In 1819, High Chief Kalanimōkū, an advisor to the first three Kamehameha kings, was baptized Catholic upon a French ship, the *Uranie.* Shortly thereafter his brother, Chief Boki, Royal Governor of Oʻahu was baptized. Pioneer Catholic missionaries Bachelot, Armand, and Short arrived in 1827, three priests from the French-based Congregation of the Sacred Hearts of Jesus and

Mary. Their party sailed on the ship *Le Heros* from Bordeaux, France. They were greeted by powerful converts such as O'ahu Chief Boki (who was already a Catholic). The priests and their converts ran into religious persecution, were banned, and then forcibly exiled by Ka'ahumanu in 1831, not allowed to return for another eight years.

Due to the insistence of French officials, King Kamehameha III allowed the priests to return and gave them lands upon which to build a church. The priests laid out a plan to build multiple congregations and open over one hundred Catholic schools. A century later, in 1941, the vicariate was designated to be a diocese, and a bishop was named. The Catholic religion thrived as groups from countries with Catholic traditions arrived to work on the plantations, comprised of Portuguese, Polish, Puerto Rican, and Filipinos immigrants, along with others.

Due to the many foreign arrivals of merchants, religious factions, and otherwise, Hawaiians contracted measles, smallpox, and typhoid, diseases for which they had no immunity. Within twenty years, the Hawaiian population dropped by half. Leprosy is believed to have spread to Hawai'i from China around 1848. By early 1866, cases had grown, and those afflicted were shipped to Kalaupapa where they were isolated and forced to live in caves and rudimentary shacks. Here again, the Catholic church played a major role. Responding to pleas from King Kalākaua, the church sent priests and nuns to tend to the afflicted. Most famed among those to arrive were Father Damien from Belgium and Mother Marianne Cope from New York. Their work and sacrifices were greatly respected and appreciated.

Kalākaua was instrumental in urging other countries to allow immigrant groups to come to Hawai'i to work on the burgeoning sugar plantations. Sugar plantation owners, some of them children of New England missionaries, had started the industry in Kōloa, Kaua'i, in 1835. The sugar industry was "king" for over one hundred years. In its prime, sixty-three plantations thrived on the land.

The plantations needed land, water, and manpower. Starting in the 1850s, laborers were encouraged to come to Hawai'i, and it is estimated that nearly 340,000 people arrived over five decades. The first workers came from China, followed by workers from Japan, Puerto Rico, Portugal, Korea, Scotland, the Pacific Islands, and the Philippines arriving on ships arranged by Kalākaua and his men. They were usually segregated by ethnicity or camps and spoke mainly their original language, only speaking pidgin English to communicate between camps. The cultural diversity of Hawai'i is part of their lasting legacy.

Statues

Exploring Hawai'i's history of origins and arrivals in the nineteenth century through historical statuary figures starts with Kamehameha and Ka'ahumanu. The statue of Kamehameha in Kapa'au is the first Western-style statue ever made for installation in Hawai'i. It was commissioned by King David Kalākaua, fashioned in Paris, France, by Thomas Ridgeway Gould, and meant as a centennial monument to Captain Cook's arrival. It arrived too late for that celebration, due to being lost at sea, then accidentally found, returned, and repaired. Meanwhile, a second version was commissioned. When both arrived around the same time, it was decided to place the original in Kapa'au near Cook's birthplace in Kohala, the second was placed in Honolulu. Amid great pageantry, both versions were installed as part of the coronation of King David Kalākaua and Queen Kapi'olani in 1883, although he had reigned since 1874.

The distinctive statue, standing seven feet in height, shows Kamehameha in a warrior pose and apparel, pointing toward his people. What differs is that the Kapa'au version has since been painted over the gold leafing, a practice that continues to this day. A third version, this one forged at a foundry in Italy, can be found in Hilo. Originally meant for a hotel in Kaua'i, local objections there led to it being stored and removed from public view. A Kamehameha School Alumni Group petitioned to have it sent to Hilo where it has occupied an honored position since 1993. A fourth statue of Kamehameha is found on Maui, this one created by the highly respected Herb Kawainui Kāne. It graces the entrance of the Grand Wailea-Waldorf Astoria Hotel. To this day, there is no statue of Kamehameha on Kaua'i.

Maui is the only island with a statue of Ka'ahumanu. She was born on Maui and lived there for many years as ruler while her husband Kamehameha was off at war. Upon Kamehameha's death, the role of king passed in turn to each of his young sons, at which point Kaumuali'i became Kuhina Nui (regent), sharing the power with them.

Kaua'i cherishes their last king, Kaumuali'i, and has two statues honoring him, one in Līhu'e at the Kaua'i Museum, and one near his home in Waimea. Kaumuali'i married Ka'ahumanu in what was a forced political alliance, but it helped to keep things peaceful after the death of Kamehameha.

Other royal figures are not honored as frequently in statue form on Kaua'i, Maui, and Hawai'i islands as they are on O'ahu. By 1850 the capital had moved from Lahaina to Honolulu and most royals resided there. However, the sacred birthplaces of Kamehameha III (Kauikeaouli) in Kealakekua and of Kūhiō in Kōloa are marked with plaques and a bust for Kūhiō. There is also a bust of Kamehameha III at a school in Lahaina which is located on the site of his home.

Statues of religious saints Damien and Cope are found in Maui and Moloka'i, where these two tended to the leprosy patients in schools, hospitals, and the communal homes that they built. The variety and number of statues stands as testimony to how beloved and admired they are. The statues are made from precious materials such as marble and koa wood.

There are no statues or memorials to the missionaries who preached and converted people for forty years, perhaps reflective of their stoic demeanor and non-lavish lifestyle. Their descendants, however, built up the sugar industry, and several of them are memorialized in stone with bronze medallions and plaques near their homesteads. Many fountains and gates were built and named for missionary families, as well as buildings, streets, and other places.

A great number of monuments honor the immigrant groups who arrived in Hawai'i to work in the plantations. Such workers are celebrated in the assembly piece by Jan Gordan Fisher which depicts five groups of sugar workers, each in their native dress and working with their tools. In time, their hard work and contributions were honored by descendants who placed memorials dedicated to the first arrivals. These can be found in abundance on almost every island.

Moving into the twentieth century, we see the types of elements that are memorialized begin to change. That century experienced two world wars and major conflicts in Korea and Vietnam, leading to the loss of many lives. Families, veterans, and other loved ones placed war memorials that included statements that their loss shall not be forgotten. The many peace memorials in Hawai‘i placed during this period celebrate non-violence, negotiation, and peaceful ways of living in hope that wars would never come again. One important peace statue is of Senator Spark Matsunaga in Hanapēpē, Kaua‘i. A plaque depicting the face of Dr. Martin Luther King, Jr. was etched in Maui. Other peace symbols include bell towers, some of these replicas of bell towers in Japan.

The information in the pages that follow is organized by island to help situate the statues, memorials, and markers examined. This chapter's short presentation of Hawai‘i's history shows that it is a tapestry, weaving together people, times, and ideas. Focusing on only one thread does not allow one to appreciate the full picture. Hawai‘i today is the sum of all that has come before.

CHAPTER TWO

STATUES, BUSTS & MEMORIALS ON HAWAIʻI ISLAND

Ola Na Moku—The Islands Prosper

—from the County of Hawaiʻi seal

Hawaiʻi Island has the greatest land area among the populated chain and is often called the Big Island because of this. Despite its population of just over two hundred thousand living on 4,028 square miles, it remains a place where everyone seems to know each other. The spirit of confidence fills the island, and its people display resiliency and fierce pride. Wide-open spaces, farming and ranching, and the ocean's borders help create that independent islander identity. This is also the location for several active and dormant volcanoes, which dominate the landscape.

Kamehameha I was born in Kohala, rose to power to become the island king, and lived out his life in Kona. Statues can be found of him in both Kapaʻau (Kohala District) and Hilo. Also in Hilo is a statue of King David Kalākaua in a county park named for him. A major iconic bronze of Ikua Purdy and dedicated to the paniolo culture sits in the middle of Waimea Town. Religious statues include three of Shinran Shonin (Hilo, Waimea, and Keaʻau) and Saint Benedict (the Painted Church) in Captain Cook in Kona. There is a statue of Damien in Pāhoa and a bust of him at St. Benedict Church.

STATUES, BUSTS & MEMORIALS ON HAWAI'I ISLAND

SUBJECT	TYPE	LOCATION	ARTIST	YEAR
King Kamehameha I	Painted Bronze	Kapa'au (Kohala)	Thomas Gould	1883
King Kamehameha I	Bronze statue	Hilo	R. Sadrin	1997
King David Kalākaua	Bronze statue	Kalākaua Park Hilo	Henry Bianchini	1988
Hawaiian Cowboy/ Ikua Purdy	Bronze statue	Waimea	Fred Fellows	2003
Shinran Shonin	Bronze statue	Hilo Betsuin	Unknown	1985
Shugyo Daishi	Bronze statue	Hilo Hooganji	Unknown	2007
Shinran Shonin	Bronze statue	Puna Hongwanji	Unknown	
Shinran Shonin	Bronze statue	Waimea Hongwanji	Unknown	2010
Saint Benedict	Bronze Statue	Captain Cook	Unknown	
Father Damien, Joseph De Veuster	Bust	Painted Church	Bob Pashby & Sean Browne	Late 1980s
Albert Lyman	Medallion Cameo	Hilo Airport	Don Rich	1992
Kamehameha III Birthplace	Memorial Plaque	Kealakekua Bay	Unknown	1911
Captain Cook	Obelisk	Kealakekua Bay	British people	1877
David Douglas	Memorial Plaque	Slopes of Mauna Kea	Donated by Hilo Burns Club	1934

HAWAIʻI ISLAND

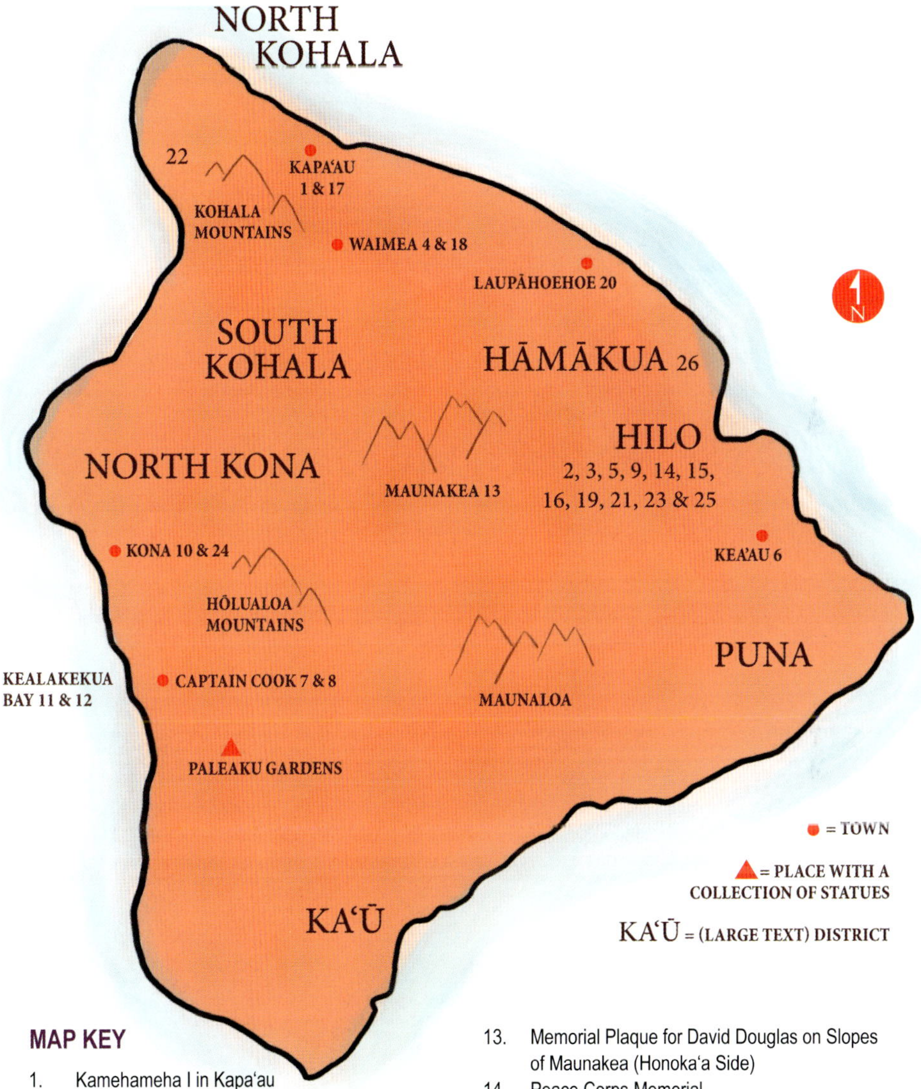

MAP KEY

1. Kamehameha I in Kapaʻau
2. Kamehameha I in Hilo
3. David Kalākaua in Hilo
4. Purdy in Waimea
5. Shinran Shonin in Hilo
6. Shinran Shonin in Keaʻau
7. Saint Benedict in Captain Cook
8. Bust of Damien in Captain Cook
9. Medallion Cameo of Albert Lyman at Hilo Airport
10. Kamehameha Helmet at Kona Airport
11. Memorial Plaque Kamehameha Birthplace in Kealakekua
12. Obelisk to Captain Cook in Kealakekua Bay
13. Memorial Plaque for David Douglas on Slopes of Maunakea (Honokaʻa Side)
14. Peace Corps Memorial
15. Kalākaua Park War Memorial
16. Wailoa Park War Memorials
17. Kohala Civic Center War Memorials
18. Tarawa Camp Memorial
19. Ka Malu Aloha Memorial to Fallen Police
20. Laupāhoehoe Tsunami Memorial
21. 1960 Tsunami Clock, Waiākea
22. Puerto Rican Memorial
23. Plantation Bell Tower in Hilo
24. Honokōhau Settlement Plaque
25. Bicentennial Memorial at Liliʻuokalani Gardens
26. Paʻauilo 88 Shrines

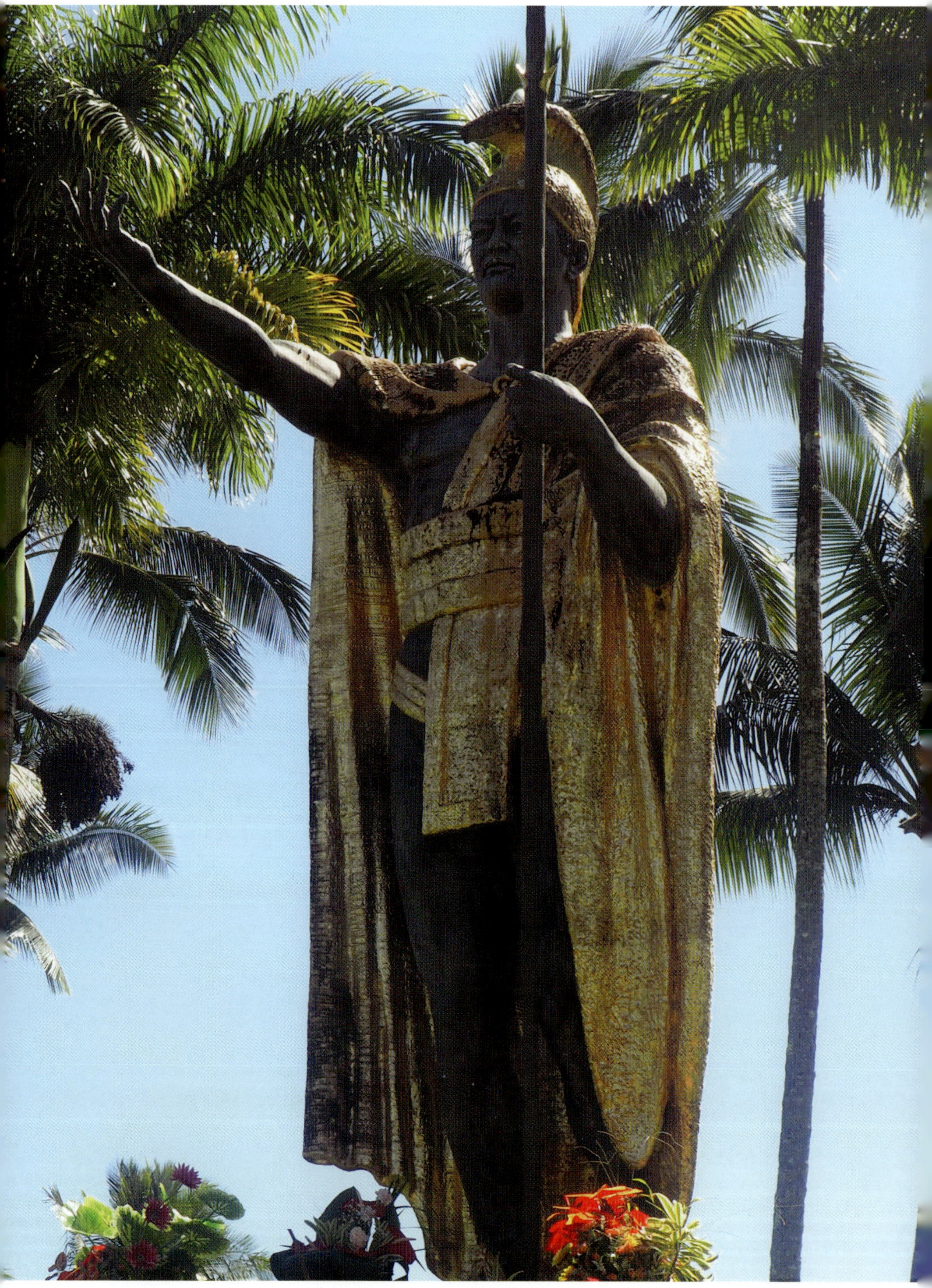

Kamehameha The Great

(c. 1758-1819)

Hawaiʻi Island is the island most associated with Kamehameha. He was born in North Kohala around 1758 and raised in that region to become a warrior. After uniting all the islands in 1810, he moved his capital back to Kailua-Kona, Hawaiʻi, until his death.

Kamehameha's life from birth was associated with rivalry, fighting, and conquest. Originally named Paiʻea, he descended from the House of Keawe on his mother's side and from a Kohala chief on his father's side, although some accounts name Kahekili of Maui as his father. Priestly dreams foretold that Kamehameha would challenge the rule of Alapaʻi. Because of this belief, his life was put in jeopardy, and he was immediately sequestered to a remote valley in Kohala until Alapaʻi died.

Kamehameha was taken into the royal court by his uncle Kalaniʻōpuʻu (chief of the Kona District), where he was trained as a high-ranking aliʻi. These skills were put to early use. Upon Kalaniʻōpuʻu's death, Kamehameha was given custody of the war god and temples, while the land went to the old leader's son Kīwalaʻō. Other chiefs were dissatisfied with Kīwalaʻō's leadership, and he was killed. At that point, Kamehameha obtained control of half the island. When a volcanic eruption wiped out parts of an opposing army, this was interpreted as confirming the prediction that Kamehameha had a "divine right" to rule.

Kamehameha was not in direct line to succeed his uncle, Kalaniʻōpuʻu, upon the latter's death in 1781. Disputes over land distribution among the chiefs, including Kalaniʻōpuʻu's two sons, precipitated continued battles for years. Kamehameha was trained as a warrior and developed great strength and abilities. Kamehameha demonstrated this strength in 1789 when in his thirties he overturned the Naha Stone, which weighed nearly three tons. The physical ability to move this massive stone was a sign of high chiefly capacity. This confirmed a prophecy that Kamehameha would be a great warrior king.

Opposite page: Kamehameha I statue in Hilo. Used with permission from King Kamehameha Celebration Commission. Photo by Ray Soon

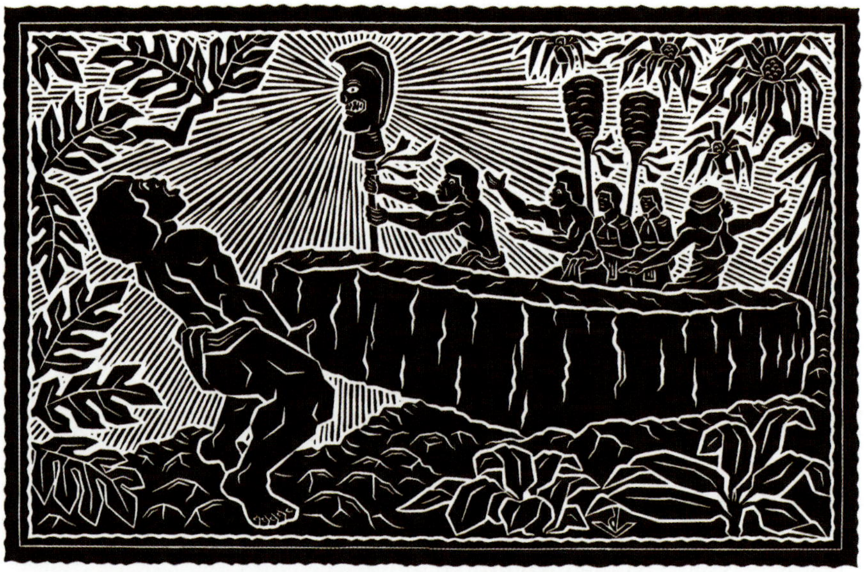

Kamehameha lifting the Naha Stone by Dietrich Varez. Used with permission.

The Naha Stone was originally located along the Wailua River in Kauaʻi. According to the legend, the Naha Stone was moved to Hawaiʻi island in a canoe by Chief Makaliʻinuikuakaaiea. Many centuries ago. It was given a prominent place in several Hilo heiau, as was the nearby upright Pinao Stone. The Naha Stone can now be seen in front of the Hilo Library on Waiānuenue Avenue where it has been since 1952.

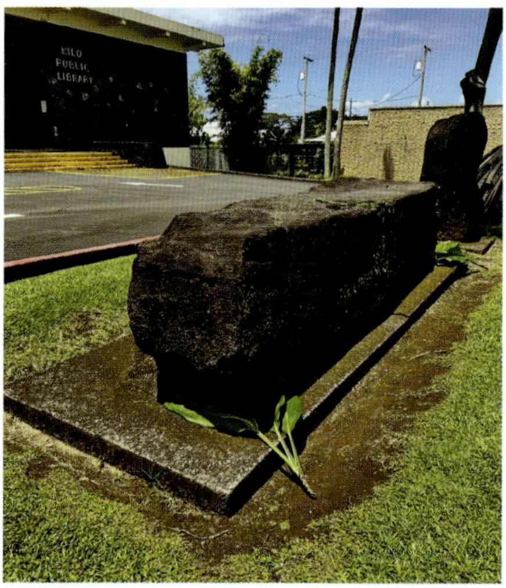

Naha Stone in Hilo. Photo by Rebecca Soon

Eventually, Kamehameha was able to rule the island of Hawaiʻi. This was partly due to his acquired familiarity with and use of Western arms. Hilo was the first capitol chosen and it is there that he built his fleet of war canoes, the waʻa peleleu.

An important goal began to emerge: to unite all the islands under single rule. This dream was shared by both Kahekili and Kamehameha, and they became rivals to achieve it. The goal of unification became more pressing as fur traders conducting business between China and North America started to use Hawaiʻi as a port of call. In 1790, Kamehameha built the impressive heiau of Puʻukoholā above Kawaihae Harbor, dedicating it to the god of war, and in fulfillment of the priestly prediction that he would unify the islands under one rule. The construction of the enormous heiau was interrupted by a sea battle with Kahekili, a conflict that severely weakened Kahekili's forces. After that, Kahekili retreated to Waikīkī where he died at age eighty-three.

In 1790, two shipmen from the trading ships were stranded when their ships were ambushed off Kohala. The two, Isaac Davis (from the *Fair American*) and John Young (who had been on the *Eleanora)*, proved valuable to Kamehameha due to their knowledge and expertise in modern weaponry. Both men would remain loyal to him throughout his lifetime. Englishman Young married Kamehameha's niece and for a time he served as Royal Governor of Hawaiʻi (1802-1812) while Kamehameha was away. Young was at Kamehameha's side when he died.

Kamehameha invaded Maui (then under the control of Kahekili) using these ships, cannons, and muskets, along with a fleet of canoes carrying several thousand warriors. His forces won battles in Hāna, Wailuku, and "Īao Valley. Five years later, after Kahekili's death, Kamehameha set off for Oʻahu, securing Maui, Molokaʻi, and Lānaʻi along the way. He positioned his canoes all along the southern coast of Oʻahu, waiting to do battle with Kalanikūpule, Kahekili's son. The battle pushed back into Nuʻuanu Valley, where he prevailed over the opposing forces.

By 1795, Kamehameha was in control of all islands except Kauaʻi, which was ruled by Kaumualiʻi. He made two ill-fated attempts to reach the island by sea. The first was interrupted by a severe storm. Six years later, a second attempt was foiled when a plague inflicted his forces. Perhaps humbled by these forces of nature, Kamehameha pursued negotiation, but was rebuffed. By 1810, Kaumualiʻi decided to surrender his kingdom to avoid a blood bath and further loss of life. Kaumualiʻi was made "vassal" which meant he would rule Kauaʻi until his death, but that foreign affairs would be solely under the governance of Kamehameha.

Kamehameha lived out his life in Kailua-Kona, Hawaiʻi Island. For many, Kamehameha came to symbolize Hawaiian independence, pride, and self-respect. A solemn celebration featuring lei draping, chants, and the hoʻokupu, or offering, occurs annually on Kamehameha Day, June 11.

Kamehameha I had eleven children with one of his wives, the high-ranking Keōpūolani, daughter of Kīwalaʻō, thus helping to ensure the continuation of the dynasty. Three children survived into adulthood, and two became king. Liholiho became Kamehameha II for five years from 1819 to 1824. The second son of Kamehameha I, Kauikeaouli, became Kamehameha III upon Liholiho's death.

Statues of Kamehameha on Hawaiʻi Island

There are two statues of Kamehameha on Hawaiʻi Island: the original in Kapaʻau, near his birthplace; the second in Hilo, his first capitol. The statues were erected nearly one hundred years apart, a testimony to his enduring influence and cherished memory.

The Kapaʻau Kamehameha was the first Western-style statue made for placement in Hawaiʻi. The statue was commissioned by the Hawaiʻi Legislature in 1878 at the request of King David Kalākaua. Its design was meant to reflect the level of esteem awarded to the deceased ruler.

Ironically, the Kamehameha statue sponsored by King Kalākaua was intended to be unveiled at the 100th anniversary of explorer Captain James Cook's arrival. The first statue (and the second as the story will show) was created after the Hawaiʻi Legislature commissioned (for $10,000) a sculpture of Kamehameha I. This led to a complicated yet fascinating chain of events.

Records stored in the Hawaiʻi State Archives were researched by Glenn Wharton and recorded in his book, *The Painted King* (2012). Wharton found key correspondences between the artist Thomas Ridgeway Gould; the primary mover in the legislature, Walter Murray Gibson; and the reigning king, David Kalākaua.

The finished statue left the German port of Bremen in August 1880 on its way to Hawaiʻi. A storm was encountered, a fire broke out, and the ship struck a reef, causing it to sink to the bottom of the sea near the Falkland Islands. The legislature quickly commissioned a second cast to be made from the plaster model. They also ordered four partial-gilt, bronze, bas-relief panels for the sides of the pedestal. Gould died while this was in progress. The relief panel work was completed by his son.

According to Wharton, officials in Hawaiʻi were surprised when the statue arrived earlier than expected, on March 27, 1882. They were especially surprised to discover that this was the first, not the second statue. It had been retrieved, apparently, by a fisherman who sold it to a junk dealer. A British captain recognized it for what it was and purchased it for a pittance. He later sold it at more than double its price to the Hawaiʻi officials. Certain damage occurred in this process, such as gouges in the cloak and the loss of the spear and the right hand but, on the whole, it was in good condition, considering what it had undergone.

The monument committee decided to install the repaired first cast in Kohala District. Ceremonies were held as part of the installation, with many dignitaries and members of the royal family in attendance.

The second cast was erected in Honolulu. By then, the Cook Centennial had come and gone. After some debate, Gibson convinced everyone to make the unveiling part of the coronation celebrations for King Kalākaua at ʻIolani Palace, which took place on February 12, 1883.

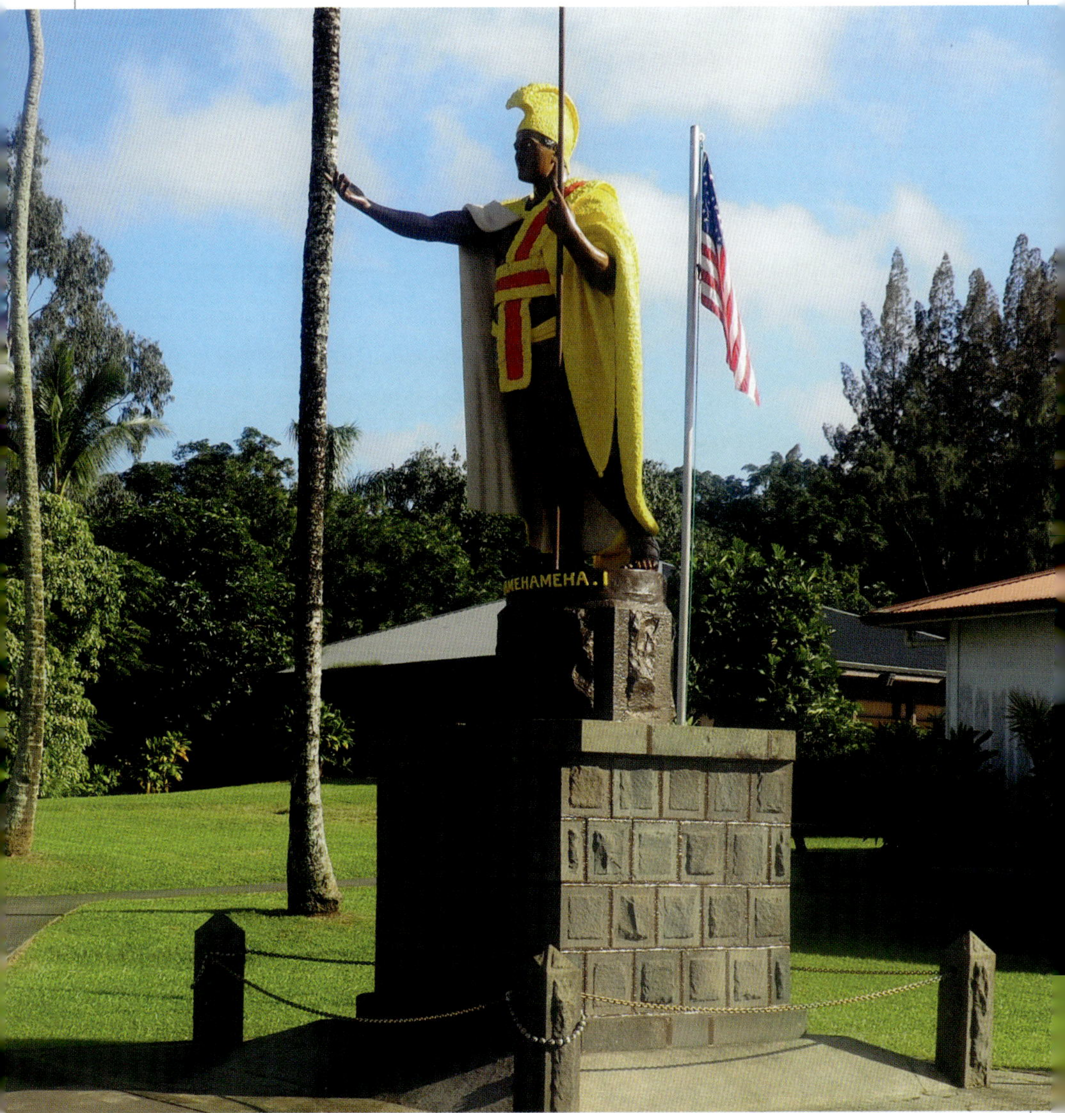

Kapa'au Kamehameha. Used with permission from King Kamehameha Celebration Commission.
Photo by Ray Soon

Statue of King Kamehameha in Kapaʻau

Owner	State of Hawaiʻi
Commissioned by	King Kalākaua and Hawaiʻi Legislature
Location	Old Courthouse, Kapaʻau
Year Erected	1883
Artist	Thomas Gould

The Kamehameha statue in Kapaʻau sits upon a round drum base with Kamehameha I in block letters painted yellow. The statue base, in turn, sits upon a rectangular base several feet high decorated as blocks within blocks, again giving a regal and commanding presence as befitting the subject. The ground there is several feet above road level, granting the statue great presence; even when driving past, one is drawn to the figure. There are four concrete short pillars connected by a minimal chain fence roping off the structure, which signifies going past it is kapu, or not allowed. Ki (ti) leaves nearby signify that this is a sacred place. The statue faces the street gazing down upon the historic main street buildings of Kapaʻau town. Two flagpoles, one with the American flag, one with the Hawaiian flag sit behind the statue. Behind those are the buildings of the old courthouse and civic center.

After viewing the original sketches, Gibson asked that Kamehameha's face be adjusted to look younger—approximately forty-five years old. The spear was originally set to be barbed at the end, not straight, a sign of peace. Hawaiians would have used a barbed spear to signify war. Other European errors in the costume were made on the cloak, which included a tassel; the length of the train; and the shoulder sash. Whar-

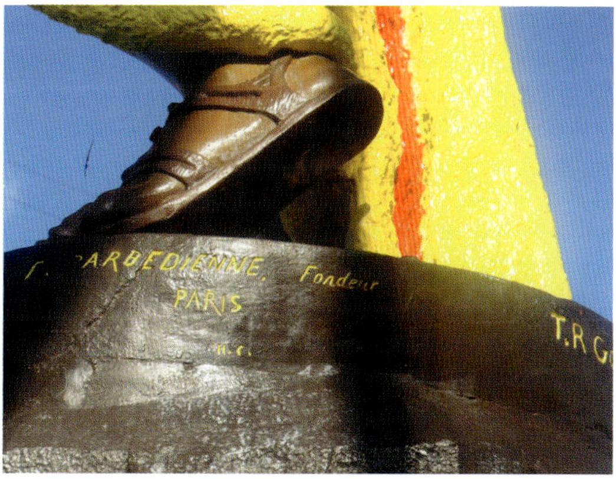

Kamehameha foot detail. Photo by Ray Soon

ton speculates that these were intentional, a "deliberate effort to celebrate a Hawaiian conversion to European values, while retaining sanitized versions of both cultural traditions…a distancing from the 'savage' and 'barbaric' past."

The base shows the name of the sculptor (Thomas Gould) and his location (Paris). Attribution would never be done in Hawaiian culture as it is thought to inhibit the mana.

Restoration

The Kapaʻau Kamehameha statue is painted regularly, usually annually, in brown with bright yellow and red paint covering the gold. Glenn Wharton, a restoration expert, was hired by the State of Hawaiʻi in 2010 to remove the many layers of paint and return the gilding. Out of cultural respect, Wharton undertook a year-long consultation process with the community, among which were descendants of Kamehameha explaining what the statue meant to them. While many perspectives were aired, in the end, the community turned to its kūpuna who pronounced that the statue would remain painted. This is recorded in his book *The Painted King* (2012), a classic read for anyone interested in restoration, history, and cultural engagement.

A close-up detail around the round base that the statue sits upon is painted brown with writing in yellow stating the name of the bronze foundry (*F. Barbedienne, Fondeur Paris H.C.)* and the name of the artist (*T.R. Gould Inv. Ct Fecit Florence 1879*). Both artists were well-renowned in that time. Barbedienne Foundry had pieces in the Vatican and in museums throughout Europe. Gould was an American from Boston who moved to Florence to pursue his interest in design. He has several pieces in public places throughout Massachusetts.

King Kamehameha Statue in Hilo

Owner	State of Hawaiʻi, DLNR, State Parks
Commissioned by	Princeville Corporation Gifted to Hilo Chapter, Kamehameha Schools Alumni Association in 1997
Location	Wailoa River State Recreational Area, Hilo
Year Erected	1997
Artist	Manufactured at Fracaro Foundry in Vicenza, Italy

The statue of Kamehameha in Hilo was erected on June 10, 1997, just before Kamehameha Day. It has a dramatic and well-manicured setting easily seen from the bay-front road. It is rooted on a rock moss base and grassed landing which in turn sits on another rock moss wall about four feet high, providing a commanding presence. The gilding and patina are similar to the Honolulu version, not the painted version found in Kohala. The Hilo statue at Wailoa River State Recreation Area, standing at fourteen feet, is the tallest of the Kamehameha statues.

This version of the statue was intended for a resort in Princeville, Kauaʻi, but after there was local opposition to its placement there, it remained in storage for two years. Upon their request, it was donated by the Princeville Corporation to the Kamehameha Schools Alumni Association, Māmalahoe Chapter who paid for it to be shipped and installed.

A statue committee worked with local officials to have it placed at Wailoa River State Recreation Area. It is said that among Kamehameha's favorite dishes were the wahoo (ono) or ʻamaʻama (mullet) that lived in the Wailoa fishpond, which is now the backdrop for this important statue.

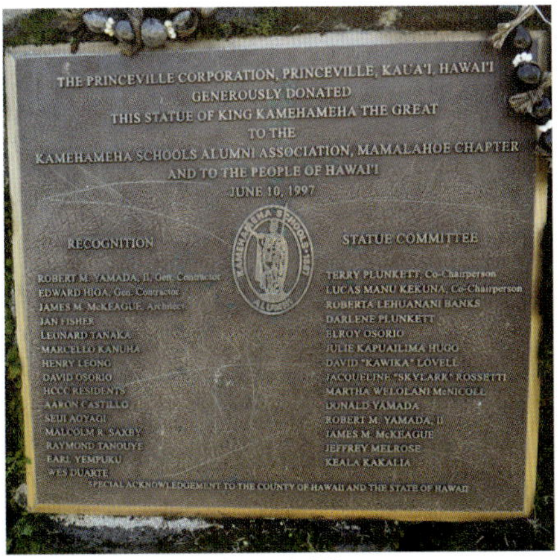

The Kamehameha plaque in Hilo. Photo by Ray Soon

The Kamehameha statue is a source of great local civic pride

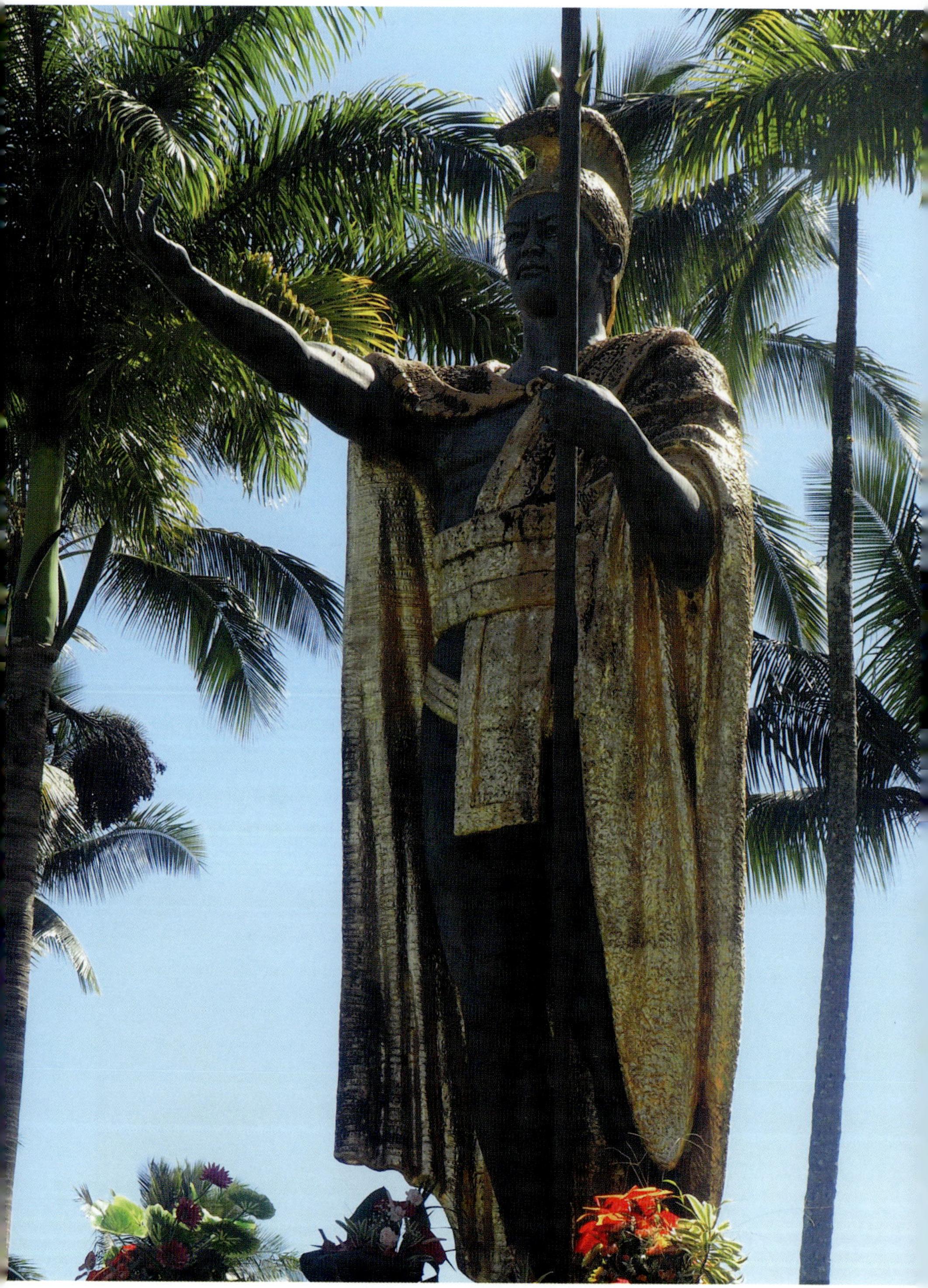

Kamehameha Hilo. Photo by Ray Soon

and is honored with lei draping during Kamehameha Day ceremonies each year on June 11. There are several plaques describing the importance of the area. One reads:

> *Kamehameha the Great was born in the 1750's and rose to become one of the most important figures in Hawaiian history. He lived during a period of great transition n Hawaiian society, having witnessed the arrival of the first Westerners when he was in his early 20's. Kamehameha was a fierce warrior and an able leader who successfully consolidated control over all the Islands by 1810.*
>
> *Kamehameha was a frequent visitor and resident of Hilo. While in his mid-40's, he oversaw the construction of his great Peleleu Fleet from the shores of Hilo Bay. The fleet consisted of over 1,000 canoes and included massive war canoes capable of carrying over 100 warriors each. Many of the great peleleu canoes were hewn from koa trees harvested from the forests of Mauna Kea. The fleet was provisioned from the rich natural resources of the Hilo area.*

A second interpretive display explains major features of Hilo Bay from the days of Kamehameha: Kanoa Heiau (one of six major luakini or sacrificial heiau on the island of Hawaiʻi); Naha Stone (used to show prowess as a warrior and foretell the future of royal born children); and the seven ahupuaʻa surrounding Hilo Bay—Hilo Palikū, Hilo One, Kaipalaoa, Waiolama, Hilo Hanakahi, Piʻopiʻo, Mokuloa, and Makaokū.

Kamehameha Markers & Sculpture

There are many locations on Hawaiʻi Island with a Kamehameha connection. For example, there is a marker in Laupāhoehoe near the tsunami memorial. The information sign explains Kanawai Mamalahoe, "The Law of the Splintered Paddle."

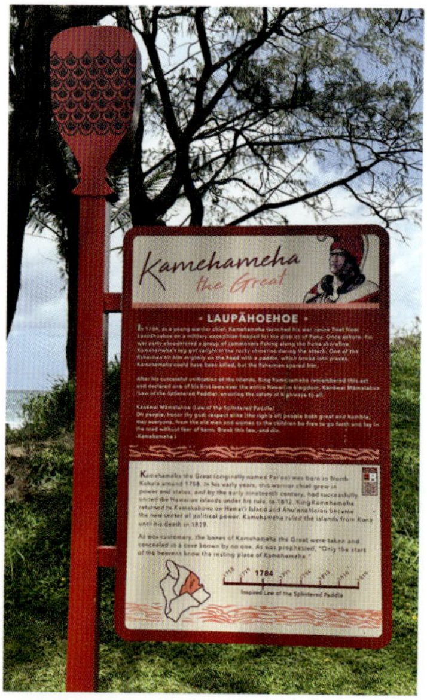

Photo by Rebeca Soon

In 1784, as a young warrior chief, Kamehameha launched his war canoe fleet from Laupāhoehoe on a military expedition headed for the district of Puna. Once ashore, his war party encountered a group of commoners fishing along the Puna shoreline. Kamehameha's leg got caught in the rocky shoreline during the attack. One of the fishermen hit him on the head with a paddle, which broke into pieces. Kamehameha could have been killed, but the fisherman spared him.

After the successful unification of the islands, King Kamehameha remembered this act and declared one of his first laws over the entire Hawaiian kingdom, Kanawai Mamalahoe (Law of the Splintered Paddle), ensuring the safety of passage to all.

Mahiole Sculpture at Kona Airport

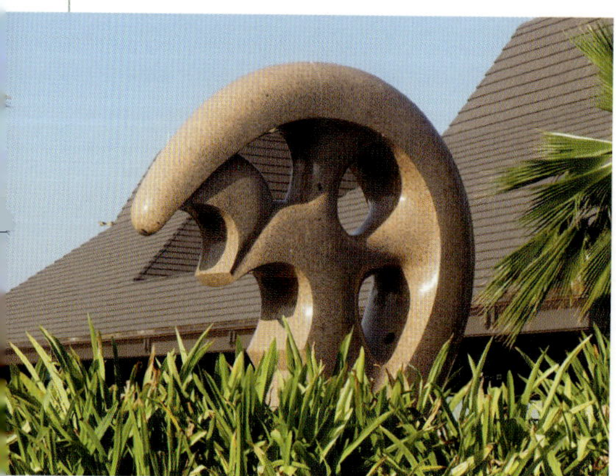

Mahiole by Sean K.L.L. Browne at Kona International Airport at Keahole [CO431]. Red granite figure completed in 2000.10'2"x10'2"x2'9". Hawai'i State Foundation on Culture and the Arts. Photo by Ray Soon

Another important piece that honors Kamehameha is the sculpture "Mahiole" which is a headpiece worn by Hawaiian royalty. It is symbolic of Kamehameha I on his home island of Hawai'i and was made from red granite by Sean K.L.L. Browne. The sculpture was installed in 2000 at Kona International Airport at Keahole.

King Kamehameha III

(1814–1854)

Owner	Daughters of Hawaiʻi
Commissioned by	Daughters of Hawaiʻi
Location	Keauhou Bay, near Kona, Hawaiʻi Island
Year Erected	1914

Upon the death of Liholiho in 1823, Kamehameha's other son Kauikeaouli became King Kamehameha III. He was only twelve years old at the time. He was robbed of a father (Kamehameha died when he was five), mother (Keōpūolani died when he was ten), and anyone else who could have served as a role model. He was guided during these times by Queen Kaʻahumanu, who continued in her role as kuhina nui until her death in 1832. After a youth spent indulging in

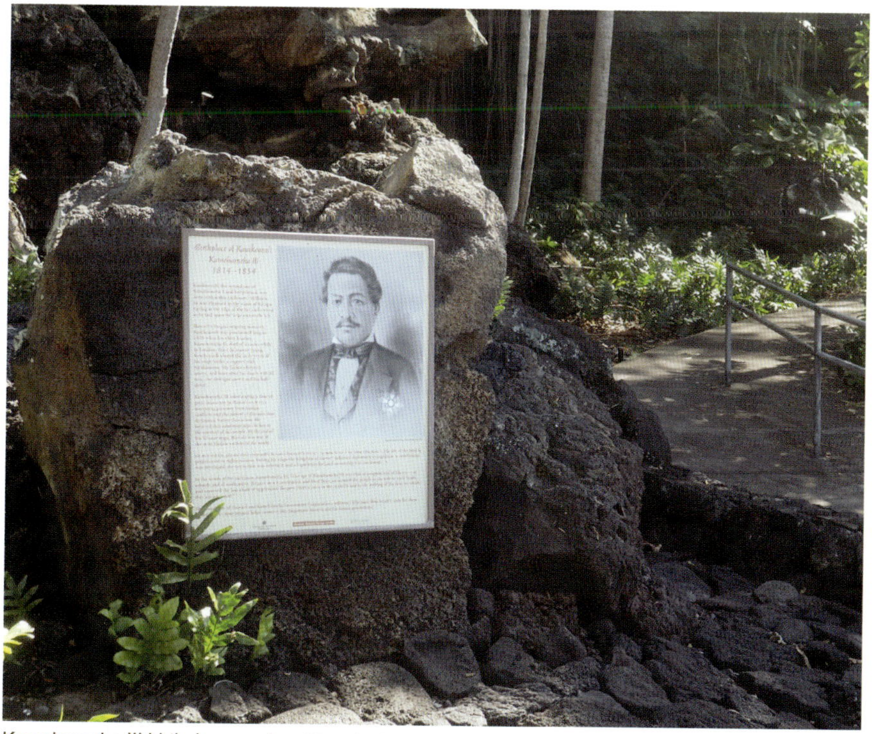

Kamehameha III birthplace marker. Photo by Ray Soon

reckless behavior, Kauikeaouli took the reins of government seriously in his mid-twenties and became an effective leader.

Kamehameha III is spoken of as a loving, gentle, and kindhearted king. He formed a constitution to grant his people the right to vote and to own land. He uttered the phrase that would become the state motto: "Ua Mau ke ea o ka ʻĀina I ka Pono" (The Life of the Land is Perpetuated in Righteousness). His reign was one of the longest, and he grew greatly during those years from an unruly youth to a man with serious governance and diplomacy abilities, both of which were required during those times.

During his reign, missionaries converted much of the population to Christianity. They set up missionary schools and created a written language from the sounds of the Hawaiian spoken language. In a short period, Hawaiʻi became among the most literate countries in the world. But during that same period, disease ravaged the population, which dropped from one hundred fifty thousand to seventy thousand. Sugar interests were starting on the islands, and crops were being planted for future trade. Kamehameha III had little direct influence over any of these outside changes.

What he did influence, with the assistance of missionary Dr. Gerritt Judd, was the creation of a constitutional monarchy (the 1840 Constitution) that established order for his people and the country's finances, replacing the former kapu system. The next step was to address standards for land distribution beyond the mōʻī, or king. This was achieved in the Great Māhele of 1848. A land commission oversaw the distribution and distinguished the lands belonging personally to the king (one million acres), the government lands for the benefit of the people (one and a half million acres), and the land grants to freehold farmers (one and a half million acres).

By the 1840s, foreign influence had become more aggressive in Hawaiʻi politics. The French demanded that land grants go to the Catholic Church. In 1843, acting unilaterally, Commander George Paulet forced Kamehameha III to surrender the kingdom to the British, contrary to the traditional role of the British as Hawaiʻi's protector, not ruler. This arrangement lasted only five months. It was protested by rivals France and the United States and reversed by the Pacific Fleet commander, British Rear Admiral Richard Thomas.

Birthplace Marker in Keauhou

This small site is against the wall of a hill that leads down to the Keauhou Bay ramp. It is the location of Kauikeaouli's birth in 1814, son of Kamehameha I and Princess Keōpūolani. According to the story, Kauikeaouli was stillborn. But one of the chiefs believed he could be saved, placed him on a rock, and chanted until he came to life.

The memorial at Kauikeaouli's birthplace is due to the vision and effort of the Daughters of Hawai'i who placed the plaque in 1914 as a monument to celebrate his 100th birthday. Celebrations began at Kawaiaha'o Church on O'ahu with Queen Lili'uokalani in attendance. She performed the unveiling of the stone tablet. On each side of the tablet stood the pūkaua (leader) and pa'akāhili (kahili bearer) in traditional style. Over 2600 persons were in attendance. There were pule (prayers) and blessings and chants; according to a nūpepa (Hawaiian newspaper) account, many were so rare they were only passed on verbally from generation to generation, never written.

Eleven years later, in 1925, the Daughters of Hawai'i acquired a small parcel of land that includes the foundation of the house and the stone where he was born. It was added to the Hawai'i Register of Historic Places (site 10-37-4383) on January 13, 1978, and the National Register of Historic Places (site 78001018) on July 24, 1978.

For Further Reading: Klieger, P. Christiaan. *Kamehameha III*. Green Arrow Press. 2016.

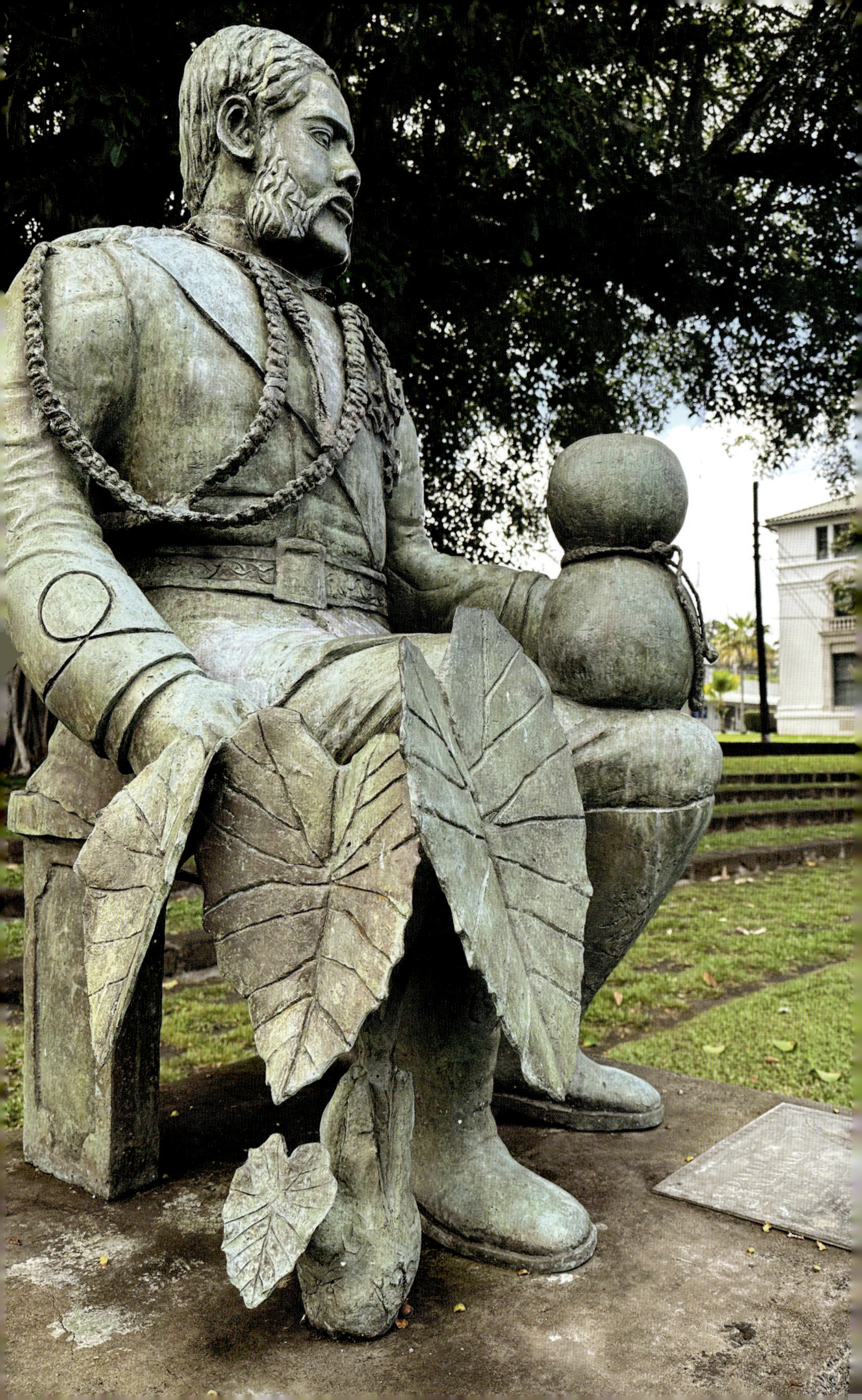

King David Kalākaua

(1874-1891)

Owner	County of Hawaiʻi
Commissioned by	County of Hawaiʻi
Location	Kalākaua Park, Downtown Hilo
Year Erected	1988
Artist	Henry Bianchini

Kalākaua was born to a high chief and chiefess, and according to Hawaiian custom, was adopted by Chiefess Kaniu, who took him into the court of Kamehameha III on Maui. He returned to Oʻahu at age four to start his education at the Royal School. He was a good student and studied law before he was assigned to various military and government positions by Kamehameha IV.

When Kamehameha V died in 1872, Kalākaua was a candidate to be elected king, but lost to Lunalilo who lived only a year. A second election made Kalākaua king in 1874.

It was widely felt that Kalākaua always had the interests of his people at heart. He was a member of Young Hawaiians, whose motto was "Hawaiʻi for the Hawaiians." Kalākaua wanted Hawaiians to broaden their education, and between 1880 and 1887, he sponsored eighteen students each year, financing their studies abroad to England, Scotland, China, Japan, and California.

Kalākaua sailed to the United States in 1874 and negotiated the seven-year Reciprocity Treaty, which eliminated tariffs on sugar and other Hawaiʻi exports. Renegotiation of the extension of the treaty included a provision that gave the United States exclusive rights to Pearl Harbor. The sugar industry prospered to the extent that the need for labor greatly increased. In 1881, Kalākaua undertook a world tour to encourage the immigration of sugar plantation workers. This resulted in thousands of Portuguese and Japanese laborers coming to Hawaiʻi.

Opposite page: Kalākaua statue in Hilo. Photo by Rebecca Soon

Kalākaua did much to restore pride in Hawaiian culture, and he brought back the ancient art forms of martial arts, lua, and surfing. He also brought back hula, mele, and chant, that act being one of his most enduring legacies, which lives on in the annual Merrie Monarch Hula Festival in Hilo. During his life, Kalākaua lived up to his nickname of "Merrie Monarch" due to his fondness for music, dance, ʻukulele, parties, food, and drink. During the two weeks of his coronation, he brought back nightly hula, which had previously been banned.

The Hawaiian Music Hall of Fame honors Kalākaua along with his brother and sisters as the Nā Lani ʻEhā (The Heavenly Four) for their contributions to Hawaiian musical culture and history. The four include Kalākaua, Princess Miriam Likelike, Prince William Pitt Leleiōhoku II, and Queen Liliʻuokalani. Kalākaua wrote the words to the song "Hawaiʻi Ponoʻī," which is now the state anthem (arrangement by Henri Berger). Several of his other songs were published. Liliʻuokalani wrote *Aloha ʻOe* (Farewell to Thee).

Impressed by the European royal lifestyle and wishing to emulate it, Kalākaua commissioned the construction of ʻIolani Palace, modeled after the royal palaces he saw in his travels. Built and furnished at a cost just over $340,000, a large sum at the time, it was the first building to have electricity. During this time, he also commissioned the statue of Kamehameha I, the first Western-style statue in Hawaiʻi.

Despite the tag "Merrie Monarch," Kalākaua's reign was marked by tragedy, pain, and dark clouds. His actions as monarch played into the hands of annexationists who wanted the United States to take over Hawaiʻi. In July 1887, an organization calling itself the Hawaiian League took control of the government and forced Kalākaua to sign a new constitution called the "Bayonet Constitution" severely restricting kingly powers. One of their first acts was to recall all the students who had gone abroad.

Kalākaua first designated his brother William Pitt Leleiōhoku as his heir, but Leleiōhoku died in 1877 while Kalākaua was still living. Kalākaua then designated his sister Lydia, who took the name Liliʻuokalani upon her ascension. Kalākaua died in his hotel room on a trip to California in 1891, paving the way for a female monarch, his sister Liliʻuokalani, who would become the last monarch Hawaiʻi would have.

Statue in Kalākaua Park, Hilo

Here Kalākaua is depicted in uniform and military braids. He is in a seated pose with his head turned, looking up at the chains of the islands. The statue is near a banyan tree which he planted over a century ago. Beneath the statue sits a time capsule (from 1991 during a solar eclipse), designed by Bianchini, set to be opened during the total solar eclipse in 2106.

Bianchini won the commission after a competition. Speaking with Kristin Zambucka, author of a book on Kalākaua (*Kalakaua: Hawaiʻi's Last King*, original 1983, reprint by Mutual Publishing, 2022) he came to appreciate Kalākaua's talents including his skills as an inventor. Bianchini inscribed three versions of Kalākaua's submarine invention on the back of his belt. In Bianchini's original concept for Kalākaua, he wore a helmet on his head, held a torch, and lacked facial features. Upon consultation with elder Pua Kanahele, Bianchini added the taro root in one hand and an ipu heke (double gourd musical instrument) in the other, signifying Kalākaua's love and devotion to the sustenance of the people of Hawaiʻi and to their culture. The model was Gabriel Kealoha, Jr.

The piece was carved and the molds were made by Bianchini in Hawaiʻi. The bronze casting was done by Alf Peterson at a foundry in Venice, California. The pieces were returned and Bianchini completed the welding in Hawaiʻi. The piece has proven popular, and always has lei placed upon it with extra attention during the Merrie Monarch Hula Festival, which is named in his honor. The community received a grant from the Historic Hawaiʻi Foundation to improve the setting of the park, the stairs, and other features, symbolic of the ongoing commitment to the space and the subject.

For Further Reading: Allen, Helen G. *Kalakaua, Renaissance King*. Mutual Publishing. 1995.

Zambucka, Kristin. *Kalakaua: Hawaiʻi's Last King*. Original 1983. Mutual Publishing. Reprint 2022.

Monument to the Hawaiian Cowboy and Ikua Purdy

(1873-1945)

Owner	Paniolo Preservation Society
Commissioned by	Paniolo Preservation Society
Location	Parker Ranch Shopping Center, Waimea, Hawai'i
Year Erected	2003 near Post Office; moved to current location in 2006
Artist	Fred Fellows

The Hawaiian Cowboy Monument and statue in the middle of Waimea is one of the more important and significant pieces in Hawai'i. It represents a revered culture and way of life that has existed for more than 150 years and continues to this day. This story is one of brotherhood and community, of pride and aloha.

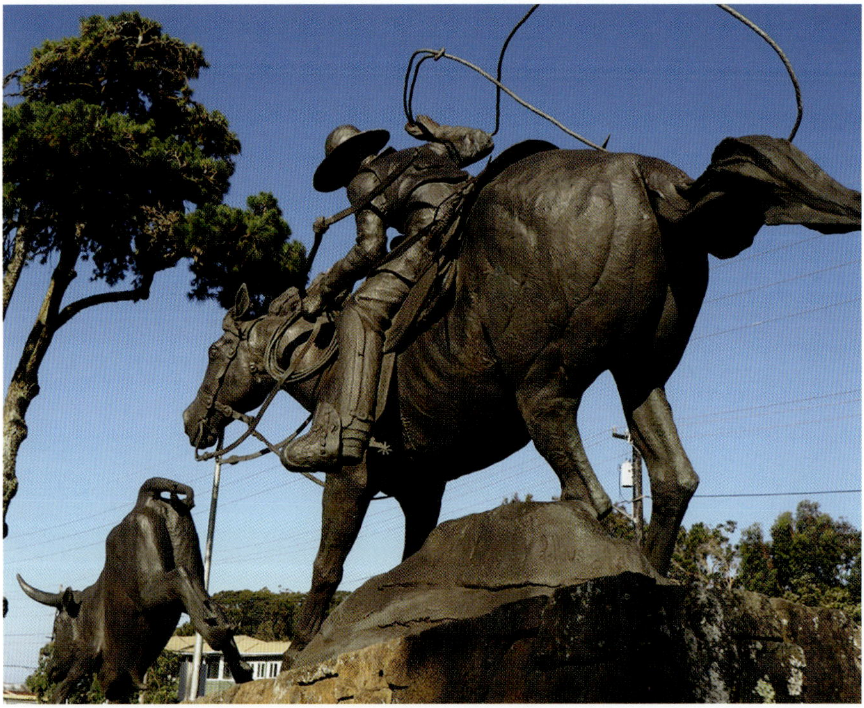

Hawaiian Cowboy Ikua Purdy. Photo by Ray Soon

The heroic bronze statue depicts a Hawaiian cowboy roping a wild bullock on the slopes of Maunakea, an enormously difficult and risky chore, but typical of paniolo life. The cowboy portrayed is Ikua Purdy, a legendary paniolo (cowboy) who worked for Parker Ranch at the time. He herded cattle, moving them through steep hills and down into the harbor, where the steers were corralled before being transported to the Hawai'i Meat Company in Honolulu for slaughter.

Known locally for his skills, Purdy earned his U.S. mainland reputation when he took first prize in steer roping at the 1908 Frontier Days Rodeo in Cheyenne, Wyoming, known as the "Daddy of 'Em All." He was inducted into the Paniolo Hall of Fame in 1999, the Rodeo Society Hall of Fame at the National Cowboy & Western Heritage Museum in Oklahoma City (2000), and the Cheyenne Frontier Days Cowboy Hall of Fame (2008) a century after his championship feat.

To memorialize that achievement, the Paniolo Preservation Society commissioned a twenty-seven-foot statue depicting Purdy that now stands proudly in the center of Waimea Town for everyone to see. While depicting Purdy, the statue is truly meant to honor all persons, male and female, associated with the paniolo culture.

Two important features were added in 2006 when the statue was moved, placing more emphasis on its educational purpose and giving wider credit to the statewide ranching community. The separate memorial bronze-plated plaque explains Hawaiian cowboy history. It is mounted on its own matching stone wall. The lei of bronze brands surrounding the pedestal is a tribute to the families who contributed to ranching throughout the state.

How the Statue Came to Be

Dr. Billy Bergin, retired State and Parker Ranch veterinarian, credits the honoring of the Hawaiian cowboy culture as a grass roots effort. In the 1990s several efforts were put forth to recognize the importance of ranching in Hawai'i's culture and economy. The State Foundation on Culture and the Arts (Executive Director Sarah M. Richards) and the Honolulu Academy of Arts (Director George R. Ellis) sponsored a traveling exhibit celebrating paniolo folk arts and the history of ranching in Hawaiʻi. The exhibit and subsequent book (*Nā Paniolo of Hawaiʻi*) were coordinated by SFCA Folk Arts specialist, Lynn Martin. Also, Hawaiian independent filmmaker Edgy Lee created her documentary, *Paniolo O Hawaii Cowboys of the Far West*, in 1998 which helped to bring deeper awareness of Hawaiian culture both locally and beyond. These artistic and educational contributions were followed by then-Governor Ben Cayetano naming 1998 the Year of the Paniolo.

A group of people started to meet and ask themselves what more they could do to preserve and honor the cowboy culture. Within a year, a nonprofit organization called the Paniolo Preservation Society was formed with a charter, by-laws, and dues-paying members. Upon the advice of two respected ranchers, Freddy Rice and Peter Baldwin, the nonprofit decided to 1) become statewide and 2) make sure genuine cowboys were at the table. They also decided to ensure that there was a female perspective. Founding board member Leslie Milne Agorastos mentioned that a sculpture of Purdy was long overdue. The idea of creating the sculpture was enthusiastically endorsed, and members went further, deciding it was their obligation to make sure they completed the task.

Dr. Bergin was assigned to gather five quotes from different artists. When Fred Fellows forwarded his maquette, the members agreed to halt the competition and award the commission to Fellows. Fellows, a noted sculptor, a painter who specializes in Western-themed pieces has won many awards and is featured in magazines and art collections worldwide. Fellows' submission reflected what the members wanted. Fellows had been annually visiting Waimea for twenty years and was an experienced roper. His attention to detail quickly becomes obvious.

Fellows helped further the effort by making fifty table-sized maquettes and four four-foot ones which were quickly sold to raise money toward the effort. They needed $360,000 to pay for the statue and its transport. The funds came from donations, fundraisers, and ultimately, a small loan from the bank, which was paid off quickly with the proceeds from a special Willie Nelson concert in Waimea organized by Freddy and Gail Rice.

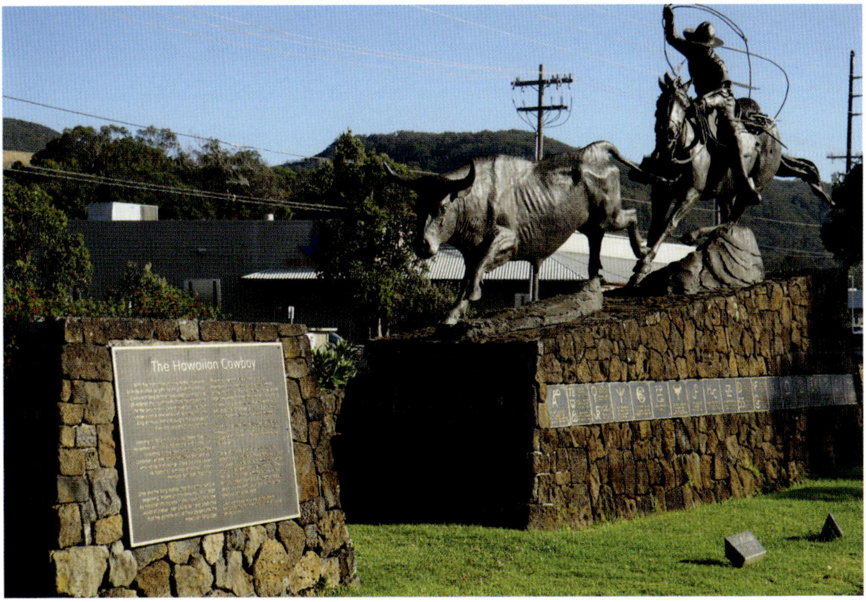

The Hawaiian Cowboy and plaque. Photo by Ray Soon

The Statue

The committee started working with Fellows to create the statue as they wanted it to look. It depicts Purdy in the mountains, riding his horse down a hill, and roping the bullock in front of him. The mounting is on a slant to add a downward feeling. Fellows was able to fashion the figure of Purdy based on pictures provided to him by Billy Bergin. Two of Purdy's sons, Martin from Waimea and Dan of ʻUlupalakua Ranch on Maui came to critique the facial elements, the mustache, hat, saddle, lariat, leggings, and sitting position and adjustments were made to everyone's satisfaction and pride. A local ranch family (formerly of ʻUlupalakua Ranch) living in Montana at that time had Purdy's saddle which Fellows used to inform his work.

Casting was done in multiple pieces, then welded and ground smooth, and the patina was added at a foundry in Kalispell, Montana. The finished sculpture weighs sixty-five tons and is twenty-seven feet long.

Too large for a container, the statue sat atop a Matson container ship and must have presented quite a sight. After the 1.25 life-sized (called "heroic-sized") sculpture arrived at Kawaihae Harbor, it was transported to town and placed on a lot offered by Parker Ranch near the post office. A ceremony and blessing by Reverend Billy Paris were held in 2003. The blessing was followed by hours of hula, music, a lūʻau, and story-telling.

Three years later, M & J Wilkow Ltd. of Chicago bought the Parker Ranch Shopping Center. They recognized the statue's cultural significance and wanted to position it alongside the highway where everyone could see and enjoy it. M & J Wilkow paid for it to be moved to its current location. At the same time (2006) the memorial was added giving a longer explanation of the history of the cowboy in Hawaiʻi. There was great relief when three months later it was unharmed by the earthquake that rocked the region.

Brief History of Ranching in Hawaiʻi

The story of ranching begins in 1793 when British Captain George Vancouver gifted King Kamehameha with six longhorn cows and one bull. Vancouver's predecessor, Captain James Cook, had similarly gifted the king with goats and pigs. Although goats were new, the pigs just added to the stock that had already been brought by Polynesian voyagers. Kamehameha placed a kapu that prohibited the cattle from being hunted or killed and they were left to roam the hillsides, multiplying to the point that they became a dangerous nuisance. The first horses came to Hawaiʻi in 1803, the gift of Captain William Shaler and commercial officer Richard Cleveland. Hawaiians took quickly to riding horses.

With the wild cattle becoming a serious nuisance, in 1812 Kamehameha allowed them to be captured, giving birth to the ranching life. The cattle hunters, on foot, with big dogs and large bore rifles, dispatched the animals in the forest or in the plains far from the villages. Rendering the meat, which was packed with salt in shoulder carried kegs, the product of their hunt was taken home for processing, a very inefficient method to say the least.

New methods for raising and herding cattle had to be invented. As he had done in so many other enterprises, Kamehameha III sought knowledge for improving how things were done, and he invited Mexican cowboys from California called *vaqueros* to come to Hawaiʻi to teach their skills.

Billy Bergin explains how the *vaqueros* taught the Hawaiians methods to rope the feral stock, keeping them hog-tied or tethered to a nearby tree base for an overnight "cooling off" session. Early the next day, the horseback *vaquero*/paniolo would lead the bullock to the village for processing, genuinely enhancing the depopulation of the wide hordes while creating a market export for salted beef near the shoreline.

The *vaqueros* taught Hawaiians how to slaughter, breed, part, and process corralled cattle for branding, ear marking, and neutering. They encouraged the Native Hawaiians to use their skills in weaving, splicing, and carving to make their own bridles, lariats, whips, and saddle trees (frames). Thus, they could convert from being on foot among the wild cattle to being horse mounted and well-equipped. These new skills paired well with their native talents for growing grass and making fences and paddocks.

The Hawaiian's excellent eye-hand coordination proved a boon for apprehending the feral bullocks by roping, casting, and tying. The *vaqueros* taught them how to tether a wild bullock to a gentle homebound ox that would lead his feral cohort to the village. This is referred to as the "pini" (pinned) method, which is slower than other methods, but more humane. Both the roping and pinning methods are of *vaquero* origin, bringing efficiency to the depopulation mission desired by Kamehameha III.

According to information supplied by the National Park Service, the Hawaiians quickly became skilled and created their own distinct cowboy culture, which included "Hawaiianized" saddles, wide-brimmed hats, leggings, belted knife cases, and other gear along with music and songs accompanied by a slack key guitar or a ʻukulele.

Ranching was difficult due to the rugged lava terrain, which was riddled with pockets and holes. As incredible as their success in rounding up the cattle over such challenging land, even more amazing were their methods for getting the cattle onto a steam ship with longboats that ferried cattle from shore to ships. The shoreside-corralled cattle were individually roped with non-choke lariats and led through the waves by a roper mounted on a stout horse. Once water-borne, the steers readily

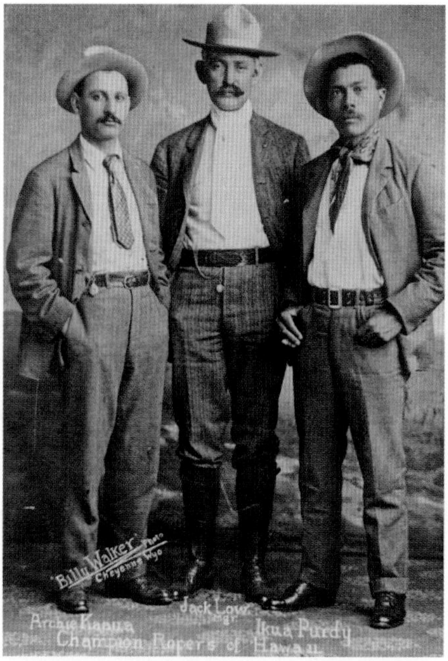

Photograph (L-R) of Ka'au'a, Low, and Purdy, at the Paniolo Heritage Center in Waimea, used with permission. Photo by Cheryl Soon

followed the horse thirty to forty yards out to the waiting long boat manned by former cowboys who "pitched" at the lariat end and drew the steer alongside for snubbing to the gunwale. The paniolo literally rode their horses into the surf, leading the cattle along with them. Four steers, "snubbed on each longboat side" would be drawn by power "winched" out to the steamship for crane-lifting aboard the waiting ship. The cattle were tied by their heads to the sides of the boats.

The skills of the Hawai'i paniolo were extraordinary. In 1908, rancher Eben "Rawhide Ben" Low of Pu'uwa'awa'a Ranch sponsored three top cowboys—Ikua Purdy (Low's cousin), Archie Ka'au'a (Low's half-brother), and his brother Jack Low—for entry into the Cheyenne Frontier Days Rodeo in Wyoming. Authors David Wolman and Julian Smith describe Frontier Days as "a blend of Wild West skits, light-hearted games, and dead serious sporting contests." This was a prestigious cultural showcase and rodeo competition promoted by such famous names as Buffalo Bill, Annie Oakley, and Theodore Roosevelt.

Promotion was widespread. The town received the trio warmly but with skepticism as they rode in with their colorful shirts, wide hats, and flower leis. By the end, everyone was stunned as Purdy won first place in steer roping with an astonishing time of fifty-six seconds. Ka'au'a placed third, and Low placed sixth. The local newspaper stated that the three "took the breath of the American cowboy."

Purdy never returned to the Cheyenne rodeo, remaining a legend in history. He moved to Maui where he worked on the 'Ulupalakua Ranch for many years. He died in 1945 at age seventy-two. Archie Kaʻauʻa died following a tragic roping accident near Waimea.

Parker Ranch is one of the largest cattle ranches in North America and one of the oldest, currently celebrating its 175th year of continuous operation. It has been a working ranch since 1847 when it was started by John Palmer Parker (1790-1868). Parker was one of Kamehameha's Western advisors who was given permission to shoot the cattle, thus creating the salt beef industry. Parker married Kamehameha's granddaughter, Chiefess Kipikane and was given two acres, which started his domain. Paniolo Preservation Society hopes to one day have a full-sized statue of Parker in the town. A proof maquette of Parker with his dog has been made by Deborah Fellows, wife of Fred Fellows, and a sculptor in her own right.

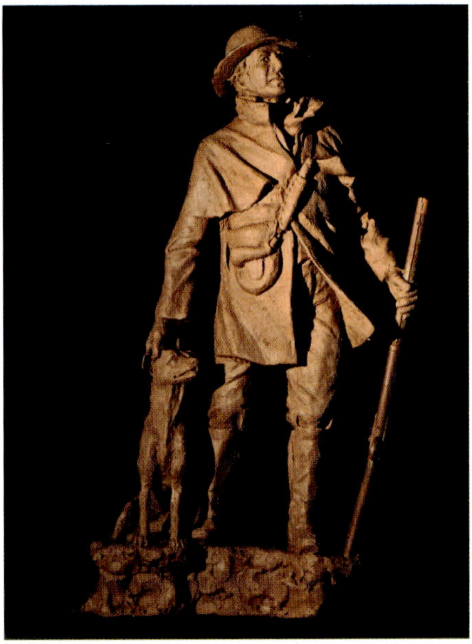

John Palmer Parker maquette. Artwork and photo by Deb Fellows

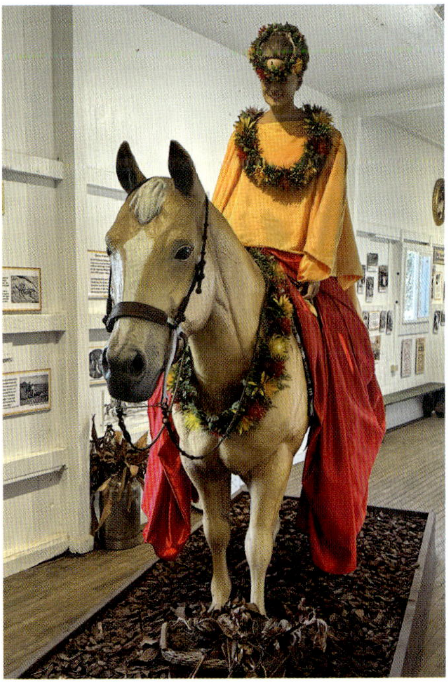

Pāʻū rider. Photo by Cheryl Soon

Today, the Paniolo Preservation Society continues to preserve the history, traditions, practices, and narratives of the paniolo while encouraging its modern manifestations and pursuits such as rodeos, parades, and festivities. They manage the

Paniolo Heritage Center at the Pukalani Stables in Waimea, telling important stories of paniolo, the making of saddles, and more.

On the other side of the stables is the Pāʻū Museum which displays paintings of many of the great pāʻū riders of the past decades and provides exhibits explaining hats, lei, and the elaborate pāʻū costumes (made from nine to twelve yards of cloth), and pictures from the past. The Pāʻū Museum is centered with a full-size horse mounted by a beautiful and graceful pāʻū rider with the likeness of Anna Perry Fiske gesturing her welcome.

Rodeos were held around the state in Kona (Hōnaunau), Nāʻālehu, Panaʻēwa (Hilo), Waimānalo (Oʻahu), and, formerly, during a three-day event in Makawao (Maui). Parker Ranch's Fourth of July Rodeo is among the biggest of them all. Pāʻū riders are a highlight of every parade, and the riders in full regalia sit upright and proud on their horses with both rider and horse adorned with flower garlands and insignia worthy of their honored place.

The Waiomina Boot

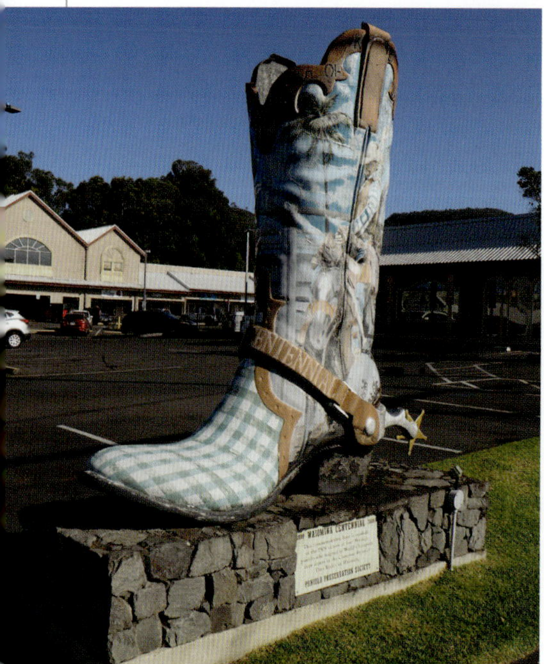
Waiomina Boot. Photo by Ray Soon

Another colorful activity of the Paniolo Preservation Society is the Waiomina Boot located in the KTA shopping center, almost directly across the street from the statue. The Waiomina Boot furthers the sister-city relationship between Waimea and Cheyenne. Here is the story of how it came to be.

Purdy's induction at the 2008 ceremony in Cheyenne was attended by a party of more than forty from Hawaiʻi who organized the 20008 Waiomina Centennial Celebration (Waiomina is the Hawaiian word for Wyoming), ably led by kamaʻāina Waimea historian Dexter Keawe Vredenburg. They hosted a barbecue creating great excitement.

Pat Bergin (wife of Billy Bergin) and other cowboy wives helped organize the pāʻū activities. During her visit, Pat noticed artful boots throughout Cheyenne City. Pat wanted one back in Waimea! She discovered one unpainted spare among the eighty boots commissioned. Before leaving Cheyenne, Pat had the boot painted by Ross Lampshire, a Colorado artist, who adorned each side with a rodeo action picture, then shipped it to Hawaiʻi, destined for display along the Waimea thoroughfare across from the Purdy monument.

In 2022, local artist Patrick Ching redecorated the weathered paint, changed the palaka color to light blue and added two new scenes. On one side, an image of Champion Dusty Miranda riding a big red bull called Shadow. On the other side that faces the shopping center, a young Holi, honoring the Bergin's late son, is seen roping a calf on his buckskin mount, Sugar, and sliding to a stop. The plaque on the boot's stone platform reads: *This commemorative boot is symbolic of the 1908 victory of four Waimea paniolo who reigned as World Champion steer ropers in the Cheyenne Frontier Rodeo in Wyoming.* A bronze version of Holi in his boyhood days riding a calf at a keiki rodeo, made by Deb Fellows, sits in the lobby of the North Hawaiʻi Community Hospital.

Like the statue, the Waiomina Boot and the smaller bronze celebrates rodeo and ranching for everyone. Ikua showed Hawaiʻi how.

For Further Reading: Martin, Lynn. *Nā Paniolo o Hawaiʻi*. State Foundation on Culture and the Arts. No date.

David Wolman and Julian Smith. *Aloha Rodeo*. William Morrow (Imprint of Harper Collins Publishers). 2019.

Billy Bergin. *Loyal to the Land: The Legendary Parker Ranch* (4 volumes). University of Hawaiʻi Press. 2003.

Saint Benedict

(c. 430-547 AD)

Owner	St. Benedict Church
Commissioned by	Unknown
Location	St. Benedict Catholic Church (Painted Church), Hōnaunau
Year Erected	Unknown
Artist	Unknown

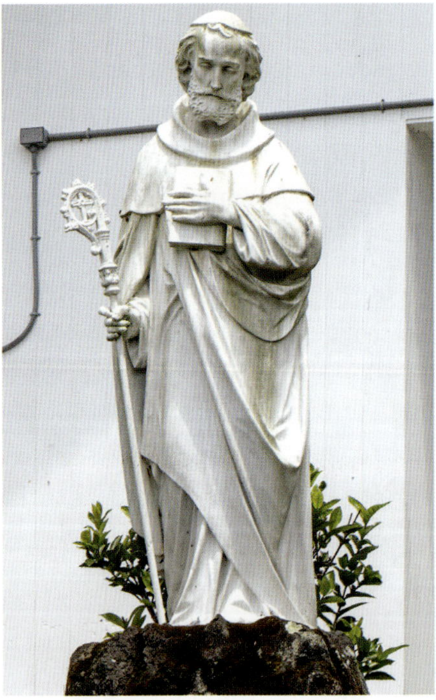

Photo by David Pillow, Dreamstime.com

Saint Benedict of Nursi was an Italian monk, a writer, a theologian, and the founder of twelve monasteries that served as centers of prayer and learning, including the great one in Monte Cassino for the Benedictines. His main achievement was the creation of a set of rules for monks to follow, written to help them maintain a spirit of balance, moderation, and reasonableness. He was named patron protector of Western Europe in 1964 by Pope John Paul II.

St. Benedict Church in Hōnaunau was built in 1899 by Belgian missionary Father John Velge and is patterned after a cathedral in Spain. The Belgian priest sought to overcome language barriers through pictures and paintings similar in nature to how stained glass is used in churches. Although not trained as an artist, Velge created frescos on the inside walls and ceiling that earned it the name Painted Church. Subjects include biblical scenes and the lives of saints, along with palm trees and other tropical images in bright rose blue and reddish-brown colors. The church is on both the Hawaiʻi and the National Register of Historic Places.

According to the church website, the first Catholic church in the South Kona District was started in 1842, near the City of Refuge, and was known as the St. Francis Regis Chapel. Residents started moving away from the beach to cooler places and to lands with more fertile soils. In 1899, the church was dismantled and moved by mules to the current location. By 1902, the church, which had been made larger, was consecrated and renamed to honor Saint Benedict. From 1983-85, the works were restored with the help of the Bishop Museum. Again, in 2002, more renovations were made and a koa wood altar and matching pulpit were installed.

St. Benedict's Church, or the Painted Church, in Hōnaunau offers a picturesque scene with multiple features. The outside of the white-and-green trimmed church is charming with gingerbread details and a prominent steeple on top. Inside, the walls and ceiling are painted with Hawaiian scenes. Each column is topped by painted coconut fronds rising towards the altar.

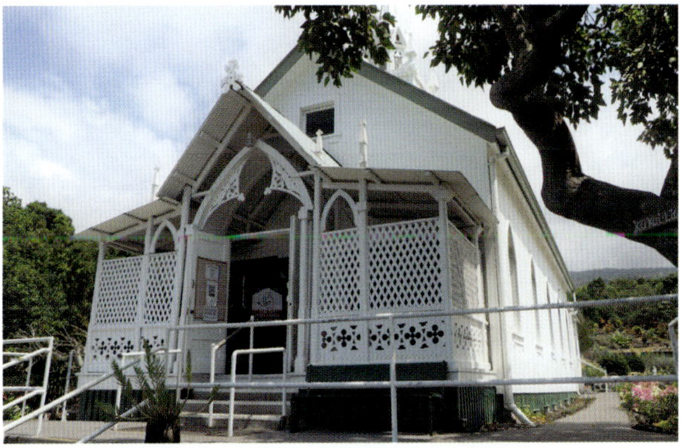

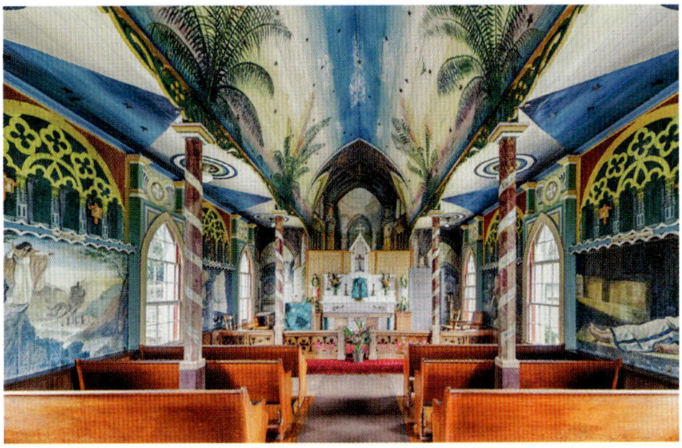

St. Benedict's Church (Painted Church). Top photo by Ray Soon. Bottom photo by Marek Poplawski, Dreamstime.com

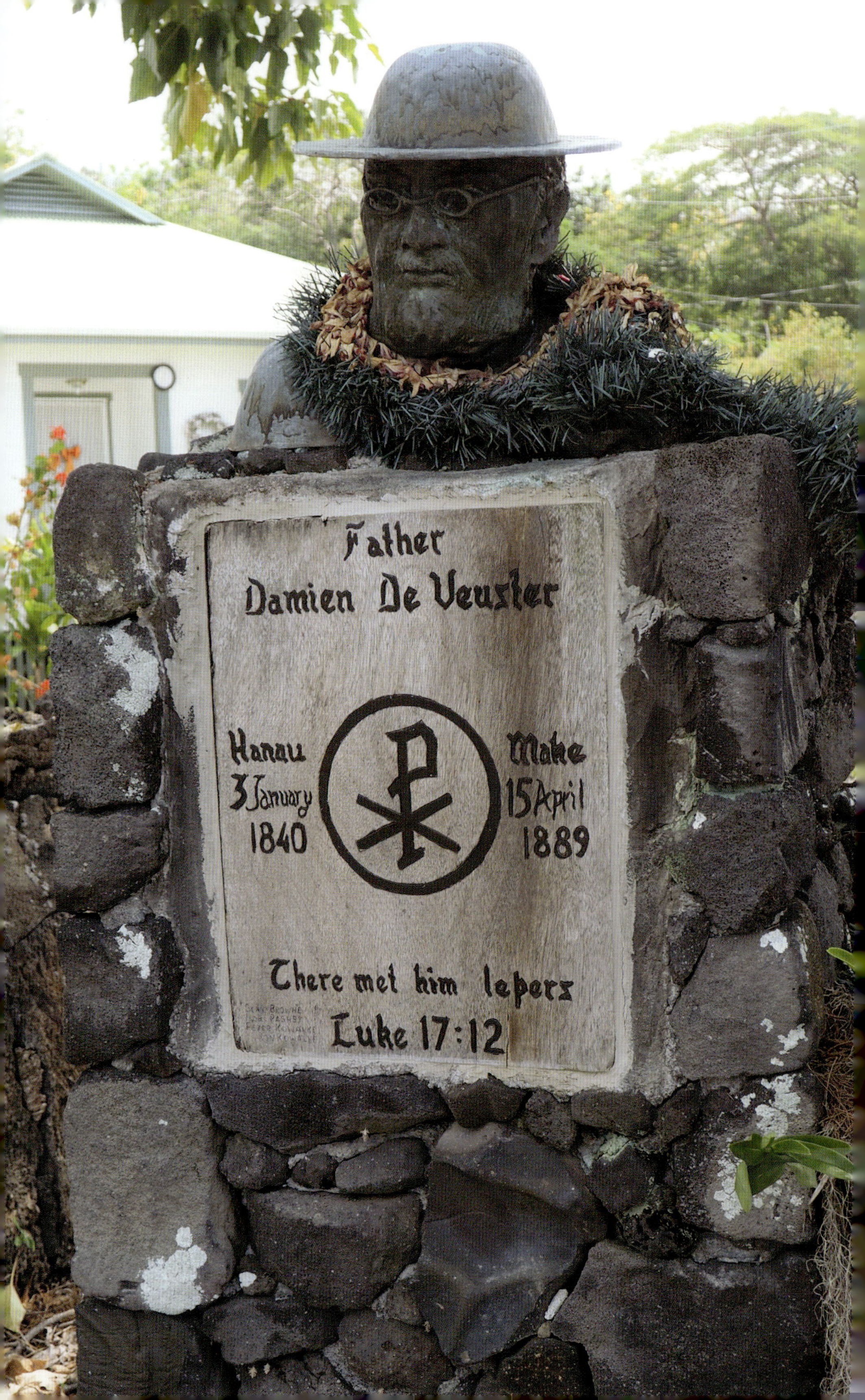
Father
Damien De Veuster
Hanau
3 January
1840
Make
15 April
1889
There met him lepers
Luke 17:12

Saint Damien (Joseph Damien de Veuster)

(1849-1889)

Owner	St. Benedict Church
Commissioned by	St. Benedict Church Parish
Location	St. Benedict's Catholic Church (Painted Church), Hōnaunau
Year Erected	c. 1983-4
Artist	Bob Pashby/Sean Browne

Father Damien was a Catholic priest from Belgium who became a saint due to his work with leprosy patients in Hawaiʻi. He is associated with many places in the Hawaiian Islands and remains a beloved figure. See Chapter 4 (Maui) for a lengthier description of his life.

Prior to going to Kalaupapa, Damien spent nine years on the island of Hawaiʻi, immediately following his ordination at Our Lady of Peace Church in Honolulu. He was assigned to Puna District for six months and then moved to Kohala/Hāmākua District. Damien built many churches of the native thatched hut variety. These were later replaced by permanent structures. While in Puna, church records show Damien baptized nearly 100 people and performed seven marriages. The Sacred Heart Church in Pāhoa has a Damien piece to honor his time in the district.

A bust and plaque for the beloved Damien was started by Bob Pashby, who did the clay modeling, and finished by Sean Browne when Pashby became ill and needed assistance. Browne completed the wax casting and finish, and he delivered the bust to the site. Damien is shown wearing his missionary hat and glasses. The bust always has lei decorations and other offerings left at it. Set upon a simple rock wall, beneath the bust is a wooden plaque that shows his name and birth and death dates. Also inscribed upon it is a passage from Luke 17:12: "There met him lepers."

Opposite page: Father Damien de Veuster bust. Photo by Ray Soon

Buddhist Temples in Hawai‘i Island

Buddhist practice started in India 2500 years ago. Buddhism spread to Japan by the mid-sixth century. Shingon Buddhism practice is of East Asian origin (India, China, and Tibet), and spread by traveling monks. It expanded through Japan by Kobo Daishi, or Kukai.

Most of the immigrants from Japan who came to Hawai‘i were practicing Buddhists. Buddhist propagation in Hawai‘i differed by denomination. Sometimes it started with laymen in their homes, moving later to home-style Daichi-do. In the final years of the nineteenth century, ministers were dispatched from Japan to provide spiritual comfort and support to the immigrant communities. Shortly thereafter, temples started to be built in Hawai‘i. The oldest, in Hāmākua, is among the most beautiful, following the roof style of a Hawaiian hale, and beautiful interior features carved and polished koa wood.

Today, there are 90 Buddhist temples remaining in Hawai‘i serving five dominant denominations of Shingon Buddhism doctrine. Jōdo Shinshu has thirty-seven Hongwanji temples of both western (Nishi) and eastern (Higashi) branches. According to Tanabe & Tanabe (*Buddhist Temples in Hawaii*, 2013) other major denominations in Hawai‘i include Jōdo (with thirteen temples), which is especially prominent along the Hāmākua Coast where there were large concentrations of Japanese on the plantations; Sōtō Zen (eight temples remaining); Rinzai Zen; Nichiren; and the latest sect, Tenchi. While the temples have common elements, each is unique resulting in an amazing diversity.

In the latter part of the twentieth century, statues were erected in front of some temples in Hawai‘i. The statues' artistic origins are rarely known, though they are likely to have come from copper foundries such as Kinjudo in Shiga Prefecture, Japan. This is also where temples purchase the bronze bells for their distinctive sound. The copper factories were re-purposed during World War II, but started making bells and statues again after the war.

For Further Reading: Tanabe, George J. and Willa Jane. *Japanese Buddhist Temples in Hawaii: An Illustrated Guide*. University of Hawai‘i Press. 2013.

Hāmākua Jodo Mission and Bust of Reverend Gakuo Okabe

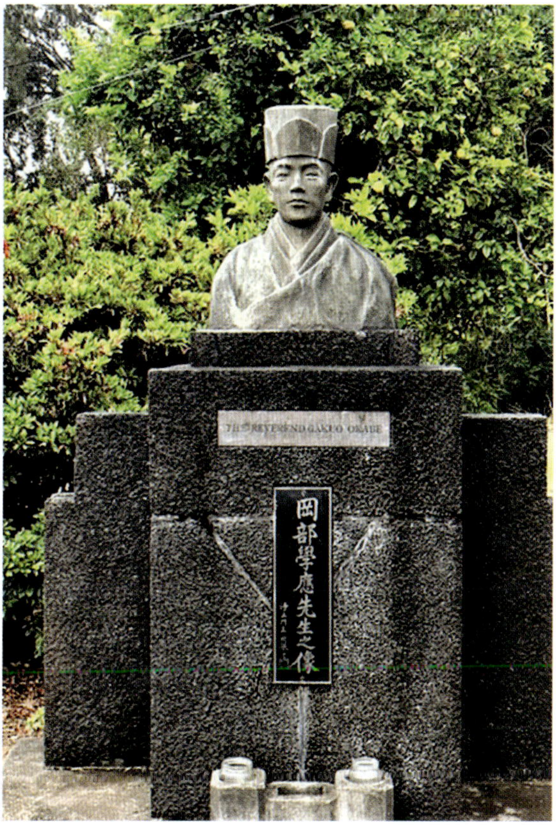

Reverend Gakuo Okabe. Photo by Cheryl Soon

The Hāmākua Jodo Mission is the oldest Japanese Buddhist temple in Hawaiʻi. In 1894 Reverend Gakuo Okabe was sent from Japan to Oʻahu as a Jodo Shu priest. Within two months he was on Hawaiʻi Island in Hāmākua district where he garnered a strong following. Okabe traveled throughout the district carrying an Amida Buddha statue on his back encouraging others to join his teachings.

When Hisashi Shimamura, the Imperial Consulate General of Japan, visited Hawaiʻi, he supported and encouraged their wishes to build a temple. Reverend Okabe and others walked door to door to raise the funds. Thus, the first sanctioned Buddhist Temple in Hawaiʻi was built in 1896 at Pāʻauhau Mauka, the current location. The original building became a kitchen and social room when the current *konpondo* temple was built in 1918. Set in a large open field overlooking the coastline and Pacific Ocean, it is a beautiful and architecturally significant building similar in style to the Hāwī Jodo Mission (1909).

According to the Society of Architectural Historians Archipedia project, the temple is the sole surviving Buddhist Temple in Hawaiʻi

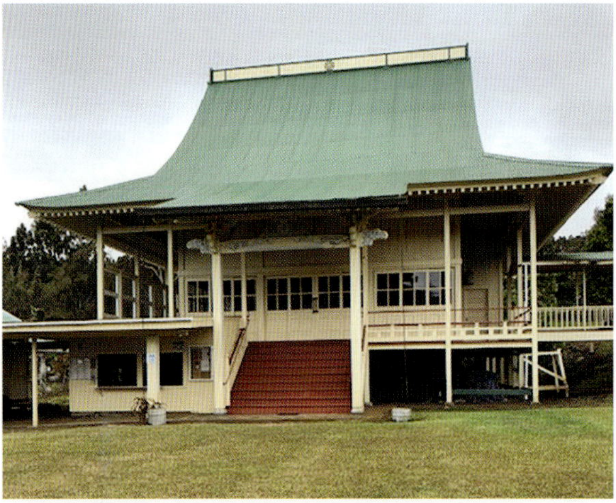

Hāmākua Mission Temple Photo by Cheryl Soon

that follows the traditional Japanese *kiwari* (proportional) system. It is made using traditional methods of wood joinery (*sashimono*) entirely without nails. Raised six feet off the ground, it is forty-three feet high, with an imposing *irimoya* roof. The *engawa* (verandah), traditional *kōran* (railing), along with the ornately carved *mizuhiki koryo* (front beam) and *ebi koryo* (lobster tie beam) are ties to Japanese architecture. Interior decorations such as the carvings in koa wood on the transverse beams and koa pillars, connect the building to Hawaiʻi and the plantation setting. The carpenter, Umekichi Tanaka, was trained in Japan by his father as a *miyadaiku* (builder of shrines and temples). Tanaka worked as a carpenter at Pāʻauhau Plantation, working on the temple after work hours.

The adjacent cemetery is the burial site for Katsu Gotō who was killed attempting to moderate a labor strike. He is still remembered as a hero by the Japanese community.

For further reading: Hibbard, Don. J. "Hāmākua Jodo Mission." Society of Architectural Historians. Archipedia.

Historic Hawaiʻi Foundation. "Hāmākua Jodo Mission: Past, Present, and Future." HHF Website Blog. October 22, 2021 and May 26, 2022.

Hilo Hooganji Temple and Statue of Shugyo Daishi

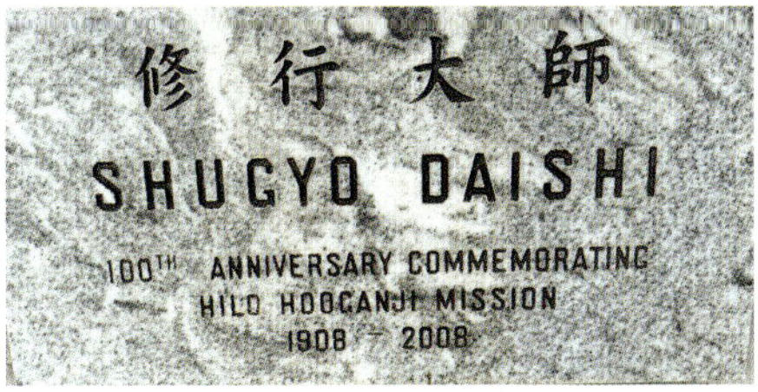

The Hilo Hooganji Mission is part of the Koyasan Shingon sect of Buddhism. The statue honors Shugyo (774 AD–835 AD), founder of Shingon in Japan. He is shown as a mendicant. This portrayal is known as "Shugyo Daishi" The Great Practitioner. He later was given the title Kōbō Daishi.

The statue came from the Toyama Factory and was sponsored by Reverend Shoryo Tanimoto of Ehime, Japan. It was installed during the Mission's Centennial Commemorative Services in October 2008.

Members of the Hilo Hooganji Mission visited another statue of Shugyo Daishi, this one along the 88 Sacred Places Pilgrimage, when they went to Shikoku on a pilgrimage in 2019.

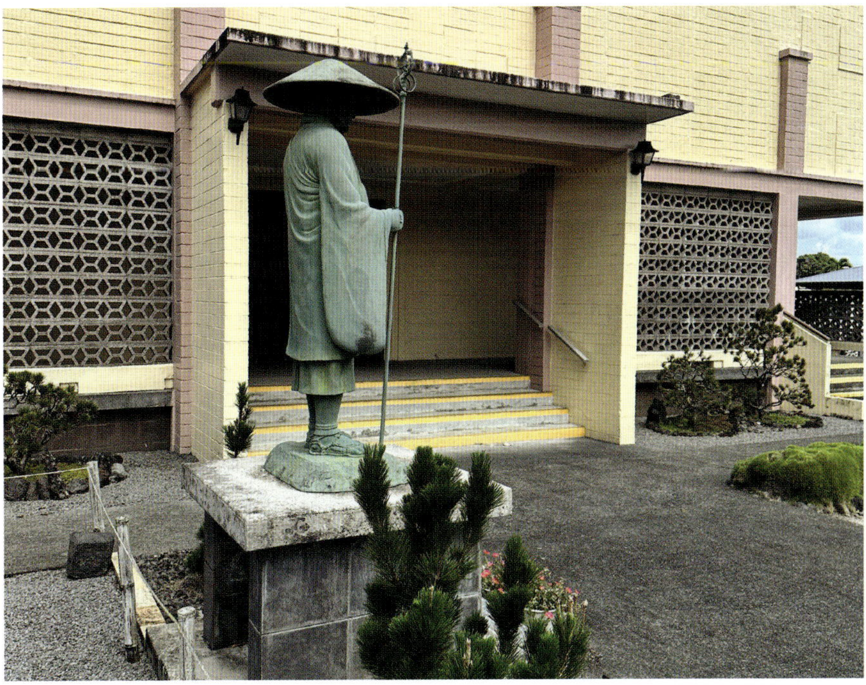

Hilo Hooganji Temple and Shugyo Daishi. Both photos by Rebecca Soon

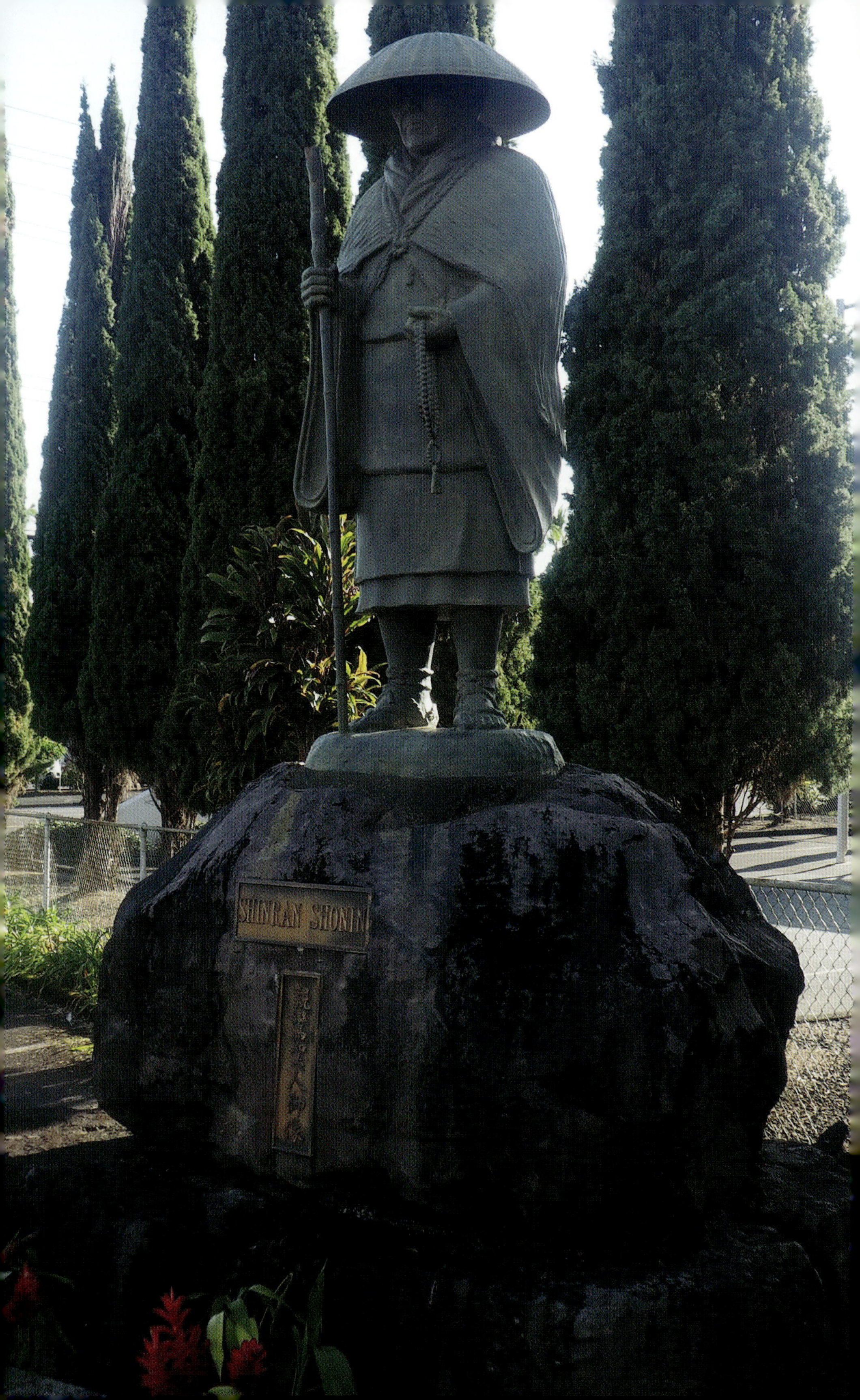
SHINRAN SHONIN

Jōdō Shinshu Buddhism and Statues of Shinran Shonin

(1173-1263)

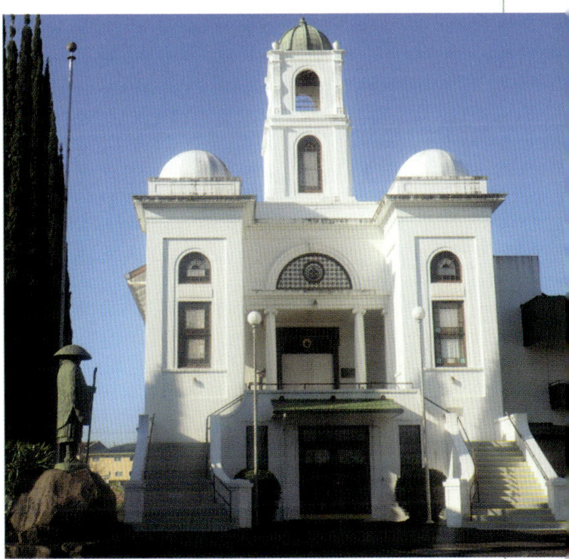

Hilo Betsuin Hongwanji. Photo by Ray Soon

Shinran Shonin lived during the Heian and Kamakura periods when political power was shifting into the hands of the warrior class and the old imperial order was falling apart. New and old schools of Buddhism were renewed and revitalized during this period. A disciple of Honen who was founder of the Jodo Sect, Shinran systematized its teachings. Shinran is considered the founder of the Jōdō Shinshu sect of Buddhism, although the sect itself was formally established several years after Shinran Shonin passed away.

Shinran was born to an aristocratic family, but at the age of nine he moved to Mt. Hiei where he lived as a monk for twenty years. After becoming disillusioned, Shinran descended Mt. Hiei into Kyoto, abandoning his *Tendai* practices, and joining with Honen. There was much rivalry among the sects at this time. The Imperial Court exiled Honen to the Tosa Province and Shinran was exiled to Kanto.

Five years later (1211) Shinran was pardoned, and three years after that, he moved with his family to the Kanto area where he taught for another twenty years. Shinran's final years, known as his writing period, were spent in Kyoto where he completed including his major work *Kyo-*

Opposite page: Betsuin Shinran Statue. Photo by Ray Soon

gyoshinsho. There are three Shinran statues on Hawai'i Island. Both the Hilo and Puna temples use the Indian Western architecture style, with towers, pillars, domes, and flared stairways.

The Honpa Hongwanji Hilo Betsuin statue sits in the front and to the left side of the temple. The metal plate on the base states it was donated in 1985 by Betty, Harriet, and Susan Takeda in memory of Reverend Byakudo and Sueko Takeda, Kikujiro and Hana Muroda, and Doro Takeda, presumably relatives. Plates beneath the front face state his name in both English and Japanese.

In Kea'au, the Shinran statue is at the Puna Hongwanji Mission. It includes some English signage, though it is limited to the name and dates. The base of the statue has Japanese characters which according to the Mission President indicates it was made by Metal Casting Master Oigo in Takaoka City, Japan.

In the same area as the Shinran statue is the Centennial Memorial Rock Garden, the War Memorial, and a peace pole. This constitutes a living and evolving collection of memorial features.

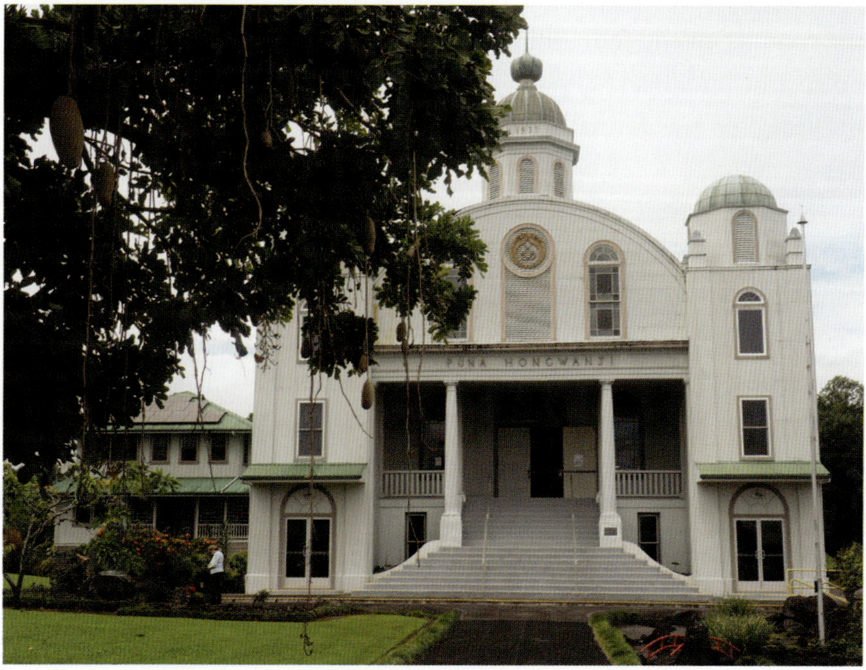

Puna Hongwanji Mission. Photo by Ray Soon

The Puna Mission is located on land donated and supported by the Shipman family. Other important features can be found there, including the Shipman Memorial Garden (2008), the Herbert Shipman Rock (1963), and the Noble Eightfold Path (behind the Shipman Rock).

The Kamuela Hongwanji Mission in Waimea is the one mission that offers a version of Shinran in his youth (age 9). The young Shinran was eager to receive ordination without delay and to embark on his life of devotion to the Dharma. According to the bronze sign, the statue was donated by Rev. and Mrs. Takanobu Koizumi in October 2010, upon the 40th anniversary of Kamuela Hongwanji.

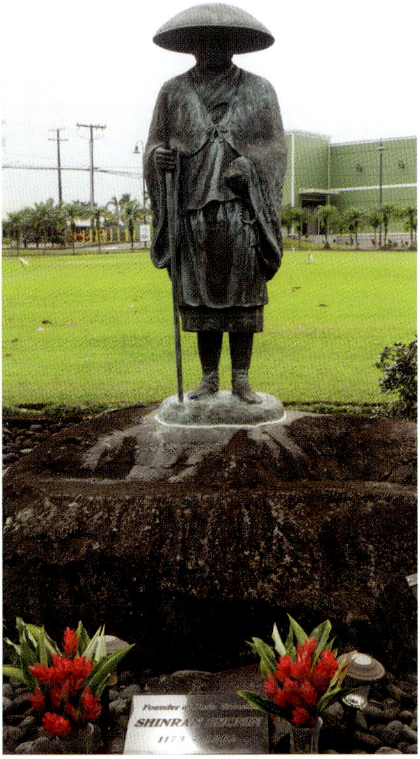

Above: Puna Shinran. **Below:** Kamuela Shinran.
Both photos by Ray Soon

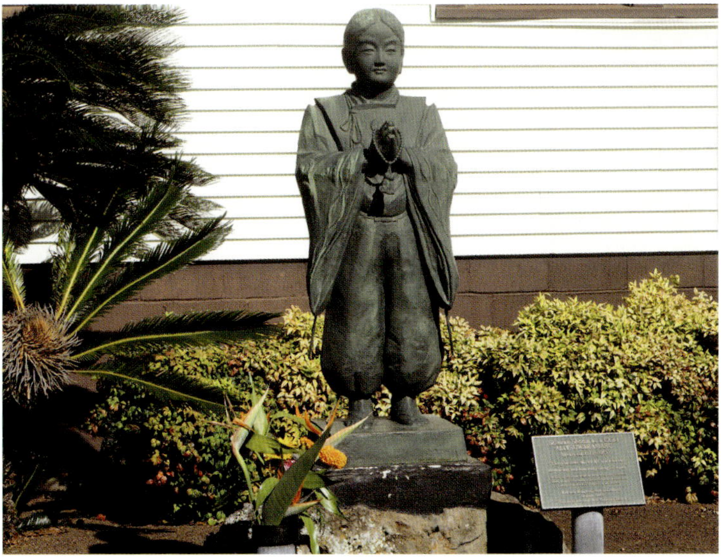

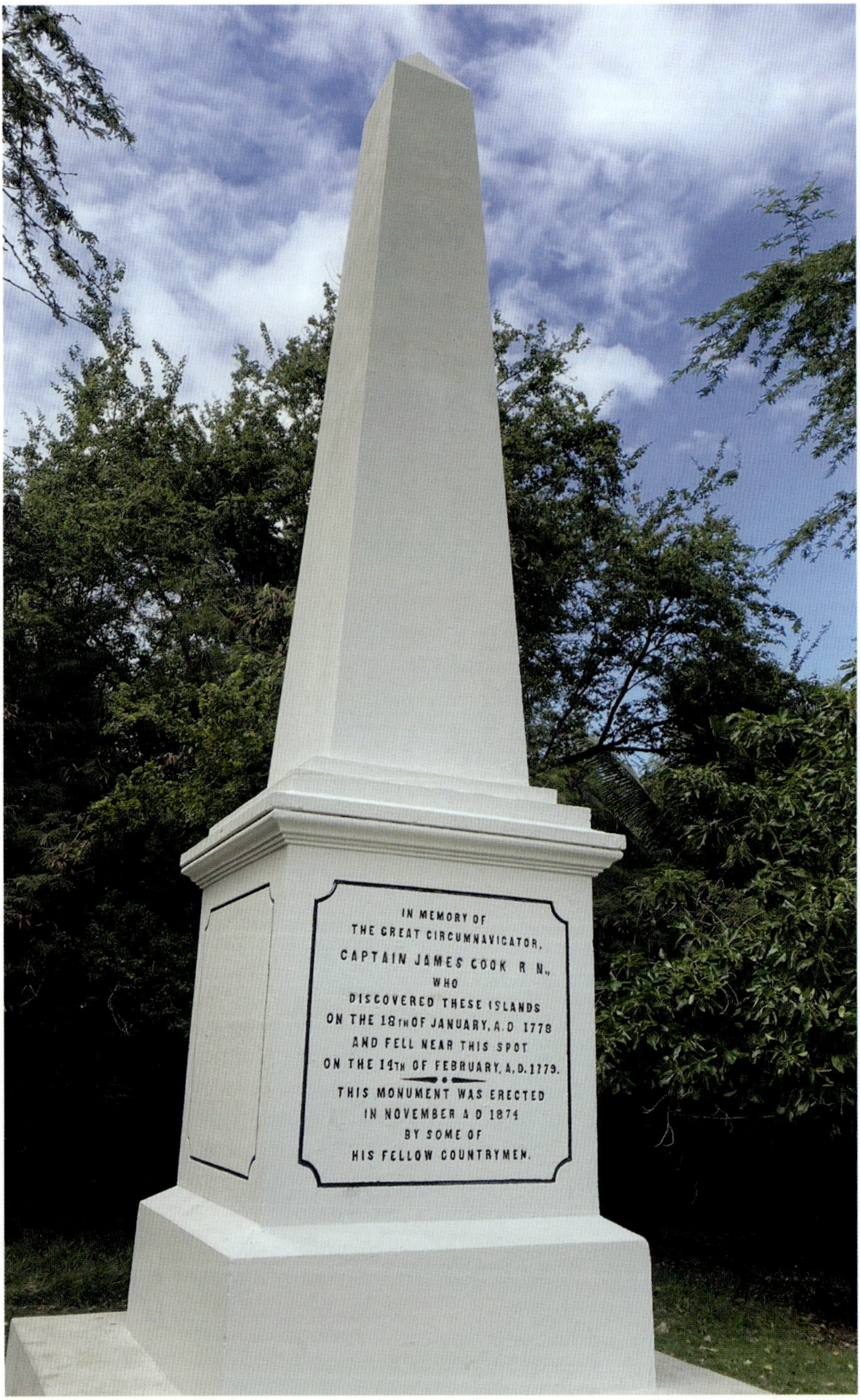

Captain Cook Memorial. Photo by Travis Ota

Captain James Cook

(1728-1779)

Captain James Cook, who sailed under the British flag, first arrived in Waimea, Kauaʻi ("First Landing") on his third exploratory voyage. Cook sailed around the islands, stopping in Kawaihae Harbor and in Kealakekua Bay. During his first interactions with the island kings who greeted him and with the king's subjects, he received lavish gifts. Eventually the Hawaiians grew weary of the drain of resources needed to keep Cook's ships and men stocked with provisions.

Cook left but soon had to turn back to repair one of his ships. The Hawaiians were less eager to see him again, and less charmed by the novelty of what he brought. There were several unfriendly confrontations, which were exacerbated by cultural differences. In one of those conflicts, Cook and four of his men were killed. The remaining crew were eager to leave and began their long journey home, shooting cannons into the crowd on shore on their way out and killing many. This occurred along the waters of Kealakekua Bay.

In his lifetime, Cook was a worldwide hero due to his published journals of navigation, mapping, and his detailed logs cataloging native flora, which were widely read. His fame and accomplishments led to many followers who erected statues and other memorials in his name.

One of these memorials to Cook, a white obelisk, was erected in Kealakekua by the British people. The land located along the shoreline above Kealakekua Bay was deeded to the United Kingdom in 1877 by Princess Likelike and her husband, Archibald Scott Cleghorn and given to the British Consul in Hawaiʻi, James Hay Wodehouse. The monument placed on the land is twenty-seven feet high, accessible through a difficult two-hour hike or by signing up with one of the three enterprises permitted to take people there to snorkel. The Cook monument is now part of the State of Hawaiʻi Kealakekua Bay Historical Park.

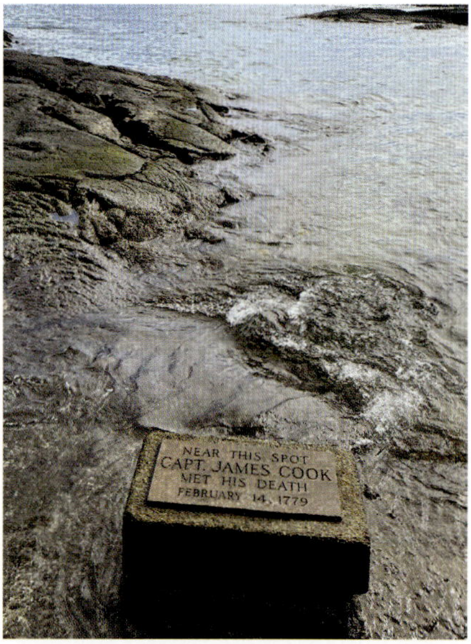

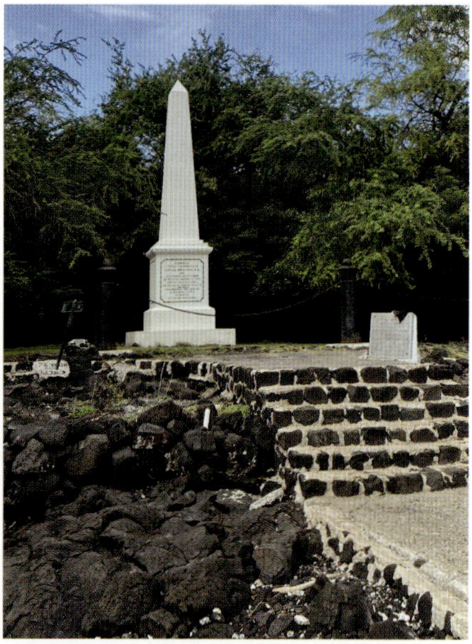

Left: Plaque marking location of James Cook's death. **Right:** Captain James Cook memorial. Both photos by Travis Ota

Another marker was placed by the jetty donors who were from the Commonwealth of Australia. The inscription on the plaque, now too worn to read, indicates it was erected in November 1874 by some of his fellow countrymen.

Also near the obelisk is a marker showing the spot where Cook was killed in 1779.

Throughout the past fifty years, many Indigenous peoples have come to dislike Cook and have expressed a desire to have his images removed, stemming from the negative effect Cook's arrival had on the health of indigenous people, introducing diseases for which they had no natural immunities, and because of the degrading way that he treated many of them.

The Hawai'i obelisk is often the subject of vandalism, and there are occasional calls for removal and requests to rename the community of Captain Cook.

For Further Reading: Moore, Peter. *Endeavor: The Ship that Changed the World.* Farrar, Straus, and Giroux. 2018

Horwitz, Tony. *Blue Latitudes.* Picador/Henry Holt and Company. 2002.

David Douglas Memorial

(1799-1834)

David Douglas was born in Scone, Scotland, and educated as a botanist and horticulturist. In the early 1800s he traveled many times to America to catalog species in the Pacific Northwest. Douglas became a famous botanist for whom the majestic coastal tree, the Douglas fir, is named.

Douglas came to Hawai'i several times in the 1830s as part of his work. He was particularly interested in the lava flows and the volcano summits which typically required a multi-day trek to reach. In the wet and rainy areas there, he collected species of ferns, moss, and other plants, while also calculating the height of Maunakea with surprising accuracy. He ultimately met his death on the slopes of Maunaloa, falling into a pit used to trap wild animals, where he was trampled to death by a bull that also fell into the pit. The circumstances of his death are fuzzy, but local legend ascribes his death to the doings of Edward "Ned" Gurney, a convicted felon, who lived near the pit and whose path crossed with Douglas'.

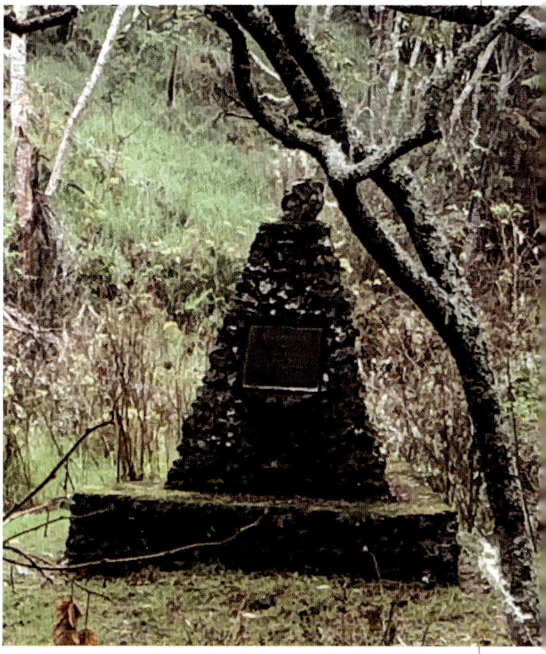

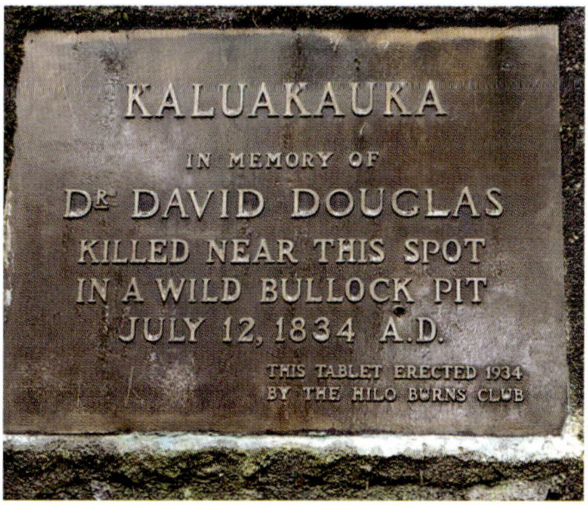

David Douglas Memorial and plaque. Both photos by David Tarnas

The memorial is located along the Hāmākua coast near a path off Mauna Kea Access Road. It consists of a rough stone spire cairn and brass plaque. The site is called Kaluakauka, meaning Doctor's Pit. The monument was installed in 1934 (one hundred years after his death) by the Hilo Burns Club, a Scottish heritage organization named for poet Robert Burns.

Dr. David Douglas was eventually buried in a common grave at Kawaiahaʻo Church in Honolulu. A plaque was added in 1856 by the church. His hometown of Scone, Scotland has an impressive memorial, and there are several places named for him in Oregon, Washington, and the Pacific Northwest.

Albert Kualii Brickwood Lyman

(1895-1942)

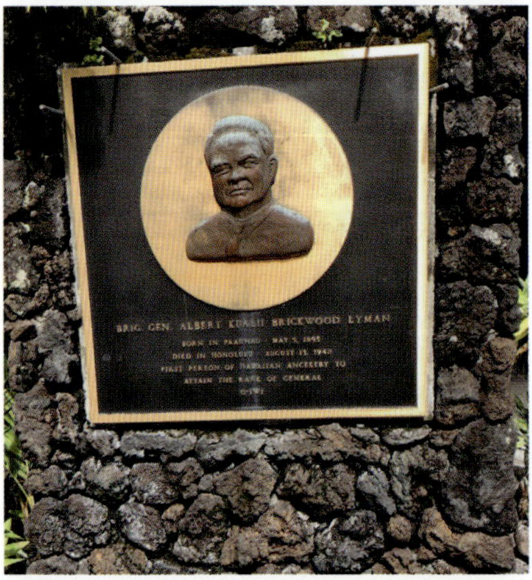

Albert Lyman by Don Rich at Hilo International Airport. Bronze cameo relief figure. Photo by Cheryl Soon

The airport and terminal in Hilo are named for Brigadier General Lyman and includes a memorial to him at the entrance to the terminal. The memorial states that Lyman was the first person of Hawaiian ancestry to attain the rank of general. The bronze monument plaque has a cameo relief of him from the shoulders up. Inside the terminal, one can find exhibits of his life.

CHAPTER THREE

STATUES, BUSTS & MEMORIALS ON KAUA'I ISLAND

The Garden Isle

— Kaua'i Epithet

Kaua'i is the second oldest island geologically (after Ni'ihau, which is also part of Kaua'i County) and the northernmost island in the State of Hawai'i. Known as the "Garden Isle," Kaua'i is naturally beautiful with dramatic cliffs, ridges, and canyons, along with plentiful beaches and a diverse ecosystem. The population of seventy-three thousand resides in small villages, many of them former plantation camps established when the sugar industry dominated economic and social life.

The persons and events that the Kaua'i populace choose to celebrate through statues are different than on the other islands. The first thing to note is the royals they honor focus on King Kaumuali'i and his mother, Chiefess Kamakahelei, who each served as ali'i nui of Kaua'i and Ni'ihau. Kaua'i is proud that it was never conquered by anyone, especially not Kamehameha, who is honored on the other islands. While Kaua'i was ultimately assimilated, credit for that goes to the sacrifices of Kaumuali'i to ensure there was no bloodshed. The Kaua'i Museum in Līhu'e honors the stories of Kaumuali'i and the complex family trees from the period of 1800-1900.

A statue of Captain James Cook marks the "first encounter" of the Hawaiians with Western civilization. Cook and his party were greeted at Waimea Landing by Chiefess Kamakahelei along with her husband Kā'eokūlani, Kaumuali'i's father. Moving forward one hundred years, a statue of U.S. Senator Spark Matsunaga now exists in his hometown of Hanapēpē, and a statue of Jose Rizal, national hero of the Philippines, can be found at the Līhu'e Civic Center grounds. A bust of Prince Kūhiō is found in Kōloa near his birthplace. It is owned and privately maintained by the Royal Order of Kamehameha.

The sugar industry figures prominently in the memorials of Kaua'i. There are five memorials to family members of sugar planter families. The first is a large statue made in Italy which serves as a memorial to the Rice family and related families. The other four—all medallions on large stones—are very similar to each other in appearance. The medallions feature pictures of the person being honored. Most have elaborate bases, sometimes created as a platform reached by stairs, sometimes taking the simpler form with bases made of rock. The earliest is from 1904 (Isenberg), and three others were placed within twenty-five years of the first; the last was created probably around 1988 (Waterhouse).

The immigration waves brought in workers from different parts of the world to work on the sugar plantations. Their influence remains today. Each presents its own story. Twenty-five, fifty and hundred years later, memorials were erected to honor the first ethnic immigrants.

Perhaps the most notable immigrant statue found is the life-sized grouping created by Jan Gordon Fisher. It was created under a commission from the Hawaiian Sugar Monument Committee, and unveiled in 1965 to honor the 100th anniversary of Japanese immigrants' arrival. It is a tribute to five ethnicities—Hawaiian, Chinese, Japanese, Philippine, and Puerto Rican—each in their own traditional dress, and doing the work of planting, weeding, harvesting, and bundling.

Kaua'i has several collections and assemblages of statuary figures. See Chapter Eight for more information on these pieces. The Hindu Monastery has one of the finest collections of statue and sculptures anywhere in the state. One of them is the grouping of craftsmen with the Shiva Siddhanta at the Hindu Monastery in Kapa'a. This ensemble piece honors the skills and craftsmanship of the silpis (stone sculptors) working to shape white granite by hand using their chisels.

A second collection on Kaua'i is the Na 'Āina Kai Botanical Gardens & Sculpture Park in Kīlauea. This exquisite natural ahupua'a setting and collection of sculptures and artworks. Ed and Joyce Doty were the founders and creative force behind the Na 'Āina Kai.

The table shows a listing of the statues and monuments of Kaua'i covered in this book.

STATUES, BUSTS & MEMORIALS ON KAUA'I ISLAND

SUBJECT	TYPE	LOCATION	ARTIST	YEAR
Chiefess Kamakahelei	Bronze statue	Middle school in Puhi	Karen Lucas	2003
Ka Mōʻī Kaumualiʻi	Bronze statue	Paʻulaʻula State Historical Park in Waimea	Siam Caglayan	2021
Aliʻi ʻAimoku Kaumualiʻi & Wahine Kekahakula	3D fabricated prototype	Kauaʻi Museum	White Clouds Co., Ogden, Utah	2022
Captain James Cook "First Encounter"	Bronze statue	Hofgaard Park, Waimea	Replica of statue, Whitby England by Sir John Tweed	1928
Spark Matsunaga "Walking in the Garden"	Bronze statue, two figures	Spark Matsunaga Children's Peace Garden, Hanapēpē	Kim Duffett	2008
Jose Protacio Rizal	Bronze Sculpture	Līhuʻe Civic Center	Kauaʻi Filipino Community Council	1988 Replaced 1997
Shinran Shonin	Bronze sculpture	Waimea Honpa Hongwanji	Unknown	1970
Kannon	Marble Statue	Kauaʻi Soto Zen	Unknown	Unknown
Sesquicentennial Sugar Plantation Immigrants	Bronze figures in structure	Kōloa	Jan Gordon Fisher	1965
Craftsmen with Shiva Siddhaata	Bronze set of figures	Kapaʻa Hindu Monastery	Holly Young	2006
Ed and Joyce Doty	Bronze pair	Na ʻĀina Kai Botanical Gardens & Sculpture	Holly Young	2010, 2018
Prince Jonah Kūhiō Kalanianaʻole	Bust on elaborate podium	Prince Kūhiō Park Hanapēpē	Julius Rosenstein	2001

SUBJECT	TYPE	LOCATION	ARTIST	YEAR
Richard Kawakami	Bronze bust	Līhu'e Airport Kawakami Terminal	Don Rich	1988
Mayor Tony Kunimura	Bronze bust	County Building Līhu'e	Sean K.L.L. Browne	2000
Mayor Maryanne Kusaka	Plaque	County building, Līhu'e	Unknown	c. 2004
Chipper Wichman	Bronze bust	National Tropical Botanical Garden	J. Brett Grill	2019
Paul Isenberg	Medallion on stone	Rice Street, Līhu'e	Unknown	1904
Rice Family Memorial	Carved stone	Līhu'e Cemetery	Stephen Sindring	1911
William Hyde Rice	Medallion on stone	Kīpū Road	Unknown	1925
Colonel Zephaniah Spalding	Medallion on stone	Upper Kapa'a	Unknown	1930
John Thomas Waterhouse	Bronze plaque	Kīpū Kai	Unknown	c. 1984

KAUAʻI ISLAND

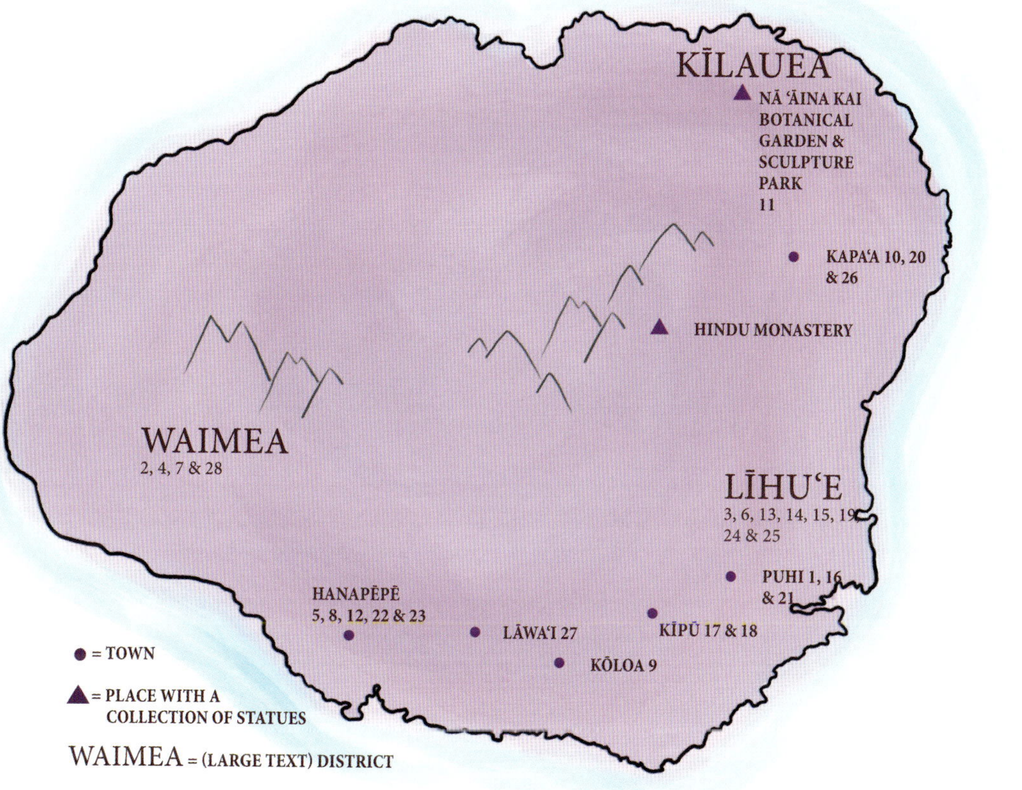

MAP KEY

1. Chiefess Kamakahelei in Puhi
2. Ka Mōʻī Kaumualiʻi in Waimea
3. Aliʻi ʻAimoku Kaumualiʻi & Wahine Kekahakula in Līhuʻe
4. Captain James Cook in Waimea
5. Spark Matsunaga in Hanapēpē
6. Jose Rizal in Līhuʻe
7. Shinran Shonin in Waimea
8. Kuan Yin in Hanapēpē
9. Sesquicentennial Sugar Plantation Immigrants in Kōloa
10. Craftsmen with Shia Siddhaata in Kapaʻa
11. Ed and Joyce Doty in Kīlauea
12. Bust of Prince Kūhiō in Hanapēpē
13. Bust of Richard Kawakami in Līhuʻe Airport
14. Bust of Tony Kunimura at Līhuʻe Civic Center
15. Plaque for Maryanne Kusaka at Līhuʻe Civic Center
16. Rice Family Memorial in Puhi
17. William Hyde Rice Medallion in Kīpū
18. John Thomas Waterhouse Bronze Plaque in Kīpū Kai
19. Paul Isenberg Medallion in Līhuʻe
20. Colonel Zephanian Medallion in Upper Kapaʻa
21. Matsunaga Peace Garden Kealaula on Pua Loke
22. Children's Peace Garden at Storybook Theatre
23. World Peace Kannon Statue
24. Puerto Rican Immigrant Memorial
25. Japanese Immigrant Memorials, Pagoda & Lantern, Līhuʻe
26. Ishidoro Japanese Lantern, Kapaʻa
27. Lawai International Center 88 Shrines
28. Waimea Hongwonji 88 Shrines

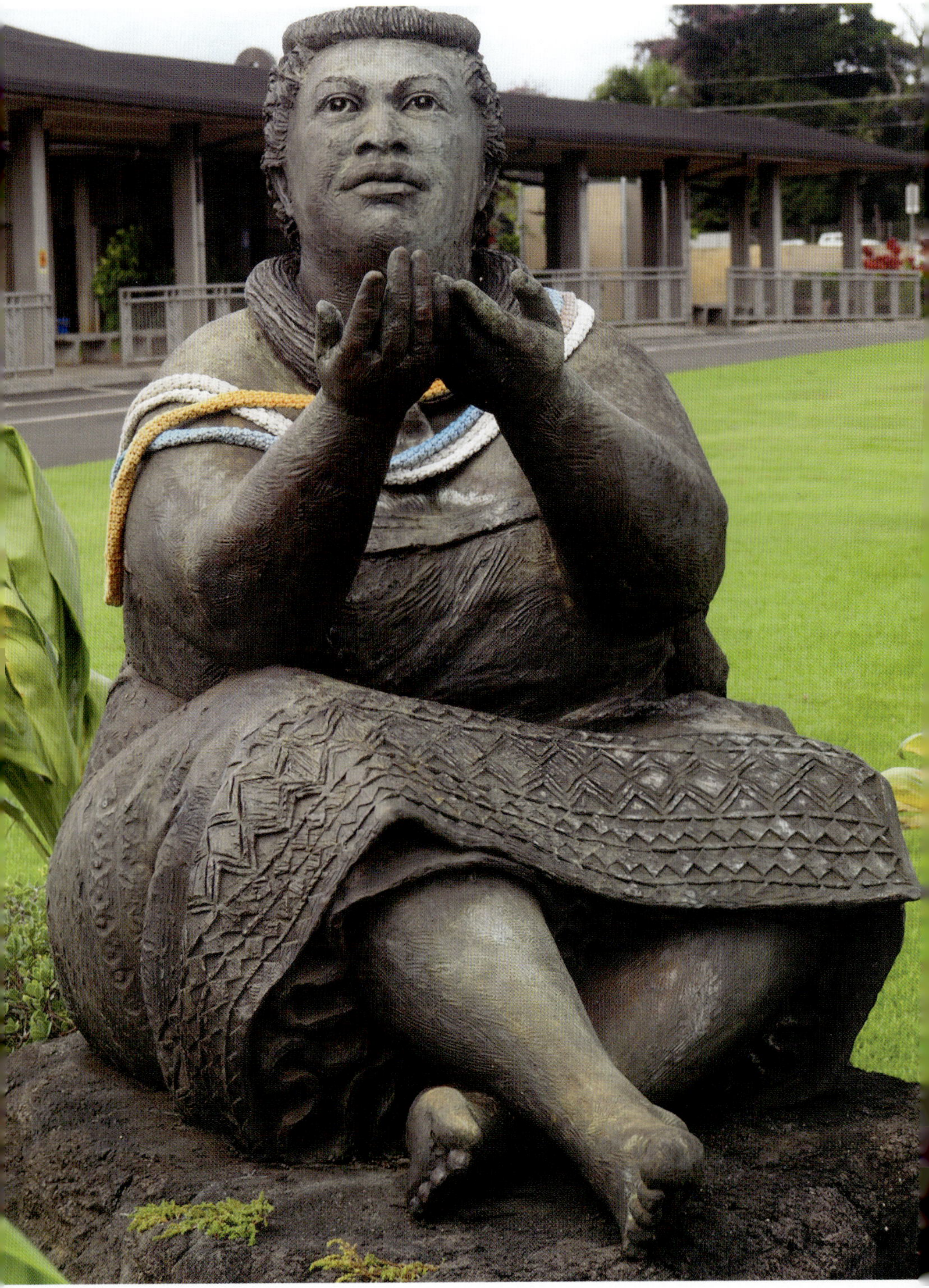

Chiefess Kamakahelei

(c. mid-1750s-1794)

Owner	Hawai'i State Foundation on Culture and the Arts
Commissioned by	Artists in Residence Program: SFCA, DOE and DAGS
Location	Chiefess Kamakahelei Middle School
Year Erected	2003
Artist	Karen Lucas
Name of artwork	E Holomua I Ka Naauao (Progress Through Knowledge)

Chiefess Kamakehelei ruled over Kaua'i and Ni'ihau from 1770-1794, a period of intense warfare among the ruling chiefs of Hawai'i. She was one of the most important ali'i nui of Kaua'i, having two high-ranking parents gave her great status. Her lineage was important to her power. She was the great-granddaughter of Kūali'i. Her own great-granddaughter would become Queen Kapi'olani, wife of King Kalākaua. Kamakahelei's son was Kaumuali'i, to whom she passed the royal title and authority. He became Ali'i Nui of Kaua'i and Ni'ihau upon her death.

Kamakahelei taught Kaumuali'i the long chants and instilled in him an understanding of his genealogical connection to the gods and his mana (sacred power). Religious by nature, she had a powerful prayer, "Aneekapuahi," which she used frequently to protect her people and to "pray to death" those who had evil intent against them. Her prayer is said to continue after her death, haunting any who intend harm to those on Kaua'i.

Kamakahelei's first marriage was to Kiha, and they had three children: a son Keawe and two daughters, Leiehoelani and Kaluaipihana. She left Kiha to marry Kaneoneo who was the grandson of Peleioholani, the ruler of O'ahu (and her first cousin). Her first husband, Kiha, then moved to Ni'ihau where he led raids against Kaneoneo until Kiha died in one of

Opposite page: *E Holomua I Ka Naauao* (Progress Through Knowledge) by Karen Lucas at Chiefess Kamakahelei Middle School. Cast Bronze figurative sculpture completed in 2003. Hawai'i State Foundation on Culture and the Arts. Photo Ray Soon

those raids. Kaneoneo was called back to O'ahu to help fight the ambitious high chief from Maui, Kahekili.

With Kamakahelei's husband absent, Kahekili sent his younger brother Kāʻeokūlani to Kauaʻi as a ploy, to woo the young Kamakahelei. The two soon married. When English Captain James Cook arrived in Hawaiʻi in 1778, his ships the *Resolution* and the *Discovery* anchored offshore at Waimea. Kamakahelei and Kāʻeokūlani were among those in the "First Contact" party. They received gifts from the voyager who was seeking favor from the native leaders. Kamakahelei advocated that they learn from Captain Cook. In 1780, Kamakahelei gave birth to Kaumualiʻi (by Kāʻeokūlani). Here was a male with impeccable lineage, "stronger than that of Kamehameha," according to Chucky Boy Chock, executive director of the Kauaʻi Museum. Kamakahelei and Kaeokulani also had two daughters, Kapiʻolani and Kaininoa.

Kaneoneo, Kamakahelei's second husband was killed by Kahekili in a battle on O'ahu in 1785. Her third husband, Kāʻeokūlani was summoned to Maui in 1791 by Kahekili, and she never saw him again. He died in a battle against Kalanikūpule (his nephew) on O'ahu, having been betrayed by two of his trusted advisors. Kaumualiʻi died in 1794 naming Kaumualiʻi the rightful heir to rule Kauaʻi.

Kamakahelei Statue

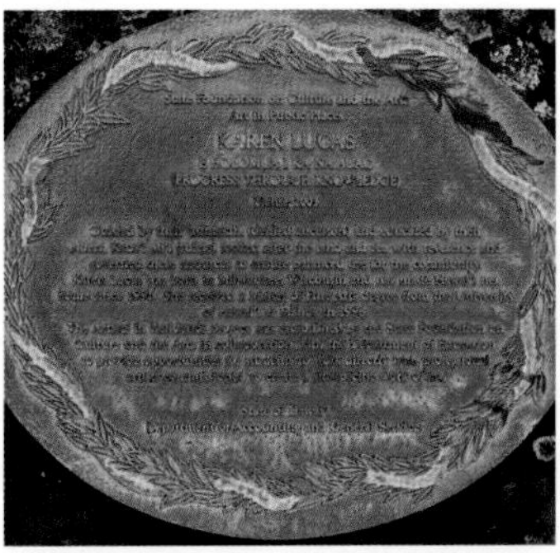

Artist's plaque. Photo by Christian R. Cook

The powerful statue of Kamakahelei at the public school named for her, depicts her sitting crossed legged with reverently outstretched arms. Her eyes gaze upward, a sign of her religious nature. Barefooted, she sits upon a lava-styled rock wearing a long kapa.

The statue created by Karen Lucas as part of the Artist in Residence Program sponsored by the State Foundation on Culture and the Arts with the Department of Education. A round bronze plaque lined with lei maile indicates the artist's name, piece name, and date.

Ka Mōʻī Kaumualiʻi Statue in Waimea

(1778-1824)

Owner	State of Hawai'i, Department of Land and Natural Resources, State Parks
Commissioned by	Friends of King Kaumuali'i
Location	Pā'ula'ula State Historic Park
Year Erected	March 2021
Artist	Saim Caglayan

Kaumualiʻi was the beloved aliʻi nui (supreme ruler or king) of Kauaʻi and Niʻihau, the twenty-third high chief, who ruled from 1794-1821. He was the last independent ruler before relocating to Oʻahu in 1821 and marrying Kaʻahumanu. Kaumualiʻi was popular among his people as well as the foreigners who visited the islands. He was deeply mourned upon his death.

Kaumualiʻi was born in Wailua (Holoholokū Heiau) to Queen Kamakahelei, the aliʻi nui of Kauaʻi and Niʻihau and her husband aliʻi Kāʻeokūlani (brother of Maui's Kahekili), the regent of Maui and Molokaʻi. His older half-brother, Keawe, was given by hānai arrangement to the family of Chief Inamoo. Kaumualiʻi was raised by his parents in Wailua. According to Croft (*Kaumualii and the Last of Hawaii's God Kings*), he learned the traditional ways that would protect his people from disasters, privation, and subjugation. He became skilled in fishing with hooks and spears and nets, could plant and harvest taro, and learned to make clothing and canoes. His water skills—swimming, diving, surfing, and paddling—exceeded those around him.

All these skills contributed to his prowess as a leader. His natural curiosity led him to learn the English language from sailors and seamen. He eventually came to call himself, as well as his son (Humehume), by the name George, after English King George III.

When his mother died in 1794, she passed her title and position to Kaumualiʻi, then only a sixteen-year-old. For five years, Chief Inamoʻo was the regent of the islands until Kaumualiʻi came of age. The transition

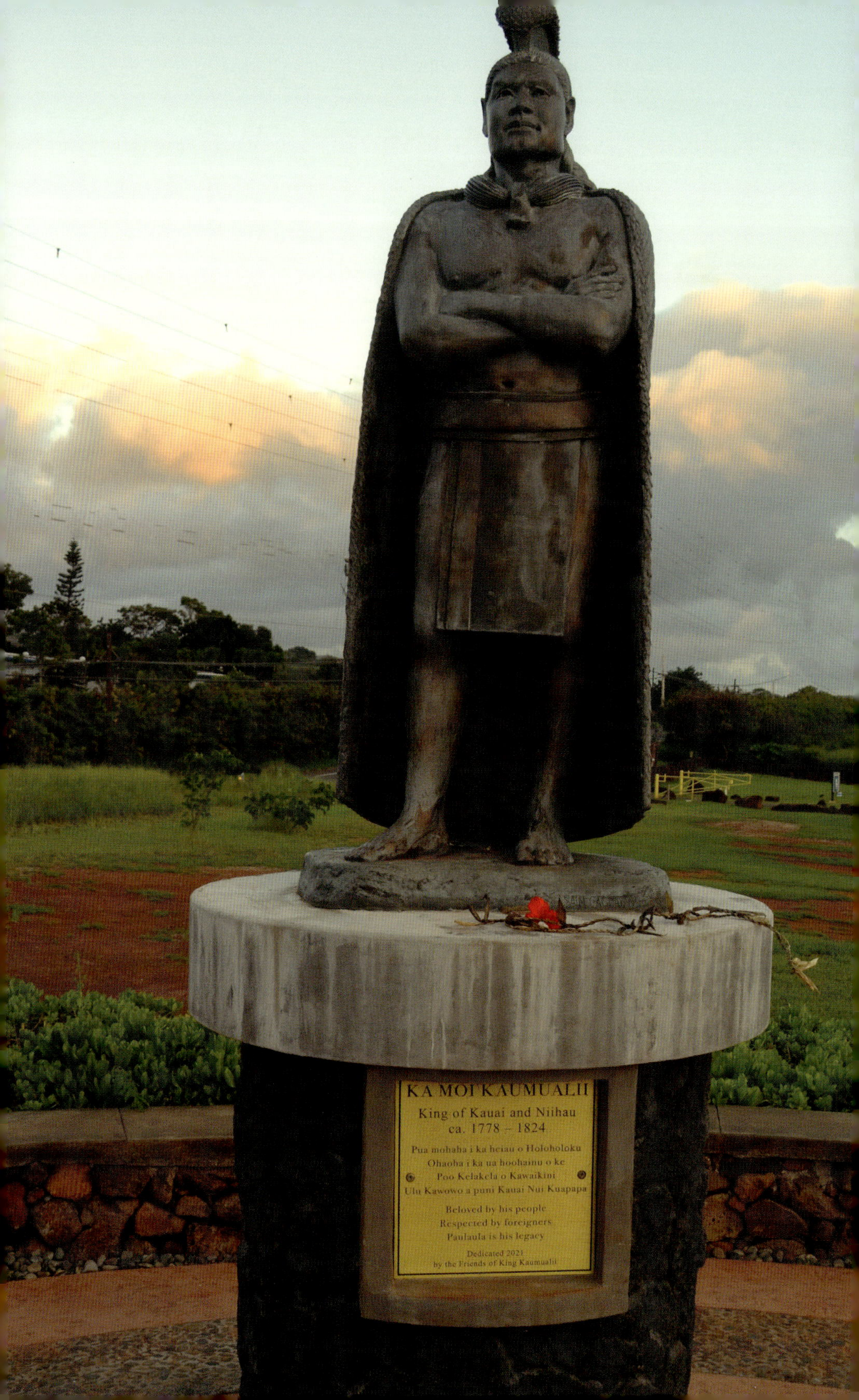
KA MOI KAUMUALII
King of Kauai and Niihau
ca. 1778 – 1824
Pua mohaha i ka heiau o Holoholoku
Ohaoha i ka ua hoohainu o ke
Poo Kelakela o Kawaikini
Ulu Kawowo a puni Kauai Nui Kuapapa
Beloved by his people
Respected by foreigners
Paulaula is his legacy
Dedicated 2021
by the Friends of King Kaumualii

was a bloody one. He was briefly captured by his brother Keawe who attempted to install himself as ali'i nui; but Keawe was shot by Ki'ikiki in Kapa'a before this could happen. When Ki'ikiki in turn was tricked into losing his guns while he was surfing, he fled to O'ahu where he was killed. Thus, in 1796, Kaumuali'i was installed as ruler, without local rivals. But there was still Kamehameha to contend with.

Kaumuali'i's rule closely tracked with Kamehameha's desire to control all the islands. Kamehameha's first attempt to seize Kaua'i and Ni'ihau came in 1796, the first year of Kaumuali'i's rule. This followed the bloody battles to take Maui and then O'ahu. The first attempt was aborted when many of Kamehameha's armada of peleleu canoes and locally built schooners were sunk in a storm. His men retreated to Hawai'i island where they were forced to defend their territory against a rebellion. Eight years later, in 1804, a second attempt to capture Kaua'i was aborted when Kamehameha's men fell to disease (believed to be cholera) and he decided to retreat. Kamehameha proceeded to amass an enormous navy that included schooners armed with cannons and large war canoes.

In the face of these vast munitions, Kaumuali'i decided to negotiate with Kamehameha, rather than sacrifice his people to inevitable bloodshed. While historical accounts suggested that they made a treaty, and Kaua'i and Ni'ihau were henceforth made part of the Kingdom of Hawai'i. However, the 1810 meeting did not result in a treaty. Research by Peter Mills published in the *Hawaiian Journal of History* (Vol 30, 1996) based on logs of contemporary traders, indicates that there was continued resistance by Kaumuali'i to Kamehameha's claim of sovereignty and he was supported in this resistance by the people of Kaua'i. According to Mills' research, he courted relations with the Americans, the British, and later Russians, constantly seeking to "align himself with any European power that would assist him in maintaining his sovereignty distinct from that of Kamehameha." There was little trust between Kaumuali'i and Kamehameha's forces.

Kaumuali'i had multiple wives, as was the custom at the time, often used as a means to solidify political power and alliances. His first

Opposite page: Ka Mō'ī Kaumuali'i, Waimea. Photo by Cheryl Anne Farrell

two wives were Kawalu (his half-sister from O'ahu), and Ka'apuwai Kapuaamohu (another half-sister, from Kaua'i). He married Kekaihaakulou in 1817. She became known as Deborah Kapule after becoming a Christian. Kaumuali'i had two sons, Humehume (also known as George Tamoree), Keali'iahonui, and a daughter, Kinoiki Kekaulike. Their descendants married other ali'i and were prominent rulers on the islands of Kaua'i and Maui as well as in the Kingdom of Hawai'i. His final wife was queen regent Ka'ahumanu, Kamehameha's former wife.

When Kamehameha died in 1819, his widow Ka'ahumanu became the effective co-ruler of the kingdom. She worried (justifiably) that Kaumuali'i might sever his relationship with the Hawaiian kingdom. When Kamehameha's son Liholiho sailed to Kaua'i in 1821, he invited Kaumuali'i to join him on his ship. Once aboard, they set sail for Honolulu, with Kaumuali'i's boat following. Some histories portray this as placing Kaumuali'i under house arrest, essentially kidnapping him, but there is evidence that he went willingly. Once on O'ahu, Kaumuali'i (by then age forty-three) married Ka'ahumanu (aged fifty-three) as did his son Keali'iahonui (age twenty-three), thus tying together the two forces through marriage. In 1822, Ka'ahumanu and Kaumuali'i took their large entourage on tours of windward O'ahu, a return trip to Kaua'i, among other places. While not a match of love, Ka'ahumanu remained Kaumuali'i's wife until his death in 1824 at the age of forty-six. Per his wishes, he is buried in the Tomb of Hale Kamani, a royal cemetery in Lahaina Maui. Ka'ahumanu lived eight more years until 1832.

Kaumuali'i is honored in many ways: Kaua'i Museum is devoted to telling his story and collecting items that belonged to him; State Highway 50 around the Kaua'i island is named for him; as is an elementary school in Hanamā'ulu, Kaua'i.

Kaumuali'i Statue in Waimea

This impressive eight-foot bronze statue overlooks the site of his royal compound. The Waimea statue had been the dream of a group of Kaua'i residents since at least 2004. The dream remained unrealized for many years as there was no image of Kaumuali'i to use as a model. It was rejuvenated when two of the stalwarts found a painting of Kaumuali'i by Brook Kapūkiniahi-Parker in a book by Lee Croft, a professor, and former Friends member. Since there were no photos of the king or descriptions, this painting of the reunion of Kaumuali'i and his son Humehume caused great excitement. When asked to explain, Parker told them that it came after contemplation of items at the Bishop Museum known to belong to Kaumuali'i: a mahiole (feather helmet), and a palaoa (whale-tooth pendant) as well as his work with Herb Kāne. Parker sold to the Friends the unrestricted rights to the image he created.

Newly inspired, The Friends of King Kaumuali'i group started up again in 2013, headed by Aletha Kaohi and Barbara Bennett. Their first objective was to achieve awareness about the importance of Kaumuali'i, later they became dedicated to placing a statue of him in Waimea. Kaohi was a sixth generation relative of Kaumuali'i. This was her family story, and it was her father's wish that she would memorialize the king.

In 2014, the Friends group connected with sculptor Saim Caglayan, a part-time resident of Kaua'i who owned an art shop in Hanapēpē. He became excited about the project and originally intended to carve it from a single basalt rock, but eventually decided to create a bronze sculpture. Dr. Keao NeSmith, who sat as the model for the work, later learned that he is a descendant of Kaumuali'i.

Caglayan first created a three-foot maquette in the spring of 2017 to show how the statue would look. It was shown around the island at schools and other public places to generate interest. The Friends worked with Bill Arakaki, the DOE complex superintendent, to distribute posters of Kamuali'i showing his timeline, teaching the children and others of his importance, and staging May Day programs featuring Kaumuali'i's story. That three-foot maquette is now located at the Visitor Center in Waimea and still travels around the island to generate interest. A small number of maquettes have been made available for sale as part of continued fund-raising.

The Friends became a 501 (c)3 organization in 2016, capable of receiving donations and grants. They raised money from donations and a lūau. They received a state grant of $220,00 and another grant from the County of Kaua'i for the work. The base lists the names of all the contributors. Volunteers from the community helped build the pā (enclosure) for the statue. Fundraising continues to create the gardens and needed security. The Friends are currently focusing on a genealogy project to find descendants and connections.

According to sculptor Caglayan, the work took over seven years and progressed as funds became available. He made early clay and bronze versions. The final was cast in gypsum in his Laguna Beach Studio and sent to the JP Art Foundry in southern California for the bronze treatment and patina finish. Caglayan said he was most "honored" to be part of Hawaiian culture in such a close way.

The finished work, at eight feet tall, was sent to Kaua'i, with NeSmith as its escort. Information signage nearby explains the celestial orientation, with the king facing the setting sun on the Spring Equinox and looking towards both Kaua'i and Ni'ihau. The king's statue is placed so that it faces the sunsets of the winter solstice on the left and the summer solstice on the right.

Friends sought and received permission from the State Board of Land and Natural Resources for the statue to be erected at the state park. Ownership of the statue was transferred to the State, and the Friends signed a ten-year agreement to serve as caretaker/curator.

Installation and site work began with a blessing in December 2020. The statue was installed in March 2021, with only 50 attendees present, due to COVID restrictions. The public dedication was held in June 2022. Events and celebrations are planned annually.

Pā'ula'ula State Historic Park

Nearby the statue are the ruins of Pā'ula'ula, a fort that Kaumualii had built adjacent to his own residence using designs supplied by Kaumuali'i's then-ally, George Schaffer, a trade representative for the Russian American Company (RAC). It included rocks from the outer star shaped wall and a few interior structures which are explained by a set of infor-

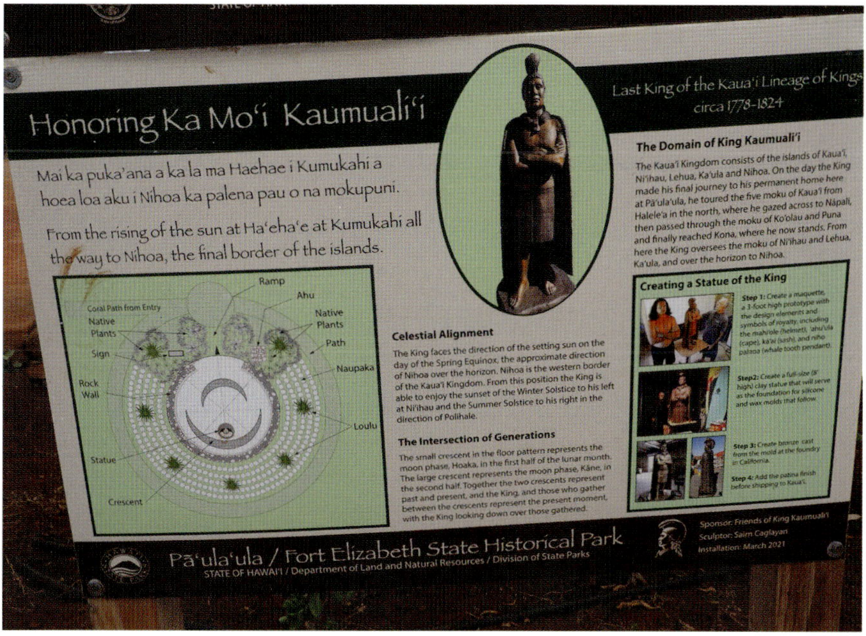

Kaumualii sign at Paulaula State Park. Photo by Ray Soon

mational panels and kiosks. Schaffer worked on it for less than a year; the fort was completed in 1817 by Kaumuali'i's forces after the RAC left.

According to historian Alexander Molodin, both Shaffer and Kaumuali'i thought it was being built for their own use. The RAC, upon learning of Schaffer's activities, distanced themselves from the rival Hawaiian kingdoms. Kaumuali'i drove Schaffer off the island on a ship that was so leaky that it was intentionally run aground off O'ahu. Once there, Kamehameha expelled him from Hawai'i.

Kaumuali'i, meanwhile, ruled Kaua'i and the fort for seven more years and, for forty years after that, his descendants occupied the Waimea fort using it as an administrative center, burial ground, and prison. The use of traditional Hawaiian building materials such as volcanic rock reinforce the view that this was the work of Kaumuali'i's men.

The fort has gone by several names, reflecting its various histories. The area was dismantled around 1864. Some of the ruins remain, including rocks from the outer star-shaped wall and a few interior structures. The area fell into a disrepair and was never restored.

For a century, the land was owned by the Robinson family, who sold it to the state in 1972 to became a state park. At that time, it was named Russian Fort Elizabeth and often called the Russian Fort. Fifty years later in June 2022, the state approved re-naming the site as Pā'ula'ula State Historic Park. Archaeologist Peter Mills used work for his doctoral dissertation to help correct the history of the site.

The corrected Hawaiian name, Pā'ula'ula, means "Red enclosure." Efforts have been underway since 2017 (the fort's bicentennial) to reconcile the history and, to replace and correct the signage. A group on Kaua'i is dedicated to telling the area's mo'olelo (story).

For Further Reading: Mills, Peter R. "A New View of Kaua'i as 'The Separate Kingdom' after 1810." *The Hawaiian Journal of History 30*: 91-104. 1996.

Mills, Peter R. *Hawaii's Russian Adventure: A New Look at Old History*. University of Hawai'i Press. 2002.

Molodin, Alexander, and Peter R. Mills. "Addressing Tensions between Colonial and Post-Colonial Histories: Modeling Hawaiian Fort Pā'ula'ula/Russian Fort Elizabeth, Kaua'i Island, Hawai'i." *Asian Perspectives 60 (1)*: 2-31. Project Muse, doi:10.1353/asi. 2020.

Mills, Peter M. *Connecting the Kingdom*. UH Press. 2023.

Zambucka, Kristin. *Kaumuali'i: King of Kaua'i*. Published by Regina Kawananakoa. ISBN-931897-03-3. 1999. No longer in print and rare to find.

Ali'i 'Aimoku Kaumuali'i and Mō'ī Wahine Kekaihaakulou

Owner	Kaua'i Museum
Commissioned by	Kaua'i Museum
Location	Kaua'i Museum, Līhu'e
Year Erected	2021, 2022
Artist	3D prototype fabricated by White Clouds, Ogden, Utah

This figure-set at Kaua'i Museum in Līhu'e was the vision of island kupuna Billy Lemn. He lamented after seeing so many statues of other ethnicities, and wanted a Hawaiian statue in Līhu'e.

He drew up a sketch with his idea and shared it with Kaua'i Museum director Chucky Boy Chock who was enthusiastic about going forward. Chock had artist Evelyn Ritter do a color drawing of Lemn's vision sketch. Models were found to pose for the statue.

The Kaua'i Museum on Rice Street in Līhu'e is dedicated to telling the story of Kaumuali'i. Stunning paintings show him as a strong, handsome, and noble man, fitting to his royal heritage. Other paintings show important events in his life, including the 1810 historic meeting with Kamehameha, and a reunion with his son Humehume. Artifacts have been collected, including many from the ship (*Ha'aeheo o Hawai'i*) which Liholiho used to capture Kaumuali'i and bring him to O'ahu. A replica of his royal 'ahu 'ula (cape) was made and now proudly hangs in the museum.

The first designer was Chris O'Connor who based the image on Lemn's vision and the later painting, estimating size and features from articles at the Bishop Museum once possessed by Kaumuali'i (his actual looks are unknown). The two figures are mounted on a metal plate set upon a short rock wall. The king stands at six-foot-four and the Queen stands at five-foot-nine, both figures are life-sized. The statue is surrounded by ti leaf plants and a short wrought-iron fencing to indicate its sacredness.

This statue set is a 3D prototype fabricated at a plant in Ogden, Utah (White Clouds). According to their website, it took White Clouds 2,500

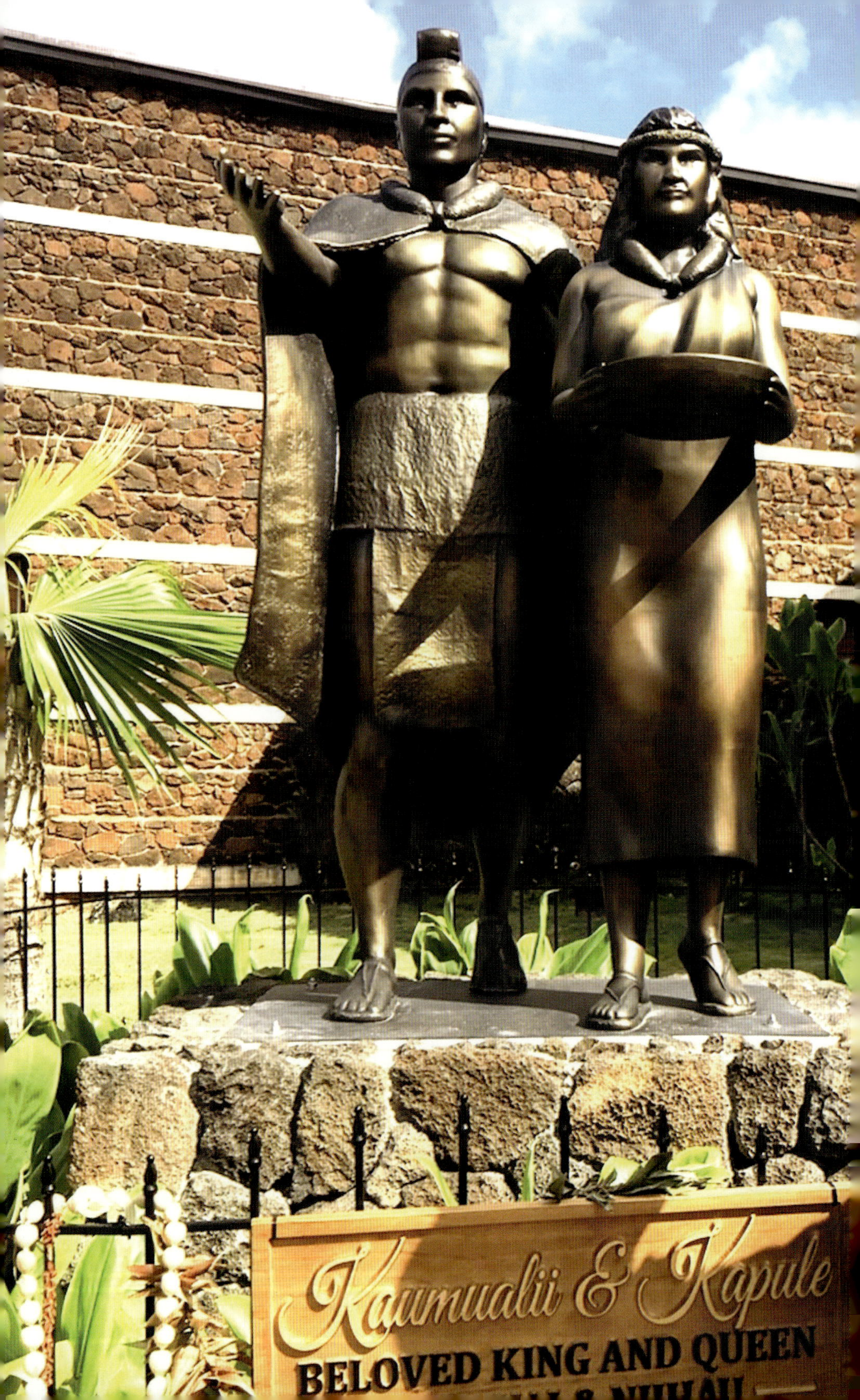
Kaumualii & Kapule
BELOVED KING AND QUEEN

hours of print time to make the eighty-three pieces from ultra-fine layers of plastic which are bonded together around an external structure. Layers of fiberglass are applied followed by airbrushing the bronze paint and satin finish and a final clear coat for extra protection. This sculpture weighs 480 pounds. The first prototype that was installed did not withstand the local climate and started to crack. The second prototype, also produced by White Clouds was installed in 2022. Efforts are underway to create a permanent bronze version.

Opposite page: Kaumuali'i and Kapule statue outside the Kaua'i Museum. Photo by Ray Soon

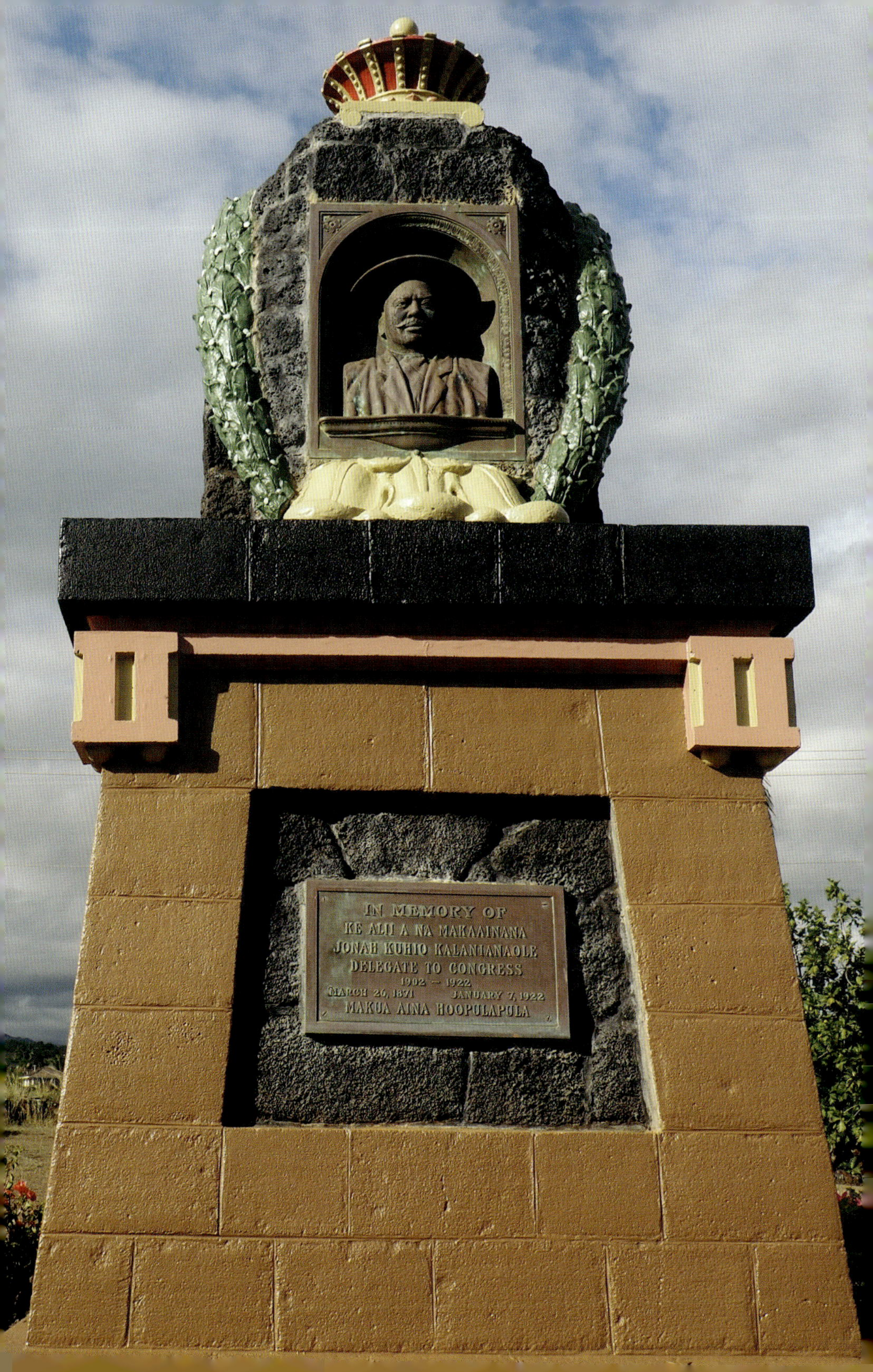
IN MEMORY OF
KE ALII A NA MAKAAINANA
JONAH KUHIO KALANIANAOLE
DELEGATE TO CONGRESS
1902 — 1922
MARCH 26, 1871 JANUARY 7, 1922
MAKUA AINA HOOPULAPULA

Prince Kūhiō (Jonah Kūhiō Kalaniana'ole)

(1871-1922)

Owner	Royal Order of Kamehameha, Chapter III Kaumuali'i
Commissioned by	Hawai'i Territorial Legislature Order of Kamehameha, Kaumuali'i Chapter
Location	Prince Kūhiō Park in Kōloa
Year Dedicated	1928
Artist	Julius Rosenstein

Prince Kūhiō was the youngest of three sons born to Kapi'olani's sister, Victoria Kinoiki Kekaulike, and to Chief David Pi'ikoi. They were descended from King Kaumuali'i of Kaua'i. When their parents died (Kūhiō was then only fourteen), the boys were brought into King Kalākaua and Queen Kapi'olani's household as hānai (adoptees) and groomed for royal duties. His boyish good looks earned him the nickname "Prince Cupid."

Kūhiō was next in line to Ka'iulani and would have become a candidate king had the monarchy not been overthrown. Kūhiō went to both the Royal School and Oahu College (Punahou), and then to business school in England in conjunction with his military training. Much of his education occurred abroad in California, England, though he also attended schooling in Japan for a year under the sponsorship of King Kalākaua.

In 1895, Kūhiō spent a year in jail for joining the revolution led by Robert Wilcox against the Republic of Hawai'i. Wilcox wanted to restore the Kingdom of Hawai'i under Queen Lili'uokalani who had been wrongly overthrown. After the failed coup against the Republic leaders, Kūhiō was charged with treason and sent to prison. Kūhiō was visited in jail daily by Chiefess Elizabeth Kahanu Ka'auwai, and they married shortly after his release in October 1896. They traveled extensively.

Opposite page: Prince Kūhiō Memorial. Photo by Ray Soon

Upon returning from his travels, Kūhiō became active in politics. He came to see annexation as preferable to the republic rule, while still arguing for the restoration of the Hawaiian Kingdom. When it was time to elect a representative to Congress, Robert Wilcox, the radical who defended and attempted to restore the monarchy, was elected to serve for a two-year term from 1899-1901.

In 1902, Kūhiō defeated Wilcox to become Hawai'i's next congressman. He went on to serve ten two-year terms. He spent nineteen years in congress generating sympathy and support for Hawaiian causes. He was an effective leader who built alliances. His achievements are well known: He influenced both the passage of the Hawaiian Homes Act and the formation of the Hawaiian Homes Commission. The act set aside two hundred thousand acres for ninety-nine-year leases to claimants who are at least 50-percent Hawaiian.

The Order of Kamehameha was formed in 1865, and in 1902/3 Kūhiō helped reorganize it. Other royal societies followed. Kūhiō helped form the Hawaiian Civic Clubs in 1918 to mobilize Native Hawaiians dedicated to elevating and promoting the social, economic, civic, and intellectual status of their citizens and leaders.

Kūhiō Memorial and Park

This site was turned over to the Royal Order with funds for clearing and restoration from the Territorial Legislature. The Royal Order commissioned Julius Rosenstein to create the bust and plaque.

Another plaque, embedded on a large rock structure several yards away, honors members of the Royal Order Chapter III "Kaumualii" with the date 2001 and the insignia of the Royal Order of Kamehameha.

For Further Reading: Kamae, Lori Ku'ulei. *The Empty Throne: A Biography of Hawaii's Prince Cupid.* Topgallant Publishing Company. 1980.

Captain James Cook

(1728-1779)

Owner	State Foundation on Culture and the Arts, Art in Public Places
Commissioned by	Kaua'i Historical Society
Location	C.B. Hofgaard Park, Old Waimea Road
Year Erected	1928, part of Cook Sesquicentennial
Artist	Replica of original statue in Whitby, England by Sir John Tweed, R.A.

Captain James Cook was a British explorer, navigator, surveyor, and cartographer who lived in the eighteenth century. He was born to a farming family in Marton, England, but moved several times in his youth trying different occupations before discovering the lure of the sea in Whitby, England. Cook was married and had six children, but none lived to child-bearing age, so he had no descendants. He spent most of his time at sea and in the service of the Royal Navy; several of his early years in service were in war settings before he later took on explorations. He was aided by his superb knowledge of astronomy, hydrology, triangulation, and his willingness to use new inventions such as the K1 chronometer for measuring longitude. His work caught the attention of the Admiralty and Royal Society who sponsored his three exploratory voyages.

Cook's detailed maps of the jagged coast of Newfoundland, the St. Lawrence River in Canada, and New Zealand, and Australia were used well into the twentieth century. These maps, along with dozens of published journals containing scientific and geographical information, remain his legacy. His collections may be found in Australia, South Wales, and England. Many memorials have been dedicated to him around the world.

Cook is credited as the first Westerner to establish contact with the Hawaiian Islands. His extensive records helped preserve important knowledge of that period and the ecology of the time. His arrival is also considered a marker in time that opened the islands to outside social, economic, political, and cultural influences which within a century to-

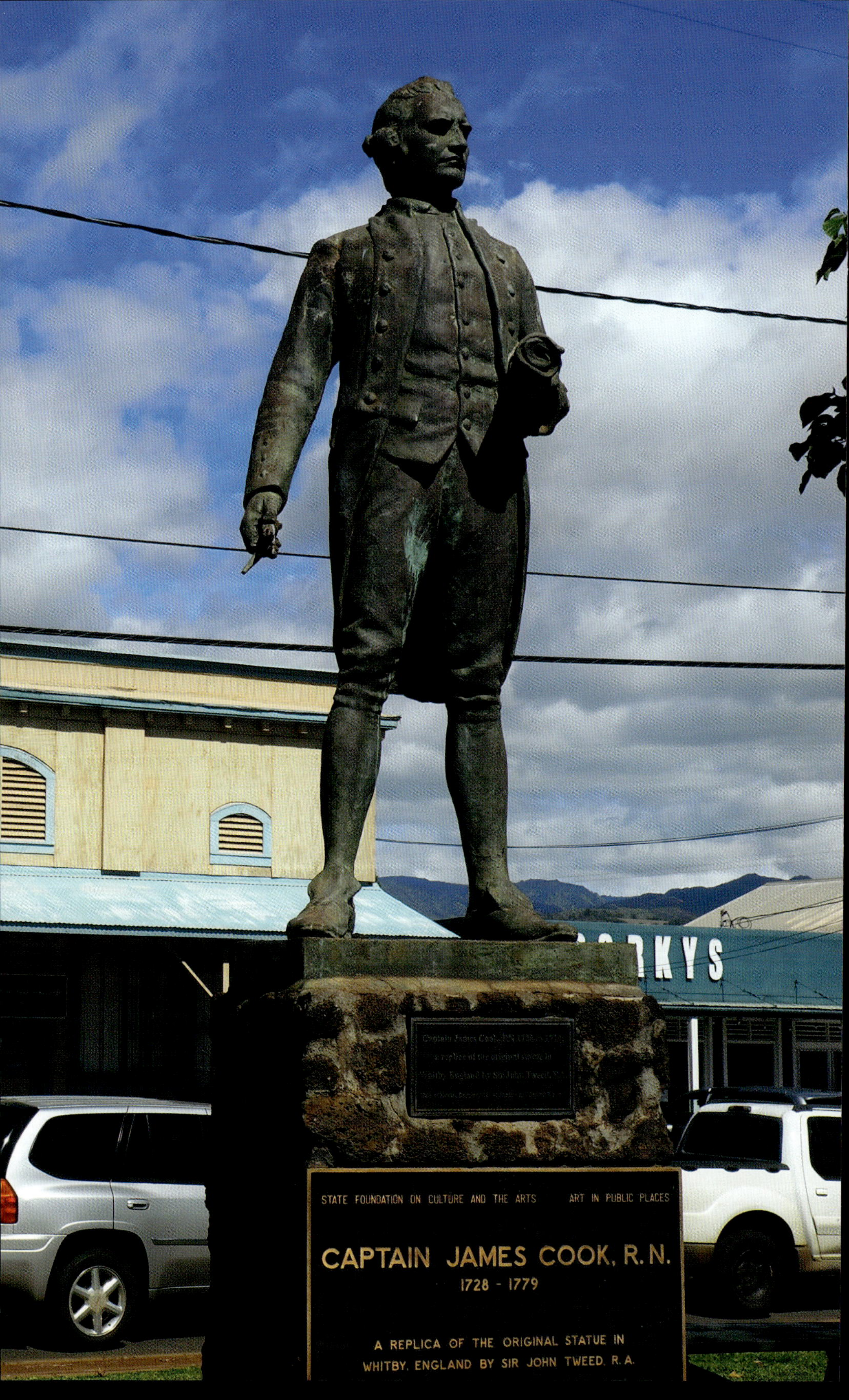
STATE FOUNDATION ON CULTURE AND THE ARTS
ART IN PUBLIC PLACES
CAPTAIN JAMES COOK, R.N.
1728 - 1779
A REPLICA OF THE ORIGINAL STATUE IN
WHITBY, ENGLAND BY SIR JOHN TWEED, R.A.

tally transformed island governance and living. Cook's voyages carried scientists, artists and cultural advisors, and many findings were documented for the first time. His botanists collected over three thousand species, and Cook's artists prepared valuable pictorial images of what they encountered. Cook himself kept careful journals, which were published and circulated throughout the world, helping to make Hawaiʻi a desirable port of call.

On his first voyage (1768-1771) Cook, then a surveyor in the Royal Navy, was commissioned as a lieutenant to command the H.M.S. *Endeavor* on an expedition to chart the course of the planet Venus across the sun, by traveling to Tahiti. He explored the coasts of New Zealand and Australia and circumnavigated the world. His second voyage and commission (1772-1775) sent him to the South Pacific where he explored many regions including New Hebrides, New Caledonia, and the Antarctic.

On his third voyage Cook was looking for a Northwest passage. He traveled through the Horn of Africa and the Indian Ocean south of Australia before shifting northward where he came upon the Hawaiian Islands in January 1778. According to the National Park Service, Cook "explored the area and its valley noting the villages, people temples, trees and crops." He named Hawaiʻi the Sandwich Islands after one of his patrons, John Montagu, the Earl of Sandwich who was the acting First Lord of the Admiralty.

The voyage was a long one, taking him first to Kauaʻi and Niʻihau, then to California, Oregon, Washington, Vancouver, and Alaska in the North Atlantic, before returning to the Hawaiian Islands again in 1779. He quickly became acquainted with the local people. The King of Kauaʻi and his high chiefs were centered in Wailua near the river, but spent their winters in Waimea where it was mild and dry. Cook's articles of trade included beads, iron, ceramics, mirrors, firearms, and cloth. He traded these for pigs, water, taro, sweet potatoes, yams, and coconuts.

By his third journey, and perhaps suffering from illness, Cook showed signs of violent behavior and poor judgment. According to officer journals from 1777 in Tahiti, Cook ordered the burning of villages and sink-

Opposite page: Captain James Cook statue. Photo by Ray Soon

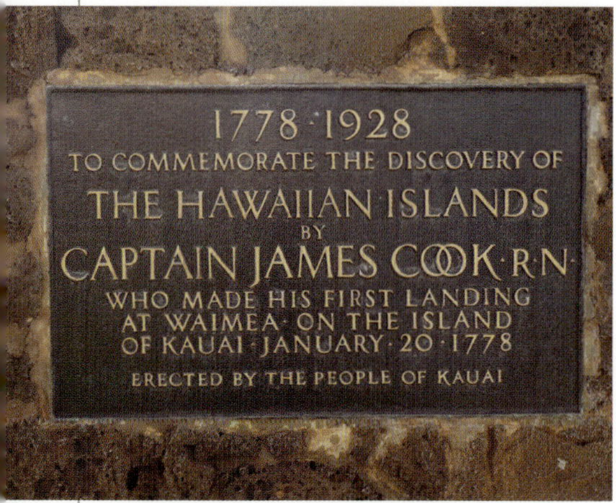

Cook Monument sign. Photo by Ray Soon

ing of canoes in reprisal for minor thefts. Therefore, his explorer legacy is marred by criticisms citing colonialism and poor treatment of natives.

Cook met his death in a conflict with Indigenous people in Kealakekua Bay, Hawaiʻi in 1779. He had arrived during the makahiki festivities honoring the god of fertility, Lono. Popular legend has it that Cook was killed when the locals learned he was not a personification of Lono, as they had thought; but this version has been contested. The islanders no longer had warm feelings towards their visitors who needed much food and supplies and, who had stolen a fence and wooden images from a burial ground to use as firewood. While he was anchored in Kealakekua Bay to fix a damaged mast, the locals stole a longboat from Cook's ship. Cook demanded it back. When the locals refused to comply, Cook attempted to kidnap the aliʻi nui, Kalaniʻōpuʻu (a tactic he had used in Tahiti and Raʻiātea under similar circumstances). When one of the lesser chiefs was shot, the gathering mob descended on Cook's party, killing him and four others. In retaliation, the departing Englishmen fired their cannons and muskets towards the shore, killing thirty Hawaiians.

Cook Monument and Statue

The Cook commemorative monument was dedicated on August 16, 1928 as part of the Cook Sesquicentennial (150th). It is made of lava rock mounted with two bronze plaques. The top one is a scene with the *Resolution* and *Discovery*, Cook's ships, and a group of Hawaiians looking towards them. The other bronze plaque contains the inscription explaining that the monument was commissioned by a group of prominent local citizen who raised the money to build it.

The nearby statue of a standing Captain Cook was once placed at Waimea Canyon School as a project of the State Foundation on Culture and the Arts. It is a replica of the Cook statue by Sir John Tweed in Cook's hometown of Whitby, England. In 1978, as part of the American Bicentennial (200th) celebration, the statue was moved to be near the 1928 monument in Hofgaard Park to give it more visibility.

The statue has Cook standing tall on a six-inch base that rests on an eight-foot lava rock pedestal, providing a larger-than-life presence. One must look up to him. His feet are apart and clad in shoes and stockings; he is wearing knickers, a vest, and a topcoat. His gaze is forward, his hair rolled up at ear length, and his face seems to have a contemplative look to reflect his scientist nature. Under his left arm, which is hooked at the elbow, is a rolled scroll, possibly symbolizing his skills in cartography. In his right hand between the index finger and thumb are calipers, a device to make accurate measure dimensions.

The statue is fiberglass cast with copper nitrate which explains the greenish hue that has overtaken its surface over time. A bronze plaque explains the particulars of the statue. Actually, there are two such signs that say exactly the same thing. The upper version is the original and somewhat faded; the newer version is larger and, at least for now, more readable. The newer version adds the name of the State Foundation on Culture and the Arts, Art in Public Places.

One of the interpretive signs explains Cook's association with Waimea Bay, starting in January 1778, when he spent two weeks there and another week in Ni'ihau. "*The British explorers were amazed at finding the Polynesian race on these remote islands, thousands of miles from any other inhabited island. Westerners had only recently learned how to travel across oceans and it was obvious to them that the Polynesians were masters of long-distance ocean travel.*"

The plaque should more accurately state that 1778 was his arrival date, not the "discovery date" as Hawai'i did not need to be discovered, except from a European perspective.

Cook's January 20, 1778 landfall is marked by a bronze plaque placed in 1969 and mounted on a stone adjacent to the breakwater at the mouth of the Waimea River beside Pakala Village at Lucy Wright Park. While the precise location is not known and the land shape has likely shifted due to sediment deposits and building the breakwater and a county park, the landing is designated a National Landmark and is on both the State of Hawaiʻi and US National Register of Historic Places.

For further Reading: Maclean, Alistair. *Captain Cook: Explorer, Navigator, Hero.* HarperCollins. 1983

Hough, Richard. *Captain James Cook: A Biography*. Norton. 1997.

US Senator Spark Matsunaga

(1916-1990)

Piece Name	"Walking in the Garden" Spark Matsunaga and Carly
Type	Bronze sculpture with adult (Matsunaga) and child figures 81.5" x 40 x 34.5"
Subject Honored	Spark M. Matsunaga
Location	Matsunaga International Children's Garden for Peace
Island	Hanapēpē, Kaua'i
Artist	Kim Duffett
Year	2008
Commissioned by	Storybook Theatre of Hawai'i

Spark M. Matsunaga was born and raised in the town of Hanapēpē. He graduated from University of Hawai'i in 1941 and from Harvard Law School in 1951. During World War II, after being interned in a detention camp in Wisconsin, he served in the 442nd Regimental Combat Team, 100th Battalion and was wounded twice in battle in Northern Italy.

Beloved by all, Sparky became a US Senator in 1977 and served six terms until 1990. Throughout his political career, Matsunaga was known for battling years-long fights, including lobbying for the creation of the position of Poet Laureate (1985) and for a US Institute of Peace (1984). His portrait is on the US Series I Bonds in the $10,000 denomination. Matsunaga was a great advocate for peace and diplomacy during the Cold War.

The Matsunaga Institute for Peace and Conflict Resolution (formerly the Institute for Peace) was established in 1990 at the University of Hawai'i Mānoa in the College of Social Sciences. Maya Soetoro-Ng (President Obama's sister) runs a program there called Ceeds of Peace: Courage & Critical Thinking Within; Compassion & Conflict Resolution with Others; and Commitment, Collaboration & Connection with Community.

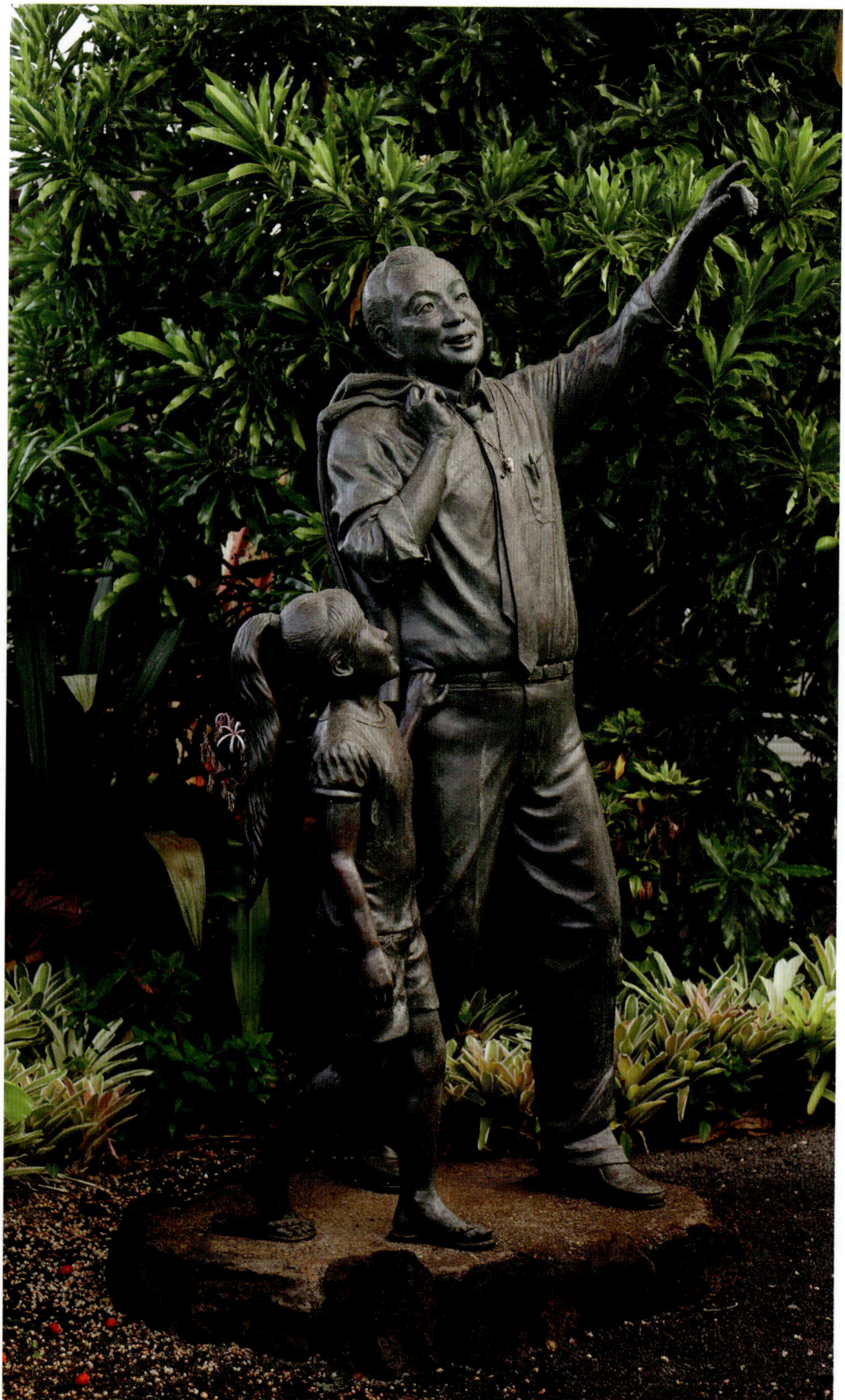

The Matsunaga International Children's Garden of Peace located in Hanapēpē is privately owned (by Mark Jeffers) and scaled for children. It includes a gazebo, a Japanese bridge, waterfall and pools, an outdoor performance amphitheater and star tapa designed roof. There is a twenty-four-foot covered entry trellis and a seventeen-foot-tall whimsical entrance gate, named Tree of Life, by the late architect Kevin N.P. Chun, who collaborated with Mark Jeffers and Kim Duffett on the garden project. The peace pole, koa plated on a gum tree base, has six sides. It was donated by the Kaua'i Hindu Temple (see Chapter Eight for more on this Temple).

Matsunaga Statue

The Matsunaga statue, named "Walking in the Garden," is 1.18 times life sized. Known for being immaculately dressed, this statue shows Matsunaga in a more casual "retirement" mode, with his jacket slung over his shoulder and his young friend's hand on his waist. He never did reach retirement, as he died in office.

Sparky's left-hand points to the sky. According to Mark Jeffers, founder of Storybook Theatre, the figurative young girl "Carly" follows his finger, looking towards the limitless possibilities above, what is separate and what is whole, the foundation for diplomacy, compassion, and peace. Duffett relates that the model for Carly was one of his neighbor's children.

The statue was funded by a grant from the 2005 Hawai'i State Legislature and through local fundraising.

For Further Reading: Halloran, Richard. *Sparky: Warrior, Peacemaker, Poet, Patriot: A Portrait of Senator Spark M. Matsunaga.* Watermark Publishing. 2022.

Matsunaga, Senator Spark with Foreword by Arthur C. Clarke. *The Mars Project: Journeys Beyond the Cold War.* Hill & Wang Publishers. 1986.

Opposite page: *Walking in the Garden.* Photo by Christian R. Cook

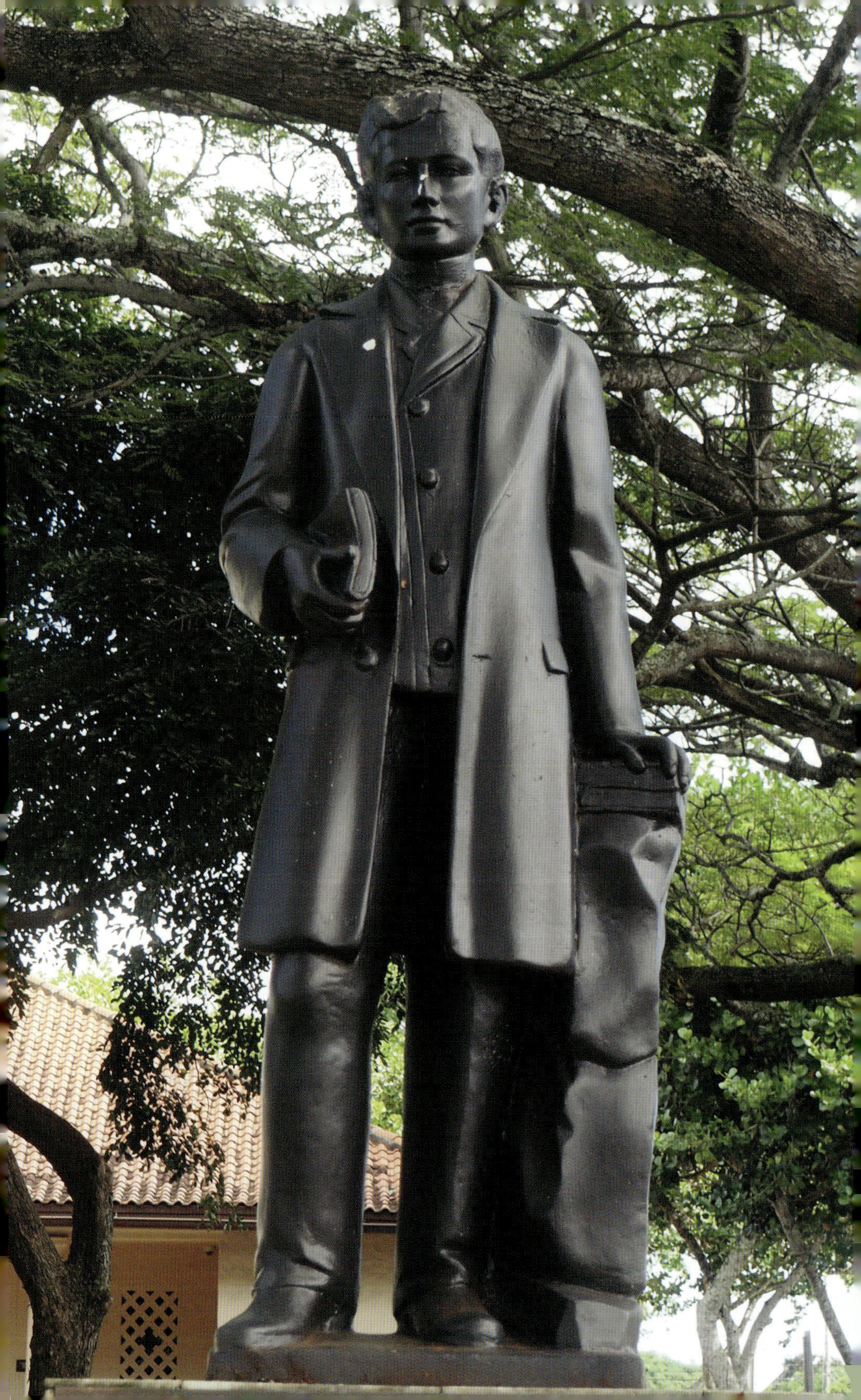

Dr. Jose Protacio Rizal Y Mercado

(1861-1896)

Owner	County of Kaua'i
Commissioned by	Kaua'i Filipino Community Council
Location	Līhu'e Civic Center Grounds
Year Erected	1984; repaired in 1997
Artist	Unknown

Dr. Jose Rizal is a national hero and martyr of the Philippines. His life is celebrated annually on December 30, the date of his death. Following his medical studies, Rizal spent ten years in Madrid and is known to have traveled extensively; some of his destinations included Singapore, Hong Kong, and Tokyo as well as many cities in America. Through his writings, Rizal led the start of a revolution against the Spanish government to attain freedom and gain control of the Philippines. He was ultimately executed by firing squad by the Spanish colonizers. In dying, he used the parting words of Jesus Christ before his crucifixion: "It is done."

Rizal was a highly talented intellectual, excelling in both science and the arts. He worked as a painter sketcher, sculptor, and woodcarver and was conversant in over ten languages. His most famous novels were *Noli me Tangere* (*Touch me Not*) and its sequel *El Filibusterismo* (*The Filibustering or Reign of Greed*) which both expose injustices against the Philippines by Spain. He sought change through peaceful means.

Rizal Statue

The Rizal statue in Līhu'e has been an ongoing project of the Kaua'i Filipino Community Council. The first monument placed was a shoulder bust. When the bust was vandalized, a youth group called Pag Asa Ng Bayan and their advisor, Ms. Rosalina Arzadon, worked to find a replace-

Opposite page: Dr. Jose Rizal statue in Līhu'e. Photo by Ray Soon

ment. The Kaua'i Committee, chaired by Alfredo Villaneuva, worked with then-first-lady of the Philippines, Imelda R. Marcos, the Minister of Tourism, and the Philippine consulate general, Trinidad Alconcel to find a statue as a replacement.

The bust was replaced by a white patina statue, which was installed and dedicated in a ceremony on June, 17, 1984. About twenty years later, cracks emerged and rebar began to show on the statue. When it was repaired, a new patina color was used, brown-black, which is the color presently displayed.

The statue depicts Rizal as a handsome young man, sporting a vest and long overcoat. He has a book in his right hand, which is crooked at the elbow, and his left arm rests on a short pedestal. On the pedestal portion immediately below the statue is a plaque with his name, dates of birth and death and the simple phrase "Philippine National Hero." The lower base is in white rock blocks upon which is mounted another plaque.

Alfredo Villaneuva, leader of the Filipino Community Council at the time, recounted the importance of Rizal and the "obligation of senior Filipinos to display this monument of Dr. Rizal in front of our County building in order to demonstrate and inform the people and especially the Filipinos, the young generations, the third generation, to show some respect for Dr. Rizal."

Rizal Elsewhere

There are two statues of Rizal on O'ahu: in downtown Honolulu, and at the FilCom Cultural Center in Waipahu and there is a bust of him in Maui at Kepaniwai Heritage Park in 'Īao Valley. There are many others throughout the world, including the first Rizal heritage monument in Daet in Camarines Norte Philippines (built in 1898 two years after his death). There are twenty-seven shrines to him throughout the Philippines, one in nearly every town there.

For Further Reading: Ocampo, Esteban. *Why is Rizal the Greatest Filipino Hero?* Manila National Historical Institute, 1996.

Ed and Joyce Doty

(1924-2008 and 1928-2022)

Ed and Joyce Doty were the founders of the 240-acre Na ʻĀina Kai Botanical Gardens & Sculpture Park in Kīlauea. The piece shown here, "The Beginning," by artist Holly Young shows the happy couple in an informal setting under a mountain apple tree, going over plans for the lagoon they planned to create. The two figures were made separately. First came Ed in 2010 (after his 2008 death), and then Joyce in 2019 when she was still alive.

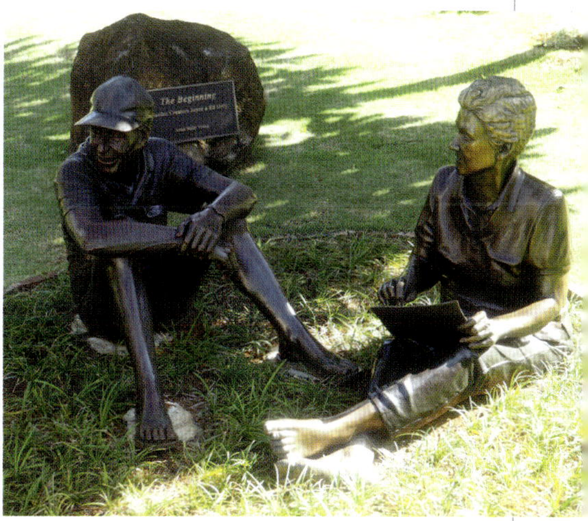

Photo by Ray Soon

Before opening to the public in 2000, these were the private gardens and collection at the retirement home of the Dotys. Joyce envisioned all the areas, "The ideas came in the night, sneaking into my thoughts, and expanding into pictures in my mind like videos." Moving them into implementation was the responsibility of horticulturist Marty Fernandes who worked with Joyce's husband, Ed, and a team of workers who often grew the plantings from seed. A dedicated crew cleans, polishes, and maintains the sculptures year-round. The sculpture collection began when Joyce "ran out of wall space for art in the house."

In 2000, the Dotys created a not-for-profit operating foundation to which they donated the land, buildings, and artwork.

See Chapter Eight for more about the sculpture collection at Na ʻĀina Kai.

Honorable Richard Kawakami

(1931-1987)

Owner	Hawai'i State Foundation on Culture and the Arts
Commissioned by	Hawai'i State Foundation on Culture and the Arts
Location	Līhu'e Airport, Kawakami Terminal
Year Erected	1988
Artist	Don Rich, Don Rich Studio
Name of artwork	"Kawakami" Bronze and steel

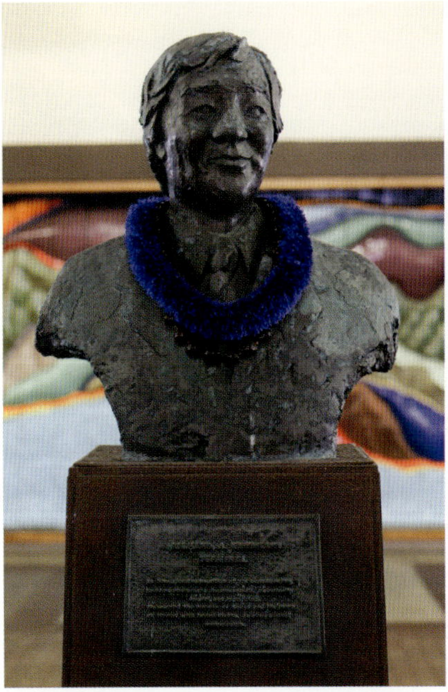

Portrait of Richard A. Kawakami at Līhu'e Airport [CO367] by Don Rich completed in 1988. Cast bronze bust. State Foundation on Culture and the Arts. Photo by Cheryl Soon

Richard Kawakami was from Waimea, Kaua'i, a Democrat who served in the state legislature for twenty-one years and was House Speaker at the time of his death. He was also president of Big Save Groceries in Kaua'i. He was succeeded at the Legislature by his wife, Bertha Kawakami, who served an additional nineteen years until 2006.

The piece named "Kawakami" is a bust commissioned by the State of Hawai'i Foundation on Culture and the Arts. It was created by Don Rich and erected in 1988. Made of bronze and steel, the bust is mounted on a concrete pedestal approximately four feet in height.

On the side of the pedestal, this verbiage is repeated in braille. The plaque on the back of the pedestal gives his name, life span, and position in the State House of Representatives.

Mayor Tony T. Kunimura

(1923-1995)

Owner	County of Kaua'i
Location	Mokihana County Building Atrium
Year Erected	2000
Artist	Sean K.L.L. Browne
Name of artwork	"Memorial Tribute to Uncle Tony"

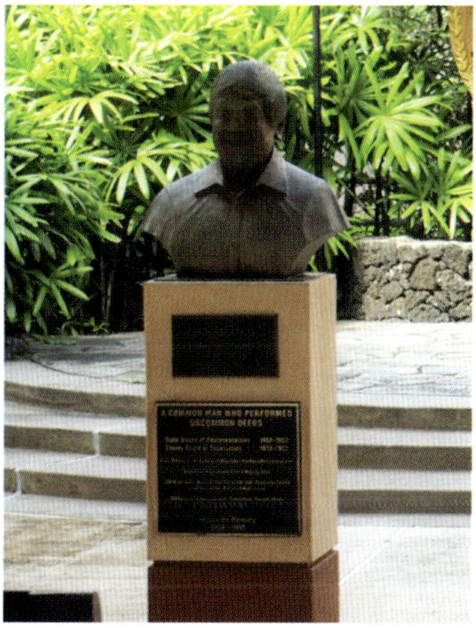

Tony Kunimura bust. Photo by Cheryl Soon

Uncle Tony" Kunimura was a colorful figure in Hawai'i politics for more than five decades. Kunimura was elected to both the county and state levels of government. He began his political career by serving twenty-eight years on the County Board of Supervisors (1954-1962), followed by twenty years in the State House of Representatives (1962 1982). He then served as mayor of Kaua'i County for six years (three terms) from 1982-1988. His career ended when he was defeated in his final mayoral race.

During his time as Kaua'i mayor, Kunimura created the vision for centralized government offices in the old Līhu'e Shopping Center and oversaw its purchase and plans for renovation. He was also responsible for purchasing the land for Wilcox School, the Convention Hall, and the Community College on Kaua'i. He was a champion for the arts, education, environment, tourism, health and safety, and Kaua'i's youth.

Upon Kunimura's death, then Mayor Kusaka, a protégé of his, formed a committee to raise funds for a suitable memorial. Upon the recommendation of the State Foundation on Culture and the Arts, they commissioned Sean Browne to create a bronze bust on a pedestal which was unveiled in 2000.

Mayor Maryanne W. Kusaka

(1935-still living)

Maryanne Kusaka was born in Kamuela, Hawai'i and raised in Hāna, Maui. Following graduation, she became an elementary teacher and moved to Kaua'i where she taught for thirty-three years. She was elected Mayor in 1994 and continued in politics until she retired in 2004. In retirement, she has followed a life of community service, including as chair of the board of directors of Kaua'i Museum.

The stone monument honors her years as mayor. It is located outside the Mokihana Building on civic grounds. The bronze plaque reads, "from the Nawiliwili garden of Shugero Kusaka in honor of Mayor Maryanne W. Kusaka 1994-2002."

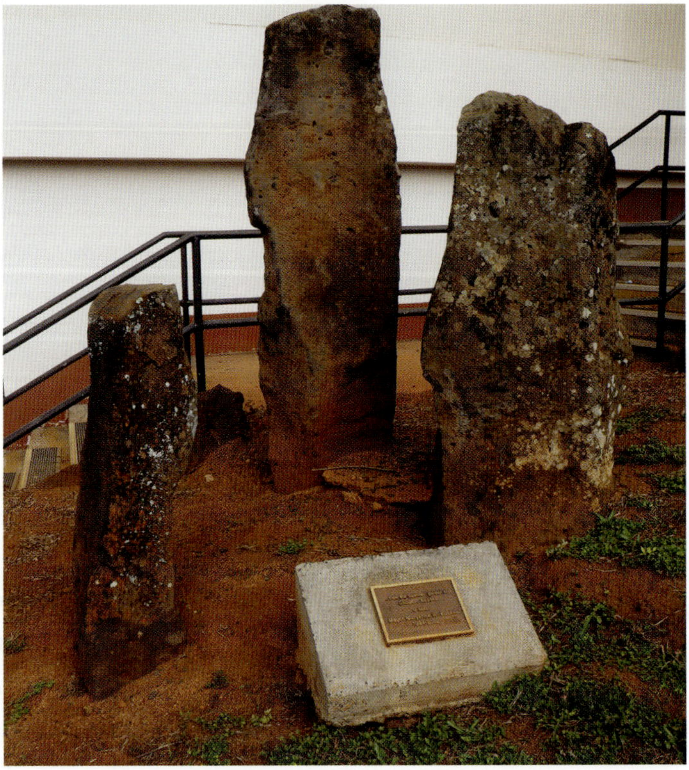

Maryanne Kusaka plaque. Photo by Cheryl Soon

Chipper Wichman

(1957-still living)

Chipper Wichman, and his wife Hauoli Wichman, dedicated their lives to creating and enhancing the National Tropical Botanical Garden. His work there started as an intern, and when he retired five decades later in 2022, he was President. A five-foot-high bronze bust and plaque was created by sculptor J. Brett Grill, donated by Trustee Thomas S. Kenan III, and dedicated November 26, 2019.

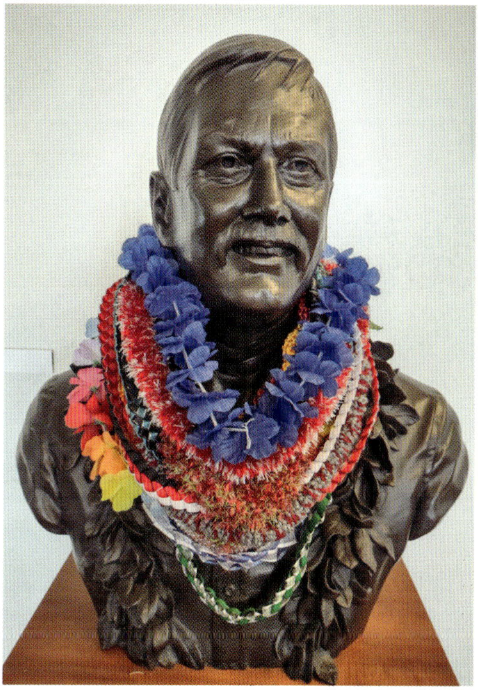

Photo Jan TenBruggencate

NTBG started as a 171-acre parcel in Lāwaʻi Valley, and grew into a conservation hub of almost 2,000 acres, the home of thousands of plant species and collections. This expanded to a network of five garden sites and preserves in Hawaiʻi and Florida. The Juliet Rice Wichman (named for his grandmother) Botanical Research Center houses a seed bank, laboratory, herbarium, and library. Chipper and his wife donated the 1,000 Limahuli Garden in Hāʻena.

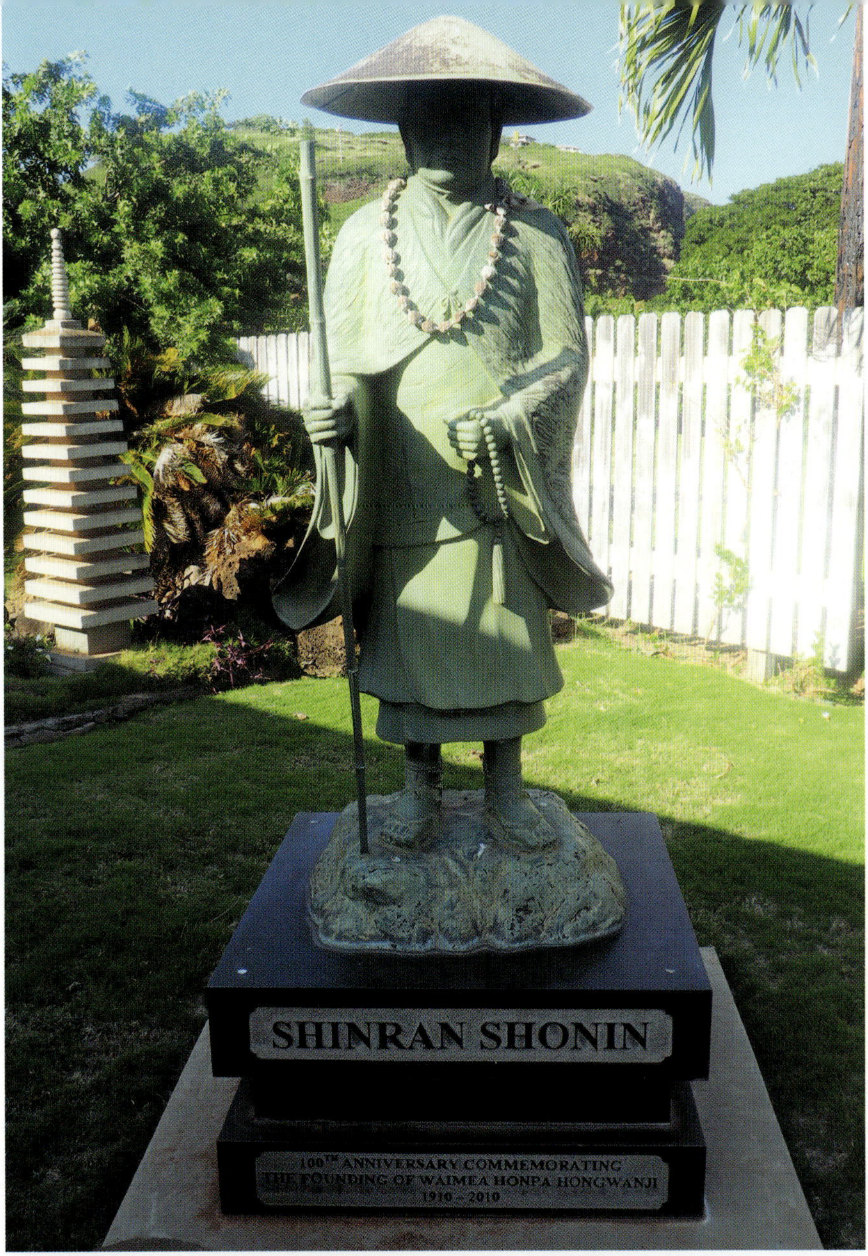
SHINRAN SHONIN
100TH ANNIVERSARY COMMEMORATING
THE FOUNDING OF WAIMEA HONPA HONGWANJI
1910 - 2010

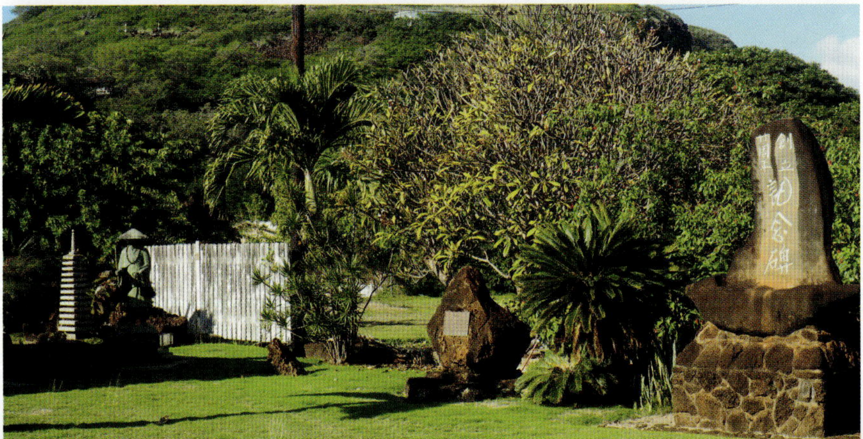

Shinran Shonin

(1173-1263)

Shinran Shonin was a Japanese Buddhist monk who lived during the Heian period. Statues of him are often found at Hongwanji Temples of the Jōdō Shinshu sect. A fuller accounting of this can be found in Chapter Two (Statues of Hawai'i Island). There are ten Hongwanji on Kaua'i Island, and three of them have statues of Shinran.

Shinran Statue

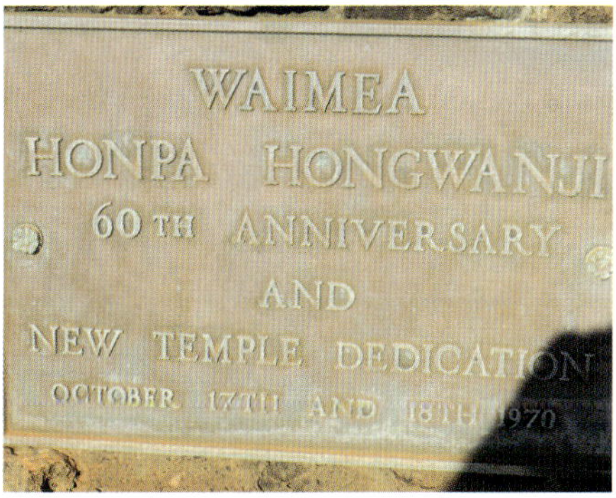

Photo by Cheryl Soon

The Shinran statue on the previous page is located at the West Kaua'i Honpa Hongwanji Waimea Temple. It was erected in 2010 as part of the temple centennial. It was purchased from Japan Memorial Corporation. The statue is on a marble base with his name and the centennial years etched in the stone. He wears peasant clothes, carries a staff in his right hand, and beads in his left hand. The statue is near two other monuments along with two rock memorials, one erected in 1930 on the 20th anniversary of the temple, the other erected in 1970, on the 60th anniversary of the Hongwanji and the year when a new temple was dedicated.

The other two Shinran statues are at West Kaua'i Hongwanji Mission Hanapēpē Temple and the West Kaua'i Hongwanji Mission Koloa Temple. In 1995, the missions of Waimea, Hanapēpē, and Koloa joined to create the West Kaua'i Hongwanji. In November 2022, the West Kaua'i Hongwanji Hanapēpē dedicated a Shinran statue to mark its 25th anniversary.

Opposite page: Shinran at Waimea Honpa Hongwanji. Both photos by Cheryl Soon

Memorials Dedicated to Sugar Planter Family Members

Kōloa, Kauaʻi has been called the birthplace of the sugar industry in Hawaiʻi. The first successful sugar cane plantation began in 1835 at Kōloa, where sugar was already growing naturally. It started with a land lease to Ladd & Company from King Kamehameha III. Within two years, they had produced enough sugarcane for export. The lands were sold at auction to Grove Farm who continued and expanded production over the next century. The plantation continued under other owners and agents with many innovations in production, irrigation, and shipping.

During the American Civil War, the demand for sugar grew and the islands prospered. At one time there were over fifty plantations on five islands. Raw sugar was sent to California, where it was refined and sold. According to Grove Farm Museum's on-line history, in 1980, Hawaiʻi supplied one-tenth of the sugar used in the United States. The demise of the industry came in the mid to late- 1900s. On Kauaʻi, Līhuʻe and Kekaha sugar operations closed in 2000 and Gay & Robinson lasted until 2009. The last sugar operation to close in Hawaiʻi was in Puʻunēnē, Maui in 2016.

Sugar family memorials are prominent on the island of Kauaʻi. The sugar families inter-married and the names of those families are seen today as street names, buildings, and major institutions. Standing memorials (mostly large rocks with bronze medallions and plaques) honoring family members with names such as Rice, Spalding, Wilcox, Isenberg, and Waterhouse are found around the island of Kauaʻi.

Rice Memorial at Līhuʻe Cemetery

This large white marble shaft with carved figures is a memorial to the kamaʻāina Rice and Isenberg families and dedicated to eight persons

Opposite page: Rice Memorial at Līhuʻe Cemetery. Photo by Ray Soon

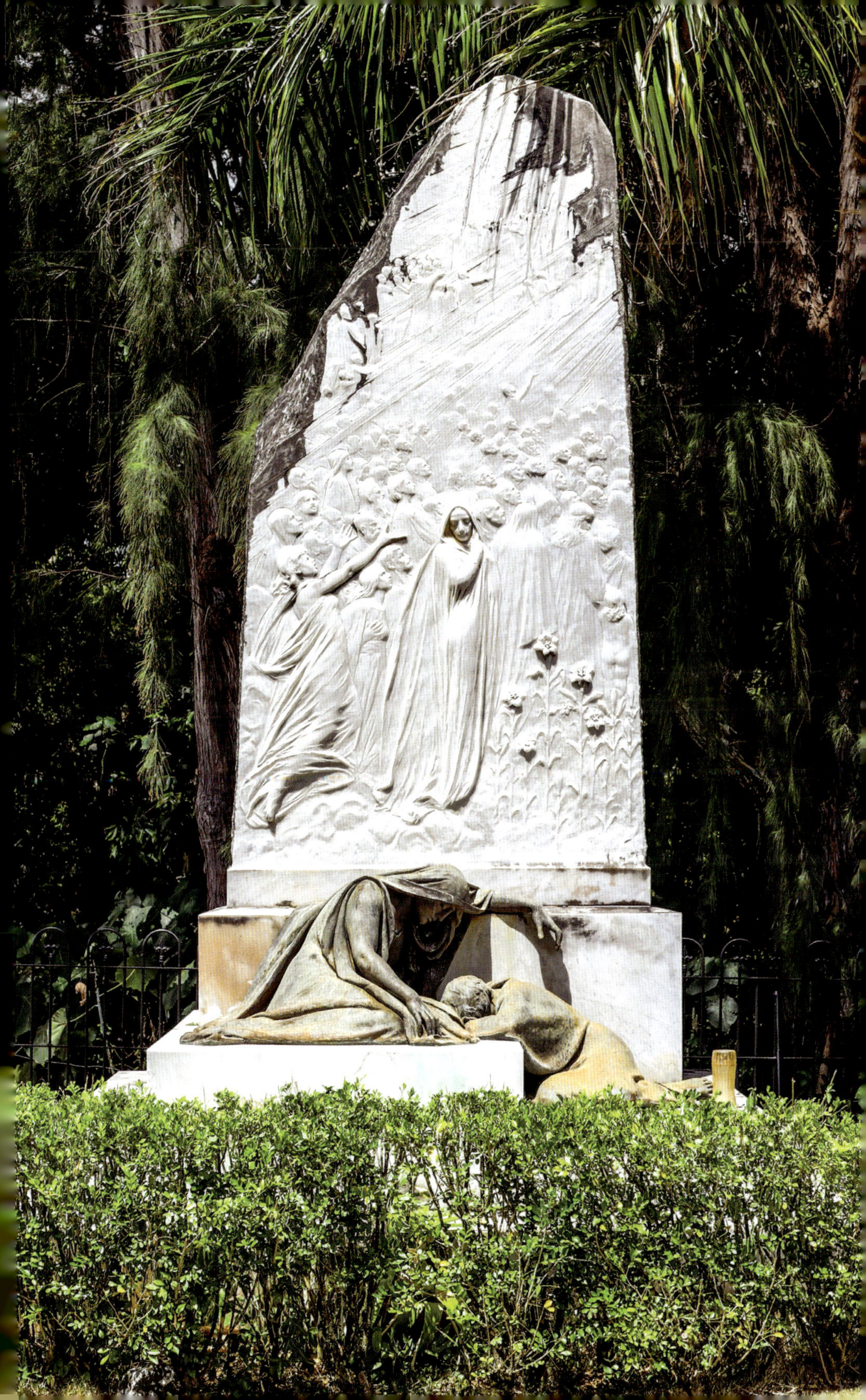

who were born in the 1840s and died in the early 1900s. It shows carved figures, their faces shrouded and turned to heaven. The female figure on the bottom represents Hannah Maria Rice Isenberg (1842-1867), wife of planter Paul Isenberg. The figures at her feet are her grieving children, Mary Dorothea Rice Isenberg and Paul Rice Isenberg.

Named "Blessed Souls Wandering Toward Light" by its creator Stephan Sinding from Norway, who finished the work in 1910, this memorial was exhibited in Paris (France) and Bremen (Germany). It was then shipped around the horn to these islands and then set up by W. Schieber, the head mason of Lihue Plantation. It was unveiled in the presence of relatives and friends by Anna C. Cook on September 1, 1911.

Medallion of William Hyde Rice (Kīpū)

William Hyde Rice (1846-1924) was the last governor of Kaua'i when Hawai'i was a kingdom. He was appointed to that position in 1891, by Queen Lili'uokalani, and held it until she was overthrown in 1893. William Rice, a Kaua'i rancher at the time, bought most of Kalapaki ahupua'a from Princess Ruth Ke'elikōlani in 1879. He ran a ranch on these lands

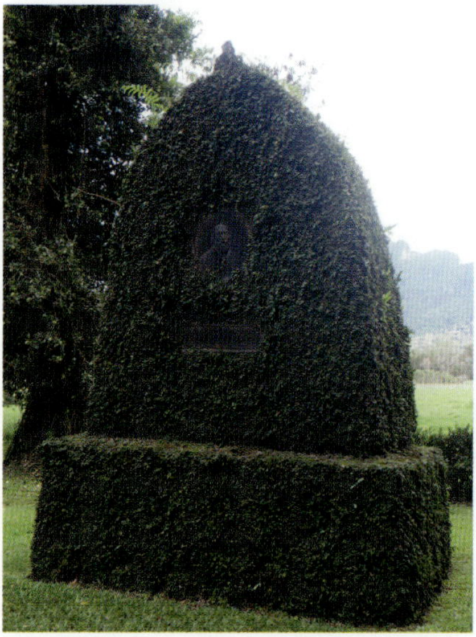

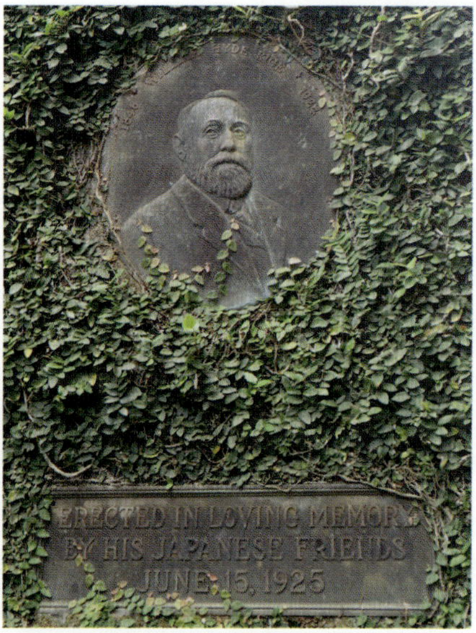

William Hyde Rice Medallion. Both photos by Ray Soon

until selling it in 1881 to the Lihue Plantation. After that, he bought Kīpū ahupua'a, where he raised cattle and grew sugar.

Rice married Mary Waterhouse in 1872 and together they had eight children. He passed away in June 1924. A year later, a monument was erected on Kīpū Road (across from the current-day ranch Zipline Tours). It is a bronze medallion and plaque affixed to a large stone with cultivated ivy. The plaque reads "Erected in loving memory by his Japanese Friends June 15, 1925."

Paul Isenberg Medallion Memorial (Līhu'e)

Paul Isenberg (1887- 1903), a German businessman who helped create the sugarcane industry on Kaua'i and in Hawai'i, was manager of Lihue Plantation from 1862 to 1878 when he became part owner of the company and later its president. He also acquired an interest in the Kōloa Sugar Company and was its president from 1892-1902. He was responsible for building the Hanamā'ulu Mill with machinery he bought from Grove Farm. Later in life, he helped form Hackfield & Company (later called AMFAC).

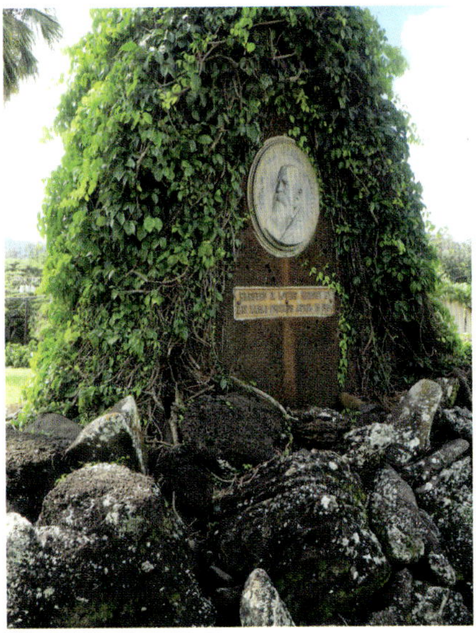

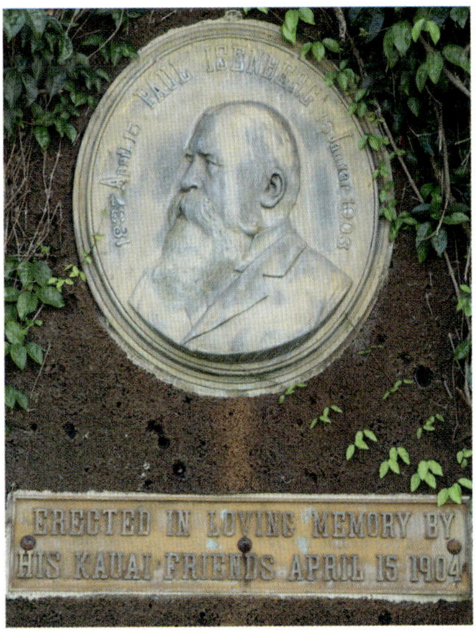

Isenberg Medallion. Both photos by Ray Soon

Isenberg married Maria Rice and they had two children. He had six more children with his second wife, Beta Glade from Germany. Paul Isenberg was appointed to the Hawai'i Legislature by King Lunalilo. In that role, he was one of the few who objected to the use of military force to compel the so-called "Bayonet Constitution" in 1887.

This monument is located on a knoll beside the Bank of Hawai'i and across from the Līhu'e Civic Center. The site overlooks what had been the Līhu'e Mill. The memorial consists of a pile of rocks and a central large rock with a medallion of his image and a low plaque that reads, "Erected in loving memory by his Kaua'i Friends April 15, 1904."

This monument was built a little over a year after his death. Similar to other sugar planter memorials, the large rock is covered in a vine that must be periodically cut back so as not to obscure the medallion and plaque. According to newspaper accounts from the time, it was unveiled in a ceremony attended by over two thousand persons.

Colonel Zephaniah Swift Spalding Monument (Upper Kapa'a)

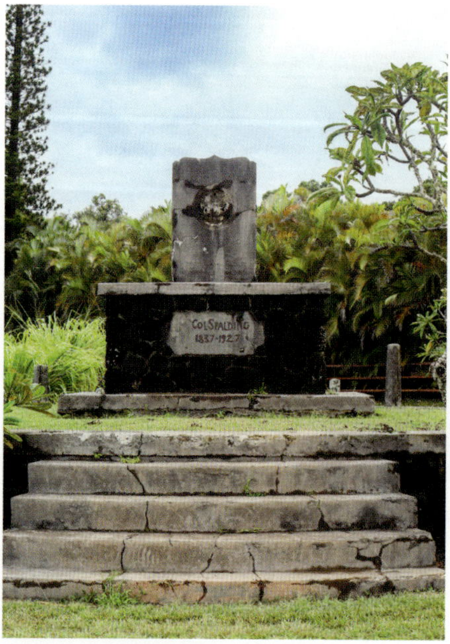

Photo by Christian R. Cook

Colonel Spalding (1837-1927) was associated with the sugar industry for over twenty-five years, first as owner of the Keālia Plantation, and later (after marrying the daughter of the then-owner), he became the owner and manager of the Makee Sugar Company. His early partners were King Kamehameha V, and later King Kalākaua. He sold Makee Sugar Company in 1916 at an enormous profit.

A man with many business interests in Hawai'i and elsewhere, in 1895, Spalding was granted $40,000 by the US government to build and maintain a telegraph cable from Hawaiʻi to the mainland. His title, colonel, was received when Spalding served in the Civil War as a Union Army lieutenant colonel. Early newspaper reports indicate that his 50th birthday celebration on Kauaʻi in 1887 drew over a thousand guests.

The Spalding monument was dedicated on April 20, 1930. According to early newspaper accounts, it was erected by Japanese residents of Keālia. Located in the heights of Kapaʻa, in a small park, it is currently dilapidated. The medallion and plaque were vandalized, restored, then vandalized again, and finally removed. What remains is the large circular rock base with five concrete steps. Upon that circular landing is another square rock wall with a cement cap and base and a concrete inset where a medallion once was affixed.

Memorial to John Thomas (Jack) Waterhouse (Kīpū Kai)

Jack Waterhouse (1902-1984) was a fourth generation kamaʻāina from a missionary family. He was the grandson of Samuel T. Alexander, one of the founders of Alexander & Baldwin (A&B), one of the "Big 5" companies of Hawaiʻi. He joined A&B in 1930, rose through the ranks, and served as Director for forty years.

In 1948, Waterhouse bought Kīpū Kai Ranch from the Rice family who were distant cousins. He developed the property by building roads and self-contained irrigation and electrical systems.

Kīpū Kai is a special place, with four beaches and rocky

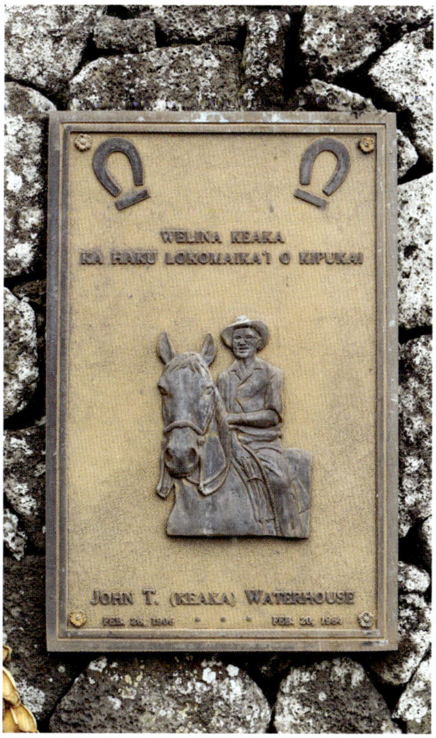

Photo by Christian R. Cook

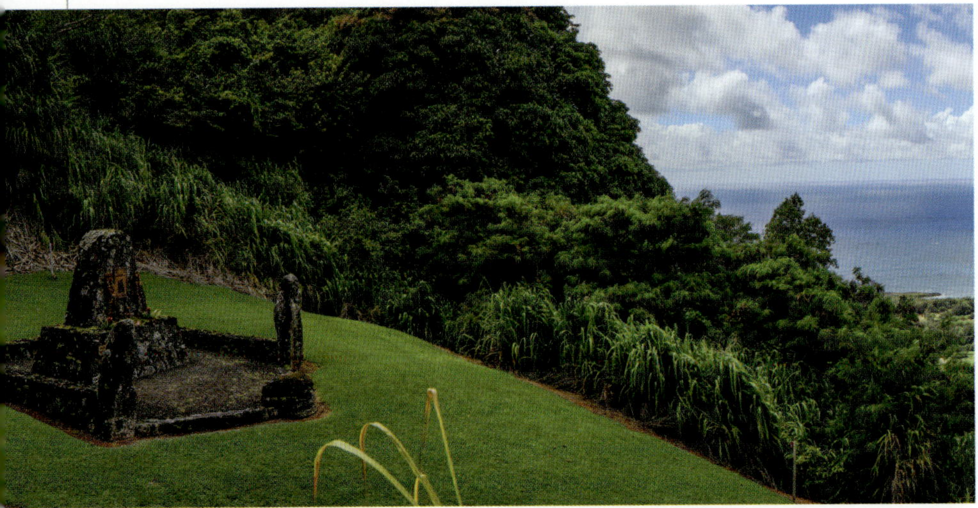

points, pastures, and cliffs. Above Kīpū Kai is the Hā'upu ridge, which is difficult to access due to steep cliffs.

In 1977, Mr. Waterhouse deeded the property to the State of Hawai'i after the lifetimes of his nieces and nephews. For now, the entire Ranch is inaccessible to the public and the roads are blocked by gates. These lands were the backdrop for several movies including *The Descendants* with George Clooney in 2011.

The stone memorial resides at the entrance of Kīpū Kai with a bronze image of Mr. Waterhouse on horseback.

G.N. Wilcox Memorial

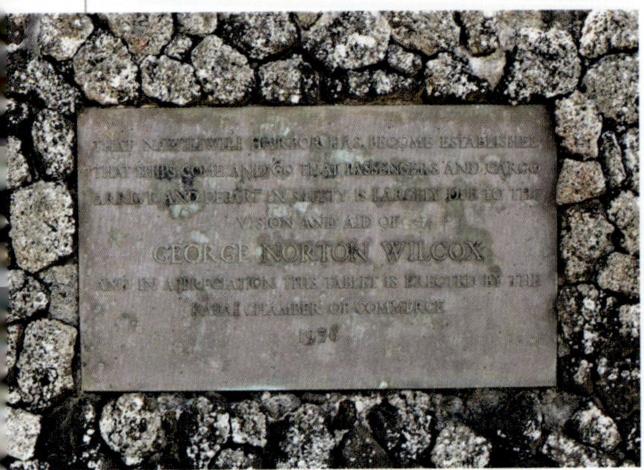

Both photos by Christian R. Cook

George Norton (G.N.) Wilcox (1839-1933) was a businessman, engineer, world traveler, and politician in Hawai'i. His parents were missionaries to Hawai'i for the American Board of Missions, teaching first in Hilo and then at the Wai'oli Mission in Hanalei, Kaua'i. After he returned from schooling on the mainland, He

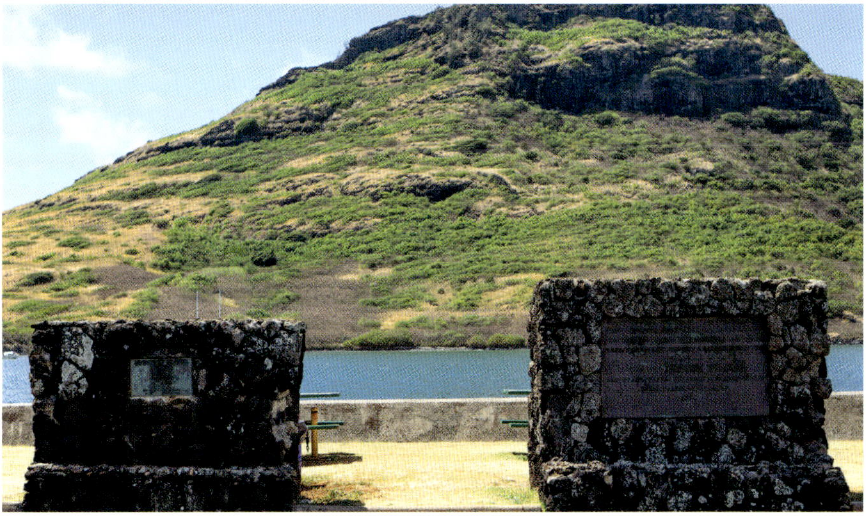

Photo by Christian R. Cook

worked for the Princeville Plantation, and then bought it. He later leased and then bought Grove Farm, both of these on Kaua'i. His business efforts continued including the Inter-Island Steam Navigation.

In 1880, he was elected to the Hawaiian Kingdom house of representatives, serving in various government positions for the next four decades. Never married, his enormous estate was left to nephews and nieces. A philanthropist and humanist, he is remembered for his extensive legacy of endowments and donations. Wilcox Hospital in Līhu'e is named for him, founded by one of his nieces (Mabel).

Following World War I, the Army Corps of Engineers proposed building a harbor at the fishing village of Nawiliwili. Wilcox bought the entire bond issue for the finance of a breakwater (1921), shoreline breakwater. The man-made harbor beneath the Hā'upu Mountain Range was dredged from Nawilwili Bay. Today it is owned by the State of Hawai'i which manages the port consisting of three piers and 1800 feet of berthing space and 16 acres of paved yard.

The memorial to Wilcox on the right honors his efforts towards the creation of Nawiliwili Harbor. The tablet is mounted on a moss rock stone wall, states it was erected in 1936 by Kaua'i Chamber of Commerce. On the left, another tablet mounted on moss rock stone wall is dedicated to the Army Corps of Engineers.

STATUES, BUSTS & MEMORIALS ON MAUI AND MOLOKAʻI ISLANDS

Maui Nō Ka Oʻi—Maui is the Best

—From an 1800s Hawaiian Mele hōʻikeʻike, a bragging chant, recorded by Reverend Paʻaluhi and Samuel Kapū of Kaʻahumanu Church, Wailuku

Maui, or the "Valley Isle," is the second largest Hawaiian island and it consists of two dormant shield volcanoes which merged to form a central isthmus, joining the "east" and "west" sides of the island. Wailuku is the County seat, while adjacent Kahului is the commercial and financial hub of the island. Maui County consists of four islands: Maui, Molokaʻi, Lānaʻi, and the non-populated Kahoʻolawe.

Until Kamehameha united the islands, Maui was ruled by its own line of chiefs; the last was Kahekili. Kamehameha's favorite wife, Kaʻahumanu, was born in Hāna, Maui and was raised on Maui where she was related to most of the island rulers there. In 1794, Kaʻahumanu became head of the ruling Maui dynasty after her uncle Kahekili died. Kamehameha had a brick palace built for her in Lahaina. Kamehameha made Lahaina the capital of the Hawaiian Kingdom in 1802.

The community of Lahaina on the west side of Maui Island is among the most historic landscapes and places in Hawaiʻi. It was an important contributor in no less than six overlapping periods of history. Pre-contact (before 1778) Lahaina was a fishing village and a gathering place for chiefs. Kamehameha I built his brick palace there and settlement continued. His wife Kaʻahumanu spent many of her adult years living there. It was the kingdom's official capitol from 1820 until 1845 when it was moved by Kamehameha III to Honolulu. Many of the monarchs are buried in the sacred burial cemetery of Waineʻe Church.

In the nineteenth century, Lahaina was the center of the global whaling industry. Ships moored on its waterfront and the sailors made merry in the town. The streets of Lahaina once bustled with myriad activities, brimming with royal persons, ship captains and sailors, whalers, and prostitutes. Lahaina was a wild place. Whaling dominated the economy from 1843 to 1860. The first New England missionaries assigned to Lahaina were appalled and embarked on the task of converting the heathens to Christianity. It remained the capital until 1845 when Kamehameha III moved the capitol to Honolulu (for its superior harbor). Captain James Cook never landed on Maui, as he could not find a suitable safe harbor there.

The first Protestant missionary, Dr. Holan from the Pioneer Company, arrived in Lahaina in 1821 aboard the *Thaddeus*. He and others built a house where he taught religion and developed a written history of the spoken Hawaiian language. The oldest church was established by Queen Keōpūolani in 1823 as Waine'e Church (now called Waiola Church) and serves as her final resting place along with other early members of the Royal family. The famous Lahaina Banyan tree was planted in the Courthouse Square in 1873 by William Owen Smith, a descendant of missionaries to mark the fiftieth anniversary of their arrival. The year 2023 marked the 200th anniversary of their arrival, and the 150th anniversary of the tree planting.

In the second half of the nineteenth century, Lahaina, like many other areas on Maui, was the locale for sugar industry's fields and mills, including Pioneer Mill. Eventually, Lahaina's dominant economic activity became tourism.

The statues on Maui reflect important events and places. The royals portrayed in statue are Kamehameha I (Grand Wailea-Waldorf Astoria); Queen Ka'ahumanu (shopping center bearing her name) in Kahului; Queen Lili'uokalani (Fairmont Hotel in Wailea); and a bust of Kamehameha III at the school in Lahaina bearing his name.

The influence and reverence for Saint Damien is highly evident on Maui, where many statues of him can be found at St. Anthony Church (Wailuku); Holy Rosary Church (Pā'ia); St. Maria Lanakila Church (Lahaina); St. Joseph Church on Moloka'i and the Damien memorial in Kalaupapa on Moloka'i. There is a statue of Saint Marianne Cope at UH Maui College Nursing School (Kahului). There are memorials, statues and other art pieces for Damien and Marianne at Kalaupapa Settlement on Moloka'i.

Other religious statues include Saint Anthony of Padua (Wailuku) and two of Shinran Shonin (Kahului and Lahaina). International subjects include Sun Yat-sen and Sun Mei (Kula, Kepaniwai and a bust in Lahaina) and Jose Rizal (Kepaniwai).

The statues on Maui are predominantly placed in commercial hotels or religious settings; very few exist in civic settings. The major civic collection on Maui is at Kepaniwai Park in 'Īao Valley. There, one will find statues of Jose Rizal in the Filipino section and of Sun Yat-sen in the Chinese section, as well as an illustrative pair of figures depicting sugar cane workers in the Japanese section. Details about Kepaniwai Heritage Park monuments are covered in Chapter Eight.

All of the historic Lahaina landmarks associated with the periods of the past two centuries mentioned in the above paragraphs were damaged or destroyed by fire on August 8-9, 2023. The bust of King Kamehameha III at the school named for him on Front Street (the school itself damaged beyond repair) remained standing, and at the appropriate time will be removed for possible restoration and re-use. The Shinran Shonin at the Lahaina Jodo Mission is gone. The temple that had moved there in 1931 is possibly salvageable. The Damien statue at Maria Lanakila Catholic Church on Waine'e Street was still standing. The Sun Yat-sen bust at Wo Hing Society Hall and Museum on Front Street (and the building which was built around 1912) is lost. With temperatures in this section of the fire reaching 2000°F, the bronze statues would have melted at 1700-1900°F. The black marble pedestal would have melted at 1200°F, cracked and crumbled.

These four statues were researched for this book and the entries are included, although some are badly damaged. The descriptions and photos remain both as a record and as a testimony to their importance and the persons who brought them to be.

STATUES, BUSTS & MEMORIALS ON MAUI AND MOLOKAʻI ISLANDS

SUBJECT	TYPE	LOCATION	ARTIST	YEAR
King Kamehameha I	Bronze statue	Grand Wailea Hotel	Herb Kāne	1990
High Chief and Chiefess of Maui	Koa wood	Kamehameha Golf Course, Wailuku	Dale Zarrella	2004
Queen Kaʻahumanu	Bronze statue	Kaʻahumanu Shopping Center, Kahului	Tom Faught Dan Skinner	1995
Queen Liliʻuokalani	Bronze statue	Fairmont Kea Lani Hotel, Wailea	Dale Zarrella	2018
Damien Memorial	Red granite	Damien gravesite, Kalaupapa	People of England	1893
Damien Bust	Bronze	St. Philomena Church, Kalaupapa	Karen Lucas	1995
Saint Damien	Bronze	St. Joseph Church, Molokaʻi	Unknown	1979
Brother Dutton	White marble statue	St. Joseph Church, Molokaʻi	Made in China	2013
Saint Damien of Molokaʻi	White marble statue	Holy Rosary Church, Pāʻia	Purchase	1976
Saint Damien	Plaster statue	Maria Lanakila Church, Lahaina	Unknown	2015
Saint Damien	Bronze statue	St. Anthony Church, Wailuku	Jean Charlot	1980
Saint Damien	Bronze statue	St. Anthony of Padua School, Wailuku	Unknown	Unknown
Saint Damien (young)	Koa wood	St. Theresa Church, Haʻikū	Dale Zarrella	2016
Christ with Saint Francis	Plaster figure sculpture	Cope memorial and graveside, Kalaupapa	Patients	1918
Saint Marianne Cope	Bronze statue	UH Maui, School of Nursing	Dale Zarrella	2022
Sacred Heart of Jesus	Bronze statue	St. Francis Church, Kalaupapa	Unknown	1907
Saint Anthony of Padua	White stone statue	St. Anthony Church, Wailuku	Unknown	1919 1994

SUBJECT	TYPE	LOCATION	ARTIST	YEAR
Blessed Chaminade	White stone	St. Anthony School, Wailuku	School Alumni	1981
Shinran Shonin	Bronze	Lahaina	Unknown	Unknown
Shinran Shonin	Bronze	Wailuku	Unknown	Unknown
Sun Yat-sen	Bronze statue	Sun Yat-sen Park, Kula	Made in China	2011
Sun Yat-sen	Bronze statue	Kepaniwai Park, Wailuku	Made in China	2011
Sun Mei	Bronze statue	Sun Yat-sen Park, Kula	Made in China	2013
Masaru "Pundy" Yokouchi	Bronze statue	Maui Cultural Center	Sean Browne	2010
King Kamehameha III	Bronze bust	King Kamehameha III School, Lahaina	Christine Turnbull	2013
Sun Yat-sen	Bronze bust	Wo Hing Museum, Lahaina	China	2012
Sun Yat-sen	Bronze bust	Kepaniwai Park, Wailuku	China	2011
Jose Rizal	Bronze bust	Kepaniwai Park, Wailuku	Unknown	1979
Ka'ahumanu Birthplace	Bronze plaque	Hāna Harbor	Superintendent DPW	1928
George Vancouver Memorial	Stone with totem poles	Ma'alaea Harbor	Unknown	1969

MAUI ISLAND

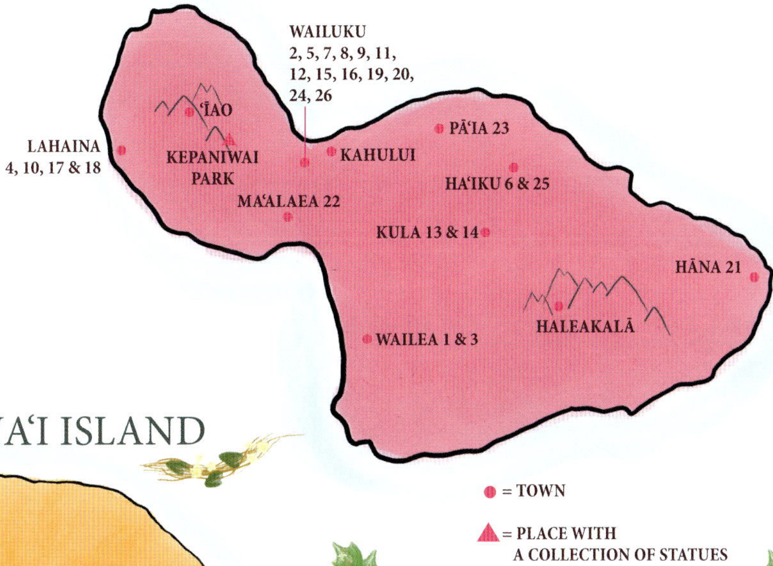

LĀNAʻI ISLAND

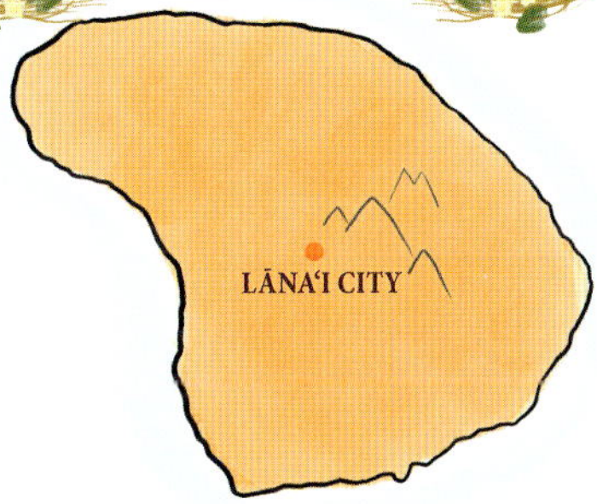

MOLOKAʻI ISLAND

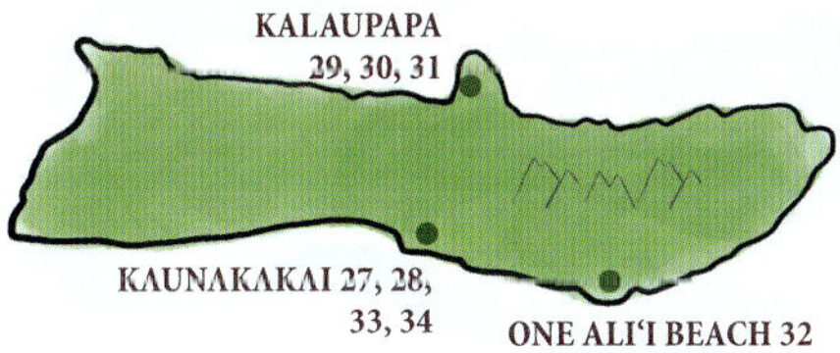

MAUI MAP KEY

1. King Kamehameha in Wailea
2. Kauaʻi Chief at Kamehameha Golf Course in Wailuku
3. Queen Liliʻuokalani at Fairmont Hotel in Wailea
4. Saint Damien in Lahaina
5. Saint Damien in Wailuku
6. Saint Damien in Haʻikū
7. Nisei Veterans Memorial Center
8. Saint Marianne Cope in Wailuku at UH Maui
9. Saint Anthony in Padua in Wailuku (2)
10. Shinran Shonin in Lahaina
11. Shinran Shonin in Wailuku
12. Masaru "Pundy" Yokouchi, Wailuku, MCC
13. Sun Yat-Sen in Kula
14. Sun Mei in Kula
15. Sun Yat-Sen in Kepaniwai Park
16. Japanese Immigrant Couple in Kepaniwai Park
17. Bust of Kamehameha III in Lahaina
18. Bust of Sun Yat-Sen in Lahaina
19. Bust of Sun Yat-Sen in Kepaniwai Park
20. Bust of Jose Rizal at Kepaniwai Park
21. Bronze Plaque, Kaʻahumanu Birthplace, Hāna Harbor
22. Stone Memorial George Vancouver, Maʻalaea Harbor
23. Montokuji Soto Mission Bell & Tower, Pāʻia
24. Dr. Martin Luther King, Jr. Memorial
25. 4th Marine Division Park in Haʻikū
26. 100th Anniversary Japanese Memorial at Kepaniwai

Molokaʻi Map Key

27. Saint Damien in Kaunakakai, Molokaʻi
28. Molokaʻi War Memorial
29. Brother Dutton Gravesite
30. Damien Memorial
31. Saint Marianne Cope Memorial on Molokaʻi
32. Japanese Immigrants Memorials at One Aliʻi Beach
33. Damien Statue
34. Brother Dutton Statue

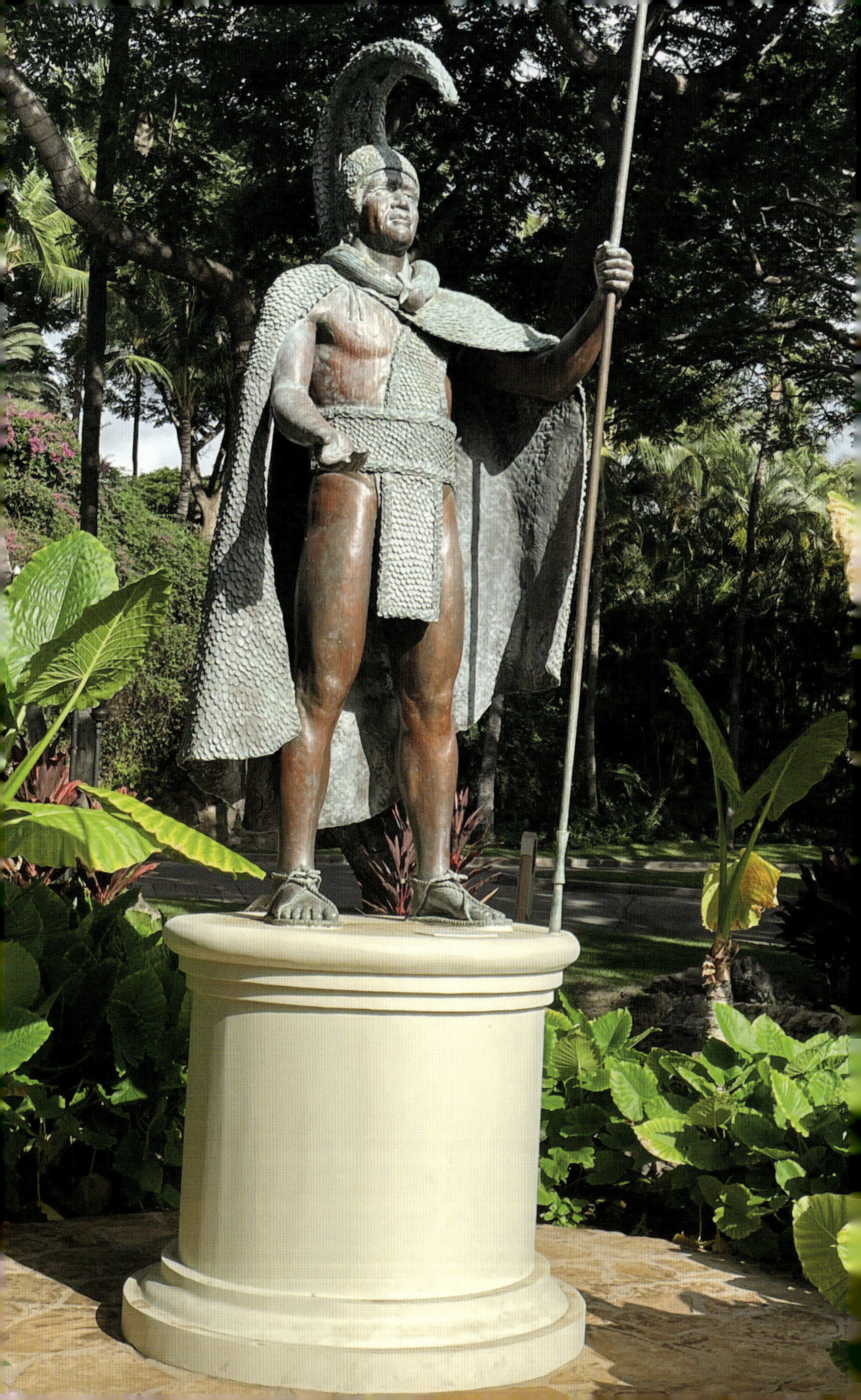

King Kamehameha

(c. 1753-1819)

Owner	Grand Wailea- A Waldorf Astoria Hotel
Commissioned by	Grand Wailea—A Waldorf Astoria Hotel
Location	Entrance to Grand Wailea - A Waldorf Astoria Hotel
Year Erected	1990
Artist	Herb Kawainui Kāne

King Kamehameha I is well remembered and honored because he united the Hawaiian Islands into one royal kingdom after years of conflict. This significant change was made even more important by the fact that if the islands had remained under separate rule, they would have been more vulnerable to competing foreign interests. This section focuses on Kamehameha's relationship with Maui Island, which he would eventually conquer. For more about Kamehameha, see Chapter Two, Hawai'i Island.

The quest to unite the islands was one that Kamehameha shared with his rival, the fearsome and skilled King Kahekili of Maui. The two battled for decades to gain control, not just of Maui, but of all the islands. The abbreviated battle history described here is based on content found in the Warfare History Network website. It starts in 1790.

Kamehameha had just captured two foreign trading ships (*Eleanor* and *Fair American*) at Kealakekua Bay on Hawai'i, gaining their weaponry, and crews (including later trusted advisors Isaac Davis and John Young). Using this equipment and expertise, he invaded Maui by land and sea. His forces won battles in Hāna, Wailuku, and 'Īao Valley. Kamehameha moored his fleet at Ma'alaea, while his forces marched to the four valleys where Kahekili's men were stationed. The majority of Maui warriors were slain, their bodies clogging the Wailuku River, earning the battle the name Kepaniwai, which means the damming of the waters. Its locus is now marked by an exhibit sign near 'Īao State Park.

Opposite page: King Kamehameha I statue at the Grand Wailea. Photo by Ray Soon

Once Kamehameha had Maui, Molokaʻi, and Lānaʻi under his control, he moved onto the southern coast of Oʻahu waiting to do battle there. This quest was interrupted by the need for Kamehameha to return to his base on Hawaiʻi Island where, in Kamehameha's absence, Keōua was ravaging the island. The battles on the east side ended when Kīlauea erupted and killed nearly four hundred of Keōua's army. This was taken as a sign that Kamehameha was meant to lead. Still, unable to conquer Keōua through fighting, Kamehameha built the massive heiau of Puʻukohalā to signify his predominance.

Kamehameha also had to fight off two alliances formed between the island chiefs. One was between the chiefs of Oʻahu and Kauaʻi who had decided to invade the west side of Hawaiʻi Island, destroying homesteads, agriculture lands, and sacred temples. A second army of invaders was led by Kāʻeo who had joined forces with Kahekili in their attempt to rule all the islands. Multiple battles ensued along the Kohala Coast and Waipiʻo Valley on Hawaiʻi Island. Kamehameha responded by land and sea, armed with superior cannons mounted on his canoes. The invaders retreated to Maui.

Kamehameha lured Keōua to his new temple at Puʻukoholā where Keōua was immediately speared to death. Having re-solidified his control of Hawaiʻi Island, Kamehameha returned his focus to Oʻahu where he fought Kalanikupule, the son of Kahekili II. The bloody battle ended on the cliffs of Nuʻuanu Valley where the defending forces suffered defeat. This was 1795.

The remaining island for Kamehameha to conquer was Kauaʻi, but this proved elusive. In 1810 Kauaʻi's King Kaumualiʻi surrendered to Kamehameha's superior military position, wanting to avoid bloodshed. In return, Kaumualiʻi was given the title of vassal with the ability to rule Kauaʻi island for his remaining lifetime, while granting Kamehameha authority over foreign affairs.

Given the history described above, it is not surprising that there is no civic statue to Kamehameha on Maui Island (or on Kauaʻi Island either). The Kamehameha statue found on Maui is at the Grand Wailea-A Waldorf Astoria Hotel in Wailea.

The Grand Wailea-Waldorf Astoria Hotel has been likened to an open-air art museum. It displays eighty beautiful museum quality pieces of art in its signature collection: eighteen bronze sculptures by French cubist Fernand Leger, nine large bronze sculptures by Columbian artist Fernando Botero, stained-glass panels by Yvonne Cheng, and glass pieces by Dale Chihuly. At the entry are two trios of hula dancers, male on one side, female on the other, and a mermaid sculpture, all by Jan Gordon Fisher. Pieces by other local artists include Satoru Abe's granite "Moon Over Trees," Shige Yamada's "Maui Captures the Sun" and Sean Browne's outdoor "Manu Lei."

The Kamehameha statue at the entrance to the Grand Wailea-Waldorf Astoria was created by Herb Kāne (1928-2011), the highly esteemed local artist known for his visualizations of Polynesian and Hawaiian culture and historical events. Equally significant to his art work, Kāne was at the forefront of restoring canoe voyaging, designing the *Hōkūleʻa* canoe, and founding the Polynesian Voyaging Society. Kāne was named a Living Treasure of Hawaiʻi in 1984 and was Historic Hawaiʻi Foundation's Kamaʻāina of the Year in 2011. Kāne's statue of Kamehameha at Grand Wailea is considered by some to be the most authentic looking because it shows Kamehameha with Hawaiian features, rather than Aryan. The towering height of Kamehameha (seven feet) is also considered authentic based on cloaks he was known to have worn.

Ali'i at Kamehameha Golf Course

Owner	King Kamehameha Golf Course
Commissioned by	King Kamehameha Golf Course
Location	King Kamehameha Golf Course Club House
Year Erected	2004
Artist	Dale Zarrella

The King Kamehameha Golf Course (KKGC) owns an amazing collection of museum-quality fine art pieces. The clubhouse itself is based on a design by Frank Lloyd Wright, with circular rooms, a domed roof, a skylight, and rooms radiating from the center. These plans were considered for several private residences at different scales (including one for Marilyn Monroe and Arthur Miller) but none of those were ever built. In 1988 the original owners of the club wanted a Frank Lloyd Wright design and chose this one, while having it expanded nearly ten-fold in size. It is nearly seventy-five thousand square feet in total. Most of the rug work, etchings, and leaded glass work are inspired

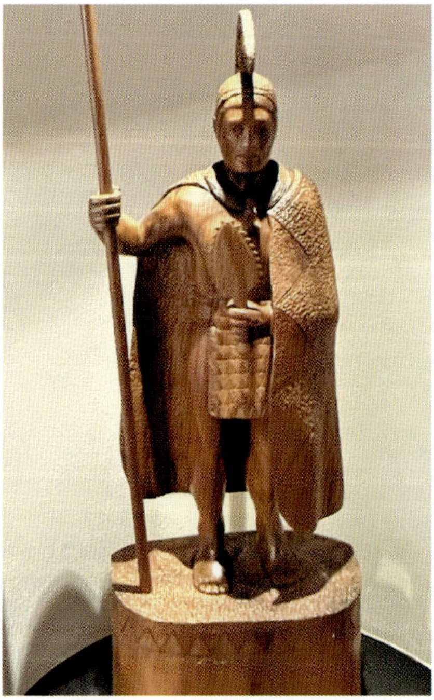

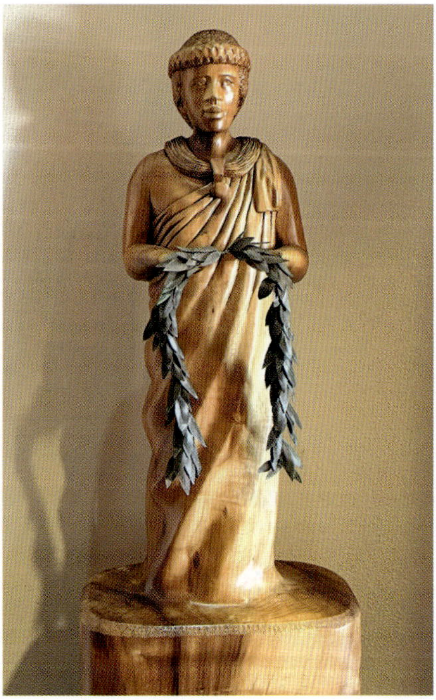

Left: Ali'i Kāne. **Right:** Ali'i Wahine. Both photos by Ray Soon

by Wright's works on other properties.

The statues of a high chief of Maui, another chief, and two female royals, neither of them named, were created by Dale Zarrella. Each was made from a single log of koa wood. Zarrella also created the Conch Blower sculpture at the clubhouse entry, the Healer bronze sculpture, and all the perpetual trophies used by the club for tournaments. Zarrella lives and works in Maui.

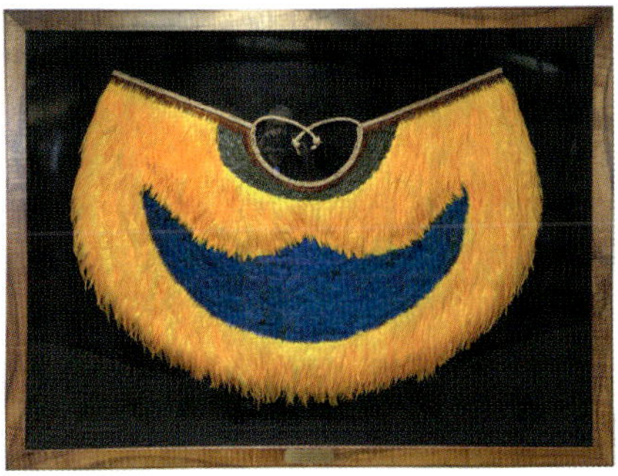

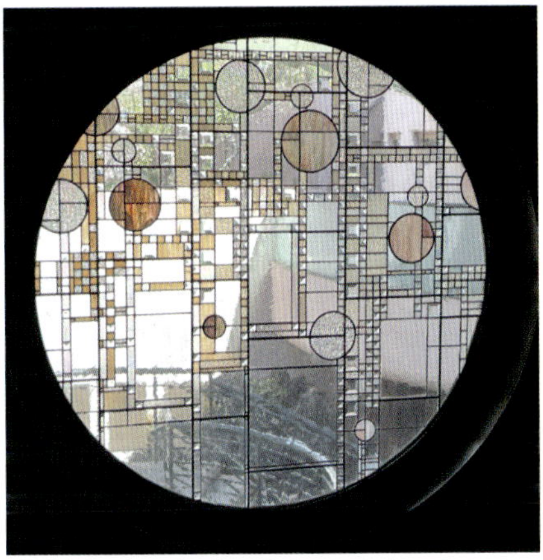

KKGC feather cloak and glass window. Both photos by Ray Soon

The KKGC art collection is spectacular and priceless. It includes Herb Kawainui Kāne's wood panel "Nā Ali'i-A Gathering of Chiefs," a summit of ancient Hawaiian chiefs in their 'ahu'ula and mahiole. Kamehameha's yellow feathers cloak is resplendent in its glory. Another feather cape made by Jo-Anne Kahanamoku-Sterling hangs in the entry gallery. Kapa master Puanani Van Dorpe created eleven exquisite pieces of keiki kapa moe (baby blankets) showing the genealogy of Maui's chiefs, each with a unique patten identifying his lineage. A portrait of Frank Lloyd Wright by Maui artist Tonia Marks Baney hangs in the stairwell.

Major statues of Kamehameha elsewhere in Hawai'i include those on O'ahu (1883), at Statuary Hall in Washington DC (1969), and two on Hawai'i Island in Kapa'au (1883) and in Hilo (1997).

For further reading: Seiden, Allen. Hawai'i: *The Royal Legacy*. Mutual Publishing, 1992.

Wolforth, Tom. Warfarehistorynetwork.com/king-kamehameha-conquest-of-hawaii.

King Kamehameha III

(1814-1854)

Owner	Department of Education
Commissioned by	King Kamehameha III Elementary School
Location	King Kamehameha III Elementary School, Lahaina
Year Erected	2013 (School Centennial)
Artist	Christine Turnbull

Kauikeaouli was the second son of Kamehameha I to rise to the throne. He became King Kamehameha III in 1823 when his brother Liholiho (Kamehameha II) died. Having become king when very young, the actual ruling of the islands, until he came of age, was handled by Kāhina Nui Ka'ahumanu, Kamehameha's trusted wife and Kauikeaouli's stepmother.

Kamehameha III reigned from 1825 to his death in 1854. His was a long reign, nearly thirty years in length. These were challenging times, and he had to balance traditional Hawaiian ideas and lifestyle with modernizing and adopting to Western ways. In 1848, Kamehameha III enacted the Great Māhele, a system of land division that allowed for private land ownership, versus the previous system of land stewardship.

Lahaina was the capital of Hawai'i from 1802 to 1845 (when he moved it to Honolulu). During the time, Lahaina was built up to serve North American whalers. They were soon followed by the New England missionaries who attempted to convert the native population to Christianity and to tone down the bawdy behaviors of the whalers and sailors. The sons of missionaries planted sugar cane, an industry which would dominate the economy for nearly a century.

Kamehameha III's words, "Ua Mau ke Ea o ka 'Āina I ka Pono" meaning the life of the land is perpetuated in righteousness or, the sovereignty of the kingdom continues because we are righteous, has been the state motto since 1959. These words were spoken by Kamehameha III on July

Opposite: Kamehameha III. Photo by Lucas Kashtan

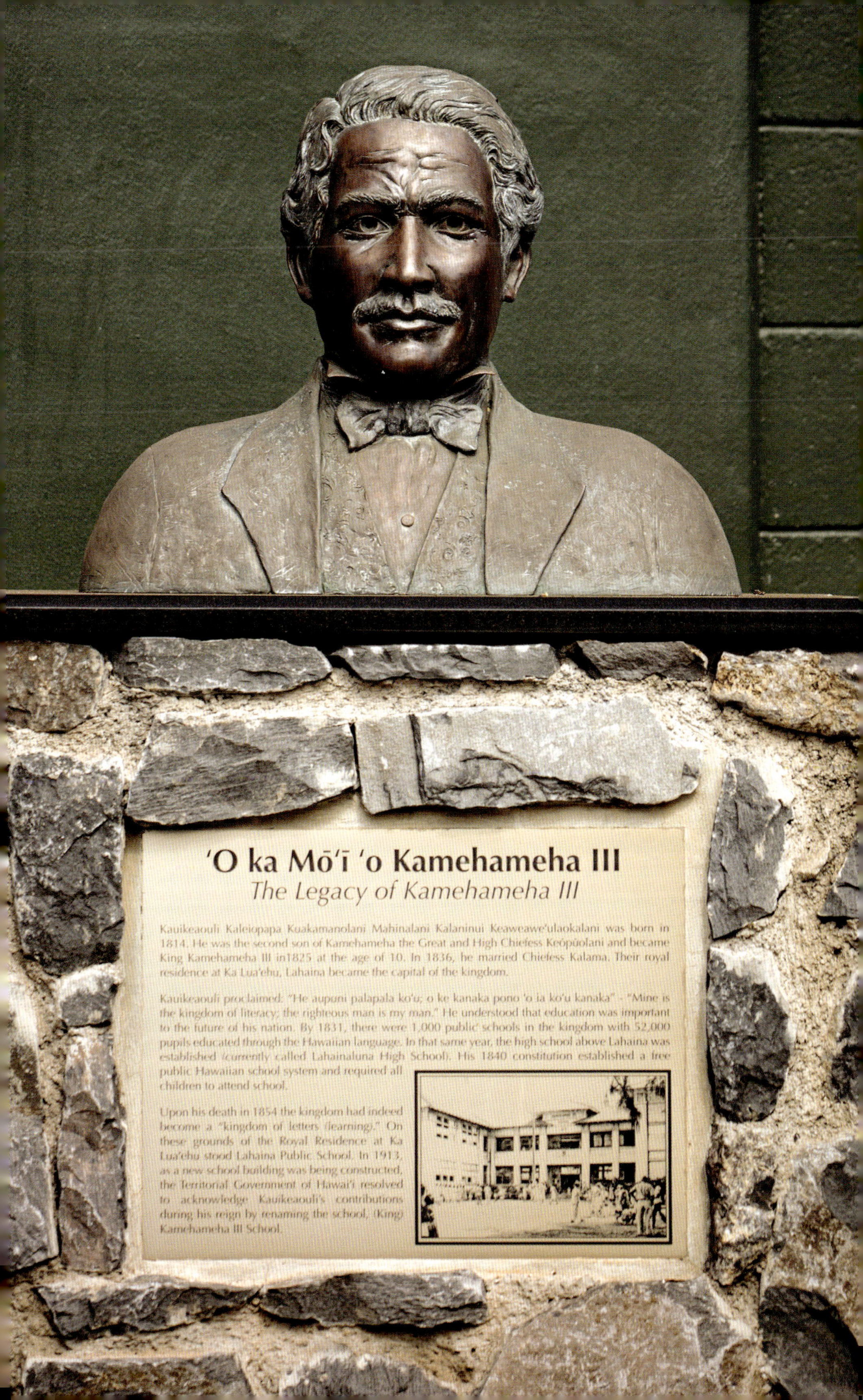
'O ka Mō'ī 'o Kamehameha III
The Legacy of Kamehameha III
Kauikeaouli Kaleiopapa Kuakamanolani Mahinalani Kalaninui Keaweawe'ulaokalani was born in 1814. He was the second son of Kamehameha the Great and High Chiefess Keōpūolani and became King Kamehameha III in1825 at the age of 10. In 1836, he married Chiefess Kalama. Their royal residence at Ka Lua'ehu, Lahaina became the capital of the kingdom.
Kauikeaouli proclaimed: "He aupuni palapala ko'u; o ke kanaka pono 'o ia ko'u kanaka" - "Mine is the kingdom of literacy; the righteous man is my man." He understood that education was important to the future of his nation. By 1831, there were 1,000 public schools in the kingdom with 52,000 pupils educated through the Hawaiian language. In that same year, the high school above Lahaina was established (currently called Lahainaluna High School). His 1840 constitution established a free public Hawaiian school system and required all children to attend school.
Upon his death in 1854 the kingdom had indeed become a "kingdom of letters (learning)." On these grounds of the Royal Residence at Ka Lua'ehu stood Lahaina Public School. In 1913, as a new school building was being constructed, the Territorial Government of Hawai'i resolved to acknowledge Kauikeaouli's contributions during his reign by renaming the school, (King) Kamehameha III School.

13, 1843 at Thomas Square when the Kingdom of Hawaiʻi was restored by the British after a brief takeover by Lord George Paulet. These words are prominently placed on a wall behind the Kamehameha III statue in Thomas Square on Oʻahu.

Under Kamehameha III's reign, Hawai'i shifted from an absolute monarchy to a constitutional monarchy through the signing of the 1840 Constitution and the 1852 Constitution, giving rights to Hawaiians for voting and holding office. In recognition of his contributions, the Hawaiʻi legislature (HR No. 134) proclaimed that "There should be a Memorial at Lahaina, Maui commemorating the signing of the said Constitution by the said Kamehameha III."

In Lahaina, the public elementary school is named for Kamehameha III. Originally named Hale Aloha Government School, it opened in 1873 with Henry Dickenson as its first principal. It moved to its current site on Front Street in the late 1880s. Over the years, buildings have been added and demolished. King Kamehameha III's home, Ka Luaehu, was once on this spot. A building replacement was approved in 1913 by the Territorial Legislature and name changed to Kamehameha III School.

Kamehameha III is credited with establishing Hawaiʻi's first public school system on October 15, 1840, making it the oldest public school system west of the Mississippi River. In 1888, all public instruction in Hawaiʻi was made free for students.

Bust of Kamehameha III

Sammy Kadotani had gone to school here and loved both the school and Lahaina. He was a longtime member of Lahaina Restoration Foundation and some called him the "honorary Mayor of Lahaina." It was his dream to have a sculpture of King Kamehameha III at the school's entrance where students would pass it daily. By the time the school had its Centennial in 2013, Kadotani was in his nineties. He and others decided it was time to move forward on the dream. A small competition was conducted, which was won by artist Christine Turnbull. Funds for the bust came from community donations.

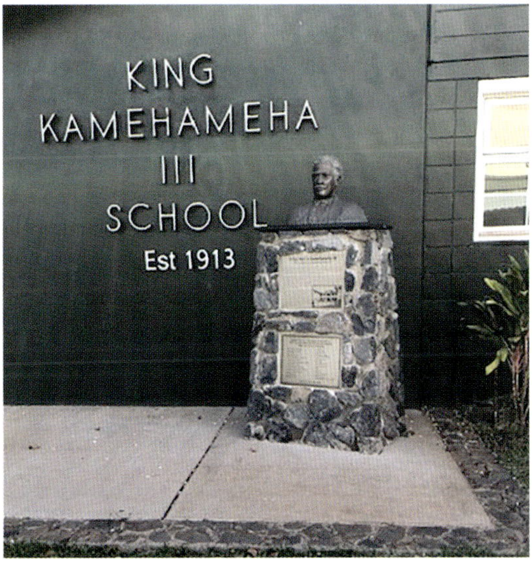

Photo by Ray Soon

Turnbull was moved by the commission, but only 2 or 3 images were available to help make an accurate 3D interpretation. She studied Hawaiian faces to ensure the bone structure was correct.

Theo Morrison and the Lahaina Restoration Foundation are responsible for the information plaques. The first plaque describes his lineage and his interest and contributions to education. The second plaque honors the donors and the 100th anniversary of the school.

The cast bronze bust of Kamehameha III sits on rock pedestal. Placement was important. He was to face mauka, looking towards his beloved island, yet not totally having his back to the sea. He would face the children as they entered the school from Front Street, and studying Kamehameha III and his contributions became part of the standing curriculum.

The bust was standing on its pedestal, but the school was damaged beyond repair in the Lahaina wildfire of August 8-9, 2023. The research conducted for this section was completed prior to the fire.

For Further Reading: Klieger, P. Christian. *Kamehameha III*. Green Arrow Press, 2016.

Queen Kaʻahumanu

(c. 1768-1832)

Owner	Queen Ka'ahumanu Center
Commissioned by	Queen Ka'ahumanu Center
Location	Center Court of the Queen Ka'ahumanu Center in Kahului, Maui
Year Erected	1995
Artist	Tom Faught with Dan Skinner

Ka'ahumanu's birth date is assigned as March 17, 1768 (dates were imprecise at that time) in Hāna, Maui. She lived for several years in Lahaina when it was the capital. Little is known of her early life, but she was likely raised near Wailuku, Maui. She was born to noble parents. Her father was high chief Ke'eaumoku from Kona; her mother Nāmāhana was related to the king of Maui. Her name means "the feather cloak."

Kaʻahumanu was given by her father at age ten to Kamehameha to become his wife, and they married when she was thirteen. Kamehameha married multiple times (again, accounts differ from seventeen to thirty), but she was his favorite wife, and he relied upon her counsel and judgment. Theirs was a tumultuous relationship marked by infidelity and argument; nevertheless, it was to Kaʻahumanu that Kamehameha turned to ensure his legacy and to assist his sons in governance after his death.

In adulthood, Kaʻahumanu was a beautiful and physically strong woman at six feet tall. She was a skilled surfer, swimmer, and canoe paddler and possessed a strong mind and intellect. Allen writes, "By birth, marriage, circumstances and personality, Kaʻahumanu was one of the most powerful persons in Hawaiʻi during a transitional period that saw the visits of many explorers and the residence in the islands of the first foreigners."

Kaʻahumanu led a complicated life, often riddled with disappointment. Kapu placed rules upon women limited that her freedoms, and she

Opposite page: Queen Ka'ahumanu statue. Photo by Aubrey Hurd

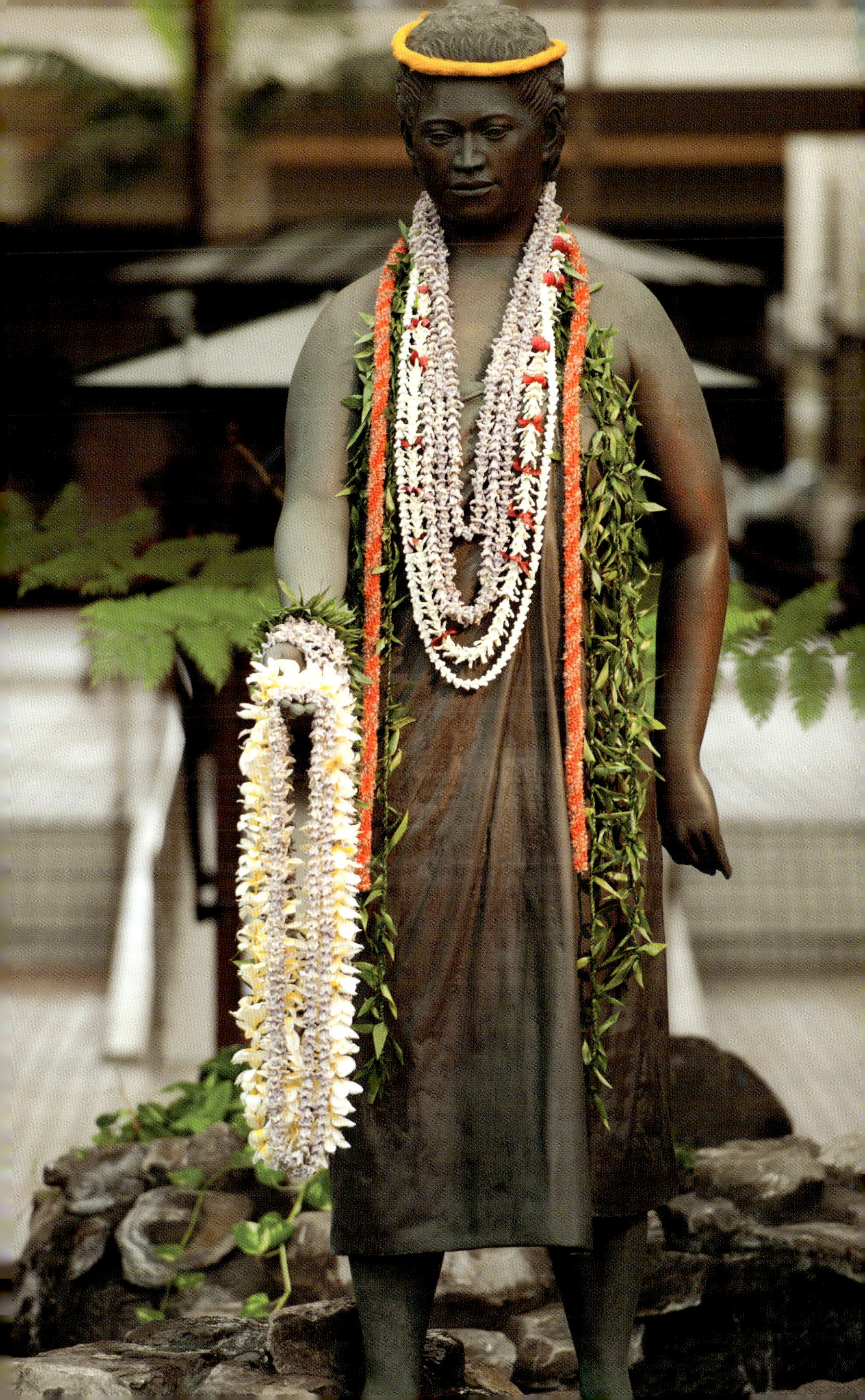

was resentful of these taboos, eventually seeking to nullify them. Powerful, influential, and highly respected by all, Kamehameha made her responsible for creating places of refuge.

Ka'ahumanu co-led the islands for thirteen years after Kamehameha's death in 1819. She served as Kuhina Nui under the young rulers Kamehameha II (Liholiho) and Kamehameha III (Kauikeaouli); their mother was Keōpūolaniʻ, the most sacred (high born) of Kamehameha's wives. Liholiho's youth and propensity toward drunkenness left most of the ruling to Ka'ahumanu. When he died in 1824, and his brother Kauikeaouli became Kamehameha III, Ka'ahumanu continued her rule as Kuhina Nui.

During her time, Ka'ahumanu was a catalyst for change. She helped break old laws and eliminated ancient kapu, including those that banned women and men from eating together. She forbade previous religious practices and ordered that heiau and places of worship be destroyed. She protected the people from foreign influences and fought for sovereignty. She promoted literacy and encouraged both aliʻi and commoners to attend schools.

Ka'ahumanu had been taught to read and write by the missionaries, and she converted to Christianity in 1825 when she received the baptismal name of Elisabet. The Protestant church in Wailuku, named for her (at her request), is located in an ahupua'a once owned by her grandmother, and was where Ka'ahumanu spent her childhood.

Ka'ahumanu died in Honolulu in 1832 at the age of fifty-two. Just before her death she was presented with one of the first copies of the New Testament translated into Hawaiian. Her services were held at Kawaiaha'o Church and conducted by Hiram Bingham. She is buried at the Royal Mausoleum at Mauna'ala where an obelisk marks her burial.

For Further Reading: Goodhue, Thomas W. *Queen Ka'ahumanu of Hawaii: A Biography*. McFarland & Company. 2022

Silverman, Jane L. *Kaahumanu: Molder of Change*. Friends of the Judiciary History. 1987.

Moore, Susanna. *Paradise of the Pacific*. Farrar, Straus, and Giroux. 2015.

Plaque Signifying Queen Kaʻahumanu's Birthplace (Hāna Harbor)

A bronze plaque marking her birth place (above the actual cave where she was born) was placed many years ago, but is difficult to reach due to steep terrain. The marker is a short walk from Hāna Harbor. She was born in a cave near the ocean right below the plaque and nursed in that cave while she and her mother hid away from a battle that raged above them. The plaque states it was placed in 1928 by the Superintendent of Public Works.

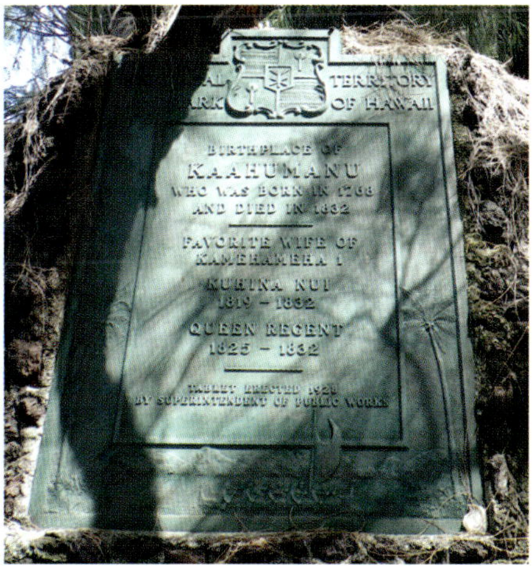

Queen Kaʻahumanu Birthplace. Photo by Travis Ota

Kaʻahumanu Statue

The statue of Kaʻahumau was created under a commission to Maui artist Tom Faught. It is made from resin and steel and stands eight feet tall on a two-foot base.

The design challenge was to develop the image of this powerful young woman, when only three etchings were available at the Bishop Museum, all showing her as aged. The earliest version of the statue, made from resin, is in Faught's Makawao studio. It is the version that he experimented with, testing poses and features and techniques. Faught wanted to capture Kaʻahumanu's compassion for her people and to portray her as mature, not girlish.

Faught crafted the right hand to be in a gesture of aloha or welcome. Her left is behind her back, once holding a mamo feather, the sign of her birth. The most difficult parts were the pose and the eyes, which are how the statue relates to the viewer.

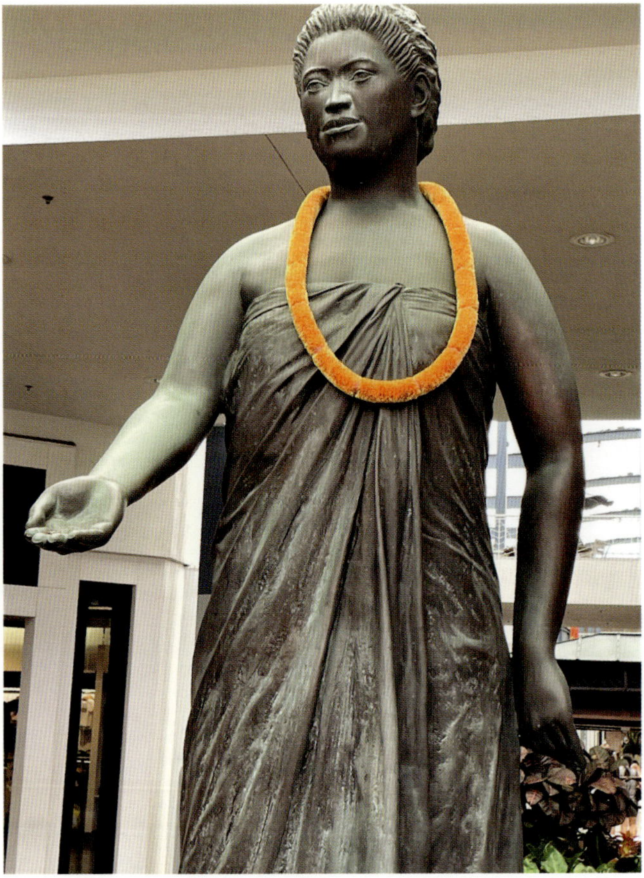

Ka'ahumanu statue. Photo by Aubrey Hurd

Faught credits others, saying that making the statue was a team effort. In particular, he worked with a Maui artist, Dan Skinner, to create the skeleton made of steel. The muscle and tissue were sculpted on the surface out of clay. Molds of the statue were made in rubber and then plaster. The molds, after being removed and used to encase the armature, were then cast with resin. The mold was then sent to the foundry in Walla Walla, Washington for the lost wax casting process. The finished statue is bronze with a honey-bronze patina.

The statue was installed at Queen Ka'ahumanu Center in Kahului in 1972. It has long served as a gathering place for events and performances and recently celebrated its 50th anniversary in 2022. Festivities included a lei draping of the statue, and a concert.

Queen Liliʻuokalani

(1838-1917)

Owner	Fairmont Kea Lani Hotel
Commissioned by	Women at Accor Generation Resort Committee & Fairmont Hui ʻOhana
Location	Hotel Lobby in Wailea
Year Erected	2018
Artist	Dale Zarrella

This striking statue of Liliʻuokalani, carved from valuable koa wood by Dale Zarrella of Maui, has stood in the courtyard of the Fairmont Hotel in Wailea since 2018. It was the vision of Women at Accor Generation Resort Committee & Fairmont Hui ʻOhana.

Lydia Kamakaʻeha, later renamed Liliʻuokalani, was born when traditional Hawaiian customs were still practiced. As was the custom, she was hānai to Pākī and Konia to inherit their mana. She was high ranking and attended the Royal School taught by missionaries Amos and Juliette Cooke. Like others of that time, she was schooled in both Hawaiian and Christian settings, and was left to reconcile often competing perspectives and values, ultimately becoming a hybrid of the two. In 1887, she traveled with Kapiʻolani to Queen Victoria's Crown Jubilee, a long trip that included a stopover in Washington to visit President Grover Cleveland and plead the importance of restoring the monarchy to its full status. She twice served as regent during the travels of her brother Kalākaua, giving her a firm understanding of governance.

Liliʻuokalani was a gifted musician. She composed over 160 mele (chants, songs, and poems) during her lifetime. The most famous of these was "Aloha ʻOe" (Farewell to Thee) written in 1878 and considered to be a lament for departing lovers. Later, the song was re-applied as a lament for the loss of her country. She played the organ and led the choir at Kawaiahaʻo Church. Liliʻuokalani married John Owen Dominis; the two had no children, although they did hānai (adopt) three children.

Described by others as well-bred, cordial, and gracious, she was also strong willed and independent, with a sense of royal inheritance. Liliʻuo-

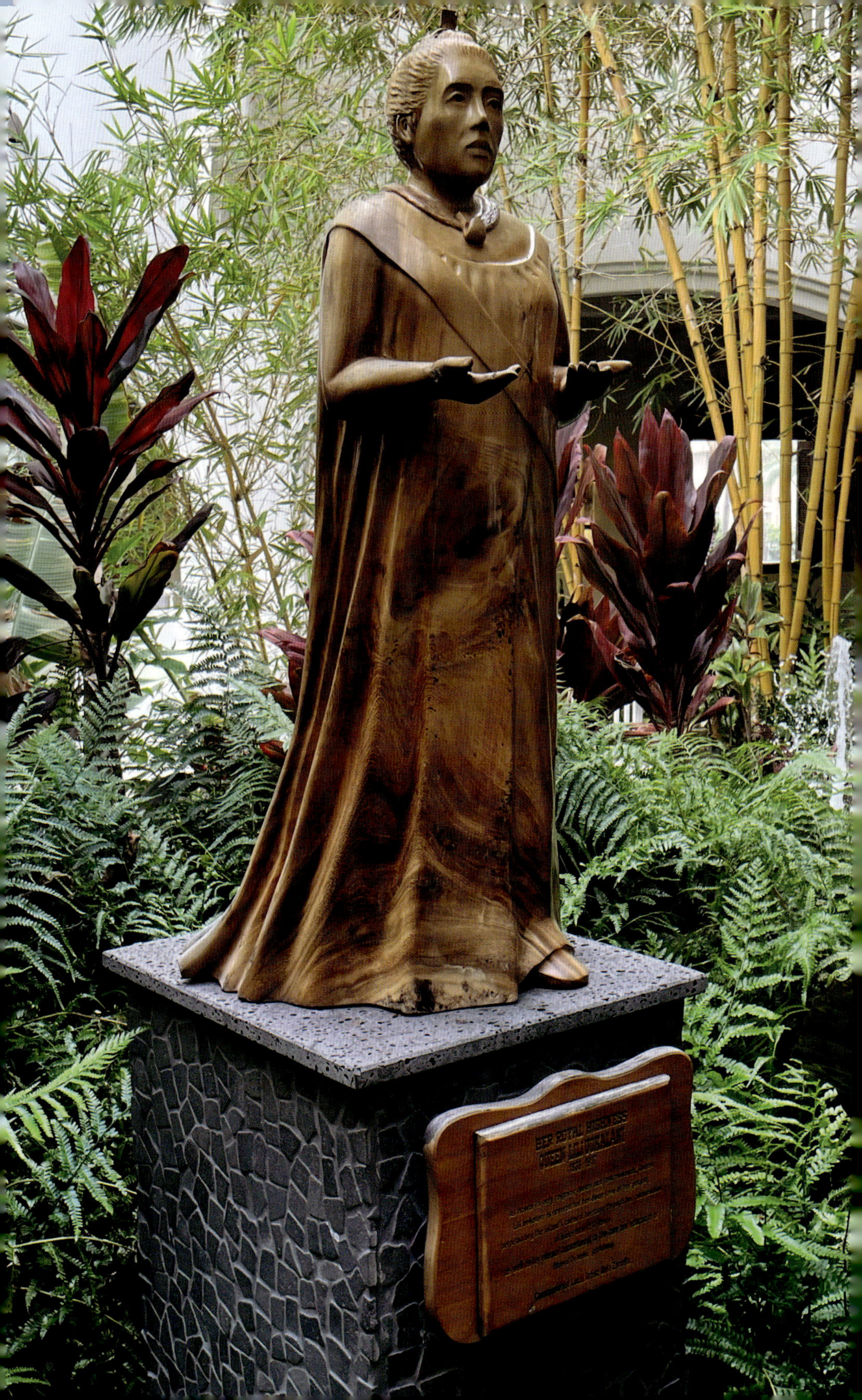

kalani was a lifelong proponent of a strong monarchy. This brought her into regular conflict with others who had economic interests in different power alliances. She ruled during tumultuous times.

When Queen Liliʻuokalani took the throne in 1891, many of the powers of the monarchy had been removed in favor of a legislature made up of businessmen and landowners, many of them American. Her attempts to return the absolute monarchy to its former status through a new constitution failed.

In 1893, a coup d'etat led by Lorrin Thurston and the Committee of Safety was staged, backed by the U.S. government, and with the aid of the U.S. Military. The Committee of Safety proclaimed the monarchy abolished and established a provisional government. Troops arrived and occupied the palace grounds. Liliʻuokalani surrendered under protest and appealed to the U.S. to reinstate her authority. Queen Liliʻuokalani moved out of ʻIolani Palace and into Washington Place. In July, 1894, a constitution for the Republic of Hawaiʻi was proclaimed, and Sanford Dole was made its first president.

In 1895, loyalist Robert Wilcox led a failed insurrection against the republic attempting to restore Liliʻuokalani to the throne. She was arrested and tried for treason, aiding an attempt to restore the monarchy. She was found guilty, fined, and sentenced. In return for a pardon for her supporters, Liliʻuokalani renounced all claim to the throne and took an oath of allegiance to the new republic. The sentence was commuted, and she was placed under house arrest at ʻIolani Palace for eight months.

Liliʻuokalani advocated for an independent Hawaiʻi through legal means and personal pleas to American officials for another nineteen years until her death at age seventy-nine in 1917.

In 1982, a statue of Liliʻuokalani by Marion Pineda was installed at the Hawaiʻi State Capitol.

For Further Reading: Allen, Helena G. *The Betrayal of Liliuokalani, Last Queen of Hawaiʻi 1838-1917*. Mutual Publishing. 1982.

Liliuokalani. *Hawaiʻi's Story by Hawaiʻi's Queen*. Original 1898. University of Hawaiʻi Press Reprint.

Opposite page: Queen Liliʻuokalani statue. Photo by Ray Soon

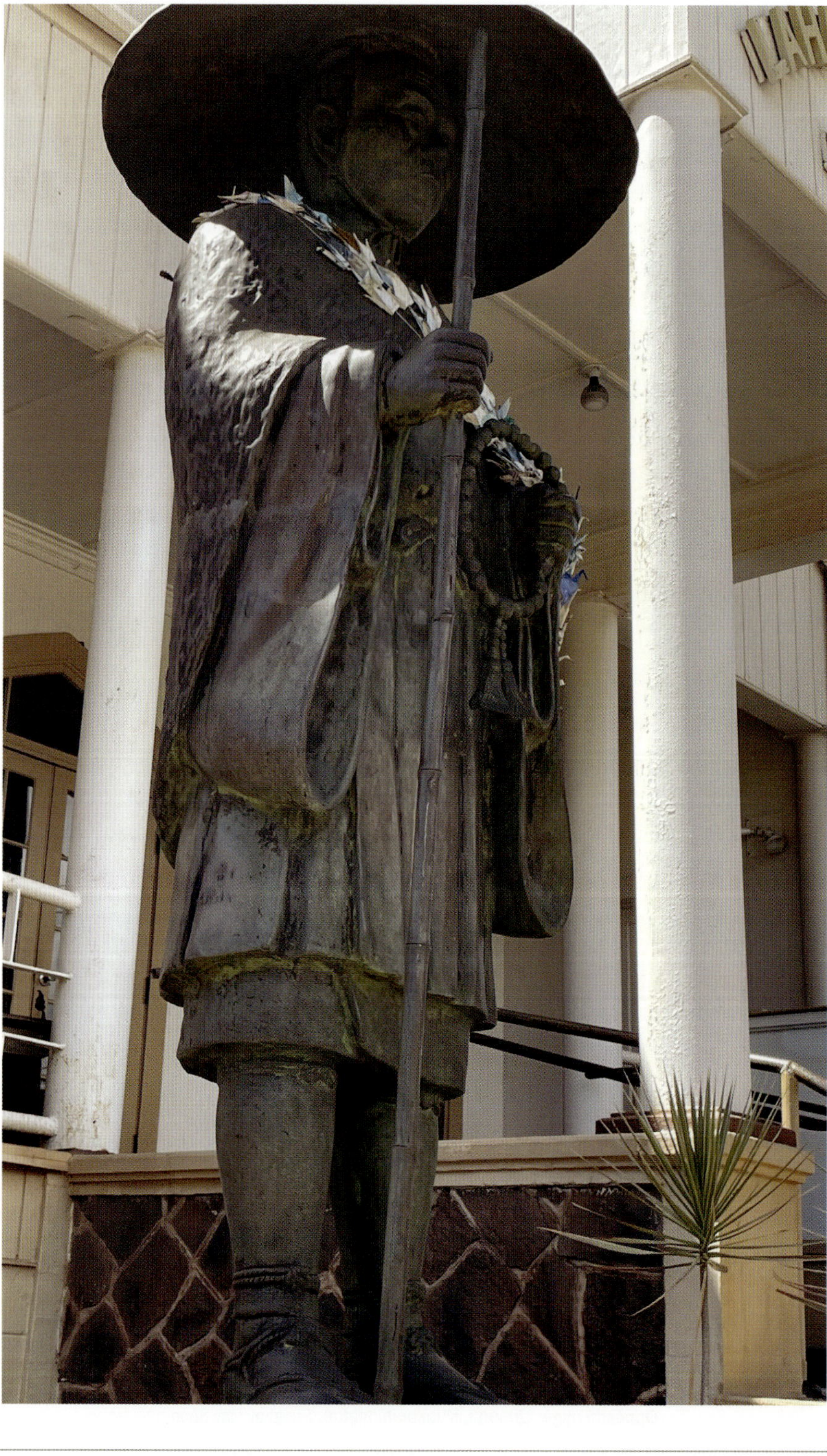

Shinran Shonin

(1173-1263)

Shinran Shonin statues are often found at Hongwanji Temples of the Jōdō Shinshu sect. A fuller description of Shinran's life is contained in Chapter Two (Statues of Hawaiʻi Island). There are five Hongwanji Missions on Maui Island, three have outside Shinran statues.

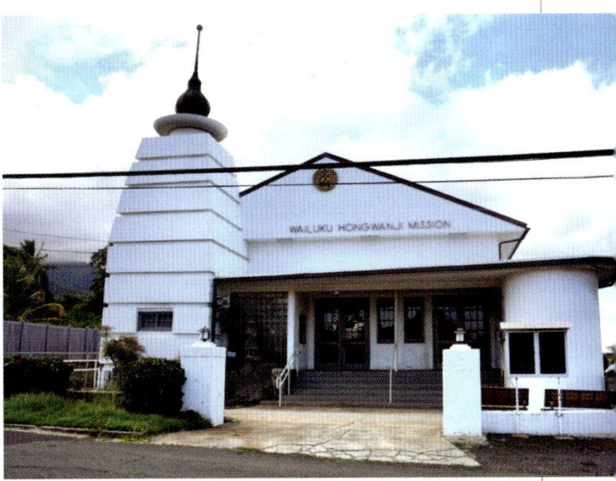

The first is at the Wailuku Hongwanji Mission, which was established in 1899. Its first temple (1902) was used by the military during World War II. The temple relocated to its present site and was given a contemporary look similar to a pagoda. The statue to the left of the entry stairs was likely added in 1974 as part of the 75th year celebration.

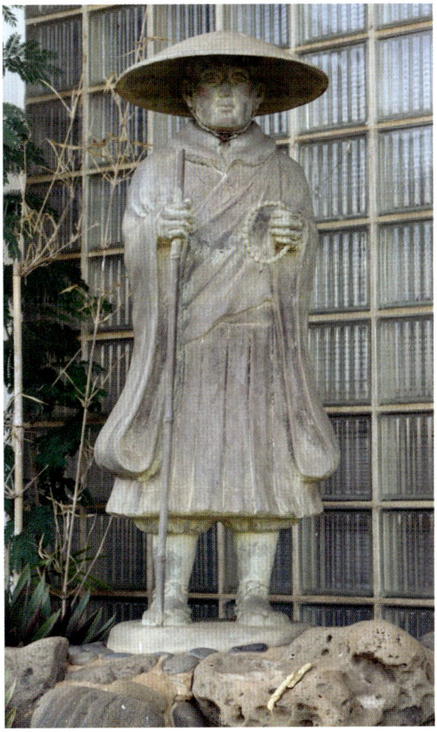

The second Shinran statue is in Kahului at the Kahului Hongwanji Mission. This community started around 1957 when the Kahului and Puʻunēnē Hongwanji merged. The temple is of contemporary design, inside and outside. The statue was dedicated in 1982

Opposite page: Lahaina Hongwanji Temple Shinran statue.
Above, top: Wailuku Hongwanji Mission. **Bottom:** Shinran in Wailuku. Photos by Lucas Kashtan

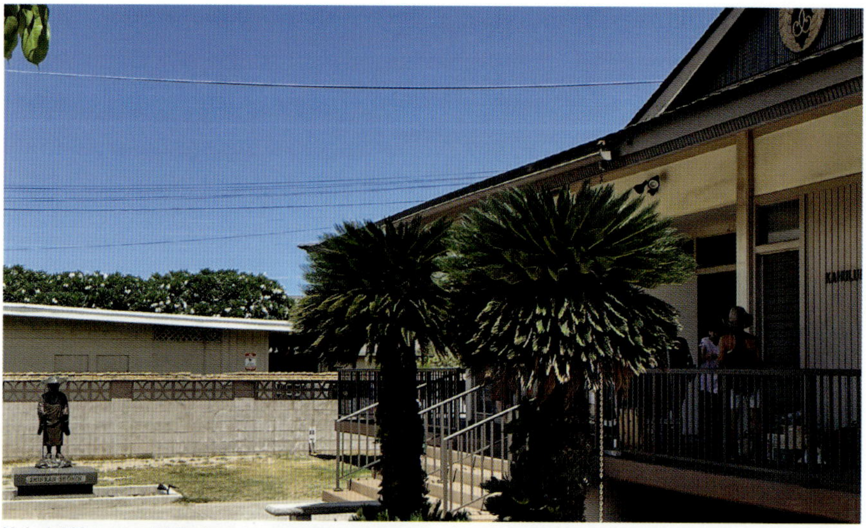

Kahului Hongwanji Mission. Photo by Cheryl Soon

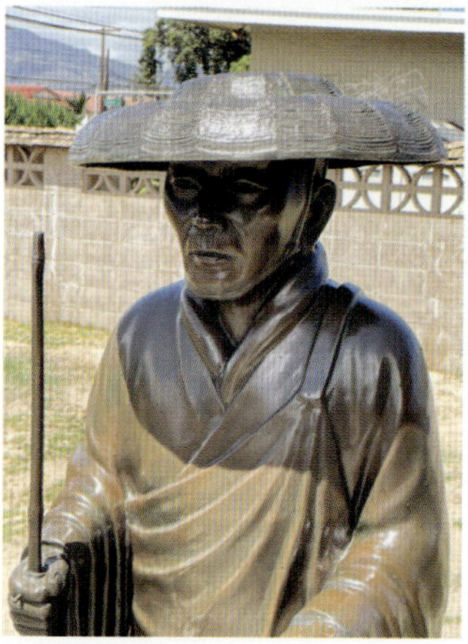

Photo by Ray Soon

and is near a bodhi tree. The base contains Shinran's name on one side and "In Memory of Masao & Takino Hiranaga" on the back side, along with the names of four relatives, possibly their children. This statue is in excellent condition, refurbished several years ago after it was vandalized.

The third Shinran in Maui is at Lahaina Hongwanji Mission Temple, which was established in 1904. The present building was erected in 1933, an excellent example of Indian Western architecture style, used elsewhere in Hawai'i including the Hongwanji Betsuin Headquarters in Honolulu. Lahaina Hongwanji had two towers, front pillars, gable roof, and was topped with domes and spires. Sadly, the Hongwanji was destroyed during the August 8, 2023 Lahaina fire. The bronze Shinran statue which stood in front on a pedestal beside the flared staircase appears in some photos after the fire, suggesting it may have survived. The condition and possibility for reuse will not be known for a while. The photo on page 134 shows the statue with a crane lei around the neck. International Peace Day (September 21) was a few days before this picture was taken.

Sun Yat-Sen and Sun Mei

(1866-1925) and (1854-1914)

Owner	County of Maui
Commissioned by	Donated by the Sun Yat-sen Foundation for Peace & Education
Location	Sun Yat-sen Park, Kēōkea Maui
Year Erected	2011
Artist	Foundry in Guangzhou, China

Two brothers—Sun Yat-Sen and Sun Mei

Sun Yat-sen and Sun Mei were brothers about eleven years apart in age. The younger brother, Sun Yat-sen was the more famous, but through his financial and emotional support, his older brother Mei made Yat-sen's way possible. Sun Mei left China in 1871 at his father's urging to escape poverty and poor agricultural conditions, meeting uncles who had preceded him to Maui. Mei prospered on Oʻahu with a store in Chinatown. After he returned briefly to China, he brought back not only a wife but 100 men to work on the sugar plantations. Mei settled in Maui and was sometimes called the "King of Kula," in part due to his larger-than-life persona and because of the size of his ranch.

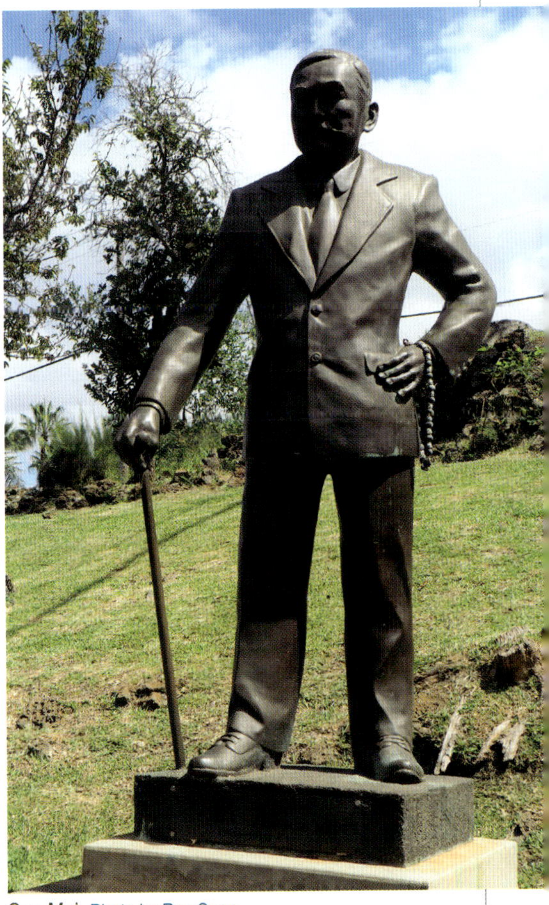

Sun Mei. Photo by Ray Soon

One of the wealthiest Chinese men in Hawai'i during the turn of the century, Mei owned extensive real estate, the Kahului General Store, and a ranch in Kama'ole. He eventually sold all his properties and businesses to support his brother's revolution, declaring bankruptcy in 1906. He returned to China around 1908, where his home was used as a meeting place for revolutionaries.

Sun Yat-Sen

Sun Yat-sen joined Mei in Hawai'i in 1879. An accomplished physician, philosopher, and a political figure, he had a magnetic personality. After he graduated from school in Hawai'i, he returned to China and was closely associated with the revolution in China. His objective was to expel the ruling Qing (Manchu) dynasty. Most people do not appreciate that the Modern Chinese Revolution was born in Hawai'i, where the Xin Zhong Hui movement was founded. The funding of the First Canton Uprising (which was unsuccessful) came from Chinese persons in Hawai'i, including brother Mei. Sun Yat-sen traveled the world six times advocating a revolution and fund raising for the cause. He is called the Founding Father of Modern China.

In 1911, Sun Yat-sen finally overthrew the Qing government (after many failed attempts) and established the Republic of China. In 1912, he was elected the first provisional President of the Republic (1911-12), a role he was again elected for and served through the years 1923-25, although he spent many of the years between those terms in exile in Japan. Sun Yat-sen is considered one of the greatest leaders of modern China and even the world. His philosophy is based on that of Confucius, and he sought to cultivate morality for universal peace and harmony. He coined the Three Principles of the People: Nationalism, Democracy, and Livelihood.

After residing in Hawai'i for many of his formative years and then leaving, Sun Yat-sen returned to Hawai'i four times between 1896 and 1910. He is revered by the local Chinese community who have erected

Opposite page: Sun Yat-sen. Photo by Ray Soon

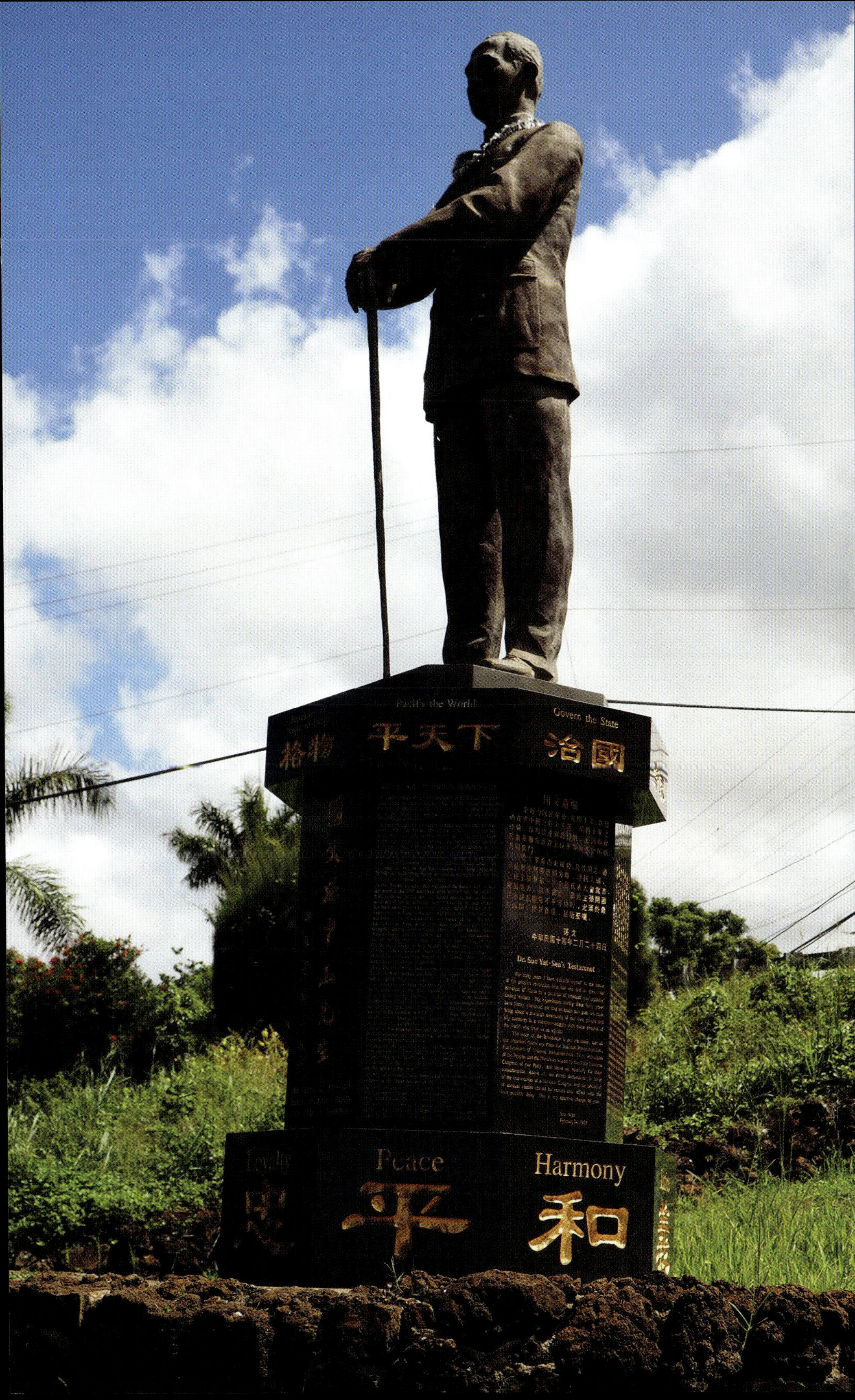
Pacify the World
格物
平天下
Govern the State
治國
Dr. Sun Yat-Sen's Testament
Peace
平
Harmony
和

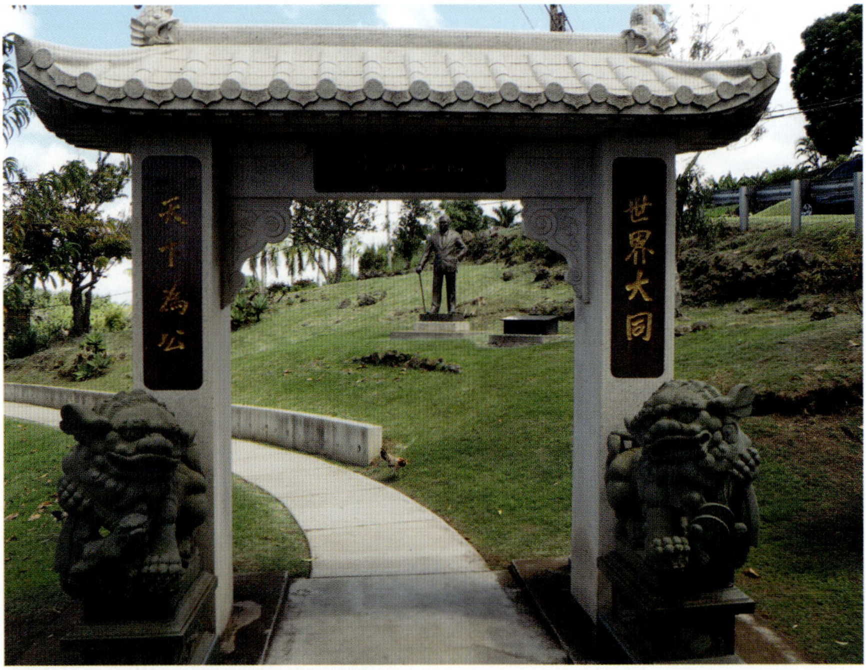

Sun Yat-sen Park Gateway. Photo by Ray Soon

many statues to him and who celebrate his birthday, November 12, each year.

There are hundreds of Sun Yat-sen statues throughout the world. The tallest (eighteen feet high) is cast in bronze and stands at Sun Yat-sen Memorial Hall in Guangxi Province, China. It shows Sun in a pose making a speech at a university. It sits on a white granite base carved with content from his important works. Other common poses include Sun Yat-sen holding an open book, holding his hat and coat, and with his hands folded atop a cane.

The Sun Yat-sen Foundation for Peace & Education, under the leadership of Dr. Lily Sui-fong Sun of Honolulu, a grand-daughter of Sun Yat-sen, vowed in 1986 to commission over one hundred statues around the world. She has exceeded that goal, having erected over 259, and is continuing to commission additional pieces. The statues erected through this foundation are made in Guangdong, Beijing, and Shanghai. The bases, typically constructed of black granite blocks with his writings in-laid in gold lettering, are fabricated in

Hui'an Province, which has a thousand-year history of stone crafting and carving.

The bases are in three pieces and provide education writings by Sun Yat-sen, often based on Confucianism. At the top are the three principles. The eight sides of the octagon show the eight virtues of Filial piety, Loyalty, Peace, Harmony, Justice, Faithfulness, Love, and Kindness.

Sun Yat-Sen Statues in Maui

All the Sun Yat-sen statues found on Maui come from the Foundation and Sun family. Sun Yat-sen Park is in Kēōkea, Maui near Kula. The park was established by the Maui Chinese Society to commemorate the 200th anniversary of the arrival of Chinese immigrants on the islands. Park land was donated by a nearby ranch in 1989, and the park was subsequently developed by the local County Parks & Recreation Department. The graceful park also has a Lion Gate (donated by Charles Wong upon the 100th centennial anniversary of the revolution), and a Peace Pole. The new statue replaced an old bronze one that had been donated in 1989 on the anniversary of Chinese Immigration to Hawaiʻi. That one was donated by Pingdong County in Taiwan, which has a sister county relationship with Maui. Unfortunately, it was vandalized. After being repaired, it now sits in the Kwock Hing society in Kula.

The new statue of Sun Yat-sen in Kēōkea shows him dressed in a Chinese suit, a cane in both hands. The pedestal is the same as the statues in Honolulu's Chinatown and at the Taiwan Economic Cultural Center, an elaborate black marble octagon with gold inlay writing.

An eight-foot bronze statue of Sun Mei was unveiled in 2013 at Sun Yat-sen Park. He was honored by descendants and government officials from China and Taiwan during the ceremony for his significant role in the revolution. The statue was crafted in China and donated by his descendant Victor Sun to the County Department of Parks & Recreation.

A plaque at the arched park entrance indicates it is an effort of the Centennial Commission, marking one hundred years after the Revolution. There is another statue of Sun Yat-sen at Kepaniwai Park and a bust. These are covered in Chapter Eight, along with a collection of other pieces honoring immigrant groups of Maui.

A half bust of Sun Yat-sen can be found in Lahaina outside the two-story Wo Hing Museum on Front Street. It was installed in 2012, another donation of the Sun Yat-sen Foundation and Dr. Lily Sun.

The Wo Hing Museum contains a collection of rare Chinese artifacts and memorabilia of Chinese in Lahaina. Recently discovered documents dating to 1906 have been preserved, photographed, translated (where possible), and documented.

According to their brochure, the Chinese started to arrive on Maui on trading and whaling ships, and helped build tunnels and irrigation systems through the mountains. Between 1852-1898, thousands came to work on the sugar plantations, in the fields, and at the mills. In the early 1900s they formed the Wo Hing Society, a chapter of the Chee Kung Ton fraternal society, to support the revolutionary activities of Dr. Sun Yat-sen.

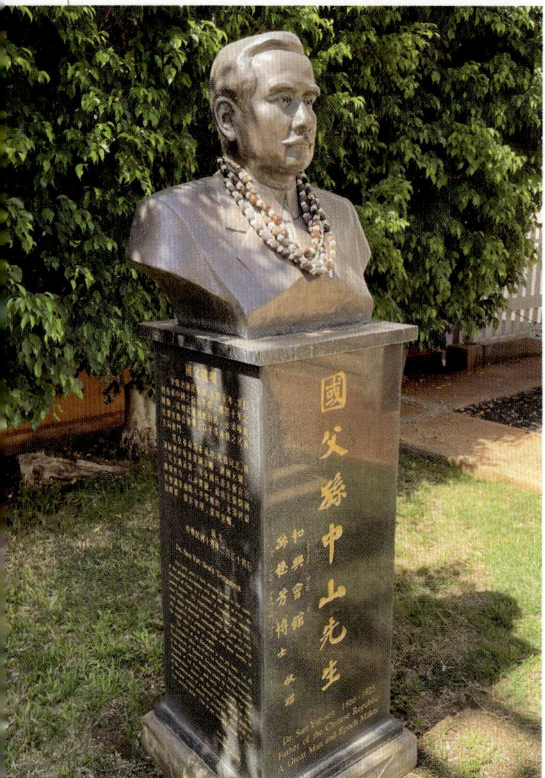

Sun Yat-sen Lahaina. Photo by Ray Soon

The Sun Yat-sen bust and the historic Wo Hing Social Club and Museum with its rare Chinese papers and artifacts were destroyed in the Lahaina wildfire of August 8-9, 2023. The research conducted for this section was completed prior to the fire.

Captain George Vancouver

(1757-1798)

This memorial is beside Ma'alaea Bay on a sandy beach near Kīhei on Maui. It is said to be Vancouver's landing site, but this remains unverified. The bay area was once a small fishing village and a retreat for Hawaiian royalty. Now deteriorated, what remains is a mount with a stone piece on top, and the bases for totem poles which no longer exist.

While greatly deteriorated, this memorial is notable from several perspectives, while ultimately leaving many questions unanswered. To start, what was Vancouver's relation to Hawai'i? While not minor, it is unlikely to be celebrated from a native Hawaiian perspective. Vancouver was on two of Cook's expeditions (the second and third). He returned to Hawai'i three more times, and completed the charting of the islands that Cook and William Bligh had started. He exchanged gifts with Kamehameha

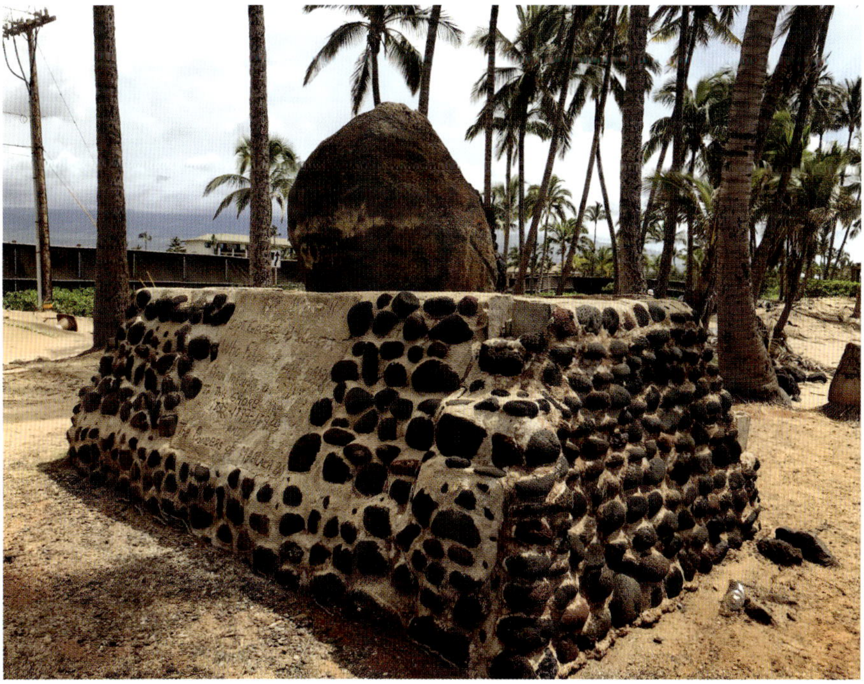

Photo by Paul K. Sensano

who in 1798, declared Vancouver "friend" having conducted himself with the "strictest honest, civility and friendly attention." This was an important statement, given that Cook was killed by the Hawaiians one year later. Vancouver explored Maui, the landing in Māʻalaea Bay, which he described in his journals.

After Cook's death, Vancouver conducted his own expeditions. He explored much of the Northwest Territory, and thus is a person of historical interest and accomplishment from that perspective. There are many places named for him, including the important coastal seaport city in British Columbia, Canada, though mountains in Alaska and New Zealand also bear his name. Statues and other memorials to him, including his gravesite in Petersham, London England, are generally maintained by the City of Vancouver, so beloved is he there (his statue sits in front of the city hall).

Given this, who erected the Vancouver memorial on Maui and why? This little-known memorial was the doing of a Canadian named James Gordon Gibson (1904-1986), a wealthy lumberman, politician, hotelier, and an author. Later in his life, he built a home in Kīhei, calling it Fort Vancouver. The home had frequent guests and evolved first into ten guest houses and later, four quadruplexes. By 1967, it was named the Maui Lu Hotel (his wife's name was Louise).

In 1969, Gibson built a memorial to Vancouver at the hotel beach. Gibson is quoted in a Spokane newspaper claiming it was Vancouver's landing site, but there is no verification of this statement. Another newspaper described the memorial as consisting of an "ancient boarding cannon and a giant clam shell. It is guarded by two totem poles from Vancouver Island." The wordings on the main memorial are hand written in rough concrete rather than inscribed on a plaque.

The two bases for the totem poles remain a few feet away.

In old undated photos the totem poles appear to the side, and upon their own stone platform. One picture shows the totem pole painted brightly and has a winged figure near the top. The carvings are said to be typical of the Nuu-chah-Nulth carvings of the Mowachaht tribe. This would make sense since that is where Gibson once lived and had his lumber business.

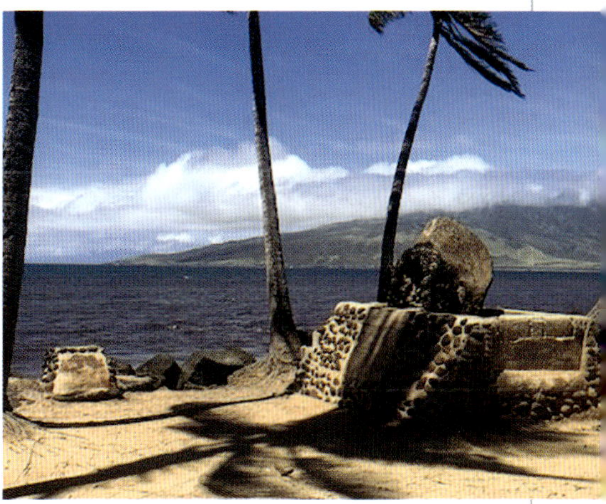

Vancouver Monument. Photo by Ray Soon

What happened to the memorial and the totem poles? A 2017 article by John Price in the Canadian publication, *Times Colonist*, states the condition as greatly deteriorated, spalling, unmarked, and difficult to find. The rock bases for the totem poles are still there. The totem poles were damaged in a storm and deemed not repairable, although they seem to have been stored under a hotel building at one point. The remains of totem poles, which likely first came from a tribe in Canada, if they still exist, are in an unknown location. They were possibly put into storage, possibly destroyed. Or possibly, as some would wish, re-appropriated to their native tribe in Canadian Pacific Northwest, which is likely their original home.

Clearly Gibson felt an affinity to Vancouver, the hero of his native homeland in British Columbia and believed he had found a connection at his new home on Maui. How he came into possession of the totem poles is unknown, but they were probably once on land he owned in Vancouver Island.

The Maui Lu Hotel was bought in 2015 and transferred to Hilton Grand Vacations in 2018, set for demolition and replacement. Contractors at that time recall seeing the memorial, already in poor shape and beyond repair. It exists on a State easement for a revetment, and the government asked that it be removed or relocated where tourists could safely access it. There were already no totem poles by 2018, just stories.

Saint Damien of Moloka'i

(1840–1884)

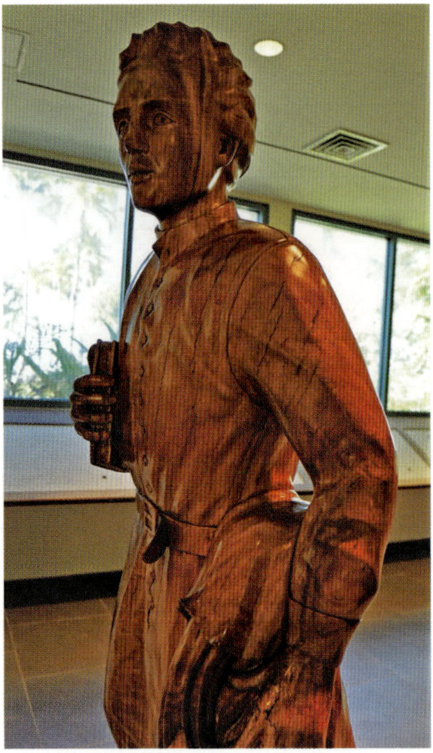
Young Damien at Heritage Center carved from koa, by permission. Photo by Sarah Yamanaka

Damien, a Catholic priest from Belgium known for his work with leprosy patients, became a saint in 2009. He had followed his older brother in religious life, came to Hawai'i by chance circumstances that involved taking his brother's place when his brother was diagnosed with typhus.

Damien arrived in Honolulu in 1864, at which time one-third of the population was Catholic. He served nine years on the Big Island and helped to build eight chapels and churches there. He preferred to build churches, to toil with others in the fields, and to tend livestock over a life of pure preaching. See Chapter Two for more on Damien in Hawai'i Island.

For years, the government in Hawai'i had been dealing with an outbreak of leprosy, likely brought by sailors and trading ships. Terrified of this epidemic, King Kamehameha V issued a law to separate those with Ma'i Ho'oka'awale 'Ohana (literally "family-splitting disease": leprosy) to a settlement on Kalawao, the windward side of an isolated promontory surrounded by the sea on three sides and sheer cliffs on the fourth. The first group, who settled there in 1866 with no dwellings, few provisions, and no doctor or priest. Their lives lacked hope, they were cut off from others, and doomed to a difficult death. Seven years later, the exiled afflicted patients petitioned Bishop Maigret, vicar of the Catholic church in the Sandwich Islands, to rotate in priests at three-month intervals.

Damien was among the first to answer the call from King Kamehameha V and Bishop Maigret to go to Molokaʻi and tend to the spiritual and physical needs of persons with leprosy (later called Hansen's Disease). He arrived in Molokaʻi on May 11, 1873, at age thirty-three, and immediately wrote back that he would remain and spend his life devoted to the needs of those afflicted. He stayed for sixteen years, became a patient himself, and died from the disease. He worked among the patients until just days before his death. King David Kalākaua bestowed on Damien the honor of Knight Commander of the Royal Order of Kalākaua, an honor he cherished.

By 1888, Damien was joined by Franciscan sisters who came to open an orphanage for girls, including Marianne Cope.

Damien's remains were exhumed in 1936 and brought to Leuven, Belgium for burial at St. Anthony Chapel. In 2009, a relic of his right heel was sent to Our Lady of Peace Cathedral in Honolulu for permanent placement. Damien was beatified in 1995 and canonized as a saint in 2009. A delegation of Church members and priests from Hawaiʻi attended the celebration in Rome, an event that drew eighty thousand devotees.

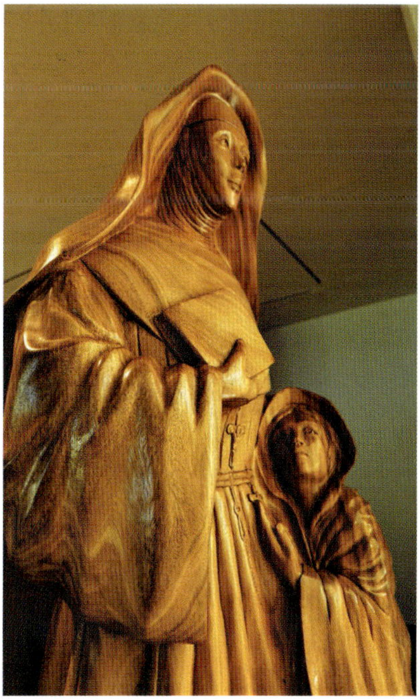

Monkeypod Cope at Heritage Ctr, by permission. Photo by Sarah Yamanaka

Maui has a strong connection to Damien, and several churches there display a variety of styles. Multiple statues of Saint Damien are described in this section. Many were added as he was on the path to being named a saint in the first two decades of the twenty-first century. This section also contains a presentation on the statues on Molokaʻi: Damien, Cope, Dutton, and other saints.

St. Augustine Church in Waikiki, Oʻahu is home to the Damien and Marianne of Moloka'i Education Center. It houses important documents, artifacts, and artworks. Dale Zarrella carved from precious woods striking figures of both Damien and Cope for the heritage center. He gave a bronze version of the Damien to the Vatican in 2012 and a bronze of the Cope to Pope Francis when the pope visited the United States in 2015.

For Further Reading: Farrow, John. *Damien the Leper: A Life of Magnificent Courage, Devotion and Spirit*. Image Books, 1954.

Daws, Gavan. *Holy Man: Father Damien of Molokai*. University of Hawai'i Press. 1973.

Damien at Maria Lanakila Church, Lahaina

Owner	Maria Lanakila and Sacred Hearts School
Donated by	Maria Lanakila Filipino Catholic Church Club
Location	St. Maria Lanakila Church Garden, Lahaina
Year Erected	2015
Artist	Not known

This striking statue stands in a peaceful garden sitting area. It portrays an aged Damien, already afflicted with leprosy. The statue, which is made of plaster painted silver, was purchased. It is dedicated to the memory of Saint Damien and placed between the church and the school building. Inside the church, a large mosaic of Damien brightens the back wall.

This Damien statue, along with Maria Lanakila Church and Sacred Hearts School, miraculously survived the Lahaina wildfire of August 8-9, 2023. This is especially amazing given the materials it is made from and the intense heat of the fire.

Opposite page: Saint Damien at Maria Lanakila Church. Photo by Lucas Kashtan

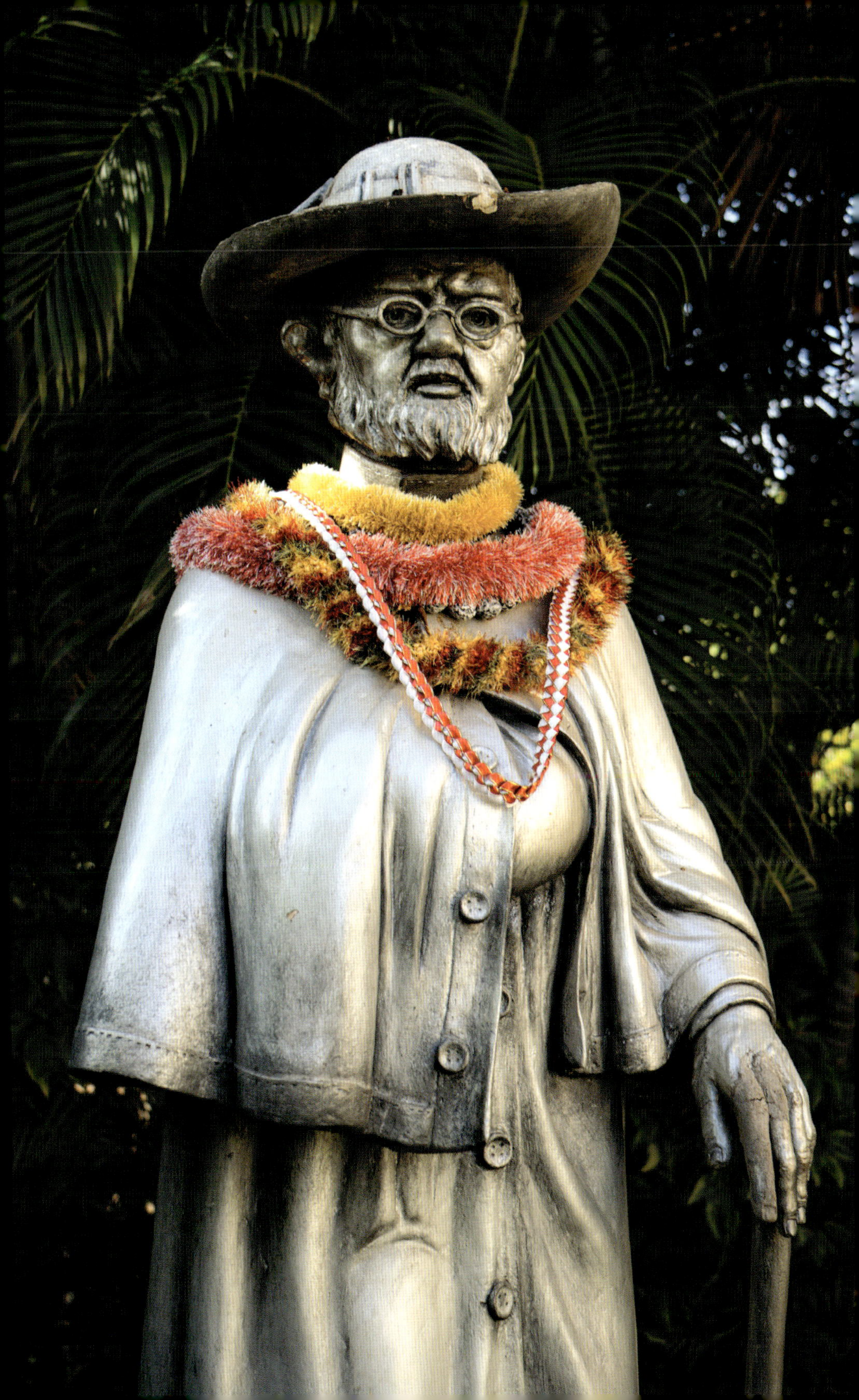

Damien at Holy Rosary Church, Pāʻia

Owner	Holy Rosary Church
Commissioned by	Sacred Hearts Father Roland Peters
Location	Holy Rosary Church, Pāʻia
Year Erected	1976
Artist	Evo Stagetti of Italy
Piece Name	Father Damien deVeuster, SSCC, Apostle of Molokaʻi

This moving monument carved from Italian marble depicts a young father Damien with his arm around a man (a leprosy patient) who is seated between his knees, his right arms resting on Damien's right knee. Damien has a clerical cape; the man has a lei of kukui.

The Holy Rosary Church was first built in 1886 to serve the plantation communities of Kūʻau and Pāʻia, primarily made up of Portuguese members. The present church was built in 1927 as a majestic Gothic structure. Among the church's other attractions are multiple stained-glass windows crafted in Belgium, and wooden Stations of the Cross carved by the Brothers of the Sacred Heart.

The Damien monument is a centennial memorial for the church. It was made by Evo Stagetti of Italy, and was unveiled on October 3, 1976 by Mr. and Mrs. Herman Calaca in a blessing ceremony by Bishop Scanlon.

The marble base is mounted on a dais with a layer of natural lava stone and a bronze plaque. Fronting the statue is an elaborate display of flowers in planter boxes. Palm trees surround the setting. A six-foot cement wall displays plaques that indicate the names of donors and tell the story of the Damien statue.

Opposite page: Saint Damien at Holy Rosary Church in Pāʻia. Photo by Ray Soon

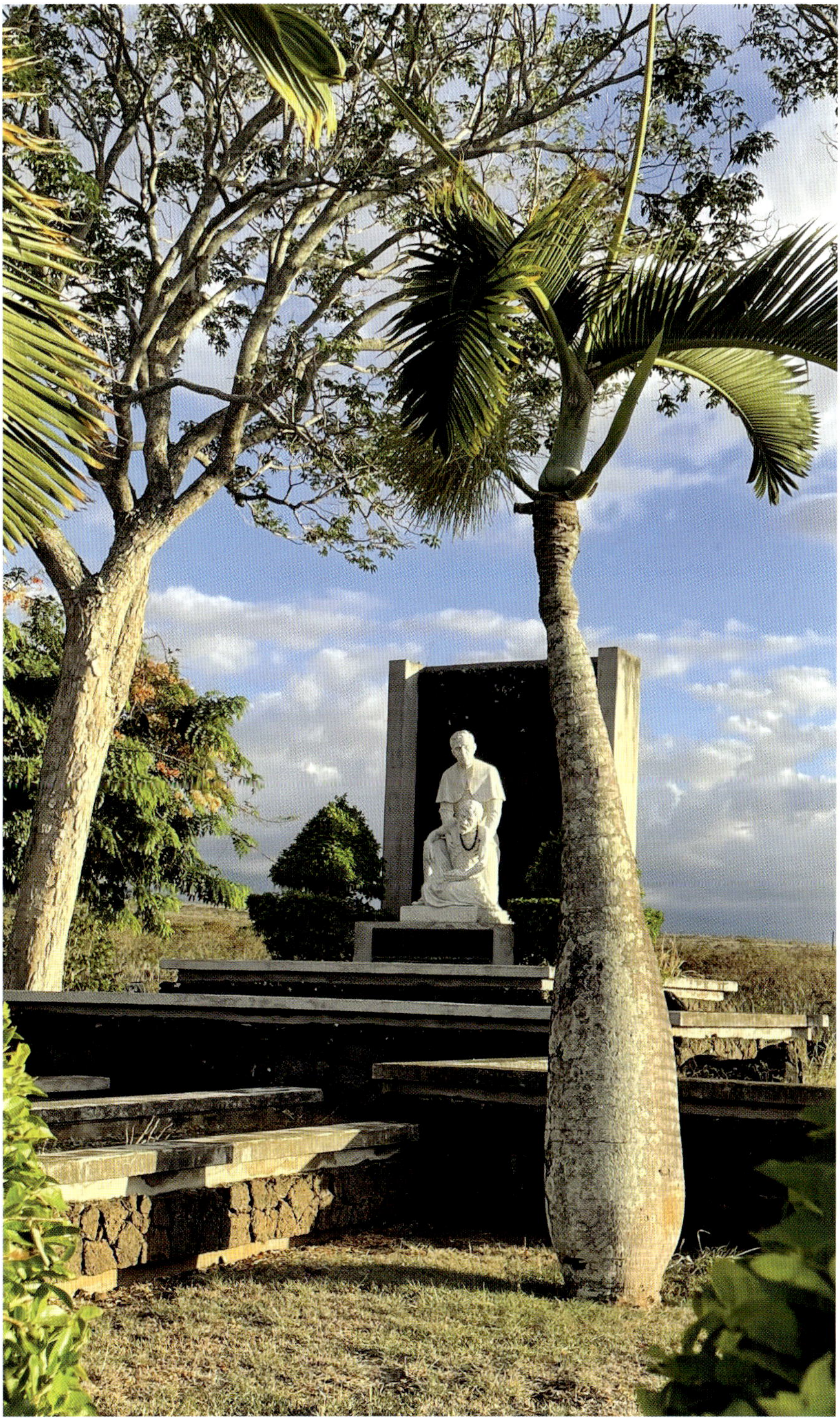

Damien at St. Anthony Church, Wailuku

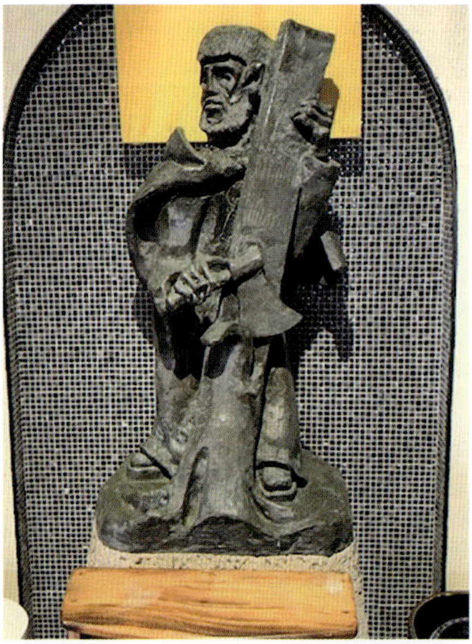

Charlot Damien at St. Anthony Church. Photo by Cheryl Soon

Inside St. Anthony Church is a significant sculpture called, Damien Builder of Churches. The 45" high bronze was created by Jean Charlot as part of the competition for the commission of a statue for Statuary Hall in Congress and the Hawai'i State Capitol (the competition was won with an entry by Marisol Escobar). It was cast in 1980 at Roman Bronze Works in New York from the ceramic model made for the competition.

The piece honors Damien, an untrained carpenter, for the grass hut village chapels he built on Hawai'i Island, St. Philomena on Kalaupapa, and four churches he built on the east end of Moloka'i: St. John the Evangelist (1876), St. Ann (1876), St. Joseph (1876), and Our Lady of Seven Sorrows.

St. Anthony Church also displays a set of block prints by Charlot representing the 14 stations of the cross, one of twenty sets. Charlot (1898-1979) was a famous French-American muralist, lithographer, easel painter, illustrator, sculptor, and author. He moved to Hawai'i in 1949 and lived the rest of his life there. The state named him a Living Treasure in 1972 for his "contributions to Hawai'i's culture and the preservation of Hawaiiana."

Damien at St. Anthony School Hall

This standing statue is located outside the school office. It is made of concrete material and portrays an elder Damien, already afflicted by leprosy.

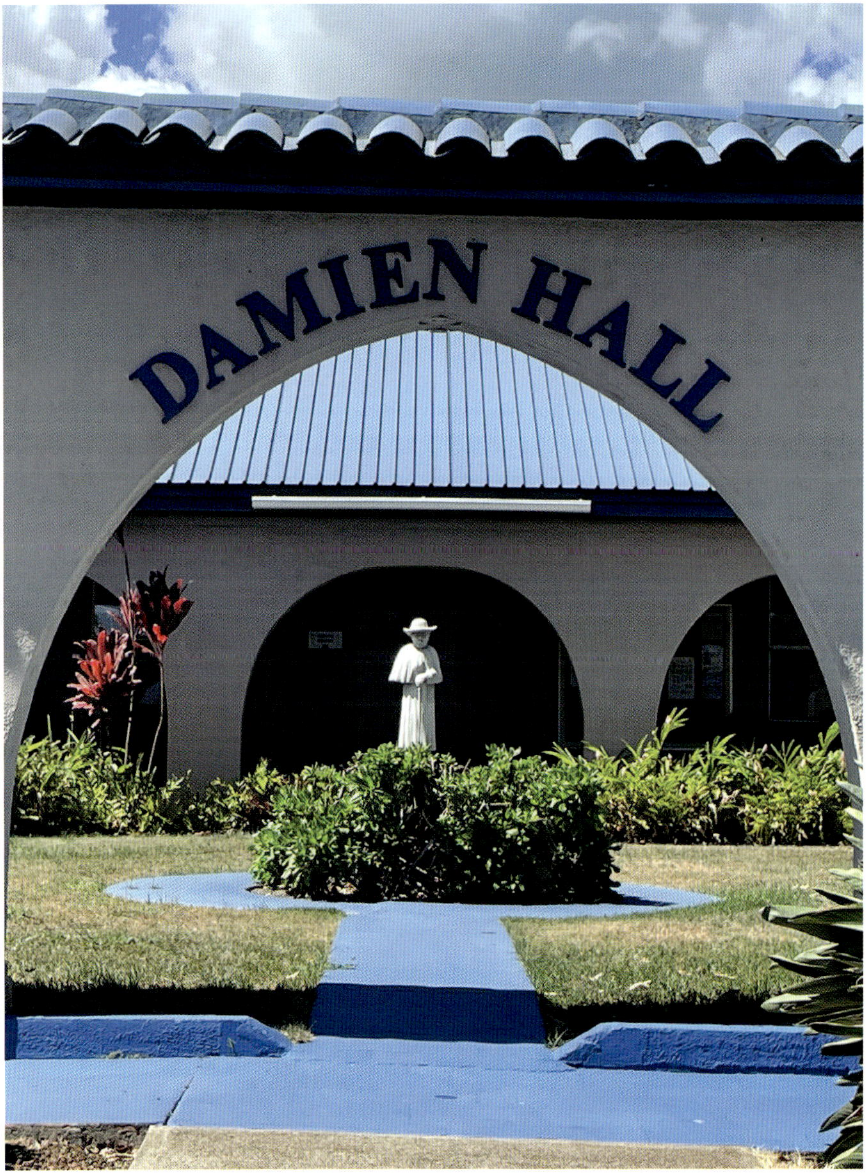

Damien at St. Anthony School. Photo by Ray Soon

Damien at St. Theresa's Church in Kīhei

Name	Saint Damien of Moloka'i
Owner	St. Theresa Church
Donated by	Dennis and Michelle Kleid in memory of Walter Joseph Myer
Location	Inside wall
Year Erected	c. 2016
Artist	Dale Zarrella

This statue of a young Damien depicts him as he first arrived on Kalaupapa peninsula in 1873 at the young age of thirty-three. Standing with an orphaned child, he observes the loneliness and suffering of the outcasts who have been abandoned. At this point of his life, Damien determined to dedicate himself to the afflicted and to live the rest of his life on Kalaupapa.

According to Zarrella, the statue depicts both the humanness and saintliness of this extraordinary man. In preparation for his work, Zarrella made several trips to Kalaupapa. He studied the letters and writings of several persons familiar with Damien, including Brother Dutton's daily journals. Zarrella has composed several versions of the saint.

There are a limited number of this sized version of Damien. The first two bronzes are at St. Teresa and at the Vatican in Rome, presented by Zarrella to Pope Francis in 2015. The seven-foot curly koa wood version was created for the Damien and Cope Education Center in Waikīkī where it will be shown along with Zarrella's statue of Marianne Cope made of monkeypod wood. The koa version (see page 146) has a natural tear in Damien's eye, the result of the grain in the wood.

The bronze version at St. Theresa's church was commissioned and donated by Michelle and Dennis Kleid in memory of Walter Joseph Myer.

Opposite page: Saint Damien at St. Teresa's. Photo by Ray Soon

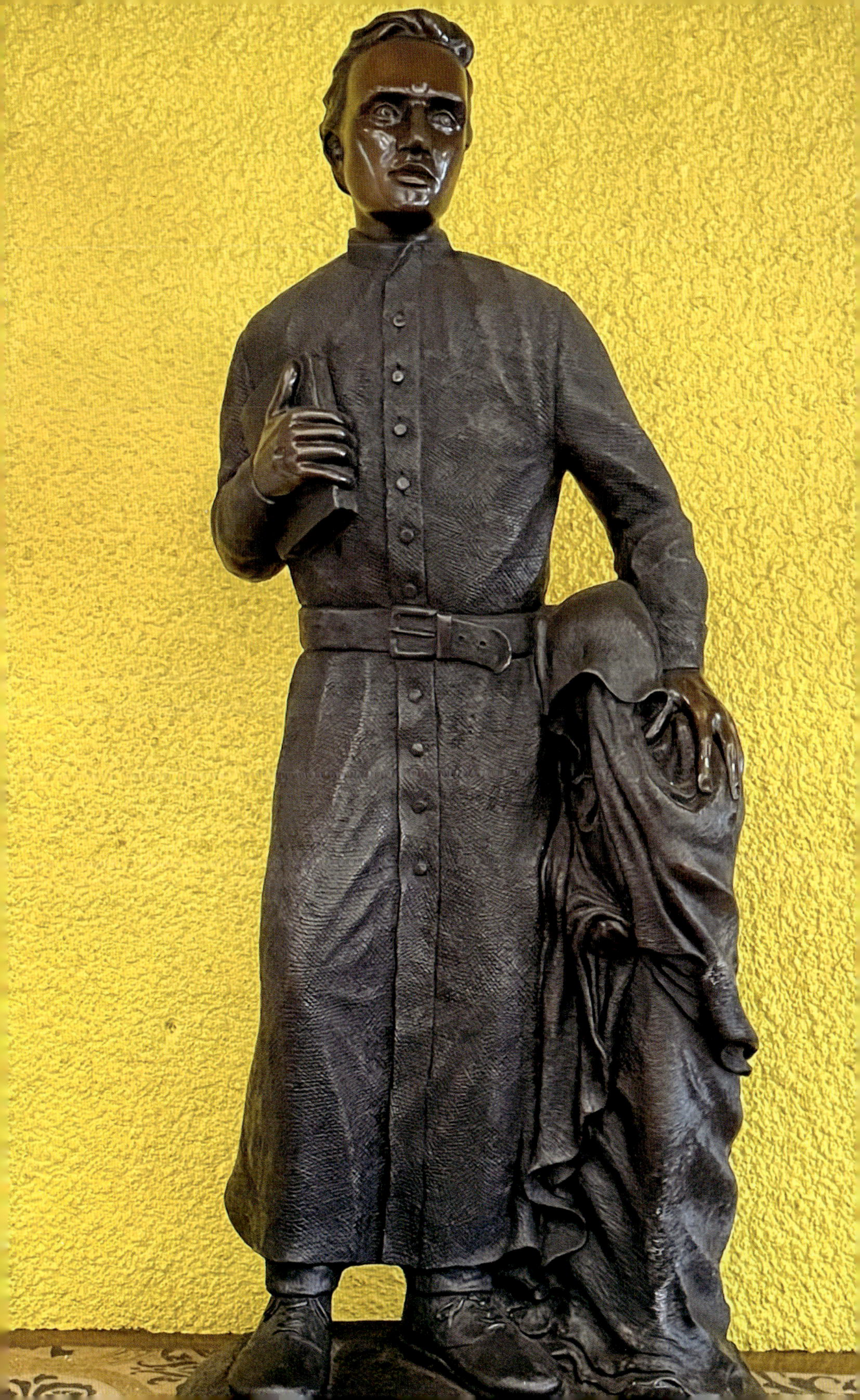

Saint Marianne Cope at UH-Maui

(1838-1918)

Owner	University of Hawaiʻi - Maui
Donated by	Michelle and Dennis Kleid
Location	Outside the School of Nursing
Year Erected	2022
Artist	Dale Zarrella

Mother Marianne Cope was head of her religious order and administrator of the St. Joseph Hospital in Syracuse, New York when she and other Sisters of Saint Francis answered a plea from King Kalākaua to come to Hawaiʻi to tend to the leprosy patients. Arriving in 1883, within one year, Cope and the others started to oversee the Kakaʻako Branch Hospital in Oʻahu where the leprosy patients were cared for. The next year (1884), she established Malulani Hospital in Wailuku beside St. Anthony Church, with a bequest from Queen Kapiʻolani. This was the first general hospital on Maui, and she served as its first nurse.

In 1885, Mother Marianne founded the Kapiʻolani House for girls made homeless when their parents were sent to Kalaupapa, Molokaʻi. This facility was located in Kakaʻako on the grounds of the convent beside Kakaʻako Branch Hospital. Marianne traveled to Kalaupapa in 1888 to tend to Father Damien and to continue her work with the medical needs of those residing in exile. There she established Bishop Home for homeless women and girls with leprosy.

Upon Damien's death in 1889, Mother Marianne agreed to head the Boys Home at Kalawao. When the Boys Home was renovated, it was renamed Baldwin Home to honor its major benefactor, Henry Baldwin. In 1895, when four brothers arrived to tend to the patients, she and the other nuns moved back to the Bishop School for Girls with Leprosy on Kalaupapa.

Mother Marianne was beatified by Pope Benedict XVI in 2005, and canonized as a saint in 2012. Her remains were exhumed and moved to

Opposite page: Marianne Cope at UH-Maui. Photo by Ray Soon

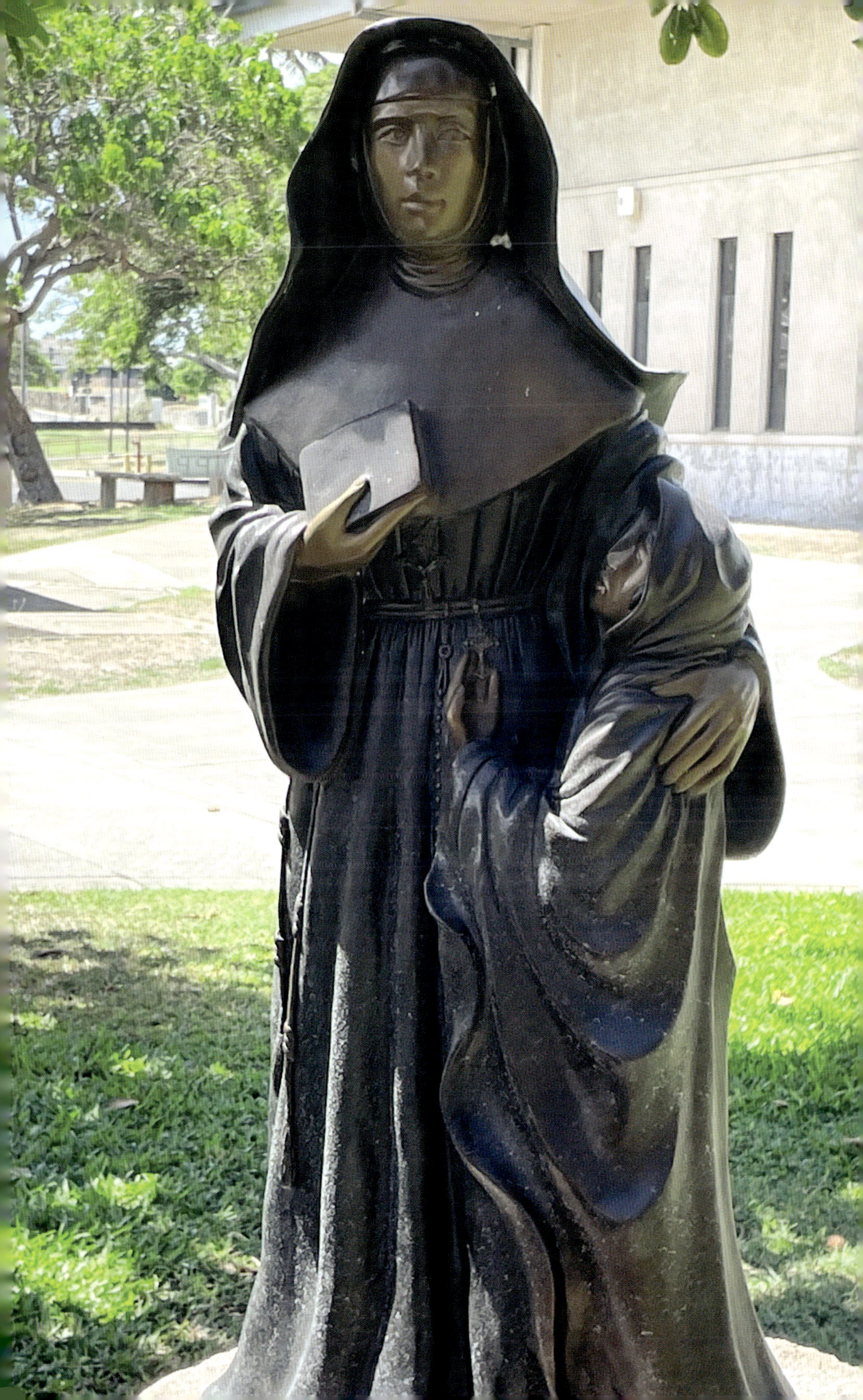

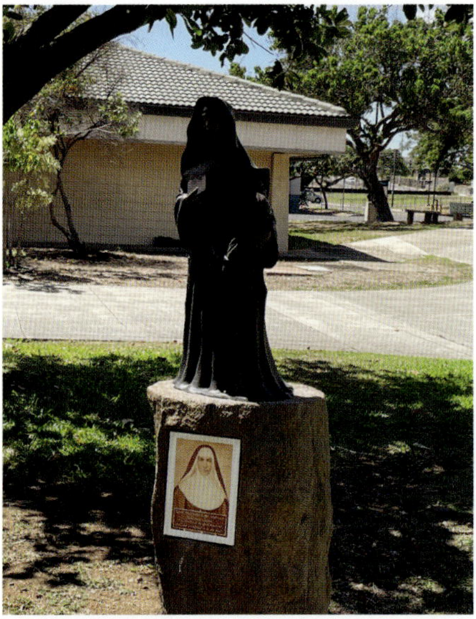

Photo by Ray Soon

Syracuse New York in 2005, but were later returned to Hawai'i and placed at Our Lady of Peace Cathedral in Honolulu in 2014, where they reside today.

This statue of Marianne is located under a kukui tree (symbol of light) near the school of nursing. It depicts her with a young child, symbolic of the many schools she opened for children with afflicted parents as well as for children who were resettled to Moloka'i. The statue was the vision of its creator, Dale Zarrella, who was inspired by a young family member attending the school. The model for the young child was Zarrella's granddaughter, and she danced at the opening.

Dennis and Michelle Kleid were the financial donors. Both Michelle and her mother are former nurses. A plaque on one side of the base is a picture of Mother Marianne. On the other is a picture of Helena Saint Martin Meyer, a former nurse and Michelle Kleid's mother, in whose memory the statue was donated.

In addition to the Maui statue of Cope and the memorial on Moloka'i, there are twin statues of Mother Marianne Cope on O'ahu. They can be seen in Kewalo Basin Park and at the St. Francis Medical Center, both in Honolulu. They were commissioned by the Sisters of St. Francis and created by one of their nuns, Sister Barbara Kopczenski. There is also a monkeypod Marianne at the Damien and Marianne Education Center, carved by Zarella.

For Further Reading: Hanley, Mary Lawrence and O.A. Bushnell. *Pilgrimage & Exile: Mother Marianne Cope of Molokai*. Mutual Publishing. 2009.

Statues and Memorials on Molokaʻi

The first twelve leprosy patients arrived on Molokaʻi on January 6, 1866. Theirs was a lonely and desolate experience. Not until a cure was found did the isolation change for them. In 1969, the quarantine was lifted with the discovery of sulfone drugs that put the disease in remission. During that hundred plus years, over eight thousand people were forced to live in the two leper colonies on Molokaʻi. First, they lived in Kalawao. Later they moved to Kalaupapa. As the population grew, so did the community's amenities. Eventually, a store, dispensary, health buildings, hospital buildings and cottages for the patients and their caregivers were built. As of the writing of this book, in 2023, four patients are still living there, in addition to two nuns, a priest, and several workers.

Three Catholic churches exist on Kalaupapa Peninsula: St. Philomena, St. Francis of Assisi, and St. Elizabeth Chapel (at Bishop Home). The Damien Parish of Molokaʻi cares for four other topside churches: St. Joseph in Kamalō, St. Damien Church in Kaunakakai, Our Lady of Seven Sorrows (1874) on the east side of Molokaʻi, and St. Vincent Ferrer in Maunaloa. Protestant churches on Kalaupapa include Kanaʻana Hou Church and its predecessor, Siloama Church. The Church of Jesus Christ of Latter-Day Saints building remains, but is decommissioned.

The lands on the peninsula are owned by the State DLNR and the Department of Hawaiian Homelands. Kalaupapa management is currently under the jurisdiction of the State Department of Health while patients are still living there. It became a National Historic Park in 1980.

While there is much of interest in the history of the peninsula, the account here is focused on the statues and memorials. Father Damien and Mother Marianne Cope were among the many who moved there to tend to the needs of the residents. Multiple statues and memorials can be found honoring both these saints as well as other religious figures. Picture shown depict the statues in their setting to give some feel for what Kalaupapa looks like. As with other features, it is difficult to maintain them in the often-windy climate by the sea.

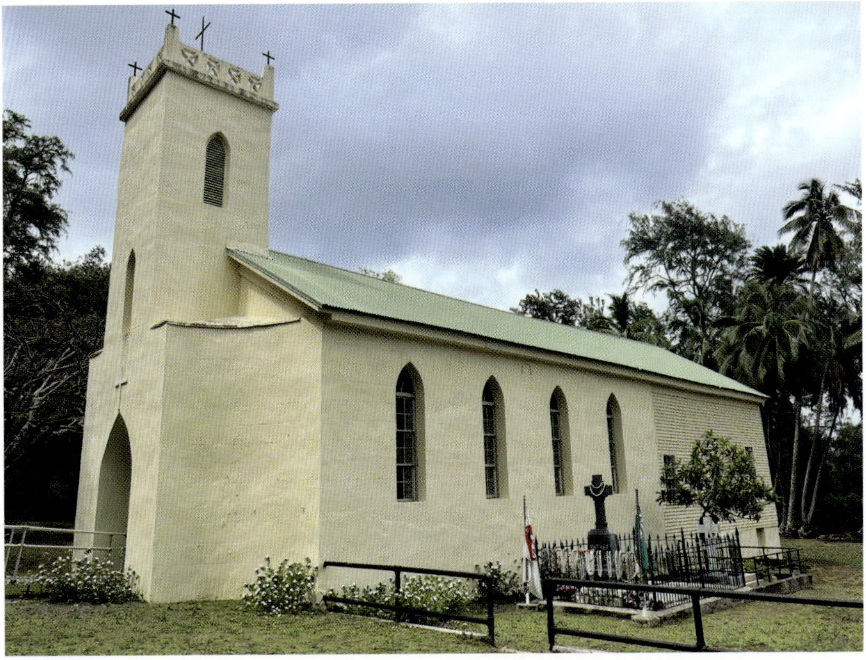

St. Philomena Church, by permission NPS. Photo by Mikiala Pescaia,

St. Philomena Church, Kalaupapa Peninsula, Kalawao, Molokaʻi

St. Philomena Church was erected between 1872 and 1889. The original church was built by the Hansen's disease patients. Damien expanded it twice; it was finally finished a year after his death. The open fields beside St. Philomena contain the unmarked burials of two to three thousand former patients.

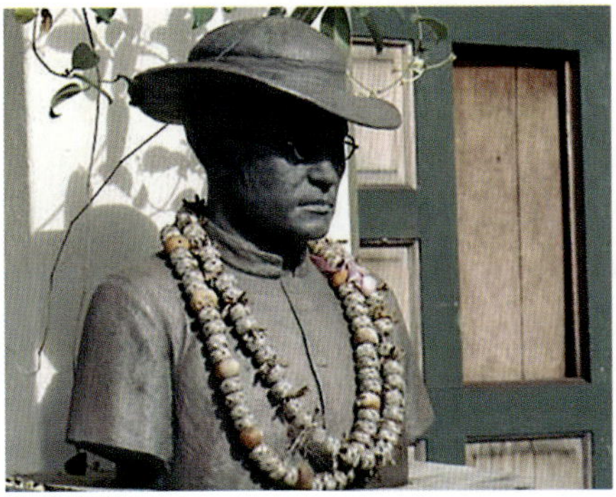

Photo by Karen Lucas

The patients buried Damien nearby when he died. His remains were exhumed and moved to his birthplace in Belgium in 1936. In 1995 a relic bone from his right hand was sent to Kalaupapa and placed in the gravesite beside the Philomena chapel. The wooden cross reads "A.C.J.S." on the top of the cross stands for his order, Apostles of the Sacred Heart of Jesus and Mary.

The cast bronze bust of Damien at Philomena Church was a gift of the artist/sculptor, Karen Lucas, and the late Richard Miller. The artist meant it to replace a Damien bust that Miller once possessed, but is now lost. A cut glass mosaic, also by Lucas, sits near a wall outside the church. "Kamiano" is the affectionate name used for Damien by the resident patients. Lucas has other cut glass mosaics of Damien at Immaculate Conception Church (Līhuʻe) and at Maria Lanakila Church (Lahaina) some made together with Sister Dorothy Santos.

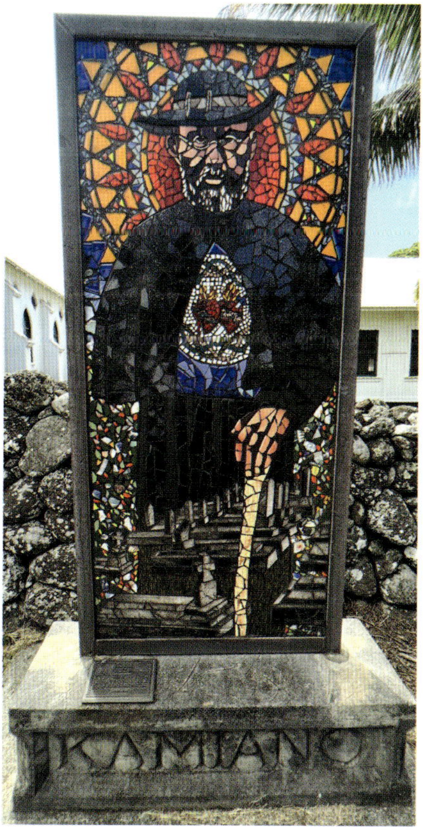

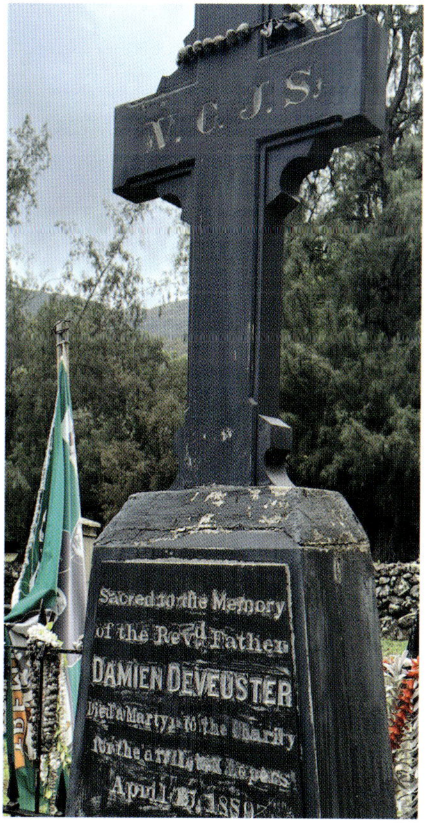

Left: Damien cut glass mosaic at St. Francis Church. Photo by Karen Lucas **Right:** Damien gravesite. Photo by Mikiala Pescaia

St. Francis of Assisi Church, Kalaupapa

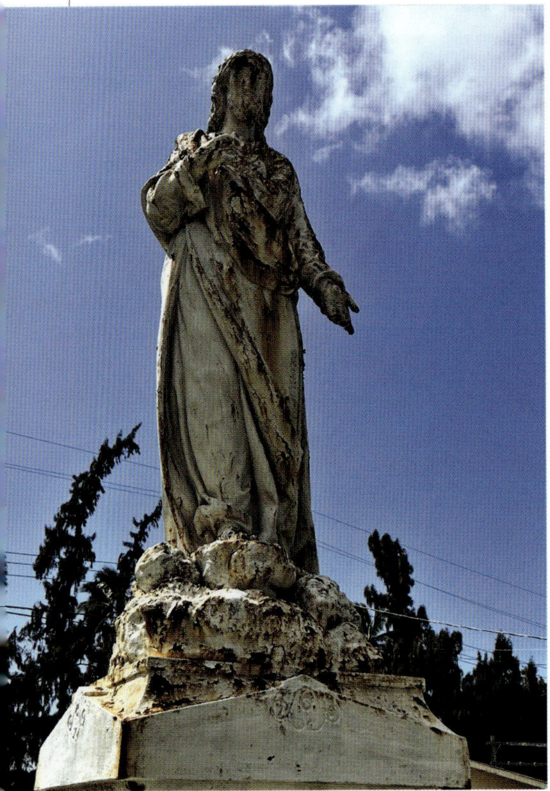

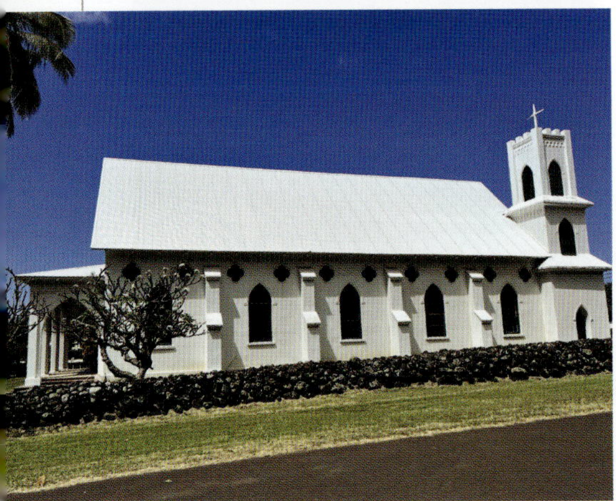

Top: Sacred Heart Statue at St. Francis, by permission NPS Bottom: St. Francis Church, by permission NPS. Both photos by Mikiala Pescaia

Patients started moving from Kalawao toward Kalaupapa, and a fishing village formed. Damien built a small church there, though he rebuilt it several times to expand it. In 1900 it was replaced again with a wooden church, which sadly burned to the ground in 1906. The church was rebuilt using a concrete Italian-Gothic style in 1908 and has a metal gable roof. The bell tower holds bells made in Tourney Belgium in 1929, one of two sets (the other is at St. Patrick Church in Kaimukī, Oʻahu).

In front of St. Francis of Assisi Church is a six-foot bronze statue of the Sacred Heart of Jesus (1907). It is a painted white and has obvious signs of deterioration. Other religious pieces at St. Francis Church include a grotto with statues of Our Lady of Lourdes and Saint Bernadette and six cut-glass mosaics telling stories from Damien's life.

St. Joseph Church, Kamalō, Moloka'i

Father Damien built four churches "topside" Moloka'i and two remain. He often scaled the steep pali to pray with them and receive their gifts. This small church was built in 1876 and is located on Kamehameha V Highway in Kamalō, Moloka'i. The church is listed on the Hawai'i Register of Historic Places.

The church ground has two statues, one of Damien (erected in 1979) and one of Brother Joseph Dutton (erected 2013).

The plaque near the Damien statue was placed in 1983 in memory of Albert D. Spielman, originally of Buffalo NY, who died on Moloka'i. The base of the Damien statue reads "1979" and "J Correale S7 de Deus" who may have been either the artist or the minister at the time it was erected.

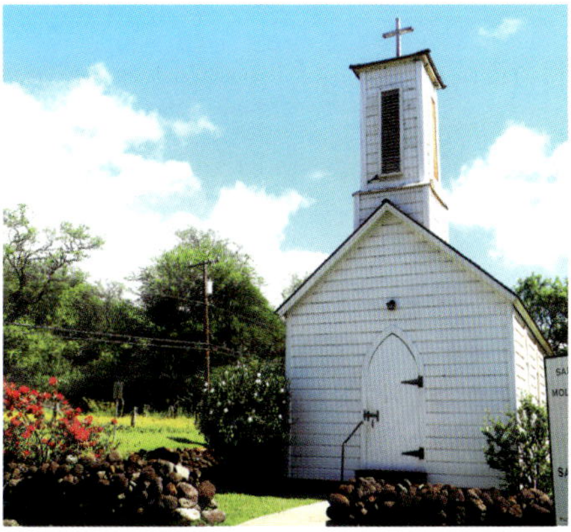

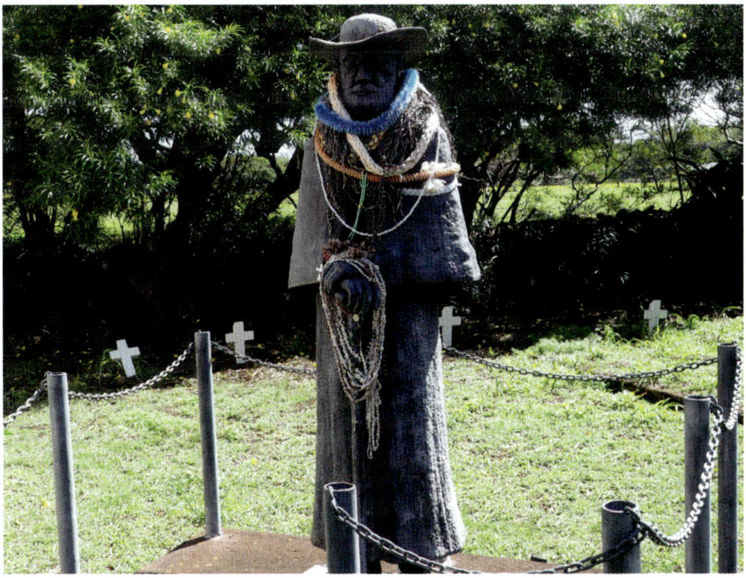

The Damien statue and St. Joseph Church, where the statue was erected in 1979 on Moloka'i. Both photos by Ray Soon

Damien Memorial

The Damien Memorial was erected by the people of England with funds raised by the Prince of Wales (Edward III). It was installed in 1893 at a site chosen by King Kalākaua. Designed by Edward Clifford, it consists of a six-foot tall rose-colored piece of granite with a Celtic cross at the top. Beneath the cross is a white marble bas-relief with Damien's head. There are three layers of writing, telling the dates of his birth and death, a scripture passage from John 15:13 and name of the donor entity. These are in both English and Hawaiian.

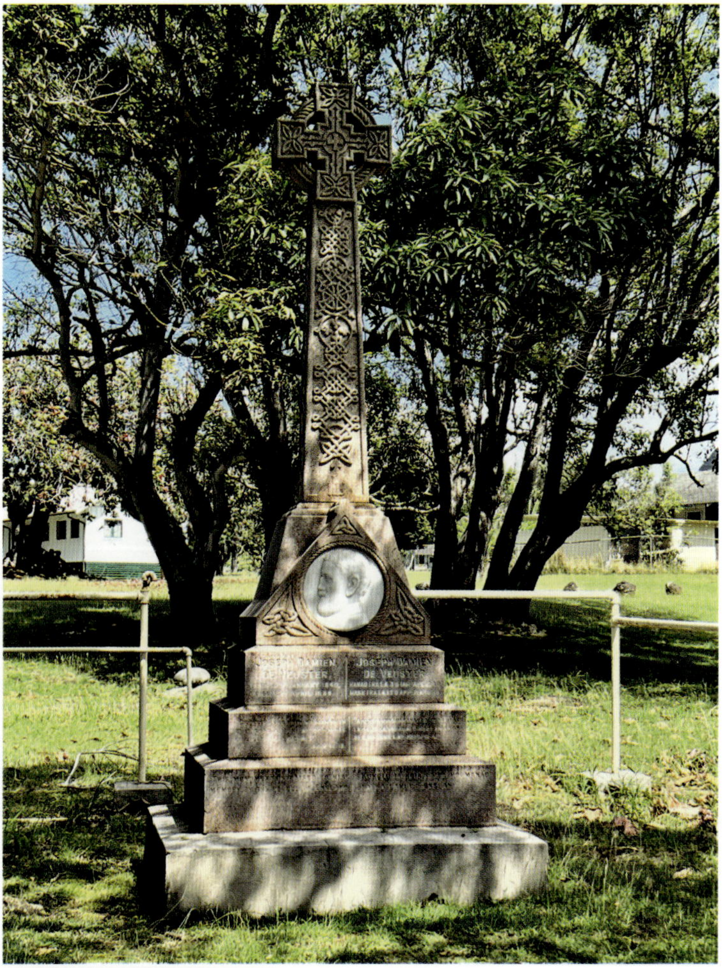

Damien Memorial at Kalaupapa, by permission NPS. Photo by Mikiala Pescaia

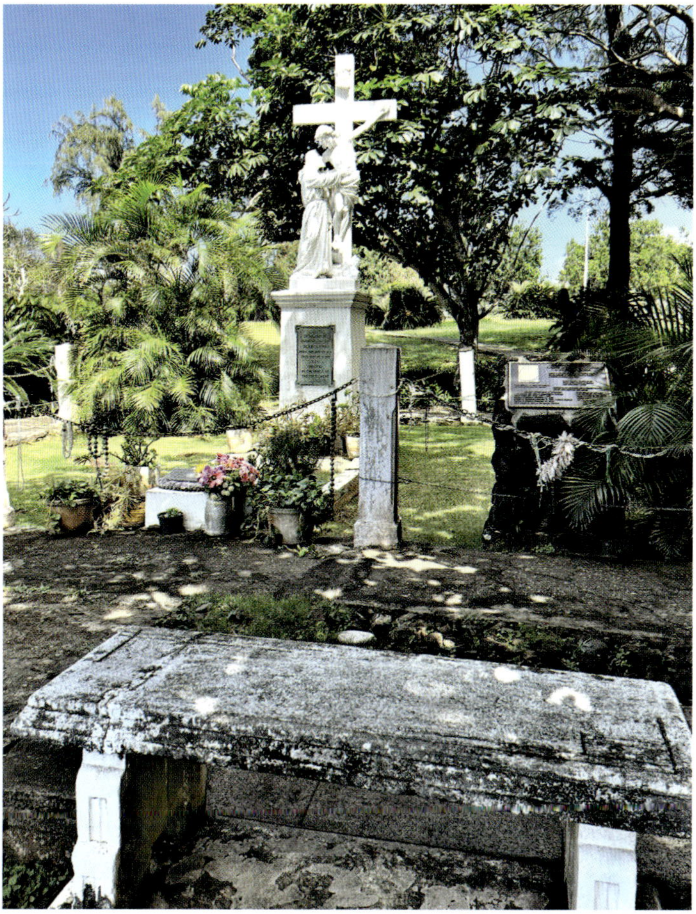

Cope Memorial & bench at Kalaupapa, by permission NPS. Photo by Mikiala Pescaia

Cope Gravesite and Memorial

Shortly after her death (1918) residents erected the monument to Marianne Cope, placed on the grounds of Bishop Home, just north of the Damien Monument. It consists of her original grave site, a formal walkway, and plantings. The six-foot-tall white plaster statue at the head of the grave and set on a pedestal is of Jesus on the cross, reaching down to embrace Saint Francis of Assisi. The base has a bronze plaque honoring Cope. There is a second bronze plaque on a rock moss pedestal, likely added around the time of her sainthood. A bench and short walkway allow for viewing and meditation.

Brother Joseph Dutton

(1843-1931)

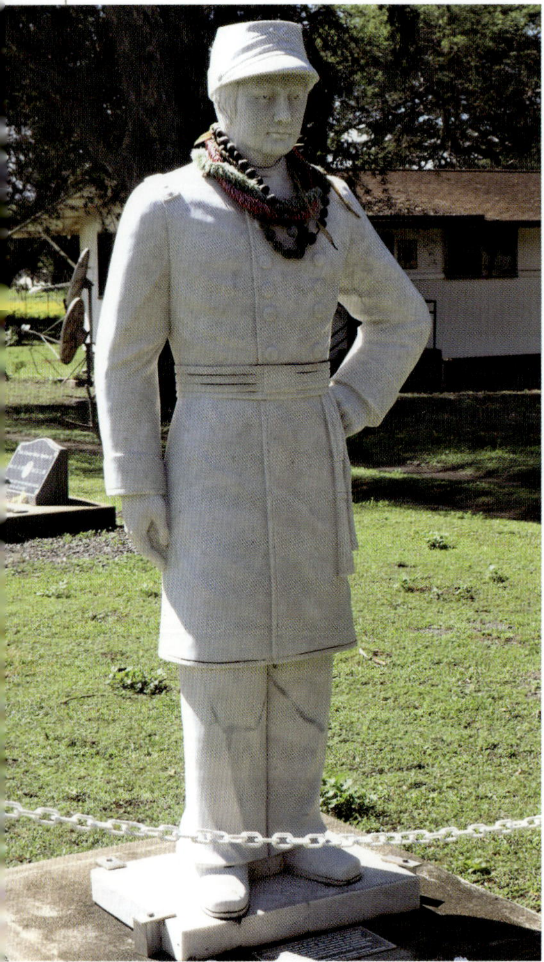

Photo by Ray Soon

While Moloka'i is already home to two saints, Damien and Marianne, efforts are underway to seek canonization for a third, Brother Joseph Dutton. Dutton, who once served in the Northern Army during the Civil War and, later volunteered to locate the dead and missing soldiers. He suffered from PTSD and drank heavily for a decade after his return from war. Then he turned to religion and, in 1886 learned of Damien's work in Kalaupapa. He volunteered to serve there, and continued until his death forty-five years later in 1931. According to the plaque, Dutton was honored in 1908 when President Roosevelt ordered the U.S. Fleet to pass by Kalaupapa in salute.

With the suggestion and encouragement of Father William Petrie, two veterans, Larry Helm of Moloka'i and John Perreira of O'ahu, both veterans themselves, paid for construction of a statue to honor Dutton.

Because permits at both the National Park and at the Veterans Cemetery involve long wait periods (Perreira was already in his nineties), the statue was given a temporary home at St. Joseph Mission Church topside Molokaʻi, installed in 2013.

The two thousand pound, seven-foot-tall marble statue of Joseph Dutton, carved in China, depicts a younger Dutton in his Union uniform rather than the older, bearded version of Dutton often seen in pictures. Sadly, Helm, who was heavily involved in the design, did not live to see it put in place.

Brother Dutton Gravesite and Memorial

Brother Dutton came to assist Damien in 1886. He died there in 1931. His gravesite sits not far from the ocean. It is marked in a similar fashion to Damien's grave with a stone obelisk topped by a Celtic cross.

Dutton is not forgotten, as evidenced by the flowers and lei left at the memorial. Efforts are underway to seek sainthood for this humble man.

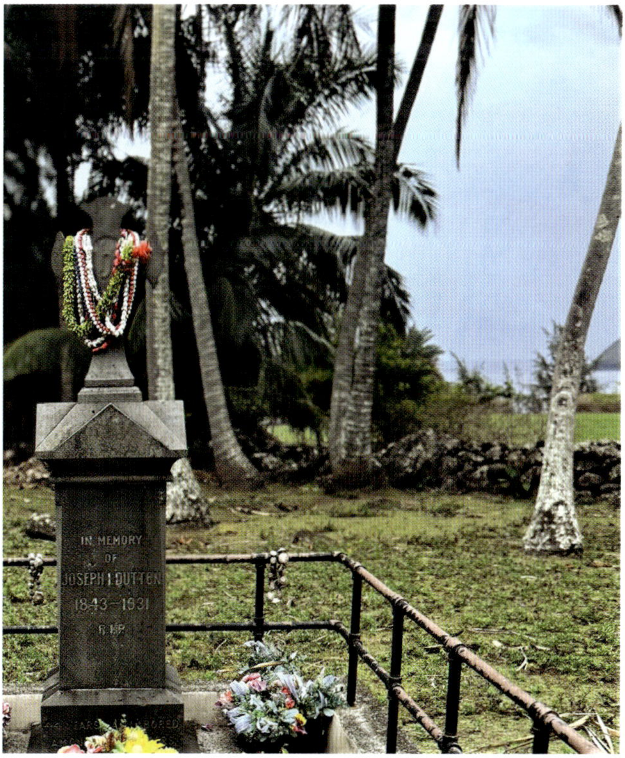

Dutton Memorial, by permission NPS. Photo by Mikiala Pescaia

Saint Anthony of Padua

(1195-1231)

Owner	St. Anthony of Padua Church
Commissioned by	Unknown
Location	St. Anthony of Padua Church, Wailuku, Maui
Year Erected	1919; rededicated 1994
Artist	Unknown

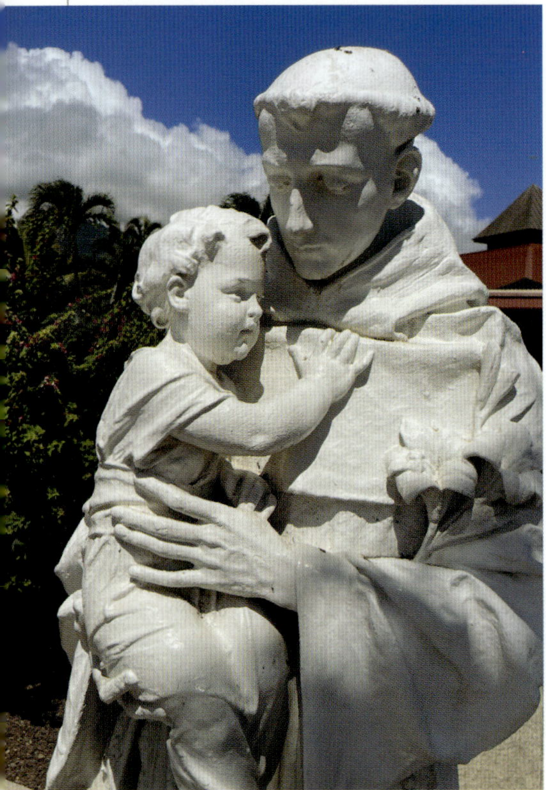

Saint Anthony of Padua statute close-up. Photo by Ray Soon

Saint Anthony was born in Lisbon, Portugal in 1195. Despite his wealthy family not supporting his chosen life, he became a Franciscan friar in 1221 in hopes of spreading the word to the people of Morocco. He was a teacher and brilliant orator. Often depicted holding the baby Jesus in his arms, Saint Anthony is considered the patron saint of the poor and oppressed as well as the finder of "lost articles and persons." He lived a short life, dying in Padua Italy in 1231 at the age of thirty-six. He was canonized as a saint only one year later.

The Saint Anthony statue shown sits prominently in a circle in front of the church. This statue once stood on the roof of the church, and was saved when that church burned down. It dates to 1919 and was rededicated in 1993.

St. Anthony Church has a long and noble history comprising the church, school, and cemetery. It is said that it is here during its dedication that Bishop Maigret called on the religious attendees to assist with the needs of the leper patients on Moloka'i. One of those in attendance who answered the call was Father Joseph Damien.

Mass services at St. Anthony started in 1848 in a thatched structure, the first wooden church was opened in 1854 when Kamehameha IV deeded 16 acres to Bishop Maigret. It was remodeled as a gothic church with bell tower in 1919, but destroyed by fire in 1977. Today, remnants saved from the fire, including the three bells are displayed.

Other Notable Features at St. Anthony Church

The church and school in Wailuku have major statues of Saint Anthony, Blessed Chaminade, and statues of Damien described above. The Chaminade is encountered just as ones enter the campus. It was presented by the St. Anthony School Alumni in 1981 in honor of the Centen nial of the arrival in 1881 of the Marianists to staff the Maui mission school.

Following the Lahaina fire, St. Anthony Church hosted funeral services for many of the victims.

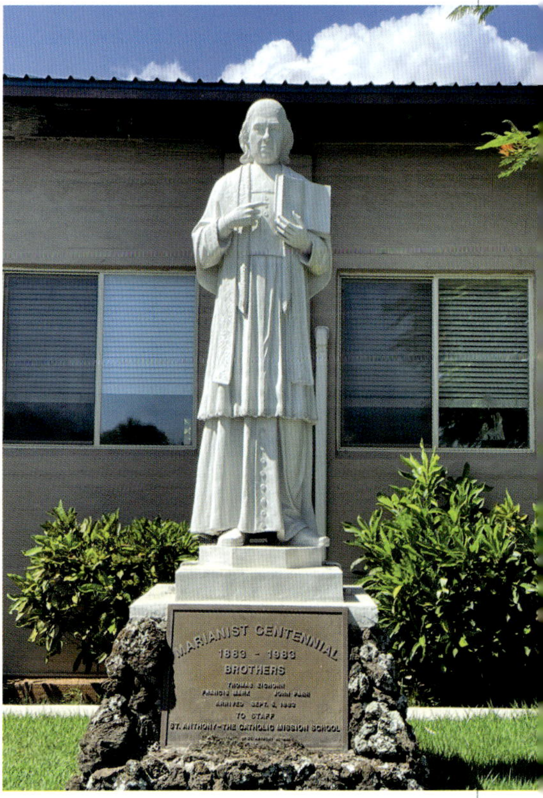

Chaminade Marianist centennial. Photo by Ray Soon

Masaru "Pundy" Yokouchi

(1925-2006)

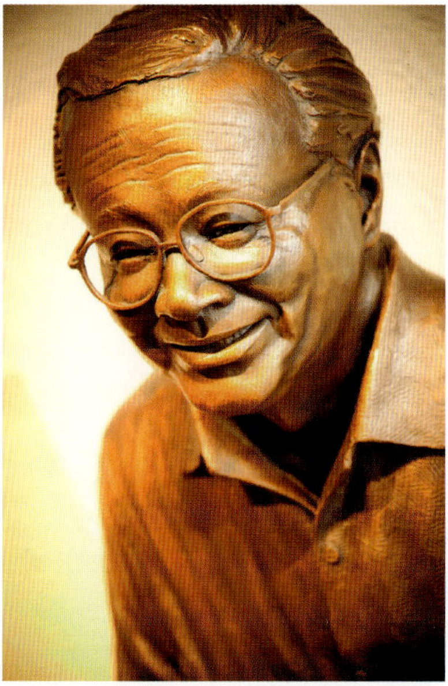

Close-up of Masaru "Pundy" Yokouchi statue. Photo by Sean K.L.L. Browne

Masaru "Pundy" Yokouchi was the driving force behind the Maui Arts & Cultural Center (MACC). It was established in 1994, the culmination of a thirty-year dream of the people of Maui. Pundy was its founding Chairman, serving for twelve years, and providing visual and performing arts as well at cultural and educational programs.

Born in Maui, Pundy became a self-made man. He was a friendly realtor, owner of Valley Isle Realty, and at the center of democratic political power in Maui and the state. His efforts were critical to development of Lahaina Town, Kāʻanapali, and Mākena as well as Nukoliʻi on Kauaʻi. Considered by some as the central figure of George Cooper and Gavan Daws' 1985 *Land and Power in Hawaii* (University of Hawaiʻi Press, 1990).

Purdy was noted as a generous, humble, and gracious person and great patron of the arts. He served as the first Chairman of the Hawaiʻi State Foundation on Culture and the Arts, instituting the 1% Arts Program.

The sculpture, the idea of his many friends and admirers, is meant to inspire future generations to do something of value by depicting his inner energy, imagination, and creativity. The slightly larger-than-life sized cast bronze statue shows him seated on a concrete bench with his legs crossed. It was commissioned by MACC in 2010 as part of a campaign to build the Yokouchi Family Pavilion. The artist was Sean Browne.

PART II
MONUMENTS

The first half of this book concentrated on statues, busts, and memorials of historical figures with some association or affiliation with Hawaiʻi. The second half is devoted to monuments that honor strong concepts, visions, beliefs, and heritage.

The monument chapters are organized by theme and each sub-chapter contains pieces from several islands.

The Monuments to Peace chapter includes gardens, bell towers, poles, and temples. Individuals honored in statue for their dedication to peace include: Spark Matsunaga, Mohandus Gandhi, and Dr. Martin Luther King, Jr. Born on Kauaʻi, Matsunaga became a six-term U.S. senator. Gandhi, who dedicated himself to nonviolence, passive resistance, fasting and meditation. He inspired another leader of peaceful resistance, Dr. Martin Luther King, Jr. (MLK), who is honored on Maui.

Interestingly, the next category of monuments, Honoring the Dead, aligns with the spirit of aloha, through an intention to remember, respect, and honor those who died, while at the same time praying for an end to bloodshed and death from violence. Honoring the Dead memorials are most frequently dedicated to groups of individuals who served in wars, and include veteran's plaques, honor roll walls, and eternal flames. Other memorials honor first responders as a class. The final examples of Honoring the Dead include memorials to victims of catastrophic events, such as tsunamis.

The monuments in the Ethnic and Heritage category honor groups of immigrant groups who came to Hawaiʻi, typically to work on the sugar plantations. These were commissioned and installed by descendants who wanted to show their pride and to remember and honor previous generations and their contributions. These were often installed in celebration of the 50th anniversary, the 75th anniversary, or the 100th anniversary of arrivals.

HAWAI'I ISLAND MONUMENTS

SUBJECT	TYPE	LOCATION	YEAR
Tsunami of 1946 Memorial	Stone monument	Laupāhoehoe Point	1947
Tsunami of 1960 Memorial	Clock and exhibit board	Hilo	1995
American Bicentennial Rock	Granite archway and gardens	Queen Lili'uokalani Gardens, Hilo	1976
Plantation Bell Tower	Bell tower with plaque	Main Street	1991
Veterans memorials World War II, Korea, Vietnam	Various	Multiple	
Memorials to World War II, Vietnam, Korea, Royal Frank	Stand-alone memorials in park setting	Wailoa River State Recreation Area, Hilo	
Camp Tarawa	Stone with bronze plaque Black marble panel walls	Parker Ranch, Waimea	1984 & 1998

KAUA'I ISLAND MONUMENTS

SUBJECT	TYPE	LOCATION	YEAR
Japanese Immigration Commemorative	Pagoda, Clock tower, Lantern, Plaques	Kaua'i Civic Center grounds	1961
Puerto Rican Centennial	Column Plaque	Kaua'i Civic Center grounds	2001
Japanese Lantern to Issei generation (Ishidoro)	Concrete lantern	Kapa'a	1915 Restoration 2018

MAUI AND MOLOKA'I MONUMENTS

SUBJECT	TYPE	LOCATION	YEAR
Ka'ahumanu Birthplace	Bronze plaque	Hāna Harbor	1928
George Vancouver Memorial	Platform with plaques	Ma'alaea Harbor	1969
4th Marine Division	Plaque	Ha'ikū	Unknown
Moloka'i War Memorial	Cannons and marble plaque	Kaunakakai	Unknown
Moloka'i Japanese Immigrant Memorial	Stone memorials	One Ali'i Beach Park	75 & 100th anniversary

CHAPTER FIVE

MONUMENTS TO PEACE

As small as it may seem, a good deed is always worth doing.

—Spark M. Matsunga, Senator from Hawai'i

The quest for peace is both an individual and a collective journey of self-awareness, inspiration, and evolution. No wonder, then, that peace is a popular theme for monument pieces. As Spark Matsunaga said, "If we emphasize the life and works of our greatest contributors, people will come to realize that moral courage is bravery of the highest type, and America will be called the Champion of Peace."

The permanent pieces in Hawai'i that represent peace are presented in the next few pages. They include gardens and sanctuaries, stone memorials, and bell towers. Some honor individuals such as the Senator Spark Matsunaga Peace Garden on Kaua'i; others represent efforts to bring world peace through action such as the Peace Corps Memorial. Some were donated by entities from other countries, Japan in particular, some are locally sponsored.

United Nations International Day of Peace has been celebrated on September 21 since 1981. The Hawai'i State Legislature established Peace Day in Hawai'i in 2002. Events are held on every island. Many of the events are organized by the Hongwanji Buddhist temples of Hawai'i. Following a moment of silence for those who have sacrificed for peace, bells are rung at 9:01 a.m. for five minutes by religious groups, community organizations and individuals. Bells range from tiny jingle bells to Tibetan meditation bowls to giant temple, church bells, and even water glasses. As they ring out together, the sounds connote harmony, happiness, and a sense of being soothed, all elements of peace.

Matsunaga Peace Gardens (Kaua'i)

Senator Spark Matsunaga was born and raised on Kaua'i. The story of the statue to Spark Matsunaga is described in Chapter Three. This chapter looks at two peace gardens dedicated in his honor.

Piece Name	Wahi Ho'omalu
Features	Peace pole, Benches, Rock garden
Location	Kealaula on Pua Loke
Year	1995 by Howard Shapiro and Marsha Hee
Upgraded	2020 by County of Kaua'i Parks Department

The peace garden located in Līhu'e was created by Howard Shapiro and Marsha Hee in 1995. It is maintained by the County Parks Department. When the County of Kaua'i built the Kealaula-on-Pua-Loke Affordable Housing project and Kealaula Supportive Housing Development homes for houseless persons, they upgraded the Spark Matsunaga Memorial Garden with walkways, landscaping, a gazebo, a peace pole, signage and peace tiles designed by keiki and kupuna.

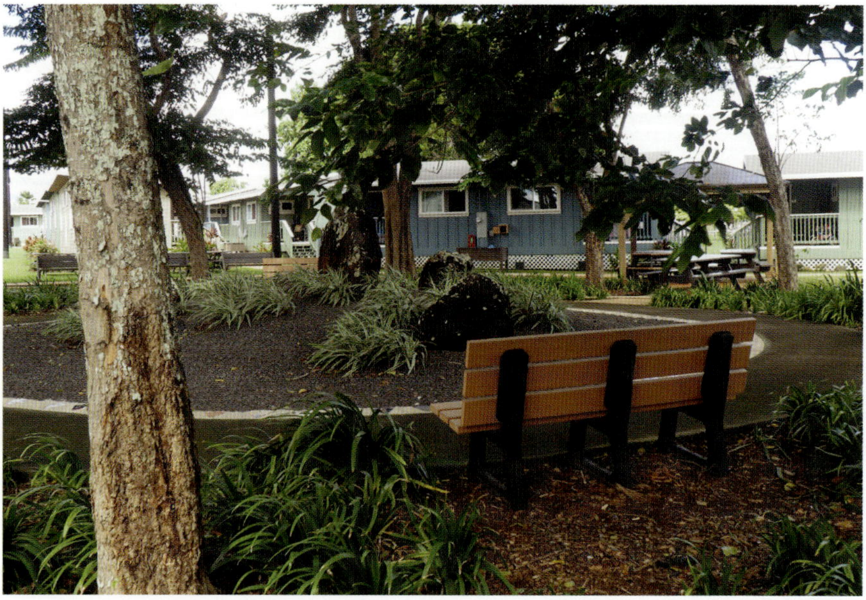

Matsunaga Peace Garden. Photo by Ray Soon

Piece Name	Children's Peace Garden
Features	Amphitheater for storytelling, Peace pole, Benches, Rock Garden, Koi pond, Statue
Location	Storybook Theatre, Hanapēpē
Artists	Kim Duffett and Kevin Chun
Year	2009

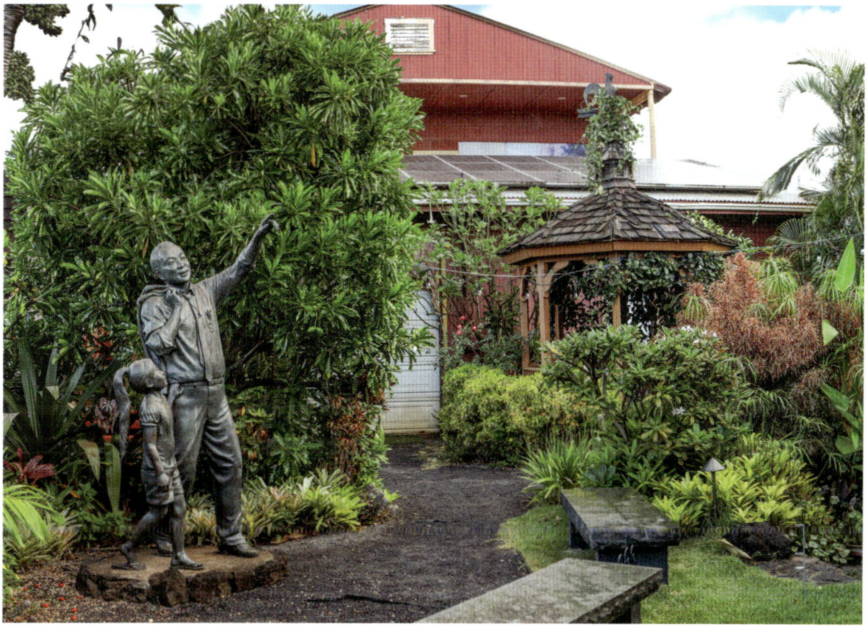
Children's Peace Garden Hanapēpē. Photo by Christian R. Cook

The second peace garden on Kauaʻi is a private one at the Storybook Theatre in Hanapēpē, the vision of Mark Jeffers. The garden was designed by Jeffers with artist/sculptor Kim Duffett and the late architect Kevin Chun. Chun formed a special gateway from stenciled metal in the form of the tree of life. While the wall is nearly nine feet high, the door is a mere four feet high to help children recognize that this is a place designed for their comfort. The semi-circular storyteller amphitheater seating is designed for the height of the average second grader. The walkway and the stone benches, like everything, has meaning. Major religions from around the world are represent from stone circles to Buddha figures.

John F. Kennedy Monument (Hilo)

Piece Name	JFK Monument
Feature	Bronze plaque on black steel
Location	Hilo Memorial Hospital Entry; moved to University of Hawai'i at Hilo
Year	Installation 1963; 2011 re-dedication with addition of granite and lava rock base when moved to UH Hilo
Commissioned by	United States Peace Corps trainees during their training in Hilo

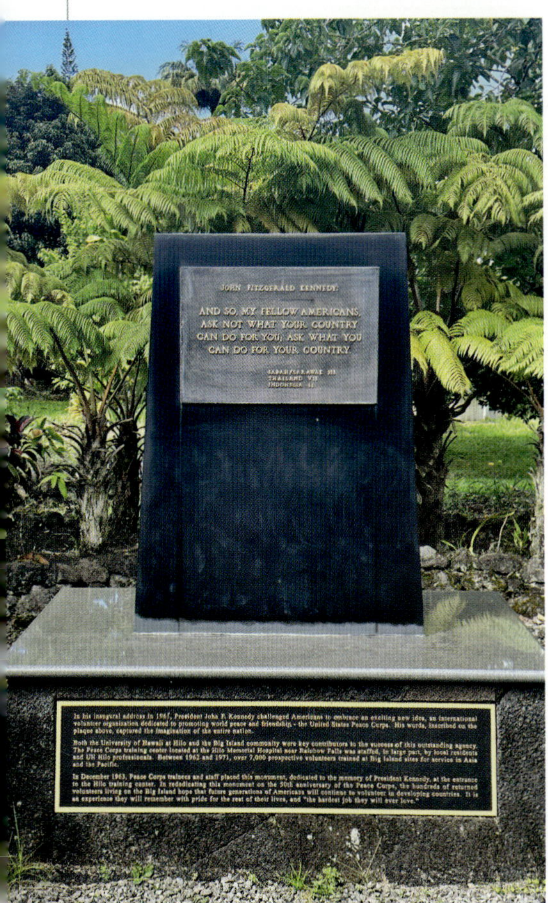

John F. Kennedy Monument. Photo by Rebecca Soon

A new and youthful President John F. Kennedy challenged Americans during his 1961 inaugural address to embrace an exciting new idea, an organization dedicated to promoting world peace and friendship. "Ask not what your country can do for you, ask what you can do for your country." These words captured the imagination of the entire nation and became the inspiration for the United States Peace Corps.

According to the plaque on this monument, both the University of Hawai'i and the Big Island community were key contributors to the success of the Peace Corps. Hawai'i served as a training center from 1962-1971. During this time, over seven thousand prospective volunteers were trained for assignments overseas. The monument was commissioned by Peace Corps trainees and staff of the Sabah/Sarawak III, Thailand VII, and Indonesia II programs. They were in Hilo for training before going overseas when President John F. Kennedy was assassinated on November 22, 1963. Trainees and staff contributed part of their daily allowance towards the monument, which was dedicated on Christmas Day, 1963.

The monument was rededicated in 2011 when it was moved to the University of Hawaiʻi at Hilo during the Peace Corps 50th Anniversary celebrations. About four hundred returned Peace Corps volunteers from across the country attended that celebration. A different plaque marks the spot where the monument originally stood at the old Hilo Memorial Hospital near Rainbow Falls.

Not far from the JFK Memorial on the Hilo campus is a red marble plaque that sits under a kukui nut tree (symbol of learning or enlightenment). The plaque is dedicated to PEACE in memory of September 11, 2001.

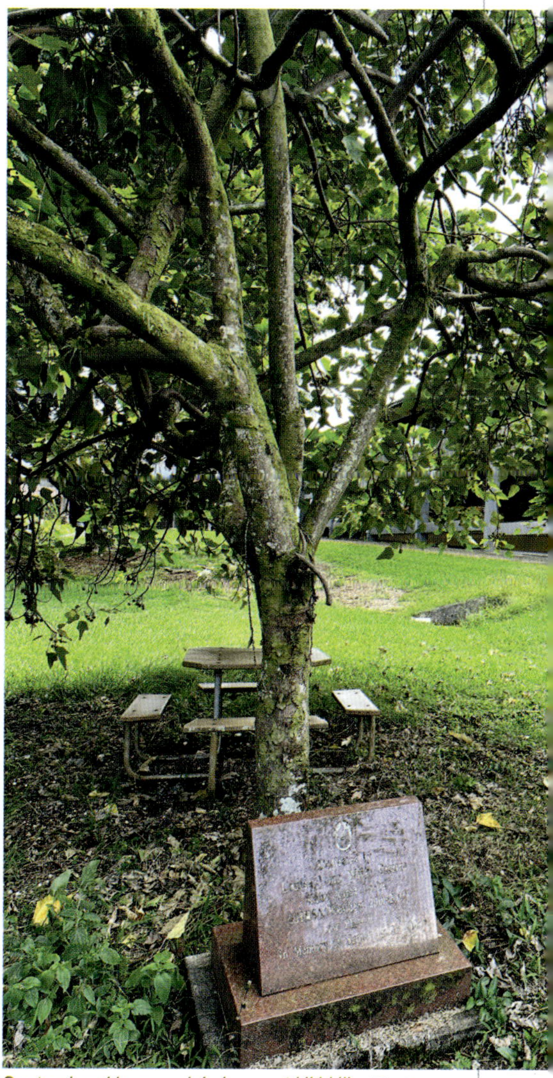

September 11 memorial plaque at UH Hilo. Photo by Andrew Graham

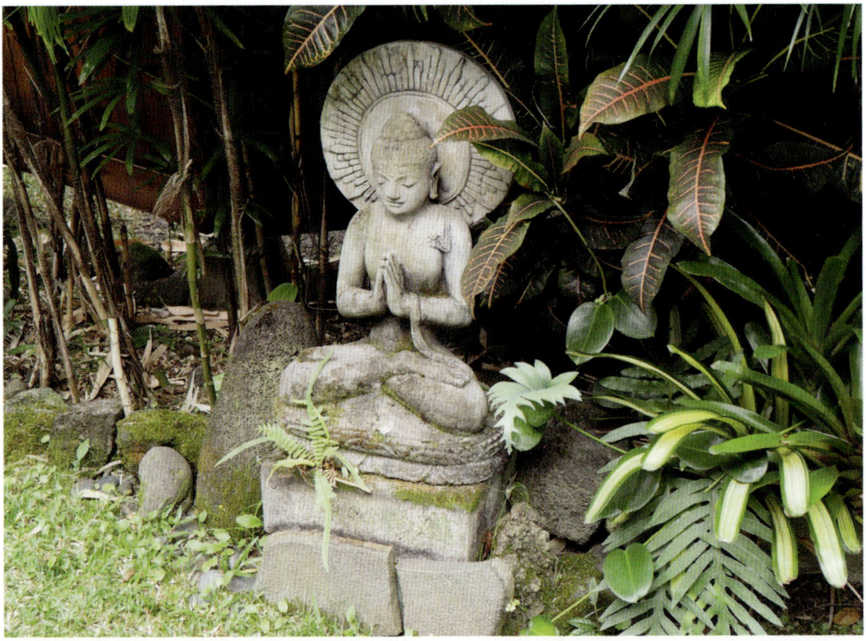

Photo by Ray Soon

Paleaku Gardens Peace Sanctuary (Captain Cook, Hawai'i)

The Paleaku Gardens Peace Sanctuary comprises seven acres of tropical botanical gardens in South Kona with expansive views of Kealakekua Bay. It is a nonprofit and was founded by visionary Barbara DeFranco. Walkways weave through tropical plants, palms, fruit trees and orchids with beautiful vistas and seating areas for contemplation and sanctuary.

Among the many features are: a galaxy garden (the first in the world to be made from plants), eight-hundred-year-old Hawaiian petroglyphs, Tibetan sand paintings, a labyrinth, a native American medicine wheel and fire circle, and a Baha'i nine-pointed star.

Many of the major world religious traditions are represented in the garden. The larger shrines include those to Tibetan Buddhist Padmasambhava, Kalachakra Stupa, and Green Tara. Feminine strength is embodied by the Ikaikai Wahine shrine and other such pieces can be seen of icons from Hindu, Christian, Islamic, and Our Lady of Guadalupe (Catholic). There is also a Thai Buddhist House, a Hebrew Tree of Life, a smaller Buddhist shrine from Bali, and a shrine to the Goddess Kwan Yin (her Chinese name; she is also known as Kuan Yin and the Asian Madonna).

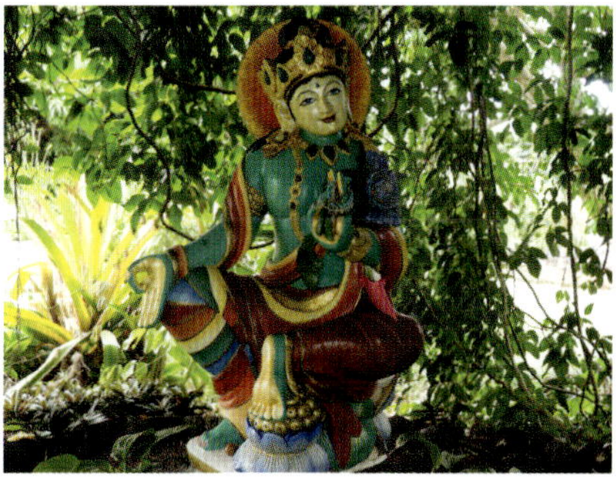

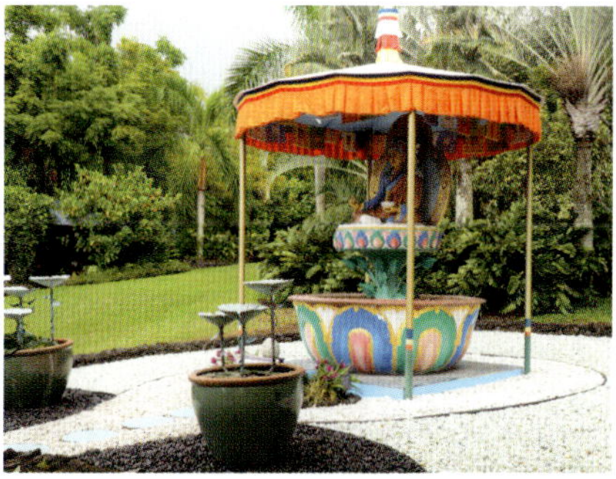

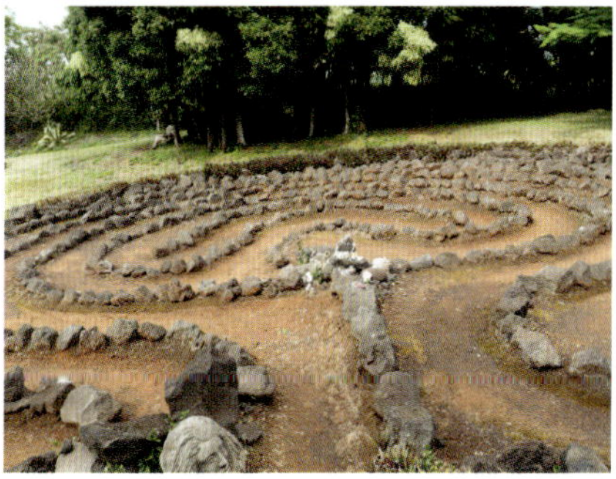

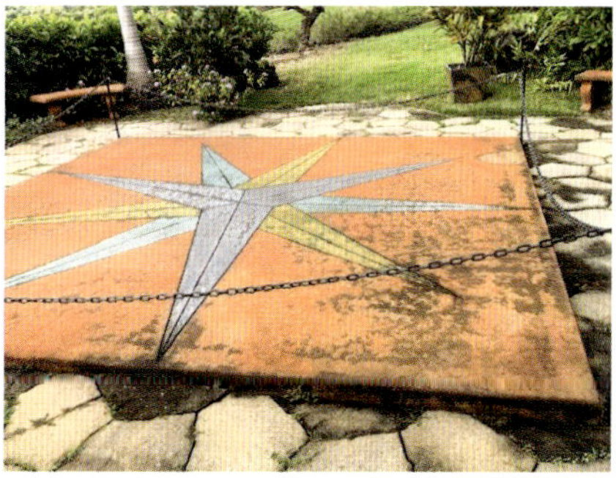

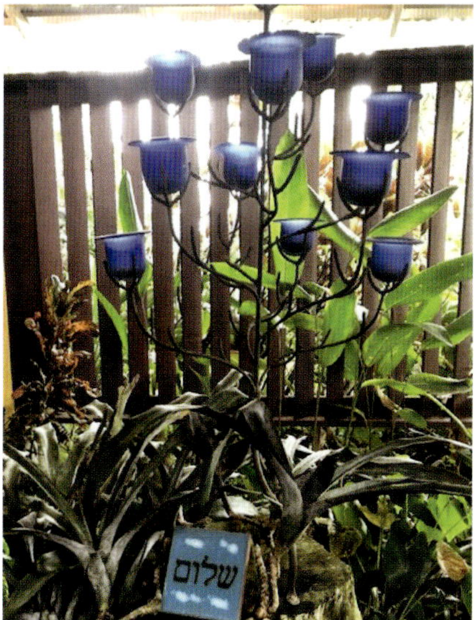

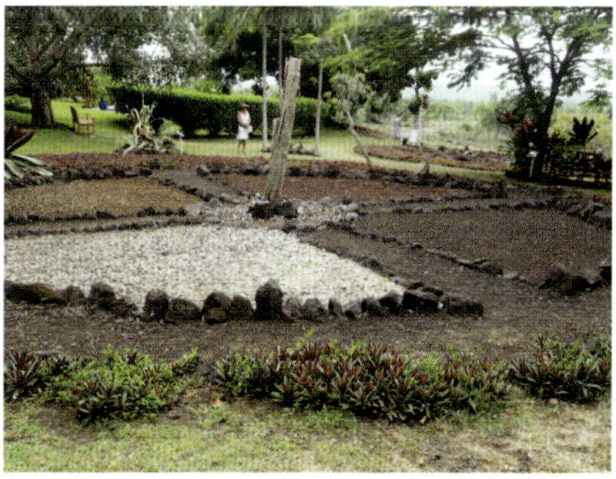

Clockwise from top: Green Tara (Buddhist Bodhisattvas); Padma Sambhava; Baha'i Nine-Pointed Star; Medicine Wheel (1997); Hebrew Tree of Life; Labyrinth (1996). Photos by Ray Soon

Dr. Martin Luther King, Jr. (Wailuku, Maui)

(1929-1968)

Piece Name	"Stone of Hope" Plaque on stone wall
Location	Maui County Building, Wailuku
Year	2006
Commissioned by	African Americans on Maui

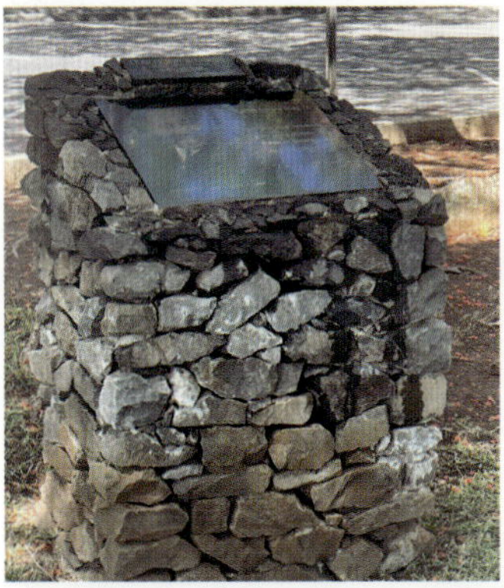

The "Stone of Hope" monument in Wailuku, Maui sits in front of the County building and is dedicated to Dr. Martin Luther King, Jr.

King's causes included civil rights, peace, and labor fairness. The plaque uses the famous quote from his "I have a Dream" speech, "Freedom is never voluntarily given by the opressor [sic: oppressor]; it must be demanded by the oppressed."

This monument, given by African Americans on Maui, was erected on December 28, 2006. The same group provided plaques explaining the history of African Americans on Maui, located about one mile away at Kepaniwai Park.

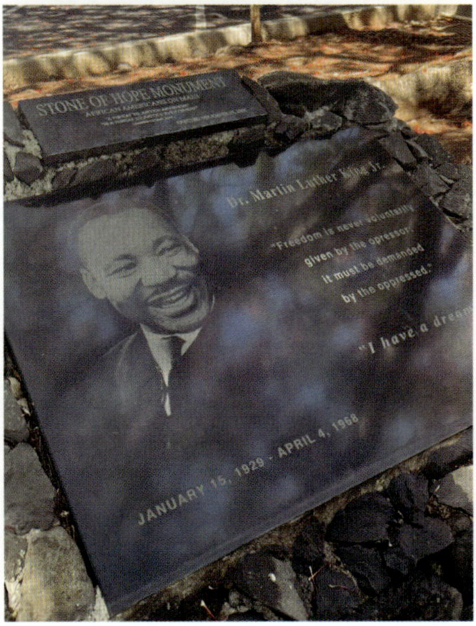

Both photos by Ray Soon

Peace Poles

Peace poles are a worldwide movement that started as a spiritual journey of the Japanese philosopher Masahisa Goi in the days following World War II. Seeking emotional and physical healing, he founded an organization to install peace poles worldwide. It started in 1983, and transcends cultural, religious, and political boundaries.

The first peace pole was planted in 1955 in Hiroshima, Japan. Since that time, over two hundred thousand peace poles have been planted in two hundred countries. Peace poles appear as painted poles, seven to eleven feet in height, with black lettering on each of four or six sides saying "May Peace Prevail on Earth" in multiple languages. Some poles have eight, twelve or more languages represented. The poles may be made of wood, vinyl, or metal and are engraved. The peace pole project is promoted in conjunction with local groups, including more than three dozen in Hawai'i. The Rotary Club of Hawai'i has taken on a project to refurbish old poles and install new ones island-wide.

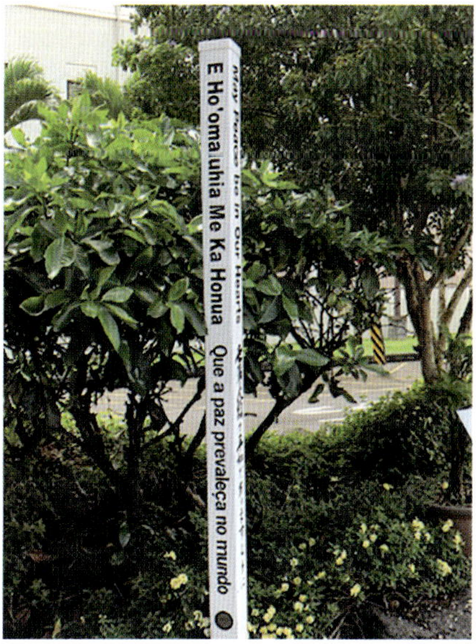

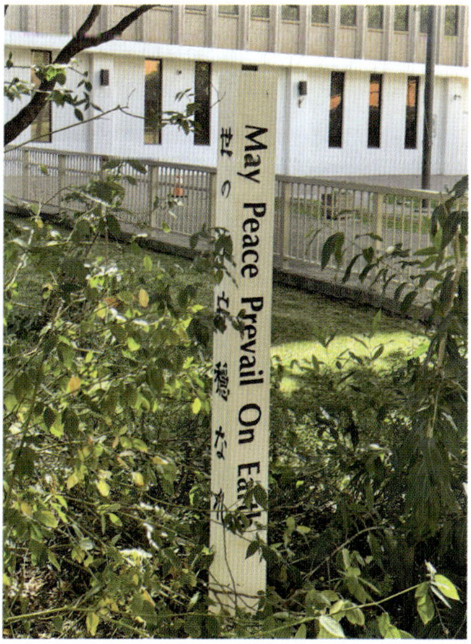

Left: Hawai'i Island Peace Pole at the Prosecutor Office in Hilo. Right: Maui Peace Pole at the County Building in Wailuku. Both photos by Cheryl Soon

World Peace Kannon

The female statue on the grounds of the Kaua'i Zenshuji Soto Zen Temple in Hanapēpē goes by the name of Kannon (Japanese) or Kuan Yin (Chinese), two figures believed to encompass the same qualities. According to legend, Saint Miao Shan, a Chinese princess who lived around 700 BC is widely believed to be the Kuan Yin. Her Sanskrit name means "Born of the Lotus." She is loved, not feared, and thought to be the model of beauty.

Kannon is a Bodhisattva, a being capable of achieving Nirvana but delays doing so due to her compassion for the suffering of other beings. Atop her head are eleven additional heads representing the stages of enlightenment. As the Goddess of Mercy, Kannon is called upon to help with daily troubles.

The Goddess of Mercy and Compassion statue was erected in 1991 as a symbol of and tribute to world peace. She is a tall slender figure, in flowing robes, holding a lotus flower in her left hand, and spreading her message of peace to everyone. A line from a Hawaiian chant confirms the statue's appropriate location on this island: Maka'i no Kaua'i, hemolele i ka mālie, "Beautiful Kaua'i so peaceful in the calm."

The Soto Zen temple site includes the temple shrine, the Kannon Peace Statue, a Bodhi Tree, and a bell tower. The Zenshuji temple was erected by a group of Japanese immigrants working at the McBryde Sugar Company and who settled in Wahiawa Camp 3. Reverend Ryoun Kan arrived in 1903 and began preaching to them in a home until the main temple was built in 1918. The families of many prominent politicians in Hawai'i were associated with McBryde Sugar including Senator Inouye's grandparents, Senator Matsunaga, and Mayor Kunimura. According to the website dedicated to this temple site, today, there is no pastor at the Soto Zen, and it is managed by a Board of Directors.

Opposite page: Kannon statue. Photo by Ray Soon

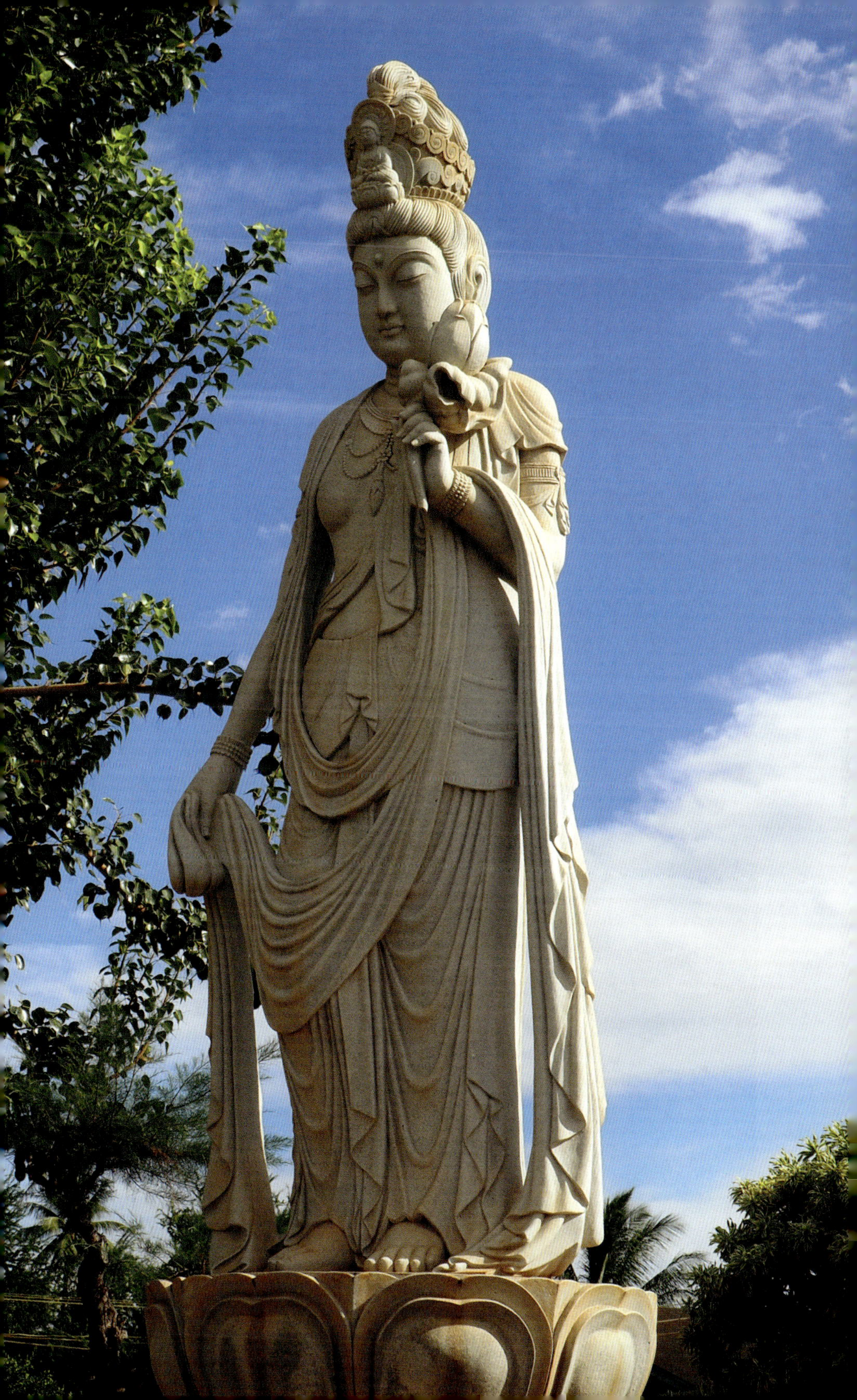

CHAPTER SIX

HONORING THE DEAD

"That their spirit may guide us to an ever-living peace among all mankind."

—Written at the Kalākaua Park War Memorial, Hilo

Humans seek meaning in life. This search intensifies when faced with unfathomable death. Memorials provide a physical place for expressing feelings of grief and for seeking meaning in group deaths, including those who fell in war, fallen police officers, and victims of tsunami and natural events.

There are many monuments and memorials in Hawai'i that honor those who fought in battles. Each island has honored its soldiers in different ways which are described here. People from around the world come to Hawai'i to visit the famous war memorials here.

World War I was a global conflict that lasted from 1914 to 1918 and fought between two coalitions, the Allies and the Central Powers. The United States was on the side of the Allies. The Central Power opposition was made up of Germany, Austria-Hungary, Bulgaris and the Ottoman Empire. While mainly fought in Europe, it spread to the Middle East, Africa and Asia. Over 10,000 men and women from the Territory of Hawai'i served, in the National Guard, Red cross or helping the thousands of orphans.

U.S. participation in World War II lasted from December 7, 1941, when Pearl Harbor was bombed to May 8, 1945. The Pacific Theater ended four months later when Japan surrendered aboard the USS *Missouri.*

The Korean Conflict between North Korea and South Korea occurred between 1950 and 1953 and marked the first military action of the Cold War. It was a proxy war between two superpowers: the United States, which supported the south, and China which supported the north.

The Vietnam War was a protracted conflict that lasted twenty years from 1955 to the fall of Saigon in 1975. Officially, it was a war between North Vietnam and South Vietnam. United States involvement on the side of South Vietnam spanned the years 1964 to 1975.

Hawaiʻi Island War Memorials

Hawaiʻi Island has been diligent in erecting memorials to those who fought in World War II, Korea, and Vietnam. They are located in public squares, cemeteries, parks, and ball fields.

Kalākaua Park War Memorial

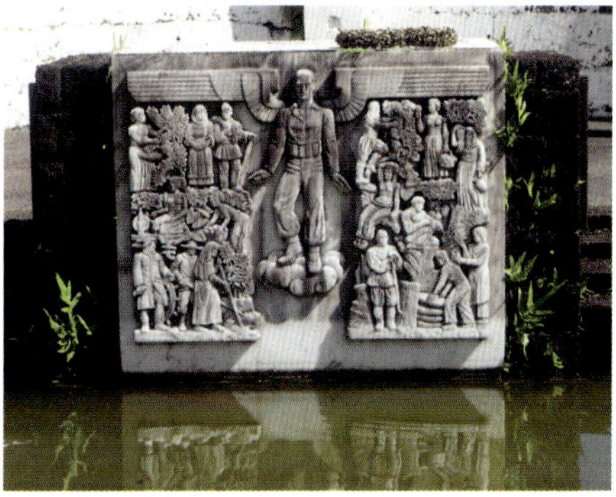

This is a memorial to those from Hawaiʻi who died in World War II. It is located at historic Kalākaua Park. Designed by Roy E. King, it is ten feet long, four feet wide and six feet high and is inscribed with 157 names. A lily pond reflects the monument and its central

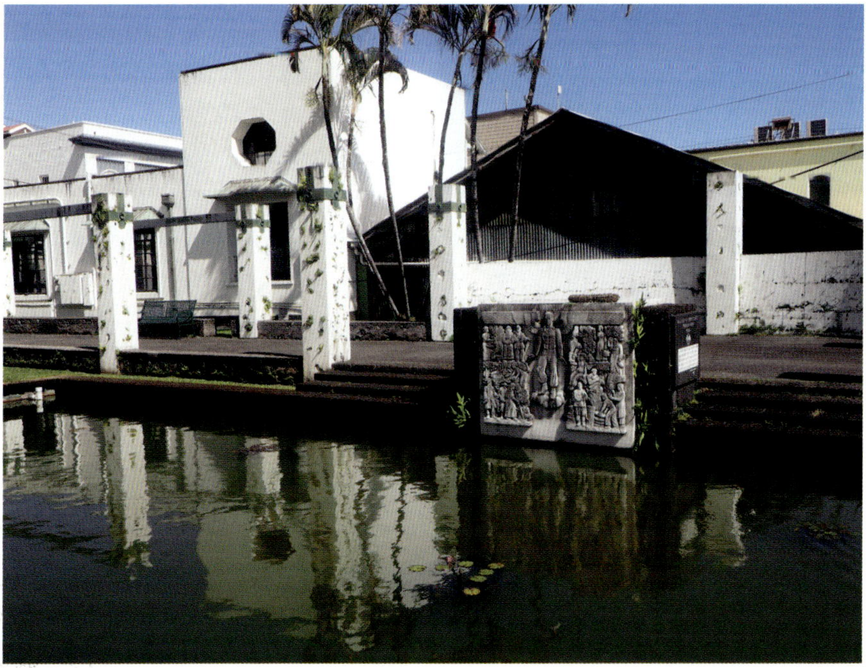

Photos by Ray Soon

figure, a winged composite fighting man who represents all combat forces and their spirit.

The project was sponsored by the Hilo Chamber of Commerce at a cost of $5,755 and was unveiled in 1948 at a well-attended ceremony. Later, two plaques were added on sides of the monument, one to honor those who fought in Korea and one for those who fought in Vietnam.

Roy E. King also designed a World War II Memorial in Honolulu located on the corners of King Street and Punchbowl Street. Both are made of Vermont Danby Imperial white marble.

Federal Building, U.S. Post Office, and Courthouse (Hilo)

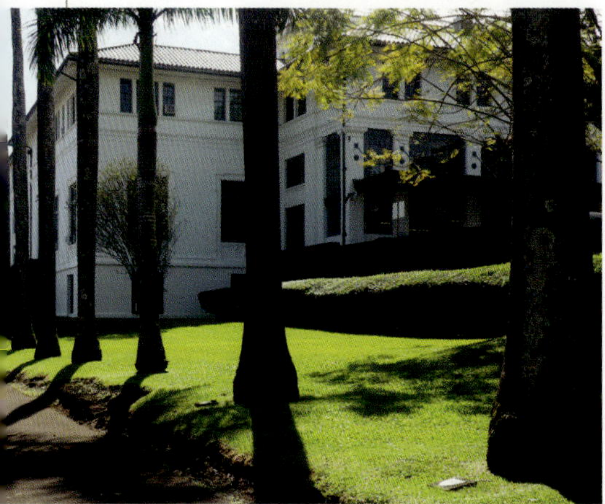

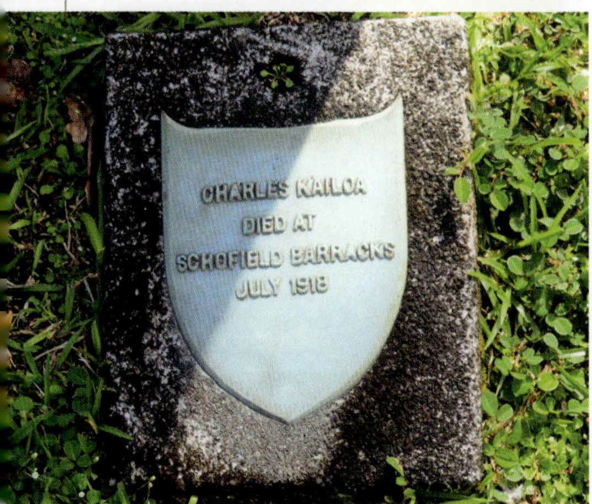

Photos by Ray Soon

The combined federal building is listed in the National Register of Historic Places. Designed by New York Architect Henry Whitfield, who had recently completed design of the Honolulu Carnegie Library, it uses a Mediterranean Renaissance Revival design style adapted to fit Hawai'i's tropical climate. It was opened in 1917. The wings were added in 1936-8.

The building landscape was purposely planted with numerous native plants. On Memorial Day in 1922, the American Legion planted seventeen royal palms on the Kekaulike Street side. Plaques in the shape of a shield at the base of each tree commemorate Hawaiian citizens who died in WW I.

Wailoa River State Recreation Area (Hilo)

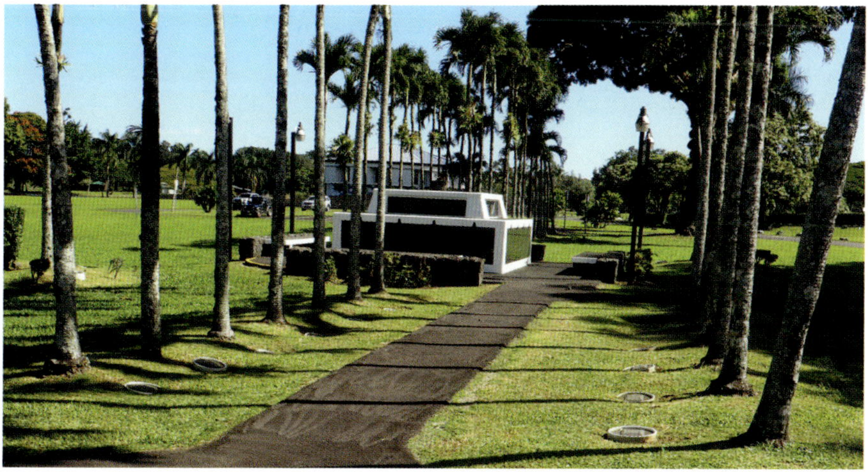

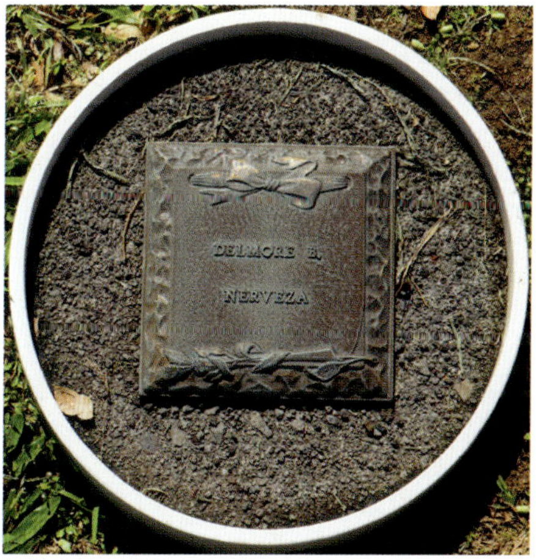

Both photos by Ray Soon

There are multiple war memorials along the Wailoa River State Recreation Area in Hilo, across the river from the Kamehameha statue. Walkways take you to each of them. The circles beneath the path of coconut trees each have a small, round plaque inscribed with the name of someone.

The largest memorial is the Vietnam memorial. Standing roughly ten feet high on multiple platforms, the concrete memorial is lined with black marble plaques etched with the names of those who served and their hometowns. Beneath the names are inspirational sayings.

The Vietnam Memorial was installed in 1986. A ground plaque recognizes the contributions of those who helped construct the memorial and the names of the Steering Committee.

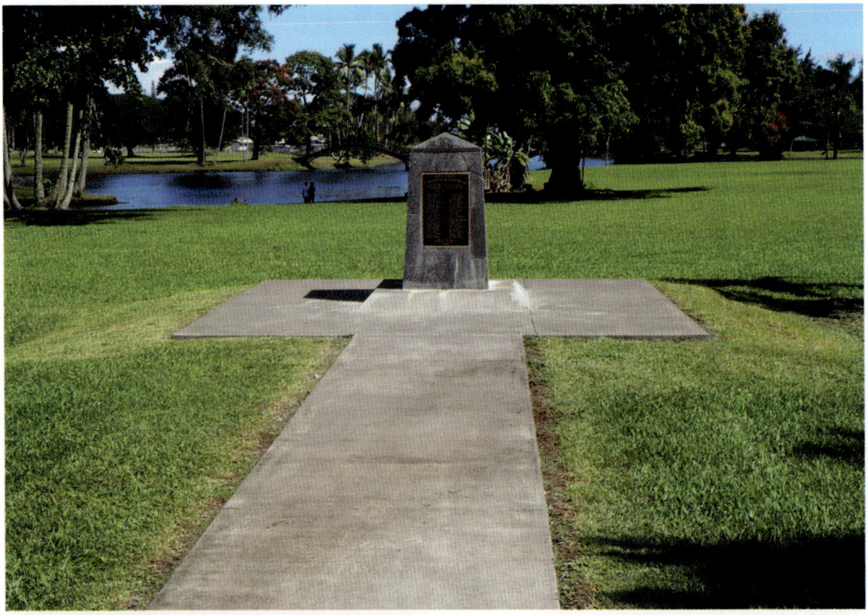

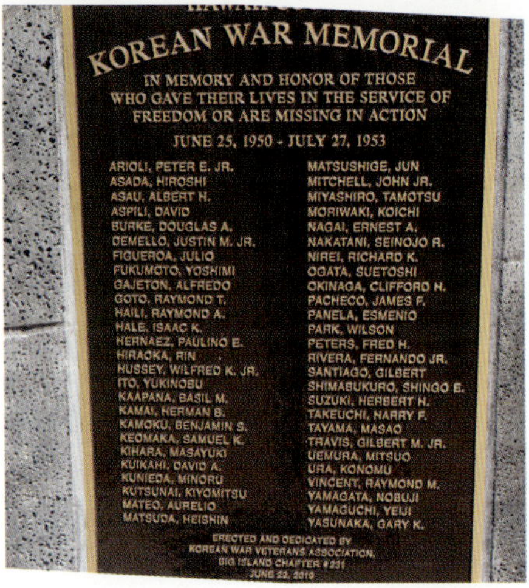

Photos by Ray Soon

Nearby sits the Korean War Memorial and a memorial to a ship that sank in World War II.

The Royal Frank Memorial (foreground of the picture) honors the ship *Royal Frank* that moved out of Pearl Harbor on January 28, 1942. It was torpedoed by a Japanese submarine and sank in the ʻĀlenuihāhā Channel between Maui and Kohala, Hawaiʻi, killing twenty-six soldiers from the Big Island. Nine soldiers survived. All are honored annually on January 28.

The Korean War Memorial was erected in 2019 by the Korean War Veterans Association, Big Island Chapter #231. It is made of concrete with a bronze plaque listing fifty-two names of those who gave their lives or are missing in action.

Civic Center (Kohala)

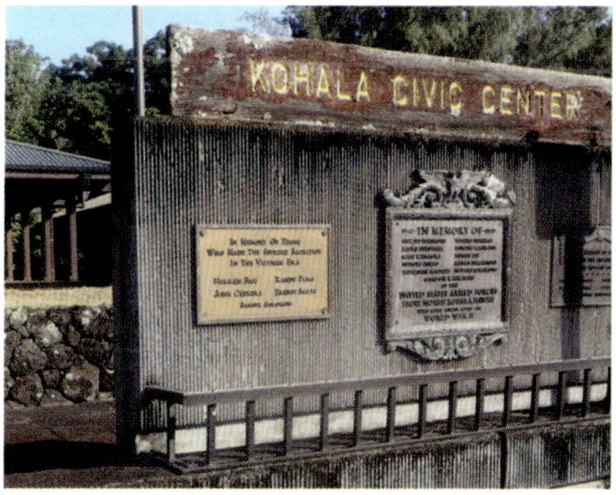

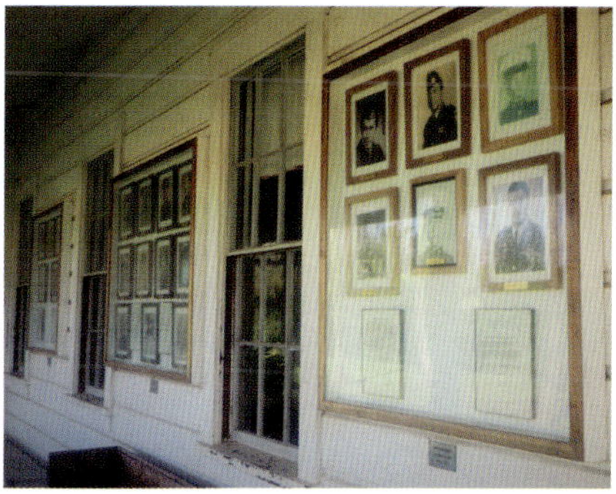

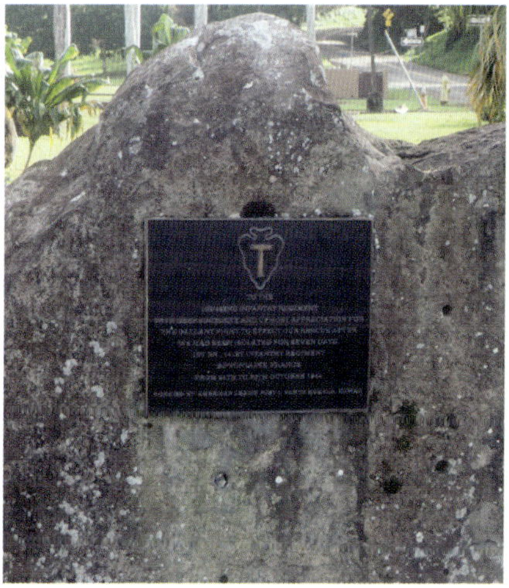

From top left, clockwise: Kohala Civic Center. Honor Roll. The 100/442nd Infantry Memorial plaque. Photos by Ray Soon

At the civic center in Kohala where the statue of King Kamehameha can be seen, are several memorial features. In the back of the civic building, near the parking lot, is a concrete monument with three distinct bronze "In Memory" plaques, placed there individually over time, for World War II, Korea, and Vietnam.

On the sides of the building are multiple large framed mural-type displays on which are the pictures of those who died in the three wars, and which ties to the names on the back plaques. An honor roll of names shows all who served in each war.

Finally, a bronze plaque on a large rock on the side of the site reads:

To the 100/442nd infantry regiment with deep sincerity and utmost appreciation for the gallant fight to effect our rescue after we had been isolated for seven days. 1st BN., 141st Infantry Regiment, Biffontaine, France. From 24th to 30th October 1944. Donated by: American Legion Post 4, North Kohala, Hawai'i.

Veteran's Field (North Kohala)

This unique memorial features an armed vehicle and a plaque.

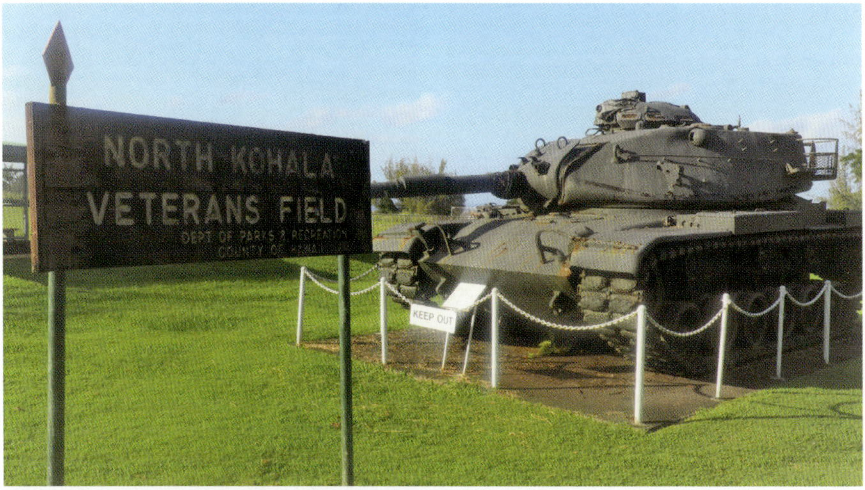

Veteran's Field in North Kohala. Photo by Ray Soon

Veteran's Park (Hakalau)

There are two memorials at this baseball field. The first war memorial is done in gray stone and etched in gold; it lists the names of those from Hakalau-Nīnole who were lost in World War I; World War II, the Korean Conflict; and the Vietnam War. It was erected in May 1961.

The second, a cinder block wall painted red, includes a glass case showing the history of the plantation camp area, including names of managers and schools. It was erected in April 2004.

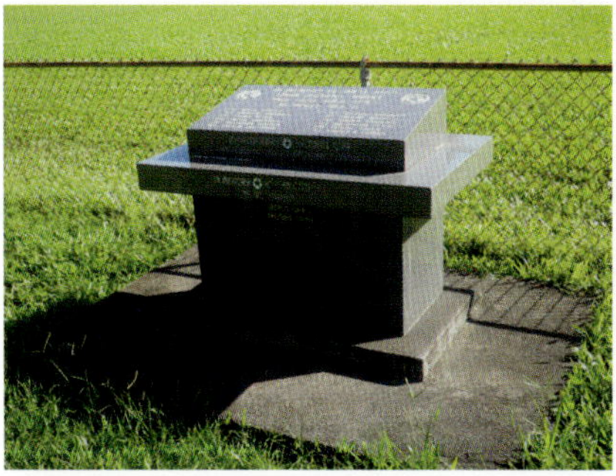

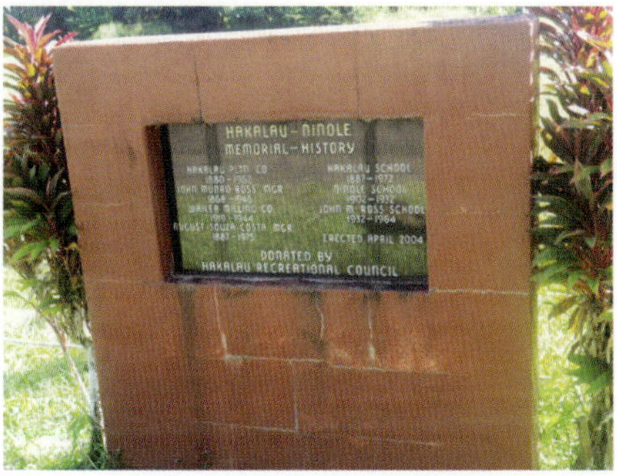

Veteran's Park in Hakalau. Both photos by Ray Soon

Obelisk at Puna Hongwanji (Kea'au)

Nearby the Shinran Shonin statue is the Centennial rock garden (2002) This constitutes a living and evolving collection of memorial features.

A granite obelisk set on a granite base sits upon a rock moss wall in the simple rock garden. The bronze inscription plaque on the marble base honors the names of fifteen persons who served in World War I. Frequently people leave flowers, stones, or other forms of remembrance.

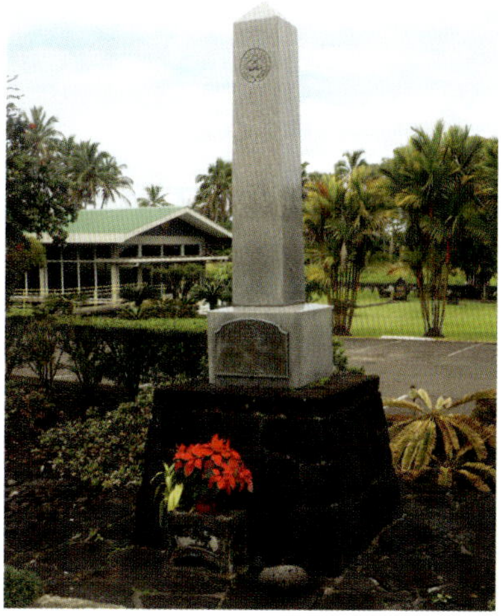

Puna Hongwanji in Kea'au. Photo by Ray Soon

War Memorial (Mountain View)

This gray granite memorial in the shape of a headstone honors thirteen names of those who "made their supreme sacrifice for our country." It sits upon a base that was likely an earlier version of the monument as that base is made from the same materials as the nearby Swett Auditorium which is dated 1937 which would make this a World War I monument.

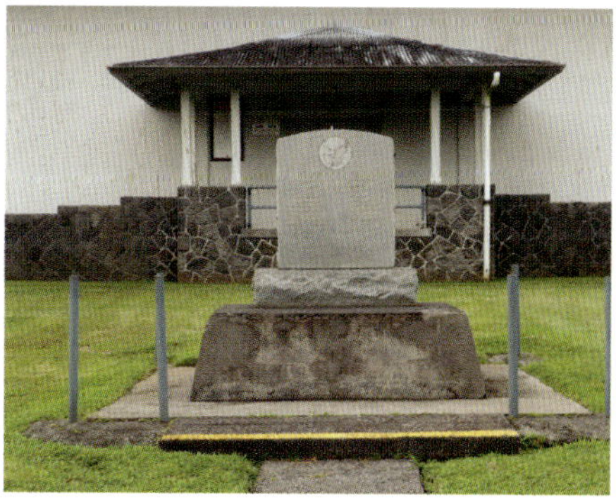

Mountain View Memorial. Photo by Ray Soon

Veteran's Cemetery (East Hawai'i, Hilo)

There are two veterans cemeteries in Hilo (#1 and #2) and each have war memorials. At Cemetery #1 in front of the pavilion and beside a flag-

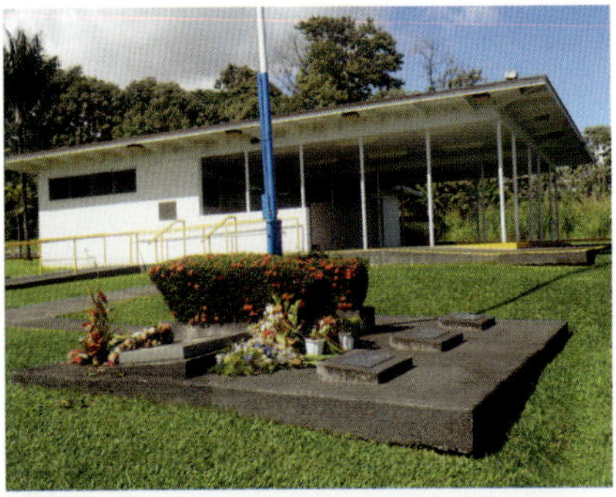

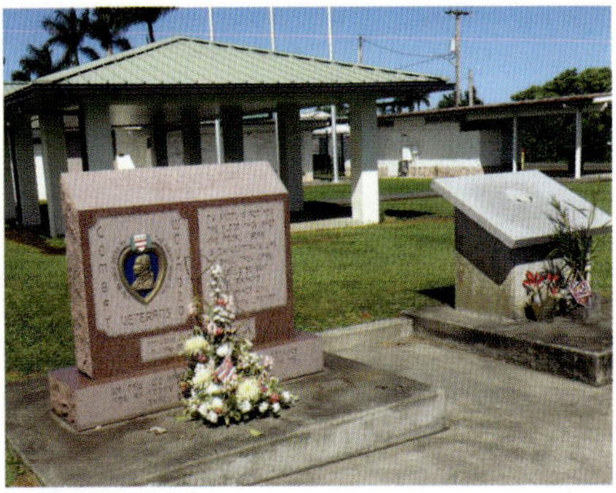

Veterans Cemetery in Hilo. Both photos by Ray Soon

pole is a concrete platform with multiple plaques. The largest is to those who served on the Royal Frank (symbolized by the crossed rifles). The plaque on the pavilion reads:

> *This pavilion and improvements completed December 23, 1951, by voluntary labor and direction of the 442nd Veterans' Club of Hawai'i. Honor all killed in action and those who served our nation's call.*
>
> *James Kealoha, Chairman and Executive Officer, Board of Supervisors; John L. Padgett, Chief Engineer. $20,000.00 appropriated by Act 170, S.L. H. 1951.*

The second East Hawai'i Veterans Cemetery is newer.

On the left is a red marble statue labeled Combat Wounded Veterans. It is dedicated to the recipients of Purple Heart, and sponsored by Big Island Chapter #731 Military Order of the Purple Heart. "My stone is red

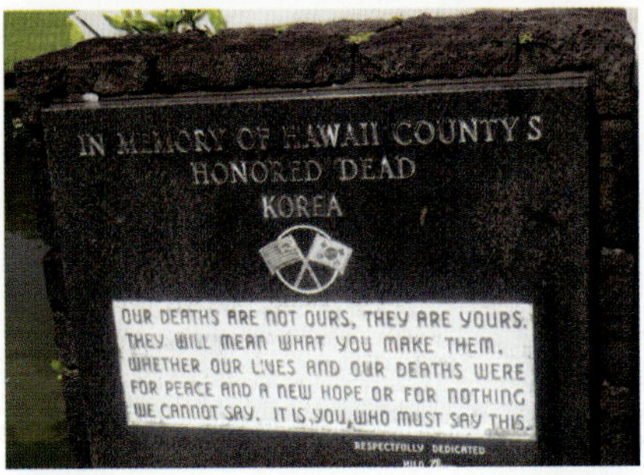

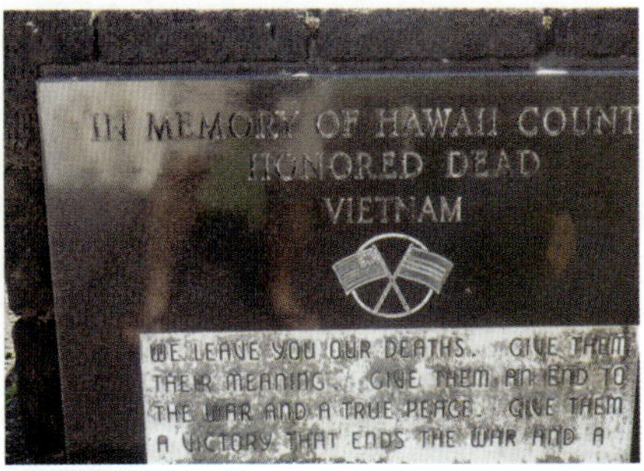

Plaques in East Hawai'i Veterans Cemetery. Both photos by Ray Soon

for the blood they shed. The Medal I bear is my country's way to show they care. If I could be seen by all mankind, maybe peace will come in my lifetime." Lower on the memorial is written, "We few, we happy few, we band of brothers for he today that sheds his blood with me shall always be my brother." On the right is the gray marble statue to Fallen Comrades of the Disabled American Veterans. Donated by Robert Kaplan, Disabled American Veterans, Hilo Chapter.

Deeper into the cemetery are short walls with plaques to those from Hawai'i county who are the honored dead in Vietnam and Korea.

West Hawai'i Veteran's Cemetery

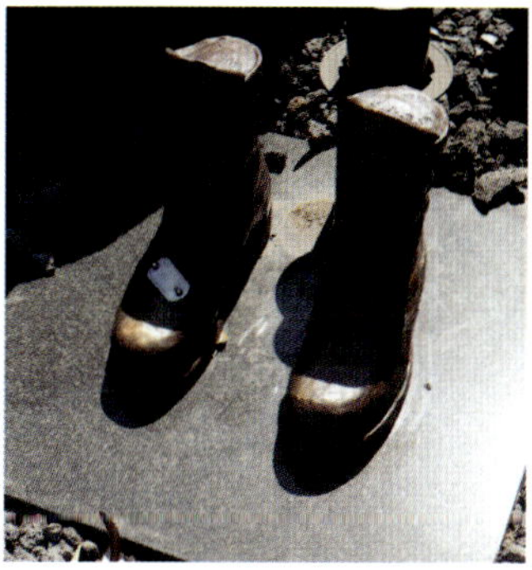

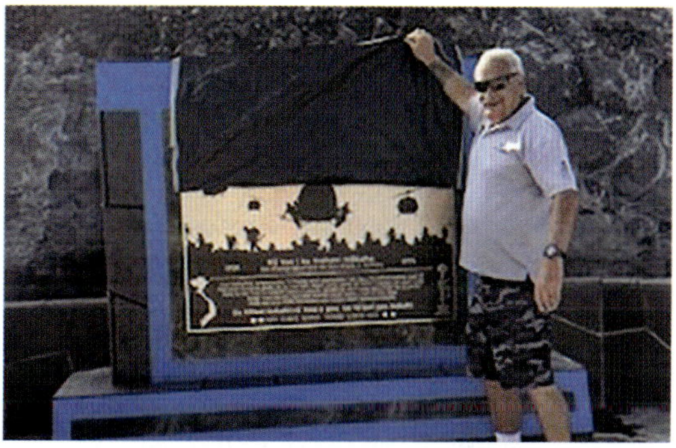

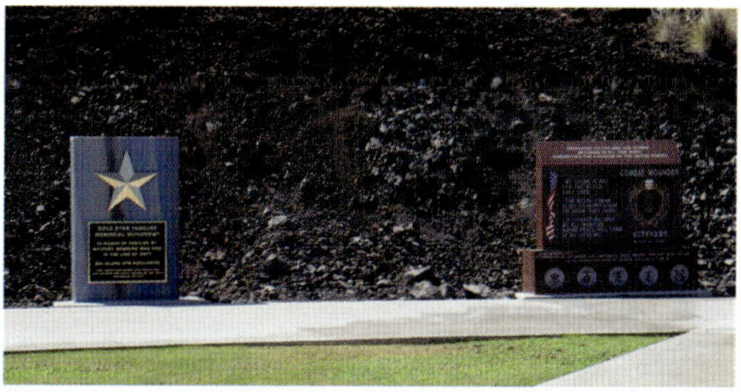

Top left and bottom photos by Ray Soon. Top right photo by Cheryl Soon.

The newest Veterans Cemetery (2008) on the island is located off Queen Ka'ahumanu Highway at a striking site on the flanks of the Hualālai volcano. In addition to the crypt area, there is a red stone memorial to Combat Wounded, along with the blue stone memorial to Gold Star Families. A POW-MIA memorial is also included, where one can find a section commemorating Korean veterans.

The latest piece is for Vietnam. It is the design and work of Billy Field (seen in photo), a Vietnam veteran and renowned maker of Hawaiian stone walls and memorial work.

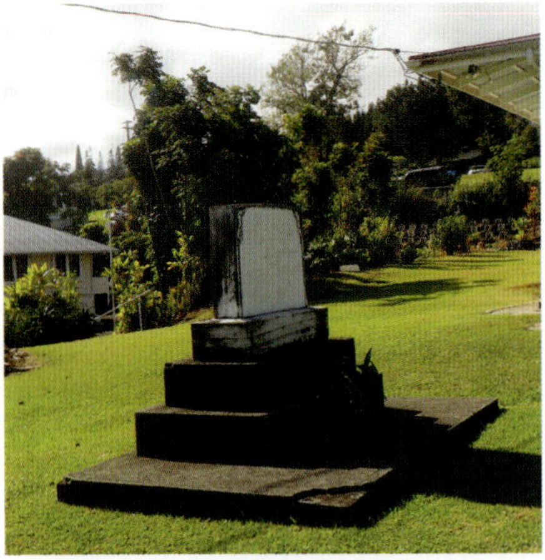

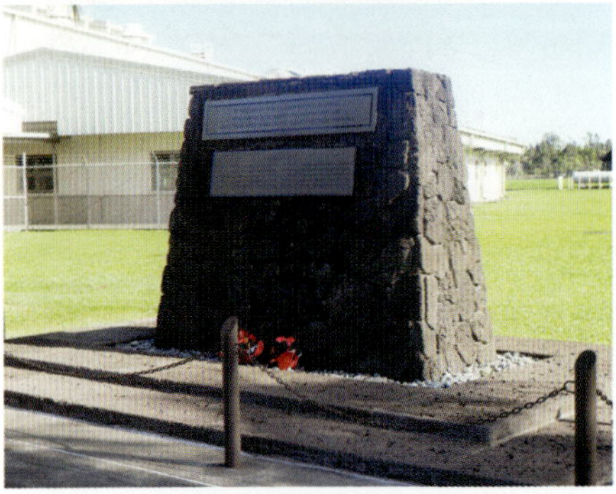

Top: Hongwanji Mission in Pa'auilo. Bottom: Vietnam Memorial. Both photos by Ray Soon

Memorial at Hongwanji Mission (Pa'auilo)

Here is a stone memorial on stacked bases showing the names of local persons who died in World War II or the Korean War.

Vietnam Memorial at National Guard Facility near Hilo Airport

This trapezoidal slab monument faced with rock honors ten servicemen from Hawai'i Island who lost their lives in Vietnam is located at the Keaukaha Military Reservation Armory in Hilo. It was dedicated in 2013.

Parker Ranch HQ for Camp Tarawa (Waimea)

This monument honors Camp Tarawa. It is on the site of a training location for the 2nd and 5th marine divisions who trained there to "bring peace to the Pacific." Tarawa was considered the beginning of the end of the war. The bronze plaque mounted on a stone shows the shields of the two divisions and the marines who "endured the pioneering amphibious assault on Betio in the Tarawa Atoll, November 20-23, 1943. Tarawa was a savage and bloody battle that tested and shaped amphibious doctrine, a doctrine that would ultimately bring victory and peace in the Pacific. Following their success at Tarawa, the Division traveled to an unfinished camp located at Parker Ranch." Camp Tarawa lasted from 1943-1945, after that the marines departed to invade Saipan and Tinian.

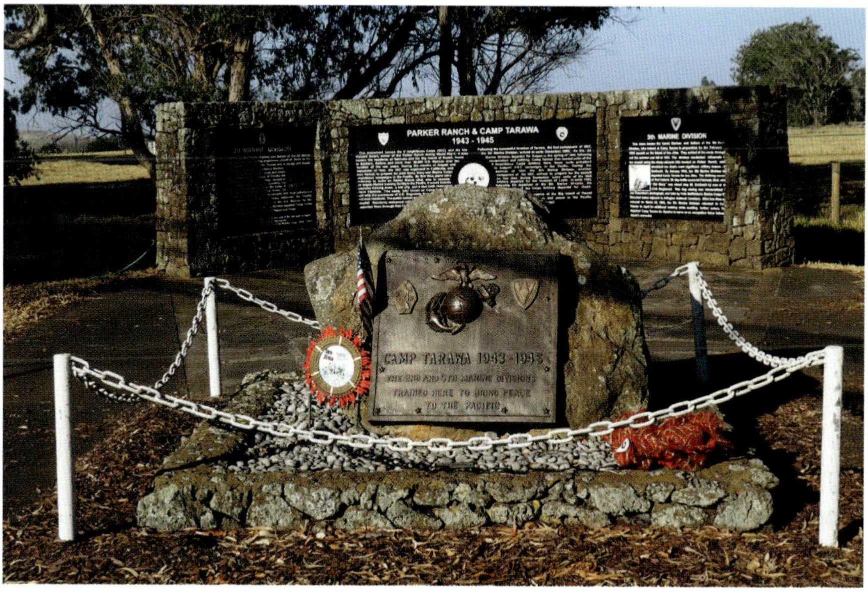

Camp Tarawa Memorial. Photo by Ray Soon

Black granite panel plaques behind the stone memorial tell the story of Camp Tarawa. The monument honors the V Amphibious Corps (VAC); the late Richard Smart, owner of the Parker Ranch during World War II; the residents of Waimea; and the Hawaiʻi Island, hosts to soldiers, sailors, and more than fifty-thousand U.S. Marines over the duration of the war years.

During the months of August and September of 1943, the VAC organized in California, and then Hawaiʻi, to prepare for joint Army, Navy and Marine Corps amphibious campaigns in the Pacific. These efforts would include extensive training areas, a tent city, and a dam above Waimea. This camp, later known as Camp Tarawa, was built with the assistance of the U.S. Engineers, Navy Seabees, Marines and local residents. The local public school and hotel served as an Army hospital. Residents welcomed military personnel into their homes and supported them through Red Cross and USO activities.

Following the successful invasion of Tarawa, the first component of the VAC, the 2nd Marine Division, arrived in early December 1943. As the 2nd Marine Division departed for Saipan in the spring of 1944, following recuperation and refitting, Camp Tarawa next hosted units of the AC Artillery who prepared to support VAC campaigns in the Pacific. During the summer of 1944, the 5th Marine Division, another component of the VAC, arrived to prepare for the assault on Iwo Jima. During September of that year, some units of the VAC Artillery departed for the invasion of Leyte. In 1945, following the departure of the 5th Marine Division, the remaining units of the Corps artillery departed for Guam.

The brass plaque monument was erected in 1984. The black granite panels behind the monument were added in 1998. There are other historic features around town that date to the period when Camp Tarawa was active. Land for the memorial was donated by Ranch owner Richard Smart.

Maui War Memorials & Monuments

War Memorial at Mantokuji Sōtō Mission of Pāʻia

This memorial honors the deceased soldiers of the Sino-Japanese War and the Russo-Japanese War. Its Japanese name is "Chikon-hi." Installed in 1911 it features a spread-winged eagle perched

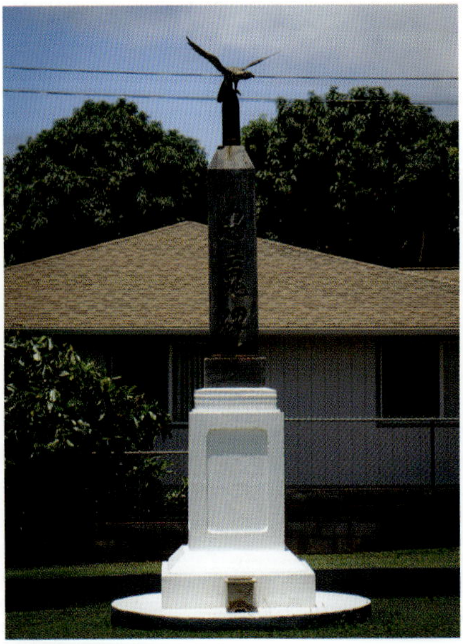

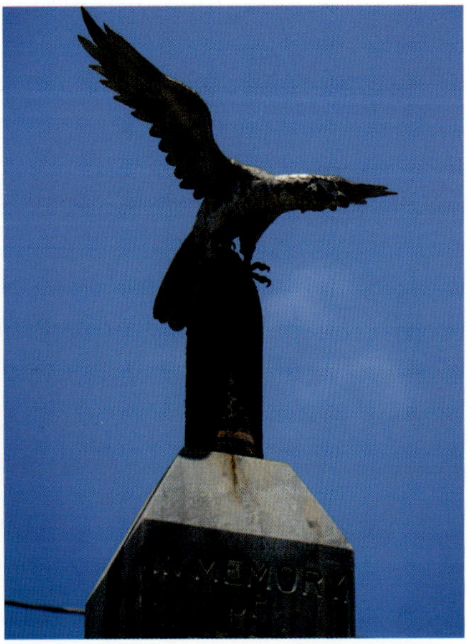

Both photos by Lucas Kashtan

on a cannon shell that was donated by the Japanese training fleet. An inscription was added to the War Memorial in 1919. The large Japanese characters read, "Monument for the War Dead." Another inscription indicates it was rebuilt in 1933 when it was moved. Every May, the Mantokuji's resident minister conducts a brief prayer ceremony in front of the memorial in conjunction with the temple's Memorial Day service.

4th Marine Division Park (Ha'ikū)

This park is where the 4th Marine Division Reserve gathered and trained during WW II. The unit formed in 1943, and went on to fight in the Pacific (Saipan, Tinian, and Iwo Jima) against the Japanese. Deactivated after the war and reformed in 1966, they were deployed to the Gulf War in 1990-91.

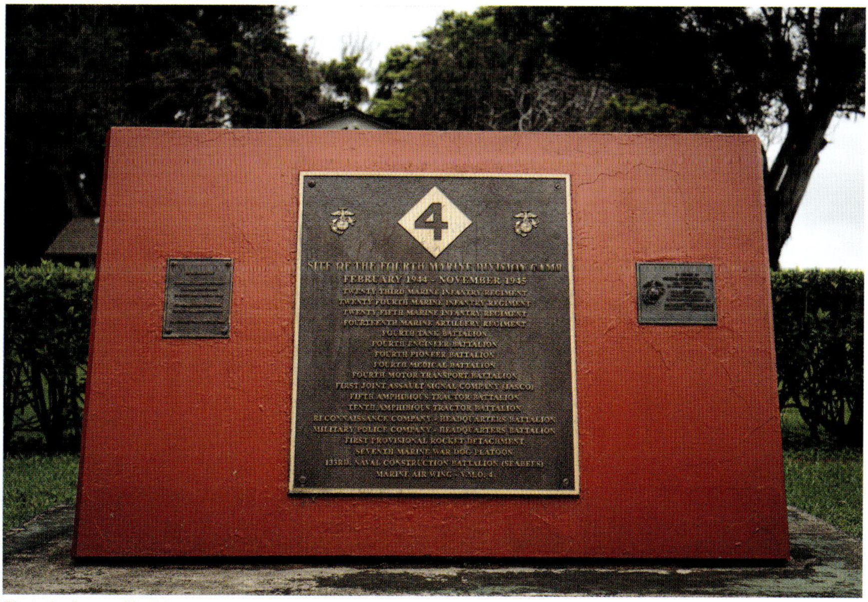

Photo by Lucas Kashtan

Makawao Veterans Cemetery

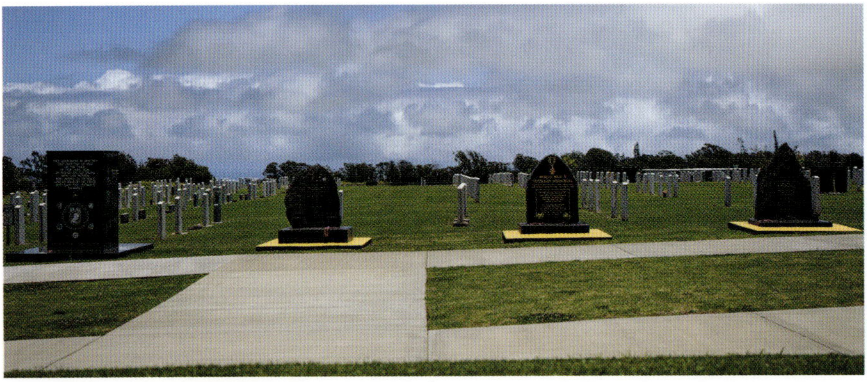

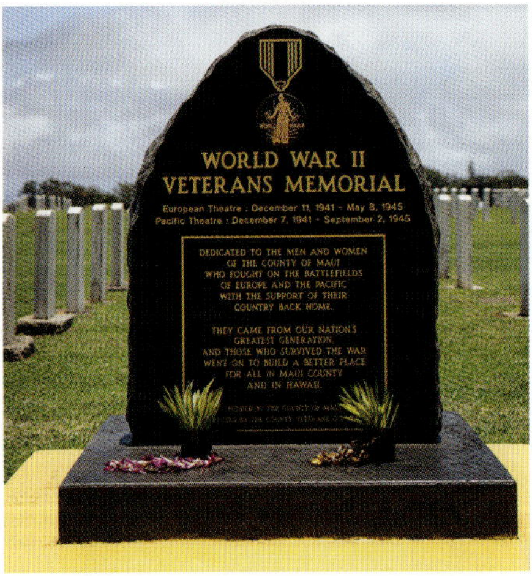

Both photos by Lucas Kashtan

This State of Hawai'i Veterans Cemetery, located off Baldwin Avenue (and across from the Makawao civilian cemetery), contains multiple memorials of varied types. Three main ones are grouped together. The World War II Veterans Memorial is a 4 ½ foot tall marble piece with gold inscriptions and a replica of the WWII Victory Medal at the top. It sits between the World War I Memorial (2010) and the Korean Memorial (2007) which is a distinctive rock taken from a Spreckelsville Camp 1. Each have bronze plaques mounted on them. The WWII memorial, installed in 2017, was the work of a monument committee led by Royal Vida and Leonard Oka of the Nisei Veterans nonprofit and made possible by a $50,000 grant from Maui County.

There is also the rose stone memorial to Combat Wounded Veterans (donated by the Military Order of the Purple Heart, Maui Chapter #729), common in several veterans' cemeteries. The latest addition to the collection is a black stone Vietnam Memorial. The Cemetery is centered by a flag pole with a plaque.

Nisei Veterans Memorial Center in Kīhei

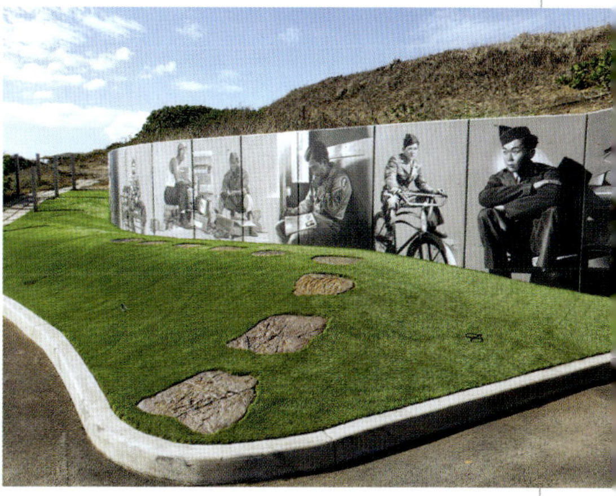

Photo by Melanie Agrabante, Research Archivist, Nisei Veterans Memorial Center, by permission.

Nisei Veterans Memorial Center is a multipurpose place built in phases starting in 2006. The educational center opened in 2013 and the Resource Centre in 2022. The center archives photos, scrapbooks, stories, oral histories, and other memorabilia from Maui veterans of World War II. They were members of the 442nd Regiment Combat Team, the 100th Battalion (aka the Purple Heart Battalion), the Military Intelligence Unit (charged with intercepting and translating Japanese communications), and the Naval Facilities Engineering Systems Command.

The center seeks to teach and inspire others using the values of these Nisei veterans which are: being selfless for the greater good, leading by example, living in gratitude, inspiring courage in adversity, and doing the right thing always.

Also included is the story of the rescue of the Lost Battalion in the Vosges Mountains in France in October 1944 as well as many internment stories. It houses the archives, books, oral histories, family albums and pictures from families of the 442nd regiment.

The mural artist was Kirk Kurokawa. The piece is named "Quiet Dignity, Everlasting Honor." Nearby is the 4.5-acre Peace Park, maintained by the Hawaiian Islands Land Trust. It focuses on native wildlife and plants.

Molokaʻi War Memorial in Kaunakakai

This stone memorial, located in the green space in the middle of town, represents tombstones and shows the honor roll of Molokaʻi citizens who died in War WW II (ten names). It was erected on May 30,

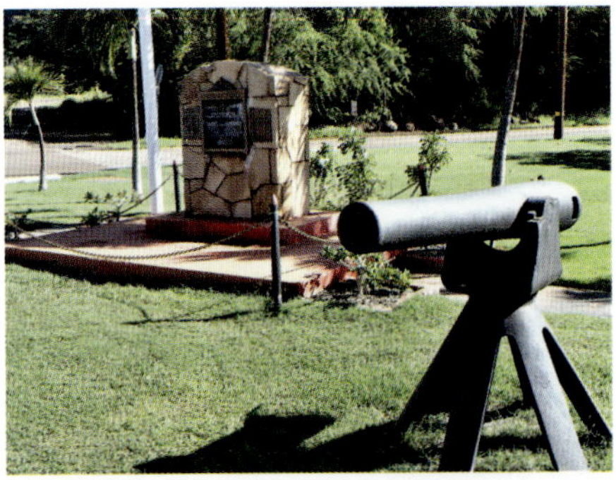

Moloka'i War Memorial. Photo by Ray Soon

1951, by the People of Moloka'i, Post 14 American Legion. Two bronze plaques were added in 1998 to the front sides, by VFW Post 3870; one for Korea (three names) and one for Vietnam (five names).

Memorial Honoring Fallen Police (Hilo, Hawai'i)

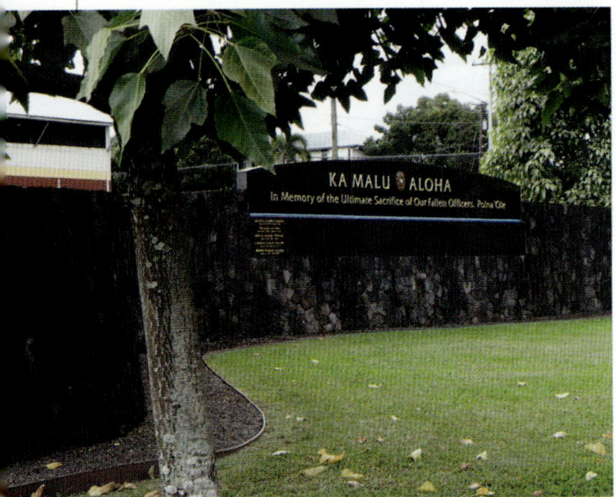

Photo by Ray Soon

The outdoor memorial, Ka Malu Aloha, means "Shelter of Aloha." It represents how their memories are sheltered with aloha. Poina'ole means "We will not forget." Police officers are symbolized by "This Blue Line" which horizontally divides the memorial, representative of how they protect people from harm. The memorial was designed by Momi Waihee Cazimero who had a policeman brother in the police force who died in duty. Funds for the memorial came from Hawai'i County, private foundations, and individual contributors. It was dedicated on May 16, 2016 during National Police Week. Currently, five names are honored, chiseled with gold lettering on black marble. Honolulu also has a memorial to fallen police on city hall grounds; and there are memorials to police, fire, and public workers, at Kāne'ohe Memorial Cemetery.

Memorials to Victims of Tsunamis

The islands of Hawai'i are subject to tsunami force waves that originate from many parts of the world. At least 135 confirmed tsunamis have hit the islands, including fifteen that caused significant damage, according to the Catalogue of Tsunamis in the Hawaiian Islands, kept by George Pararas-Carayannis. Impacts vary according to the direction they arrive from, ocean conditions, and submarine features such as valleys and coral reefs. The waves can refract and circulate throughout an island, especially those that are more circular in shape.

Tsunamis that originate in the North Pacific will generally cause the greatest damage, eastern and southern coasts are subject to damage from tsunamis traveling outward from South America, and western coasts are subject to tsunamis that originate in Japan. Tsunamis of local origin can hit anywhere. There are several memorials that honor these events and those who were lost.

April 1, 1946 Tsunami

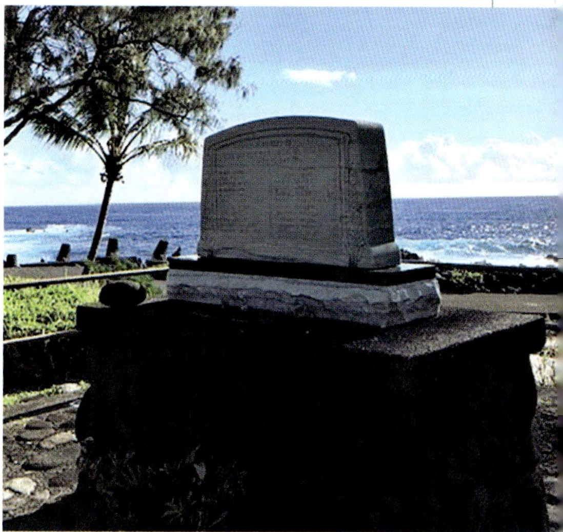

Photo by Ray Soon

On April 1, 1946 Hawai'i was hit by a devastating tsunami that originated from an estimated 7.1-8.5 magnitude (estimates vary as this time predates today's instrumentation) undersea earthquake off Alaska. It destroyed the Hilo waterfront, most of the train system, and several coastal villages, reaching a height of forty-five feet. It killed 159 people and caused $26 million in damage. In Laupāhoehoe, three teachers and twenty-five students and their schoolhouse were lost. The Pacific Tsunami Museum in downtown Hilo tells stories of the devastation that occurred throughout the island. Buildings were displaced from their footings and toppled by the huge waves. Corrective actions that followed that tsunami included the creation of a tsunami warning system, increased community awareness on how to escape the wrath of the waves, and city planning adjustments to keep buildings out of the impact zones.

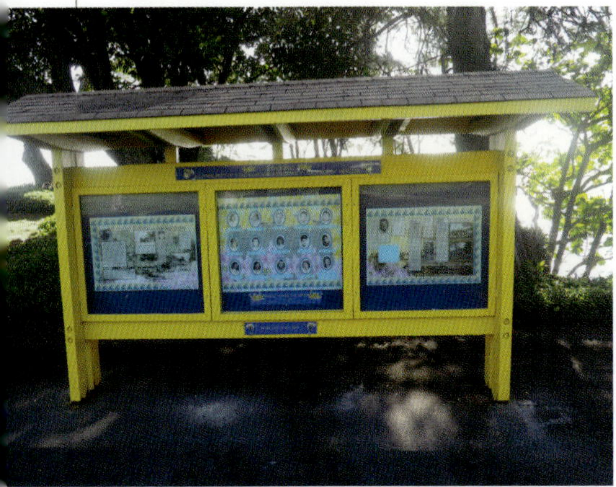

Photo by Ray Soon

Prior to the tsunami, Laupāhoehoe had been a bustling community of two thousand people, restaurants, liveries, a bakery, and even a hotel. The port at the point was an active point of entry for immigrants until the railroad was built in 1912. Now the point is a district park managed by the County Department of Parks & Recreation used mostly for fishing boats. A music festival is held at the point on April 1 of each year in honor of the tsunami remembrance.

The white stone memorial at Laupāhoehoe Point sits prominently on a bluff overlooking the boat launch ramp and offers a long-distance view of the coast. The names of those who died are etched upon the stone. Most are buried in a small cemetery near the site and beneath a large banyan tree that survived the tsunami. A short walk away is a large interpretive exhibit with information and pictures of the victims; much of it comes from Laupāhoehoe Train Museum.

> *This Monument, commemorating the victims of the April 1, 1946 Tsunami, was erected by the efforts of the Rev. Kakkusho Izumi, the presiding minister at the time of the tragedy, of the Papaaloa and the Honohina Honpa Hongwanji Missions, with the donations of the families of all the villages in the communities of Honohina, Ninole, Papaaloa, Paupahoehoe, Waipunalei and Ookala. Dedicated April 1, 1947.*

Keʻanae Congregational Church (Maui)

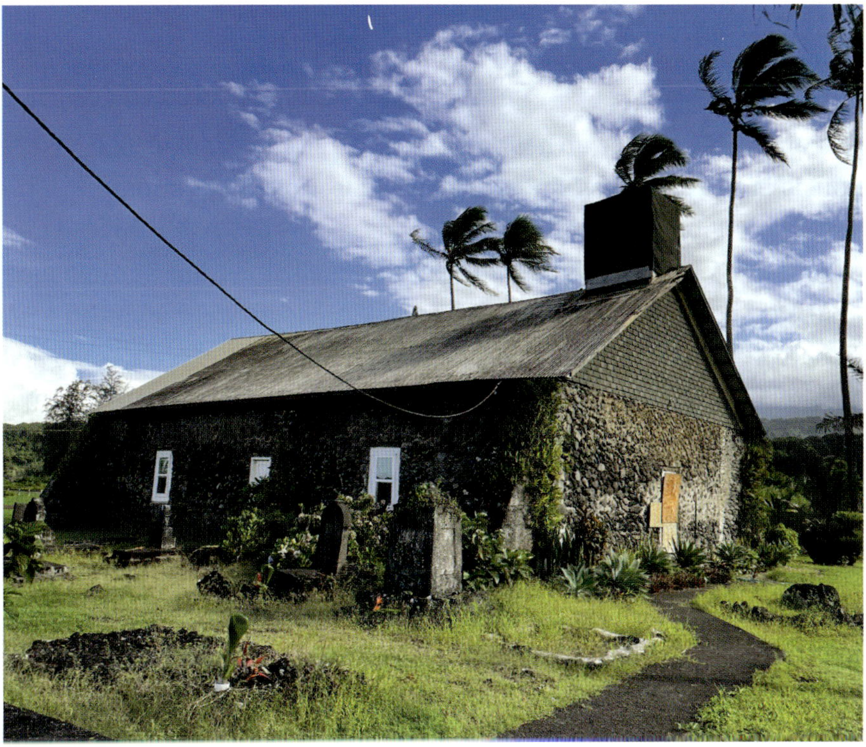

Photo by Ray Soon

The April 1946 tsunami hit elsewhere in Hawaiʻi. On Maui, damage was felt from Honokaʻa to Hāna, including the tiny village of Keʻanae Peninsula where everything was destroyed except a church.

This church, the Lanakila Ihiihi o Iehova Ona Kaua (Sacredness, Success of Jehovah, the Son of God) Church was first built in 1863. The 1946 tsunami appeared here without warning, with thirty-five-foot waves, and killed twenty-four persons. The church building features rubble lava rock walls (which had to be passed along a line of men from the sea), shingled gables and a small belfry. Buttresses were added later. Restored and rededicated in 1969, it currently appears unused.

May 23, 1960 Tsunami

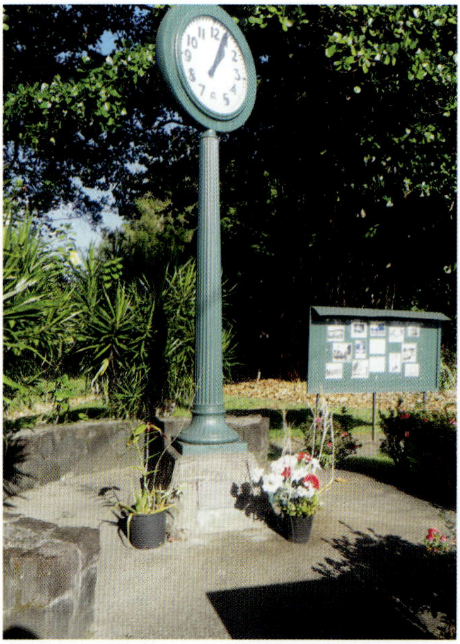

Photo by Ray Soon

On May 23, 1960, another tsunami hit Hawai'i Island, triggered by a 9.5 magnitude earthquake in Chile, the largest recorded in history. This time the worst impacted was Waiākea Village in Hilo. Sixty-one persons died. Many more had died in Chile the day before; the waves moved on to Honshu and Hokkaido, Japan, killing 180 more and leaving fifty thousand homeless.

Prior to the 1960 tsunami, the small community of Waiākea was full of homes, businesses, and schools. A memorial exhibit consisting of a green backboard with pictures and captions was erected to commemorate it sixty years later. The memorial exists on busy road against the golf course.

A major feature is a tall clock, that once stood on Lihiwai Street, now permanently marked with the time 1:05 when the third wave arrived. The Waiākea Social Settlement Clock was refurbished and re-erected on this original concrete stand by the Waiākea Pirates Athletic Club in May, 1984. Mrs. Martha E.R. Wakefield, principal of Waiākea Kai Elementary School which adjoined the settlement building, donated the clock in memory of her sister, Mrs. C. E. Richardson, in 1939. Today, it serves as a symbol of the strength, courage, and resilience of the residents of Waiākea Town, also known as "Yashijima."

Shinmachi Tsunami Memorial

Within downtown bay-front Hilo was a small community called Shinmachi, which means "New Town." The area populated by Japanese immigrant plantation workers who sought economic independence, contained shops, businesses, and homes. According to the Pacific Tsunami Museum in Hilo, Shinmachi, along with other parts of the coastline (see entry on Laupāhoehoe above) were hit by Hawai'i's most devastating tsunami. Death toll was 158, many swept out to sea. 488 buildings were demolished and 936 more damaged. Documentaries have been made featuring survivors and Shinmachi descendants who still reside nearby.

Parts of the area were re-built after the 1946, but not for long. A second tsunami in May 1960 another devastating tsunami originating in Chile, hit the same community. Following that, the area was not rebuilt, but rather made into a park, better able to withstand the terrible waves.

A memorial was erected in Waiola River State Recreation Area in 1983. The work is the creation of Iraphne R. Childs and is a circular bronze plaque with text and a large image of a tsunami wave. It was donated by the Shinmachi Club and dedicated "In the memory of those who lost their lives in tidal waves on the island." It is located not far from the Kamehameha statue mounted on a lava stone wall.

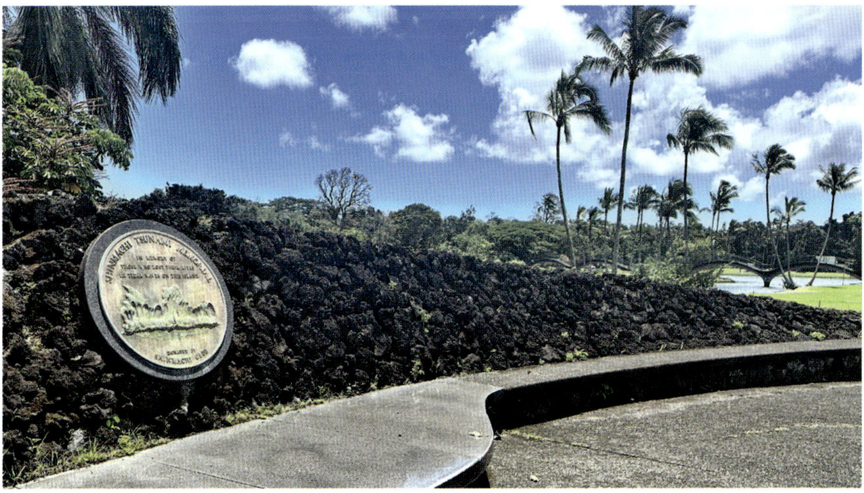

Photo by Rebecca Soon

Tohoku Earthquake and Tsunami in Japan (Maui)

On March 11, 2011, one of the most devastating earthquakes ever triggered two tsunamis in the Indian Ocean. The catastrophe took twenty thousand lives in Tokushu, Japan. Also destroyed was a forest of over seventy thousand red and black pine trees. The lone pine that survived was saved to provide a symbol of hope and perseverance. Five months later, the Japanese Cultural Society of Maui planted a matsuo pine tree and a plaque was dedicated to the resolve of those affected by the tragedy and as a symbol of strong ties between Maui and the people of Japan. It is located at Kepaniwai Park.

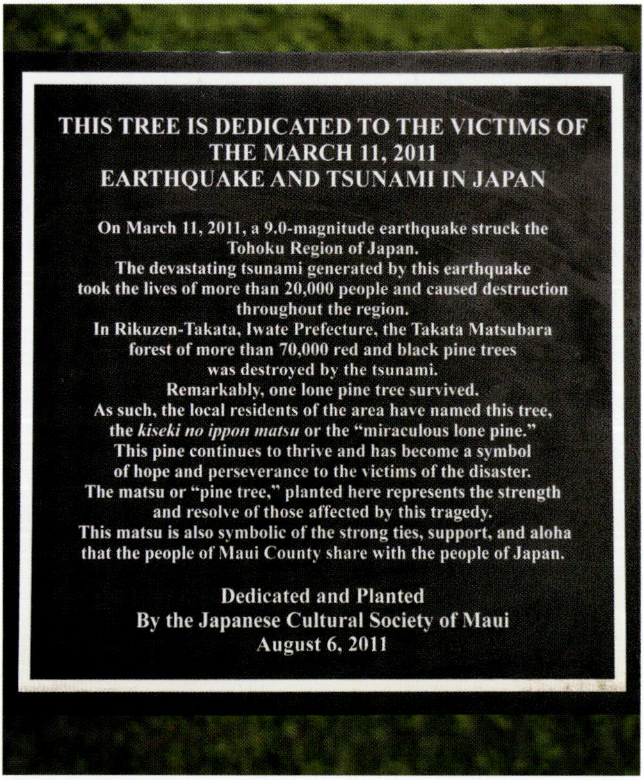

Photo by Lucas Kashtan

ETHNIC AND HERITAGE MONUMENTS

The introduction of the sugar cane industry caused great change in the ethnic make-up of Hawai'i. The industry started on Kaua'i in Kōloa, expanding rapidly both in Kaua'i and on other islands. Many of those who started this industry were younger generations of missionary families who had befriended the king and came into possession of large tracts of land needed to grow sugar cane. Memorials to individual family members, typically large stones with bronze plaques, are covered in Chapter Three (Kaua'i). This chapter's focus is on the memorials to immigrant groups and their lasting influence in Hawai'i.

The need for labor in the fields and to work mills became pressing. Hawaiians quickly lost interest in continuing this activity, preferring their own economic lifestyle of hunting, planting, and fishing for subsistence for their families. Some Hawaiians excelled as horsemen and cattle ranchers (paniolo). But the population of Hawaiian persons, decimated by disease at that point, became an unlikely source of labor in the plantations.

In 1881, King Kalākaua traveled for a year, to Asia (Japan, China, Siam, Burma, and India), the Middle East (Egypt), and Europe (Italy, Belgium, Germany Austria-Hungary, France, Spain, Portugal, England) and the United States. His objectives were to study governance, bolster diplomatic and social relations with leaders elsewhere, observe military and scientific advancements, and promote immigration. Many results came from this trip, but the most obvious was the influx of immigrant workers.

Immigration for the sake of the sugar plantation work was serious business that required the support of government. Between 1852 and 1887 thousands of Chinese came to Hawai'i, most of them from the Pearl River Delta near Macao (Canton) according to Moore (*Paradise of the Pacific*, 2015). The early Chinese laborers were indentured workers.

The initial group of Japanese workers arrived in 1868. However, for seventeen years afterward, the Meiji government prohibited immigration due to reports of harsh treatment. During his visit, Kalākaua and Emperor Mutsuhito agreed that labor could come back to Hawaiʻi starting in 1885 until 1924. Initially, only single men immigrated, then single women (to become their wives), and later, family units. This continued over a twenty-five-year period as Japanese began to settle into life in Hawaiʻi. Issei (first generation) stuck closely to their cultural roots, food, language, and customs. Nisei (second generation) grew up in a bi-cultural environment. By the end of the nineteenth century, forty percent of the Hawaiʻi's residents were Japanese.

Soon thereafter, persons from Portugal arrived. The sugar plantations and Hawaiʻi government financed transport for over twenty-five thousand Portuguese from Madeira, the Azores, and mainland Portugal. They arrived from 1878 to 1911, often serving as luna, or supervisors, of other groups.

After the turn of the century, Puerto Ricans arrived and began working on the plantations in various capacities. The sixth and final set of sugar immigrants, Filipino contract laborers (sakada), came starting in 1906, and by the end of that century, made up half the plantation work force. Most groups remained after their contracts expired, raised families, and integrated throughout all parts of life in Hawaiʻi.

Kauaʻi's rich relatively flat land was well suited to sugar production. The first sugar extraction and mill started in Kōloa in 1835, others soon followed suit. In 1877 the Makee Sugar Company opened in Kapaʻa with King David Kalākaua as one of its backers and shortly thereafter, the Lihue Sugar Plantation emerged in the Wailua area. Kauaʻi eventually was home to at least a dozen plantations, and the industry came to be called "King Sugar." Plantations boomed in the mid to late 1800s, and dominated the economy and way of life in Hawaiʻi for over one hundred years. Statehood in 1959 indirectly led to the demise of agriculture (both sugar and pineapple) when taxes and labor laws (and competition from cheaper labor in other countries) made it too costly to continue. The last plantation to close in Kauaʻi was Gay & Robinson (2009), and the last in the state of Hawai'i was HC&S on Maui.

By then, Kaua'i had become a melting pot of persons from around the world. Even today, most people from Kaua'i are descendants of immigrants who came to work the plantations from all over the world, such as Japan, China, the Philippines, Portugal, Puerto Rico, Spain, and Germany.

The immigrants not only worked in the fields, but they helped run the mills, built and operated the roads and irrigation systems. Hawai'i is not alone in this story; similar plantation diversity was occurring during the same time period in Louisiana, British Guiana, Cuba, Puerto Rico, and Jamaica where crops were being exported to other countries.

While in many ways, sugar is part of a bygone era, there is tremendous pride in the culture and contributions made both by the immigrants and by their descendants to local politics, education, and economy. In 1985 the Sugar Plantation Monument Committee and Hawaiian sugar Planters Association erected a piece that is a set of statue figures honors that effort and celebrates the importance of immigrant descendants in today's life.

Other immigrant memorials, erected by descendants, can be found on civic grounds and near major camps.

For Further Reading: Takaki, Ronald. *Pau Hana: Plantation Life and Labor in Hawaii*. University of Hawai'i Press. 1983.

Kimura, Yukiko. *Issei: Japanese Immigrants in Hawaii*. University of Hawai'i Press. 1988

Patterson, Wayne. *The Korean Frontier in American: Immigration in Hawaii* 1896-1910 and *The Ilse First Generation Immigrants in Hawaii 1903-1973*. University of Hawai'i Press. 2000.

Portuguese Immigrants 1878-1912. Hawai'i Plantation Museum. 2019.

Sesquicentennial Sugar Plantation Immigrant Monument

Owner	Knudsen Trust
Commissioned by	Hawai'i Sugar Plantation Monument Committee
Location	Kōloa
Year Erected	1985 Sesquicentennial (150th) Celebration of Kōloa Plantation
Artist	Jan Gordon Fisher

This life-sized grouping, created by Jan Gordon Fisher, is one of the islands' most notable. It is a tribute to the persons of all ethnicities, each in their own classic dress, doing the work of planting, weeding, harvesting, and bundling. Appropriately, the monument is located in Kōloa and co-located at the Old Kōloa Sugar Mill, a Registered National Historic Landmark.

The main feature is a composition of eight figures that represent the multiple ethnic groups that have worked the plantations. According to

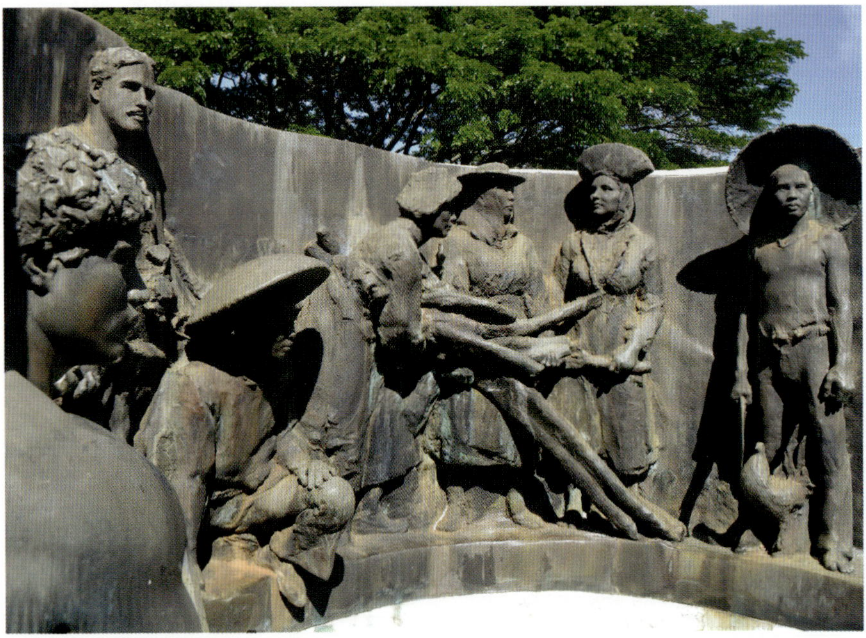

Photo by Cheryl Anne Farrell

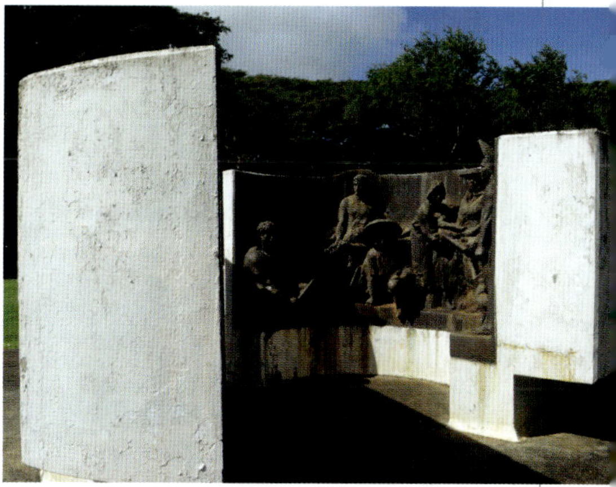

Photo by Cheryl Anne Farrell

the Historical Marker Database, "the first figure on the left is a Hawaiian, representing the first sugar workers. He wears a malo, holds an o'o and sits next to his poi dog. In the backgrounds, riding upon a horse, is a Caucasian, representing the North American and European entrepreneurs and managers who started and developed the industry. Next is a Puerto Rican man carrying sugarcane. Beside him, a Chinese man squats to pick up his hoe, attired in laborer's clothing of the Ming Dynasty. Then a Korean woman carries a large bundle of cane. A Japanese woman wears chikatabi to protect her feet and her face is shielded from the sun by a traditional hat. On her left, a Portuguese woman stands barefoot, with headgear well suited for carrying any needful thing. Finally, a Filipino, carrying a cane knife, represents the last major group to join the Hawaiian sugar industry."

Artist Jan Gordon Fisher, who won the commission, said he hoped to capture their "stances, dignity, and strength as they might have been in their earliest years in Hawai'i. Together, they represent cooperation among diverse peoples and how they helped develop the sugar industry."

The outer element of the sculpture piece is a thick white circular wall meant to suggest a mill stone. It opens slightly to reveal the bronze figures inside. The orientation was intended to call attention to the remnants of the 1841 mill. Over time, this feature has perhaps proved unfortunate, since the paint is peeling and dirty, making it easy for people to overlook entirely the beautiful sculpture figures inside. Detail plaques tell the stories of the sculpture's meaning.

Puerto Rican Immigrant Memorials

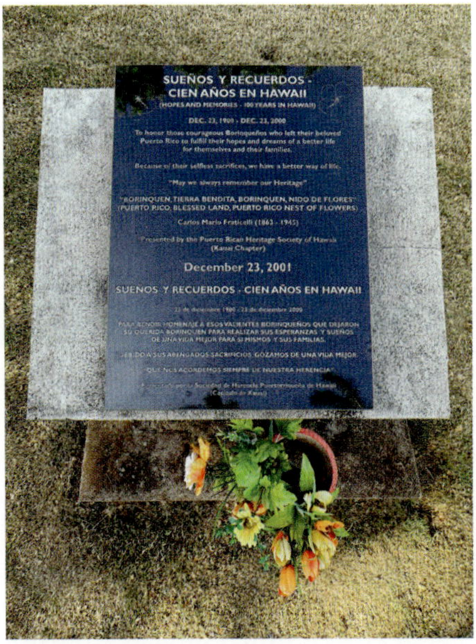

Puerto Rican Memorial on Kaua'i. Photo by Christian R. Cook

Puerto Ricans came to Hawai'i starting in 1901 following the end of the Spanish-American War. Ultimately, close to five thousand Puerto Ricans came to the islands to work on the plantations.

The black marble plaque at Kaua'i civic grounds includes a statement written twice: in English and in Spanish. It was presented by the Puerto Rican Society of Hawai'i (Kaua'i Chapter) on December 23, 2001, marking the one hundred years of Puerto Ricans in Hawai'i.

The Puerto Rican Memorial on the Big Island is in a remote location in Kohala at the ocean's edge. The memorial rock and plaque were placed in 2001 on land owned by Hideaway Holdings, LLC.

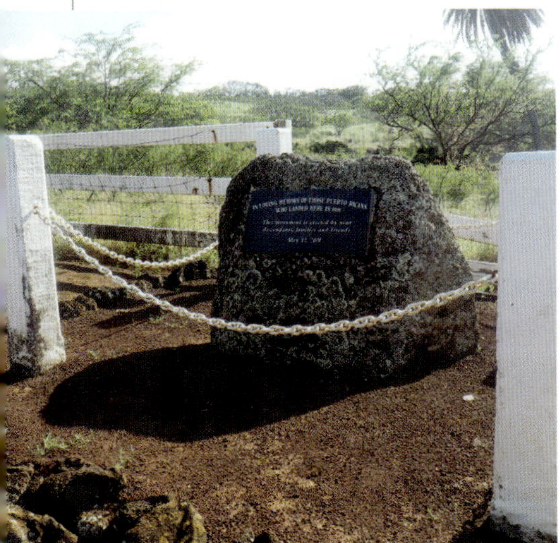

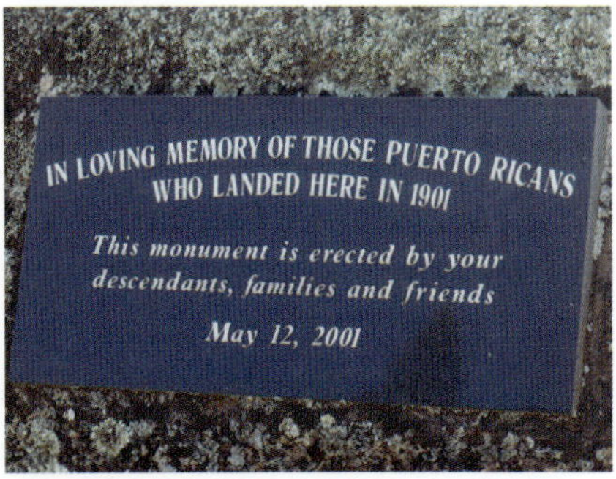

Left and above: The Puerto Rican memorial on the Big Island. Both photos by Ray Soon

Scandinavian Migration Monument

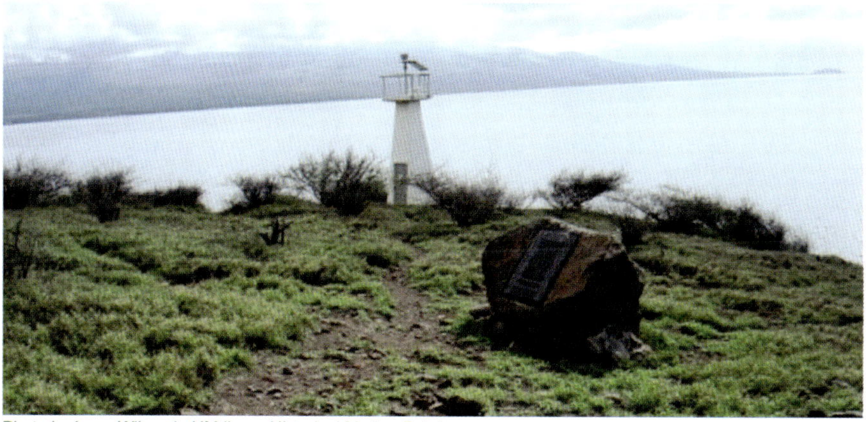

Photo by Larry Wilson in HMdb.org Historical Marker Database

Scandinavians from Norway, Sweden, and Denmark, more than six hundred in number, came to work on the sugar cane fields and mills. According to the monument plaque, they arrived February 18, 1881, in Maui on the Norwegian barque *Beta* and three months later in Honolulu on a sister ship, the *Musca,* following a difficult six-month journey. They had three-year labor contracts written in both English and their Native language, describing pay, responsibilities of each party, consequences for deviation from the contract, health care, and a guaranteed return ticket.

The monument honoring their migration and contributions was donated by the Scandinavian Centennial Commission on February 14, 1981. It is a bronze cast metal plaque mounted on a large stone about one meter in height. It was restored in 2006 on the 125th anniversary.

Located a mile past Mā'alaea, Maui, the marker is located off of Route 30 near McGregor Point and Lighthouse. While relatively unknown compared to other immigrant statues, it is situated with a commanding view of the Pacific Ocean from the bay to beyond.

Their time was not always smooth, and they participated in one of the first labor strikes. Some of the laborers stayed in Hawai'i at the end of their contract to become skilled tradesmen, craftsmen, and merchants, and their descendants remain to this day. Others moved to the US Midwest, where there are large populations from Scandinavian countries.

Filipino Worker Monument (Keaʻau, Hawaiʻi)

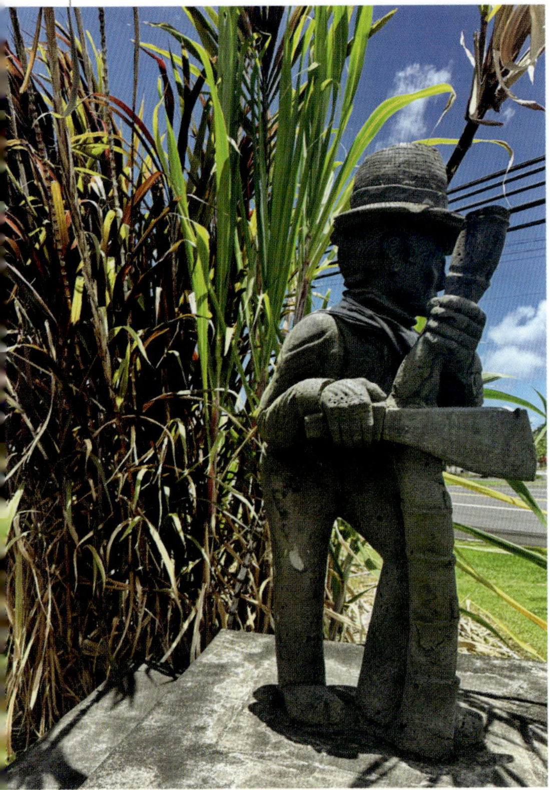

Photo by Rebecca Soon

This monument, located in Keaʻau on the former lands of ʻŌlaʻa Sugar Plantation, honors the heritage of the area. It depicts a worker cutting sugar cane. The land is located within an ahupuaʻa now owned by W.H. Shipman, Ltd, having acquired it from the estate of King Lunalilo. It is still managed by a fifth generation of the Shipman family.

The concrete stone statue on a square base was created by Dr. Fred Soriano from University of Hawaiʻi at Hilo. It was installed in 2006 during the centennial anniversary of Filipino arrival in Hawaiʻi.

There are three plaques at the base. One sign explains the Filipino Centennial Anniversary (1906-2006) and provides the names of the first fifteen Sakada (many related to one another) who were sent to ʻŌlaʻa Sugar Plantation. The second is the Sakada name plate, explaining the meaning of the statue and "from their labor and sacrifices emerged much of the Filipino community in Hawaiʻi. The third sign gives credits to the State of Hawaiʻi, County of Hawaiʻi, WH Shipman, LTD, the Big Island Centennial Committee, the Congress of Visayan Organizations, and the Big Island Filipino Community Council. Daidai Hopkins was a key community member who helped bring the statue to fruition.

Gannenmono (First Year People) Memorials to Japanese Immigration

The capital of Kanagawa Prefecture is Yokohama. Most of the early Japanese who came to Hawai'i were recruited from Yokohama, sailing on the *Scioto* out of Yokohama Harbor. The first arrivals came in 1868. Memorials to their arrival and contributions were erected during the 50th anniversary (1918). More Gannenmono memorials were placed, but the greatest number in 1968, on the 100th year anniversary. Memorials were again placed for the 125th (1993) and 150th anniversary (2018).

Japanese Immigration Commemorative Plaques at Civic Grounds (Līhu'e, Kaua'i)

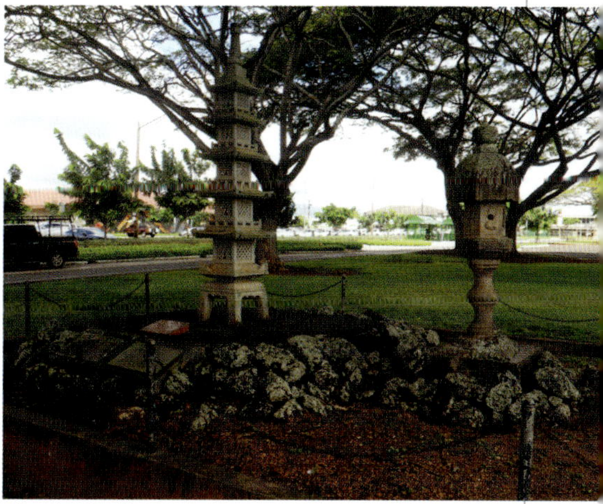

Photo by Ray Soon

Japanese memorials can be found both in front of the County Administration building and across Umi street in the Japanese Garden at the building where county offices are located.

At the Japanese section, which is roped off by a low chain fence on the lawn of the county building on Umi Street, are a pagoda, a lantern, and three plaques. Two plaques, one gray and one red, are in Japanese language, partially covered in moss, and difficult to read. The third explains that the five-storied pagoda and the stone lantern were presented in May 1961 by the Institute for Sea Training, Ministry of Transportation, Japanese Government. They were presented on the 75th anniversary of the official Emigration Agreement between the Japanese and Hawaiian governments in (January of 1886 in Tokyo). The plaque further explains:

These gifts are the replicas of the original ones at Gotokuji Zen Temple in Hikone city. Shiga Prefecture, which is the historic home of Lord Naosuke Ii Family. These gifts were made possible through the courtesy of the Temple's resident minister. The Reverend Tetsujo Hyodo, and were brought to Kauai in May 1961.

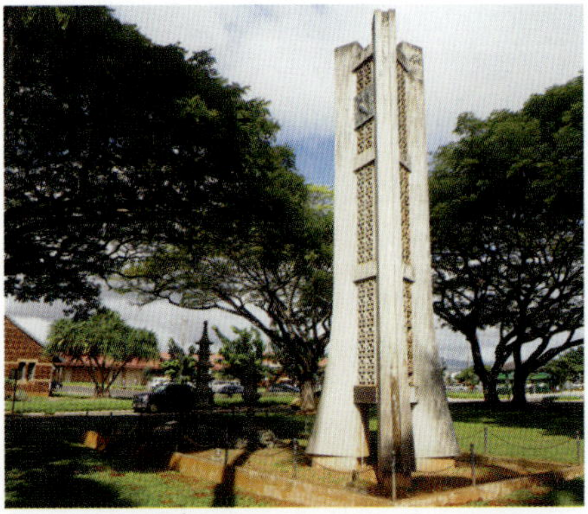

Photo by Ray Soon

An additional element on the Civic Center grounds near the corner of Umi Street and Rice Street corner is a clock tower. Its bronze plaque indicates it was erected for the Centennial celebration of Japanese Immigration to Hawai'i 1865-1965.

Hans and Dora Isenberg Japanese Garden (Līhu'e, Kaua'i)

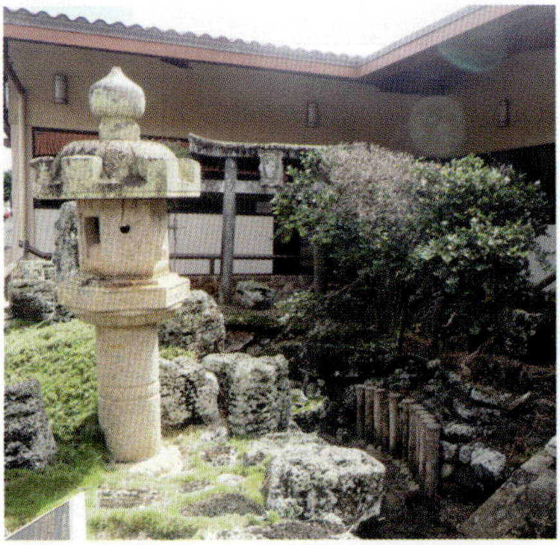

Photo by Ray Soon

Located on Molokoa Street across Umi Street and in a former shopping mall, are the administrative offices and departments of the county. In a corner of the building is the Isenberg Japanese Garden. Originally placed in various locations, several pieces were gathered when the garden was refurbished in 2018 on the 150th anniversary of the first immigrant laborers. The plaque explains:

The stone tori gate and stone lantern were brought to Lihue from Japan about 1906 by Pastor Hans Isenberg and his wife Dora. Mr. Isenberg was then President of the Lihue Plantation Company and brother of one of its founders. They were placed in the Isenberg Garden at Molokoa. Later the lamp stood in front of the Lihue Store for many years. They were generously donated by Dora Jane Isenberg Cole, a descendant of Lihue Plantation's founders. The stone bowl was donated by J.K. Shimonishi who constructed this garden for the Lihue Shopping Center.

A second bronze plaque in the Japanese Garden reads:

In honor of the 150th anniversary of the Hawaii Gannenmono—the first Japanese immigrants to arrive in Hawai'i—I humbly rededicate this historical garden, which was beautified with the help of the Kaua'i Japanese Cultural Society, Kaua'i Bonsai Club, Kaua'i Nursery and Landscaping and many individual volunteers.

May this garden be a bridge of Aloha, goodwill, and friendship with Kaua'i and Japan.

Mayor Bernard P. Carvalho, Jr. County of Kaua'i, State of Hawai'i, September 2018

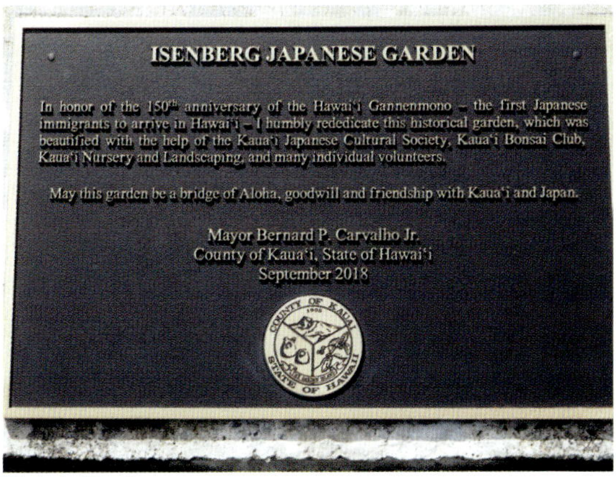

Photo by Ray Soon

Japanese Stone Lantern (Ishidoro) (Kapa'a, Kaua'i)

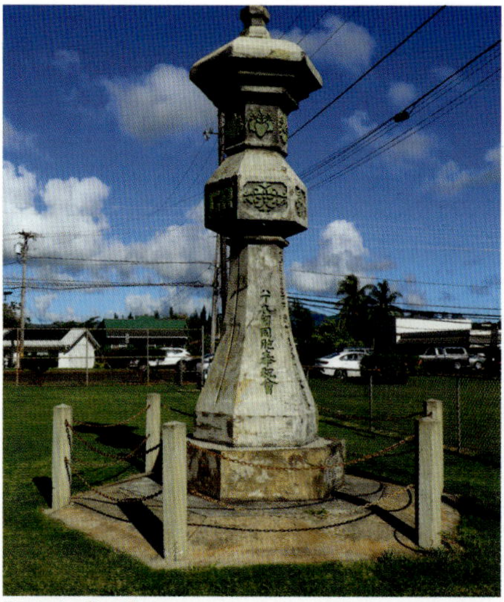

Photo by Ray Soon

The lantern was erected to preserve the history of Kapa'a's issei generation. A fund-raising event was held among local Japanese to support the mother country in the Russo-Japanese War of 1904. The war was short-lived and surprisingly, the money was returned. Several years later, in 1915, the fifteen-foot cast concrete was installed. The Ishidoro was dedicated to the Emperor Taisho of Japan, shaped like a lantern to symbolize light and enlightenment. The inscription reads, "Great Japan Emperor ascension to the throne, coronation and commemoration lantern."

During World War II, as anti-Japanese sentiment grew on Kaua'i, the lantern was buried in 1943. Almost three decades later, the lantern was unearthed in 1972 when county workers responded to complaints about a protruding metal rod in Kapa'a Beach Park. When no group was ready to assume the costs for the monument repair, it was reburied. In 1987 it was uncovered again and re-erected through a community effort led by Mayor Tony Kunimura, the Kaua'i Historical Society, and others. For the next twenty years, the lantern stood supported by heavy I-beam braces.

In 2008, with an award from the Kaua'i County, HUD Community Development Block Grant Program, the lantern was finally restored through the efforts of the Leadership Kaua'i/Lantern Restoration Committee and the Kapa'a Business Association. Restoring the lantern to its original beauty was a means of celebrating Kapa'a's unique history and multi-cultural heritage.

Kepaniwai Park (Wailuku, Maui)

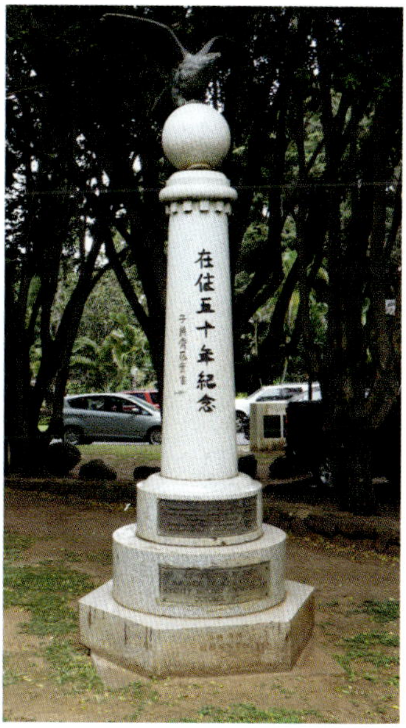

This five-storied memorial dedicated to the 100th anniversary of Japanese arrivals can be found at Kepaniwai Park in Maui along with other memorials. See Chapter Eight for more on Kepaniwai Park.

Japanese Immigrant Memorials (One Ali'i Park, Moloka'i)

Moloka'i's One Ali'i Park on the water edge has two identical memorials, one commemorating the 75th anniversary of Japanese arrival (1960) and the other commemorating the centennial (1985) of the same event. They are both made of concrete with a rounded top and are five feet tall with a one-foot base. The plaques are made of marble and simply worded in both English and Japanese.

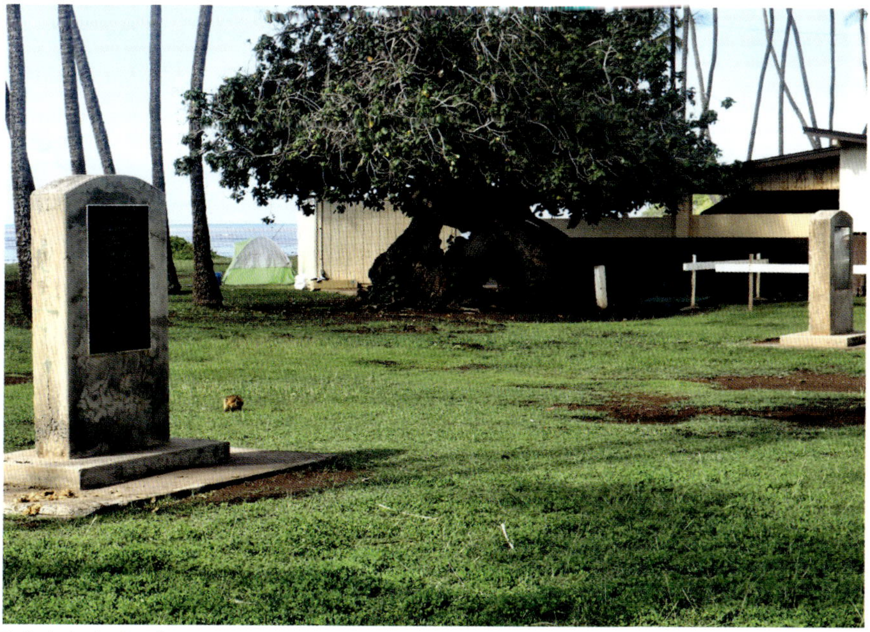

Both photos by Ray Soon

Bell Towers

Kaua'i Soto-Zen (Hanapēpē, Kaua'i)

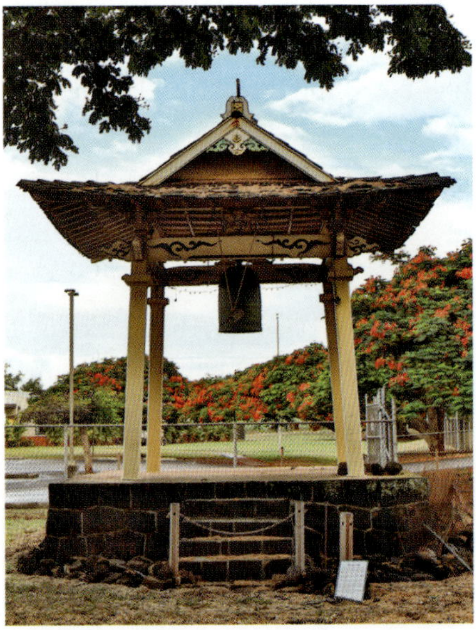

Photo by Cheryl Soon

In 1934 a young men's group raised money to purchase a bonsho, a large temple bell, from Japan. The bronze bell, which is struck from the outside using a handheld mallet suspended on ropes, is decorated with raised bands and inscriptions. The tower was built to house the bell. This bell and tower were originally sited in Wahiawā.

In 1979, the tower was replicated and the bell moved to Hanapēpē. It is rung on New Year's Eve, special holidays, and at festivals and commemorative events.

Mantokuji Soto Mission Bell Tower (Pā'ia, Maui)

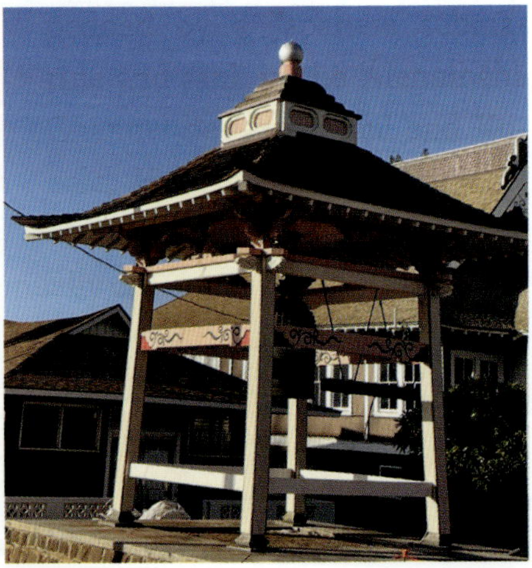

Photo by Ray Soon

The Mantokuji Soto Mission was founded in 1906 and the current temple constructed in 1921. According to the written mission history, in 1909 came a proposal to erect a war memorial monument and bell tower. The bell tower was first erected in 1912. The temple was moved in 1933 and rebuilt with contributions from Henry Baldwin and the County of Maui.

The bell tower suffered damage from the 1949 tsunami. Placed in storage for over a half century, the bell tower was restored in 2019. The structure bears the names of the artisans who built it in 1912. Workers peeled away layers of paint to reveal the original colors. Cast in Japan, the three-ton bronze bell is six inches thick, giving it a tone that carries long distances. It is contained within a teak wood, pitched roof tower that stands twenty-two feet high on a twelve-by-twelve base and a pitched roof. A log that serves as the gong hammer was also saved and outfitted with new ropes. A Mission Centennial Garden was added in 2005/6, marking one hundred years for the mission.

A recently completed $200,000 renovation project was made possible by community donations and foundation grants. The mission property is eroding into the ocean and beach restoration work is underway. It is possible that the entire facility, including the bell tower may someday have to be moved to save it.

Plantation Bell Tower (Hilo, Hawai'i)

Hilo Town Plantation Bell Tower was erected by the Hilo Main Street Program, October 12, 1991 through a contribution from C. Brewer & Company, LTD. In commemoration of its 165th anniversary. The plaque reads:

> *Dedicated to the memory of the people who have contributed to the growth of the Big Island, its economy, and its culture through their work on our many island plantations. This bell originally served the Hakalau Sugar Company.*

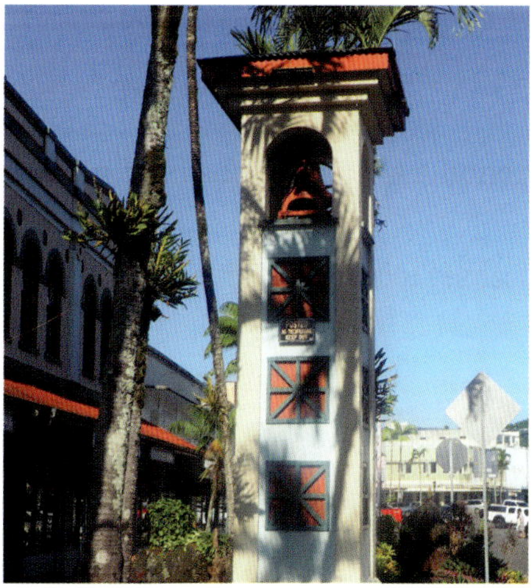

Photo by Cheryl Soon

Japanese Obelisk in Kealakekua, Hawai'i

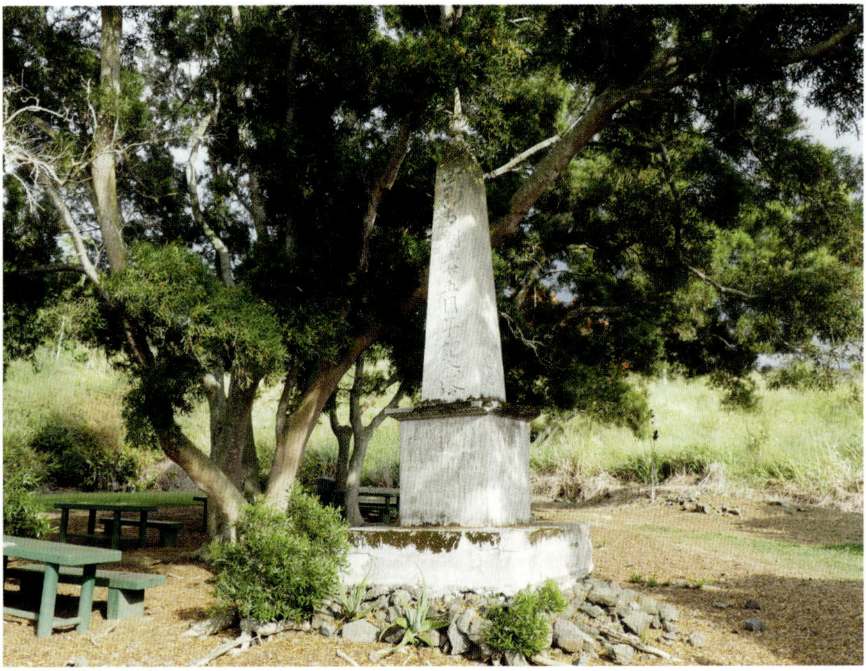

Photo by Cheryl Soon

This tall obelisk has Japanese writing on all four sides and the base. It is a commemorative piece associated with a Japanese temple once located on this site. The temple was combined with three other temples and relocated to a new site in Hōlualoa. The obelisk was moved by Kealakekua Ranch when they built the retail Ranch Center in the 1970s. Now, this is a quiet private park of about one acre with picnic tables for visitors.

American Bicentennial Memorial (Hilo, Hawai'i)

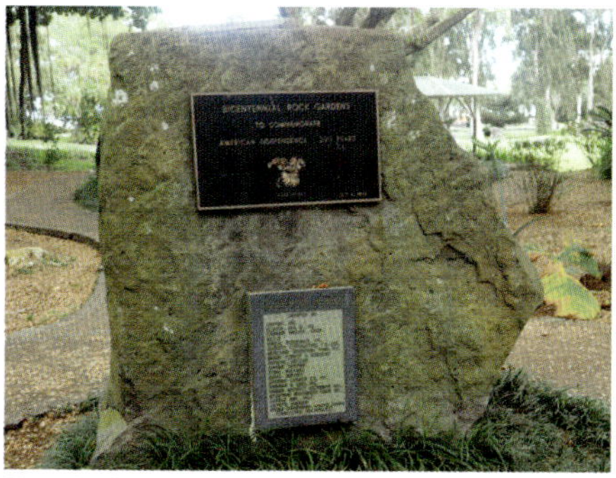

Photo by Cheryl Soon

Memorials to honor the 200th year of independence (America Bicentennnial) were placed nationwide in 1976. In Hawai'i Island, two examples are noted. The first is at Lili'uokalani Gardens in Hilo, just past a *torii* (gateway), where two plaques are placed on a large rock. The top plaque is bronze and indicates it as a bicentennial commemoration of American Independence. It was dedicated on July 4, 1976. The lower plaque is granite. The plaques state County of Hawai'i and lists names of contributors.

The second Bicentennial Memorial is a time capsule placed at the interior atrium of the county office building on Aupuni Street. The capsule contains a message from the local Bicentennial Committee to the future 2075 Tricentennial Committee.

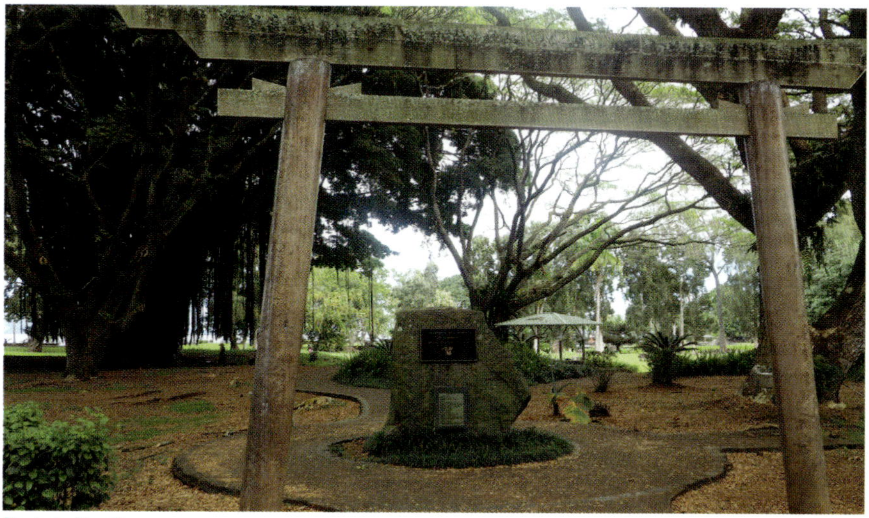

Photo by Ray Soon

COLLECTIONS

There are several places in Hawai'i that merit special attention because they are collections of individual statues and monuments that reside in the same location, lovingly assembled by patrons who have a passion for what they wish to honor, to respect, to represent. The statue figures have been melded with gardens and nature settings, setting off a sensory experience not easily forgotten. Each setting invites the visitor to toss out everything else on their mind, and immerse themselves in a new world created for the purposes of reflection, remembrance, honor, and respect. Six such places are described in this chapter.

- Kepaniwai Park and Heritage Garden in Wailuku, Maui
- Hindu Monastery in Kapa'a, Kaua'i
- Na 'Āina Kai Botanical Gardens & Sculpture Park in Kīlauea, Kaua'i
- Three locations with miniature 88 Shrines: at Lawai International Center in Lāwa'i, Kaua'i; at Waimea Hongwanji in Waimea, Kaua'i; and at Pa'auilo Mission in Pa'auilo, Hawai'i.

Kepaniwai Park and Heritage Garden (Wailuku, Maui)

This park was established in 1952 to showcase Maui's multiple ethnic heritages. Landscape architect Richard Tongg developed the master plan to include several village areas, which involve a home or structure, plantings, and sometimes figures depicting that ethnic heritage. Depictions were selected by the committee of persons from that heritage. The area was restored in 1994 and several pieces added. A September 2016 landslide inflicted considerable damage to the area, and some of it, including the Hawaiian village and grass shack, have not been restored.

The heritage park is located on sacred grounds adjacent to Wailuku Stream, where, in 1790, Kamehameha and his forces defeated Kalanikūpule, son of Kahekili, in the bloody battle known as Kepaniwai (clogged waters).

New England Area

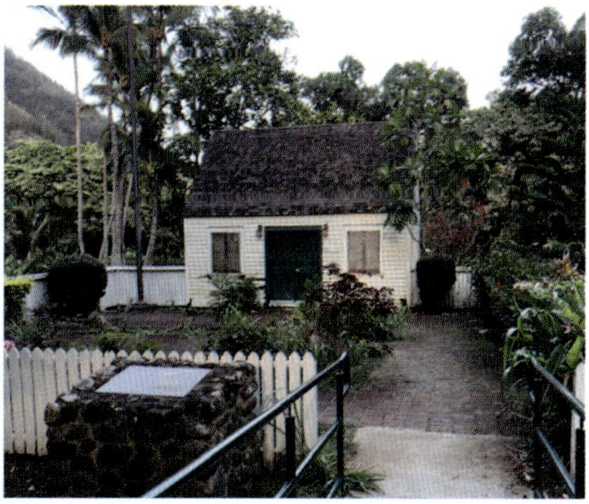

Photo by Ray Soon

From 1820 to 1863, just short of two hundred New England missionaries came to Hawai'i in twelve companies, settling in seventeen stations, throughout five islands. They were teachers, doctors, agents, and clergymen. Their influence was widespread, from teaching Hawaiians how to read to converting them to Christianity to imposing laws and mores that suited their own rather strict religious codes. Unfortunately, the changes brought by the missionaries were often destructive to the Hawaiians. Their descendants shifted to mercantile and other pursuits, rather than adhering to the stoic lives of their parents. Today, this area at Kepaniwai (as well as the Mission House Museum on O'ahu) shows the characteristics of their dwellings and gardens.

Chinese Moon Gate

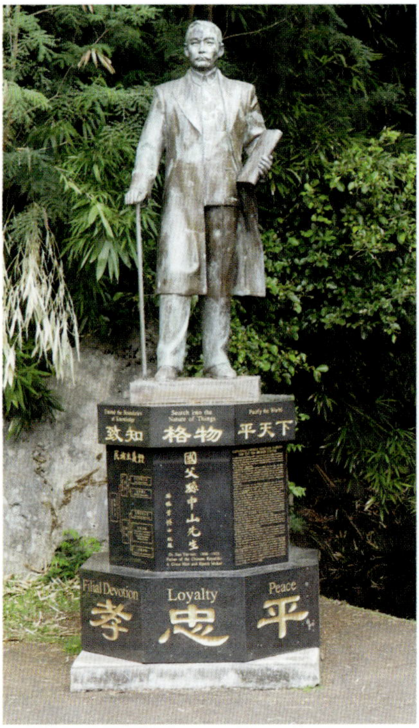

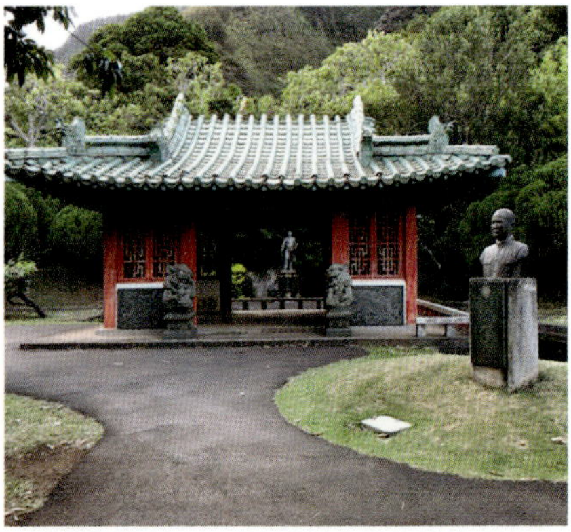

Both photos by Ray Soon

This area includes both a statue and a bust of Sun Yat-sen, in addition to the pavilion. The statue is on a black granite base with gold lettering, similar to the statues in Kula, Maui, and on O'ahu, and displays the words and principles of Sun Yat-sen.

The bust, which was added later, includes a plaque beneath the bust that is written in Chinese. The Chinese section of Kepaniwai Park is close to a Kwai Mi Lychee tree that was planted on February 11, 1989 in commemoration of two hundred years since the first arrival of the Chinese immigrants.

Japanese Village, Garden and Tea House

The Japanese area includes a teahouse, garden, and walking path. A five-storied pagoda monument and stone lanterns were placed in 1935 to commemorate the 50th anniversary of the arrival of Japanese contract laborers (although the first arrivals or Gannenmono came seventeen years earlier in 1868). It was re-erected on the 72nd anniversary, in 1957. Nearby are two figures of persons representing Japanese sugar cane workers.

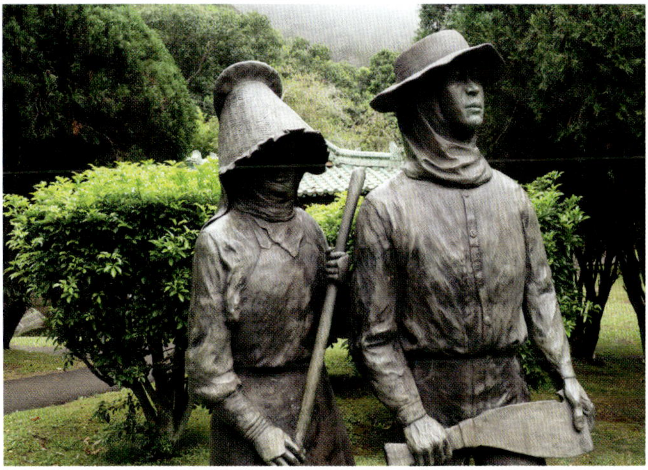

Photo by Ray Soon

These were added in 1985 during the 100th anniversary celebration of immigrant contract workers from Japan coming to Hawaiʻi. While some of the immigrants returned to Japan when their contract was fulfilled, many stayed and became part of a "pioneer generation of Japanese in Hawaiʻi." The plaque reads:

> *These pioneers had the courage to leave their homeland and to persevere in establishing themselves in a foreign land. They endured many hardships and made many sacrifices which benefitted their descendants and contributed to the development of present-day Hawaii.*
>
> *With solemn humbleness, heart-felt appreciation, and a sense of reverence, we, the present beneficiaries, dedicate these bronze statues of Japanese cane field workers so that their aspirations, hardships, and contributions—along with those of the pioneers from Hawaii's many other ethnic groups—will be remembered for generations. Our tears of gratitude now transcend time to mingle with their tears of sacrifice.*
>
> *Dedicated by the Maui Japanese Community,*
> *June 19, 1985*

Portuguese Villa

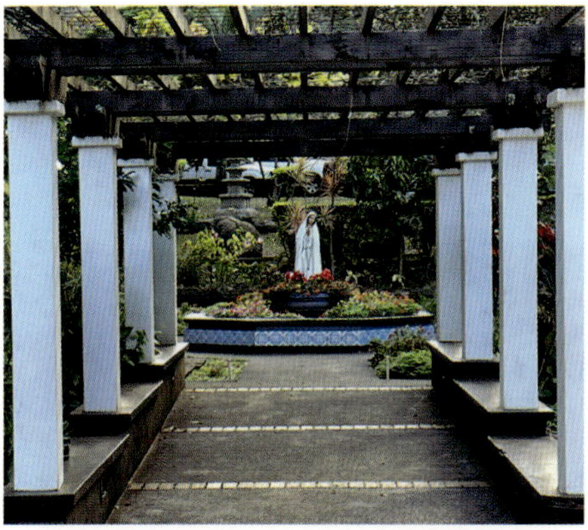

The Portuguese immigrants came to Hawai'i from the islands of Madeira and Azores started in 1870 and continued through the turn of the century. They worked as ranchers, farmers, crafters, and in the sugar cane fields. Their heritage and influence in Hawai'i can be found in food, music, ranching traditions, and politics. At Kepaniwai Heritage Park, they are represented by a miniature house and garden with a portico leading to a religious statue of Mary. Nearby is a baking oven with several plaques which indicate that it was designed by Antone Bras and constructed by volunteer craftsmen from the Portuguese Chamber of Commerce of Maui.

Korean Garden Area

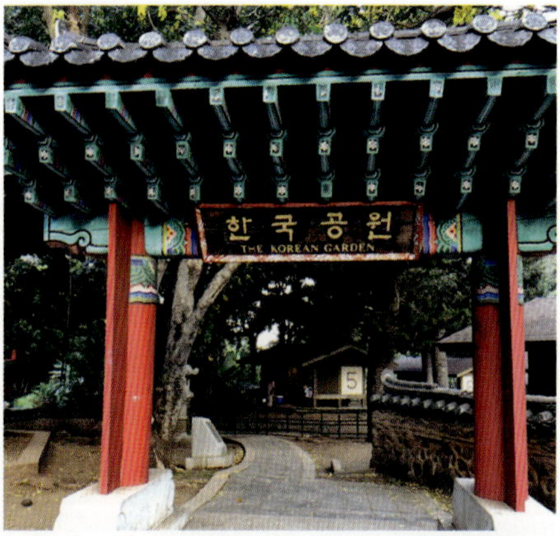

Both photos by Ray Soon

The first Koreans arrived in Hawai'i in 1903. To commemorate the 100th anniversary of their coming, and to show their pride, the Centennial Committee erected a Hexagon Pavilion and garden in the park. The Korean area also includes the pottery deck , used to store highly prized Korean dishes and delicacies that are fermented in the pots. A statue of Haitai, a mythical unicorn-lion who represents justice and triumph over evil, was donated in 2000 to commemorate the centennial of Korean immigration to Hawai'i.

African Americans on Maui

A poster board explains the history of African Americans in Hawai'i starting from before the time of Kamehameha I when Keaka'ele'ele (aka Black Jack) lived on O'ahu. Others arrived on whaling ships between 1820 and 1880, and still more came and stayed after the world war. Stories of several noted black persons are explained including T. McCants Stewart, William F. Crockett, Doris Miller, and Nolle Smith. There is also a memorial to Dr. Martin Luther King, Jr. placed by Maui African Americans. See Chapter Five (Monuments to Peace).

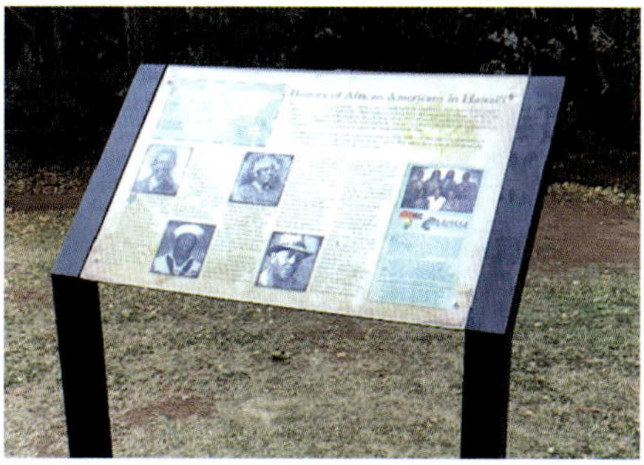

Filipino Cultural Area

The Bahay Kubo, or Nipa Hut, from the Philippines is made of bamboo and oak and is currently in the process of being restored. It sits on pond and a covered bridge leads to the garden where visitors will find a bust of Dr. Jose Protacio Rizal (1861-1898). Ten years after the original elements, the Rizal bust was donated in 1979 by the Sevilla family of Wailuku. Rizal's writings inspired the Filipino revolt against Spanish rule. Rizal is a national hero in the Philippines where statues of him appear in most towns.

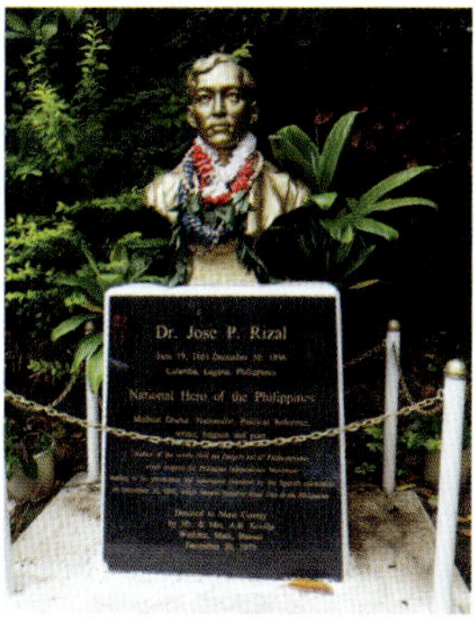

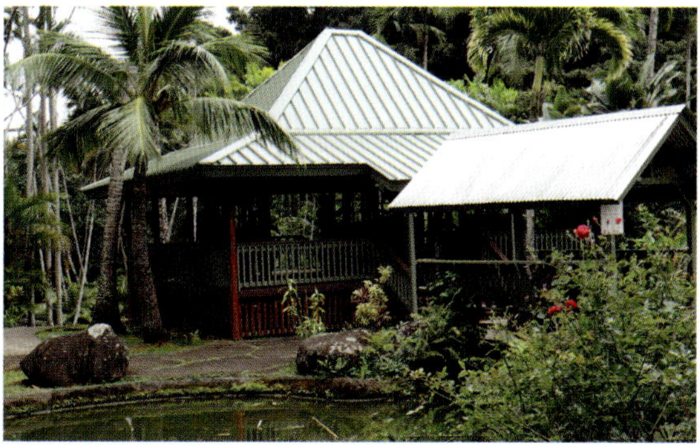

All photos by Ray Soon

Hindu Monastery of Kauaʻi

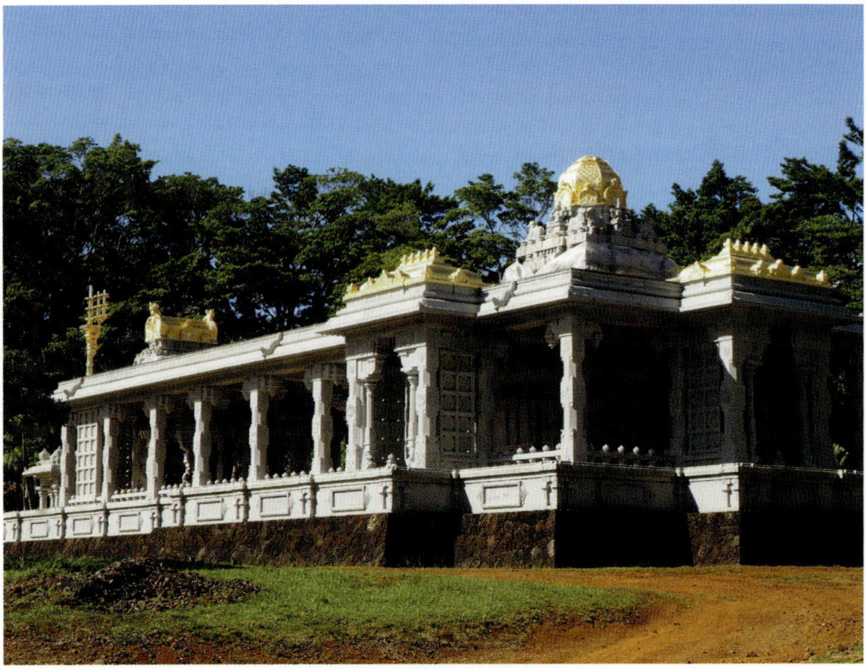

Photo by Ray Soon

A short sixteen miles from the Kōloa tribute to immigrant sugar plantation workers lies another monument honoring the skill and craftsmanship of a different set of workers: those who helped to build the Iraivan Temple at the Hindu Monastery in Kapaʻa.

First, some background. Hindu monk Satguru Sivaya Subramuniyaswami (affectionately known as Gurudeva) had the vision for a major temple to be a pilgrimage for followers. He envisioned it in the tranquil setting high in the mountainside of Kapaʻa. The work took over thirty years and was completed in 2023. It is an amazing work of art.

One day, around 1999, Gurudeva took note of the "sweet sounds" the silpis (stone mason/workers) were making with their chisels as they shaped the white granite. He realized that visitors from the future would not be privileged to see or hear this amazing process. So, he directed the monks to create a bronze memorial that would depict the ancient technology.

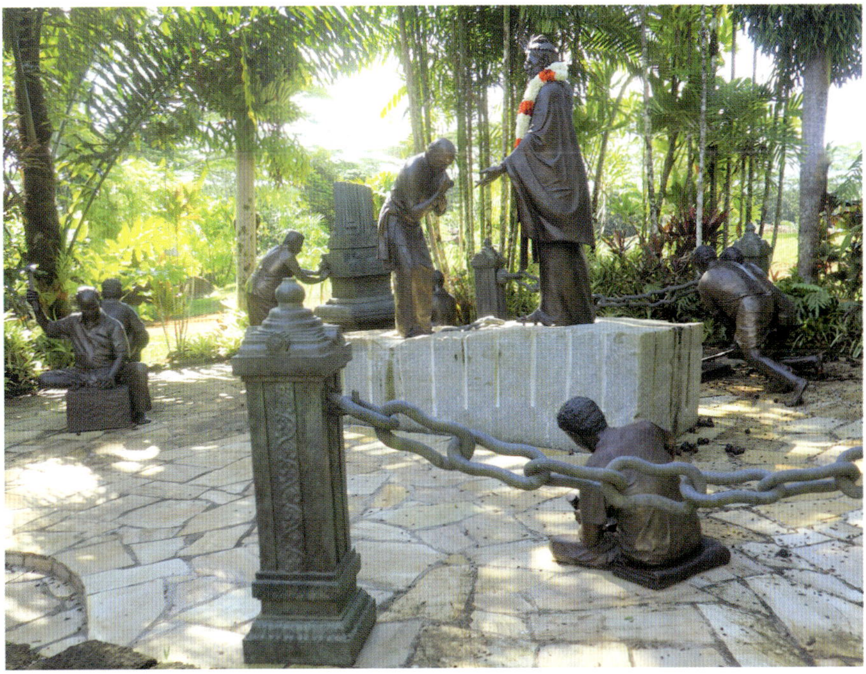

All photos by Ray Soon

Silpi Monument

Standing in the center of the monument on a raw granite stone (which still has the extraction holes drilled at the quarry) is Gurudeva, his right arm lifted, bringing the vision of a perfect Agamic Temple to Earth on Kaua'i. Bowing before him is Sri V. Ganapati Sthapati (1927-2011) the

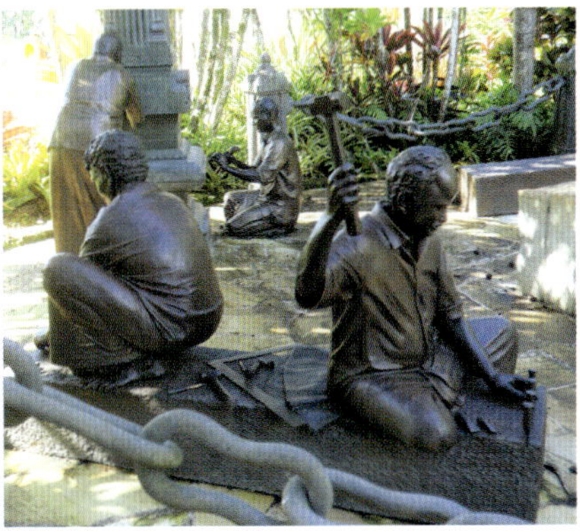

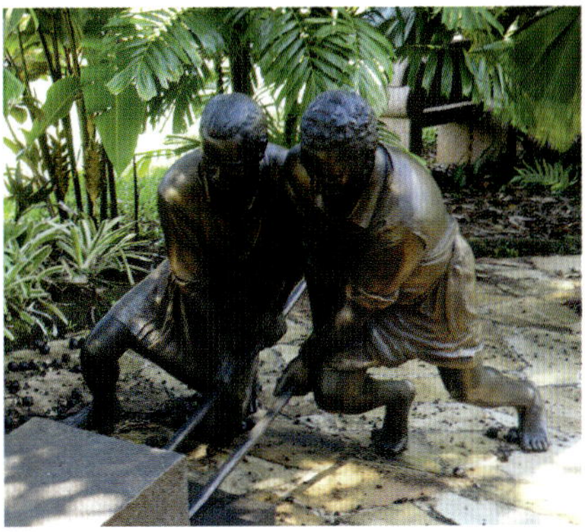

master architect, India's finest, receiving instructions from the Gurudeva in the traditional South India gesture of humility. Under his arm are the plans.

Around them in a circle are the craftsmen, marking, moving, and hewing stone with nothing but simple hammers and mild steel chisels. Gurudeva had directed that this temple, unlike any other in modern times, be entirely carved by hand, without the benefit of electric tools, in the traditions practiced in South India's Chola Empire a thousand years ago.

One of the craftsmen sits at the small forge heating the all-important chisels while nearby another hammers the red-hot iron into a sharp point, which will quickly grow dull on the hard granite. The master builder stands at the pillar, marking the stone to guide the seated carver's work. Walk through their workshop, examine their tools and marvel at the hundreds of thousands of man hours involved in building the Iraivan Temple. The giant stone chains that form the outer handrail are each made from a single, nine-foot-long granite stone. They hint at the extraordinary skills of these artisans.

It took seven years to craft these ten life-sized figures. They are the work of Holly Young, once from Kaua'i, now a resident of Hawai'i Island. She not only completed this beautiful assemblage, she also helped

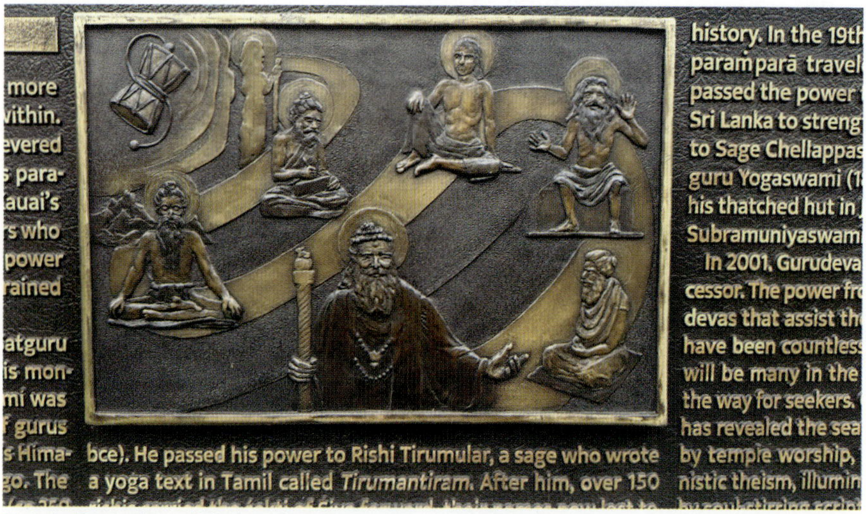

Photo by Paramacharya Sadasivanathaswami

with other works at the monastery, including most recently, fourteen-by-forty-eight-inch bronze relief panels that surround the temple's base and which contain historical and spiritual facts about the temple. Young completed thirty-five relief panels made of bronze. The one shown here is Nataraja, a traditional depiction of the dance of the universe.

Young also completed the remake of the thirteen-foot-tall bronze figure of Hanuman, Siva's right-hand man, who can fly, is intelligent, diplomatic, and resourceful. He is holding the temple in his left hand. It is located on a small knoll near the sacred Rudraksha forest.

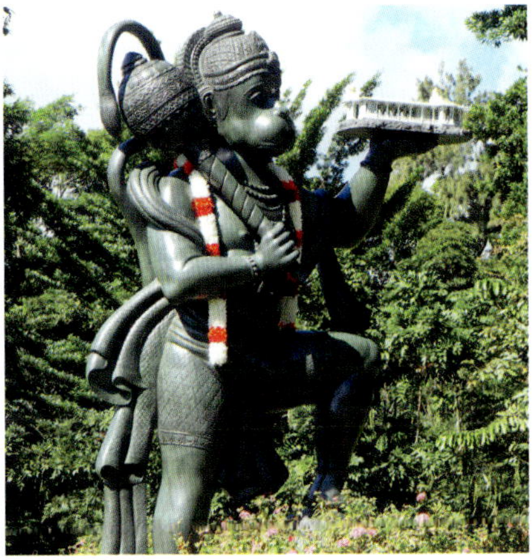

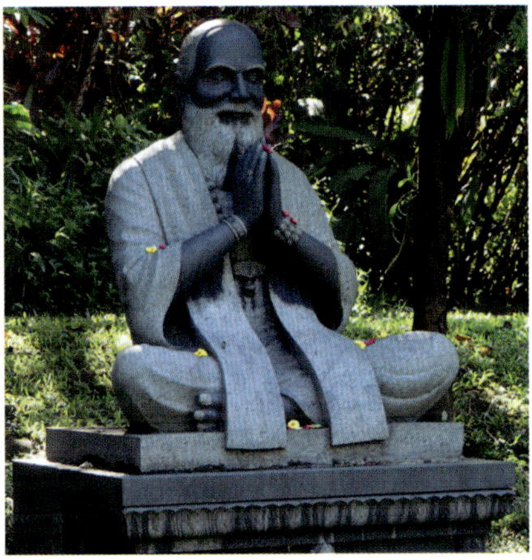

Photos by Paramacharya Sadasivanathaswami

In one of the many garden areas of the grounds are eight granite statues of Hindu spiritual leaders. All were carved in the Hindu tradition from South India at 1.2 life-size, the ratio considered necessary to make a human figure seem divine. The statue shown here is of the current spiritual leader of the Himalayan Academy, Satguru Bodhinatha Veylanswami.

For further information: www.himalayanacademy.com

Na ʻĀina Kai Botanical Gardens & Sculpture Park (Kīlauea, Kauaʻi)

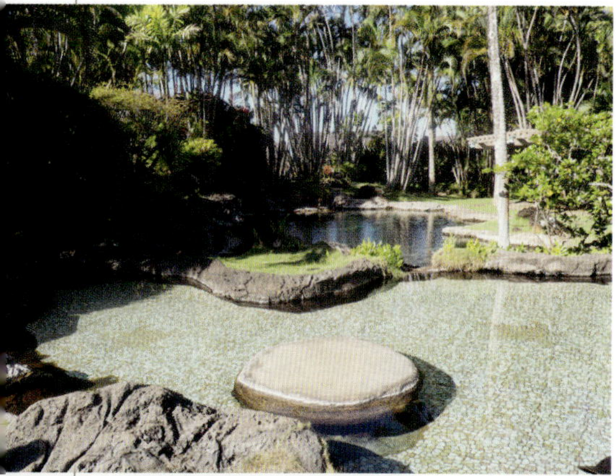

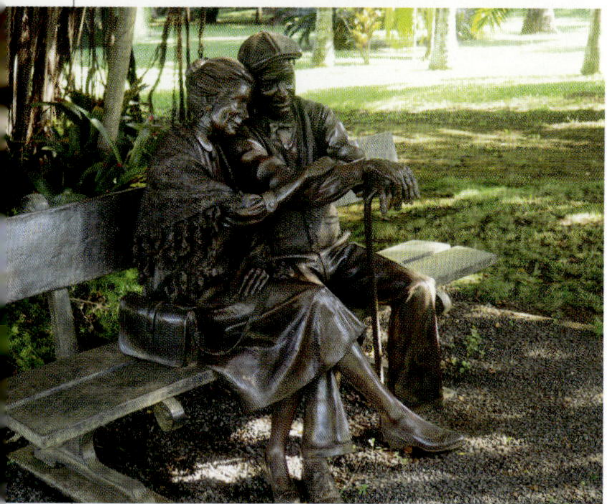

Valentine. Both photos by Ray Soon

For lovers of gardens and sculpture, a visit to Na ʻĀina Kai in Kilauea on Kauaʻi's North Shore is extraordinary and memorable. The Na ʻĀina Kai ("Lands by the Sea") Botanical Gardens & Sculpture Park provides an impressive collection of over two hundred life-sized limited edition bronze sculptures. Here the natural and more manicured man-made areas are infused with fanciful pieces of sculpture and artworks. According to founder Joyce Doty, "When I look at a piece that I like and know an exact place in the garden where it will go, only then will I buy it. Each piece is integrated into the horticultural setting where it is not competing for attention with other sculptural pieces."

The sculpture collection started in 1991 with the purchase of "Valentine" by George Lundeen. It portrays a couple in their later years sitting on a bench. He is wearing a cap and leaning on a cane. She, with her legs crossed and wearing a shawl is leaning into his shoulder holding a Valentine card. It is a beautiful and loving piece.

The property started on a twelve-acre residential lot of former pastureland purchased by the Dotys. Working with architect John Goark &

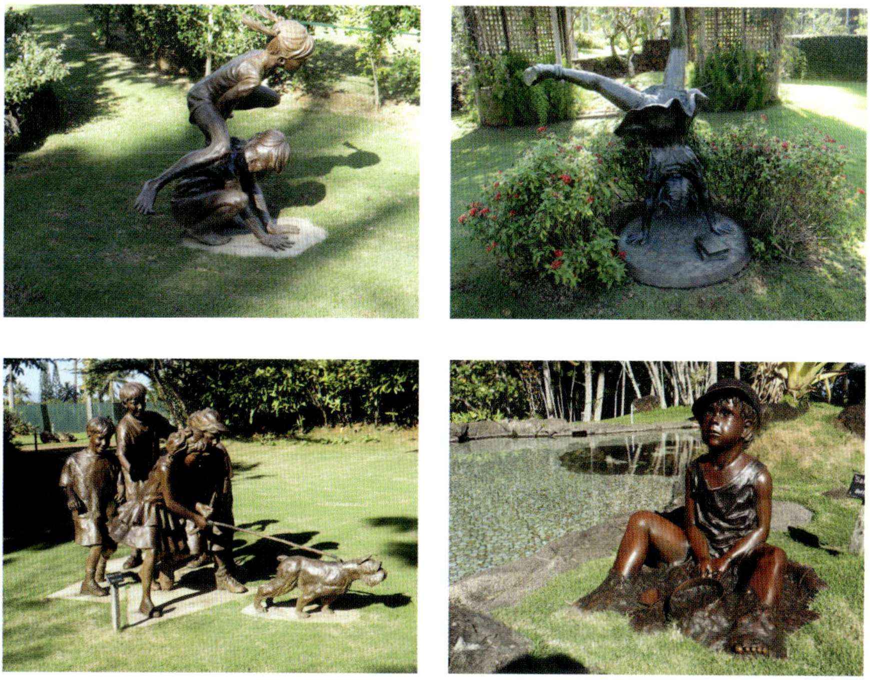

Clockwise from top left: *Frog Legs* by Gary Alsum. *Cartwheel* by Kay Worden. *Sand and Son* by Bets Lundeen. *Walking the Kids* by Rosie Sandifer. Photos by Ray Soon

Associates in 1982, the Dotys built a swimming pool, hillside garden and path to the beach. The Dotys continuously added features including the maze (ending at the royal poinciana tree with its red flowers) and the ambitious lagoon.

Next, they added adjacent lots as they became available and started growing vegetables and tropical fruits at their farm named Kilohana Farms, later adding hardwood trees, including groves of teak. Today the 320 acres of gardens and plantation are funded by a trust and managed by a Board of Directors set up by the Dotys to ensure they are perpetually available after their deaths.

Examples from the natural components and their bronze sculptures include the Hawaiian bird area with "Kia Manu" and woman, "Nīele" collecting and cleaning bird feathers, as well as five rare and colorful native bird species all by Holly Young. There is also the Koli Ridge Bird Walk, the Wild Forest Garden, the Meadow and Marsh, Kaluakai Beach, and Kuliha'ili Canyon.

The more formal sections include the Visitor Center and Orchid House gift, the Bog House, the Hardwood Plantation, the Lagoon, the Desert Garden, Shower Tree Park, Poinciana Maze, Horticulture Amusement Garden, and the Library and Art Collections.

Three Heritage Villages: Hawaiian Ahupua'a, Navajo Compound, and Alaskan Village

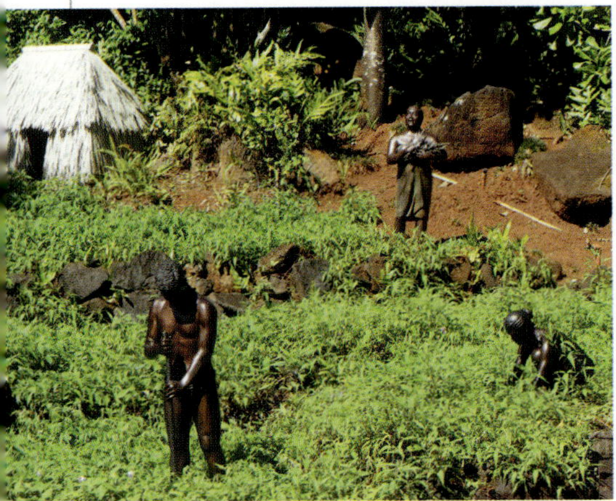

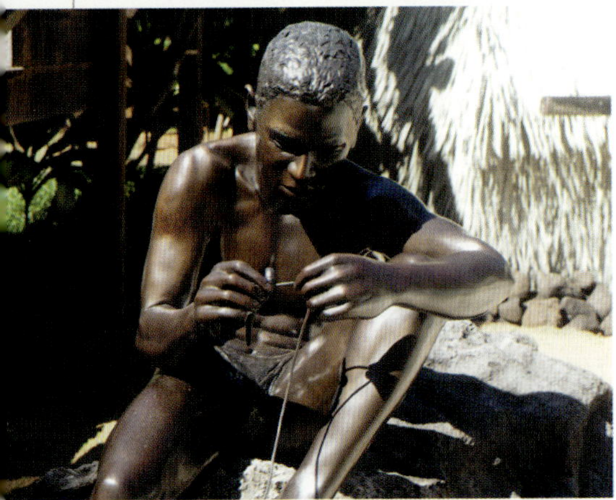

Both photos by Ray Soon

Among the pieces mentioned in this book, the statuary figures are of particular interest. Foremost among these are the human figures in the three villages which are used to depict life styles and heritage from three native groupings: Hawai'i Ahupua'a, Alaskan Athabascan Village, and the Navajo Nation Compound. Many of the figures in the three heritage groups were based on actual persons who were used as the models and represented that ethnic group or occupation.

The Hawaiian ahupua'a, "Ohana," was created by Hawai'i artist Holly Young in 2005. It contains bronze sculptures of two brothers (Kuamo'o and "Meawa'a"), each with their wives, children, and grandchildren. People are busy tending a sweet potato patch, making kapa, carving a canoe, and gathering medicinal plants. Real-life models posed for the making of these sculptures. A large mosaic depicts important scenes of Hawaiian history. A mountainside with waterfalls and streams were added and Hawaiian plants planted. An ocean with native fish were created by Alex Vupton and hale (houses) built. The Ahupuaʻa won several awards such as "Keep It Hawaiʻi" from the Hawaiʻi Tourism Authority.

A few years later (2011), the Hawaiian heritage features were expanded when Joyce Doty asked Young to create pieces that depict the practice of feather collecting to make capes for the king. Five rare (or extinct) birds were fashioned in bronze then hand painted to show their colorful plumage. The bronze figures were the included of a man collecting the feathers and his wife sorting them in a shelter. Branches and stumps were added along the short walkway. Each figure is wearing Hawaiian clothing and wearing ornaments from that culture. Bronze branches and stumps were added along the short walkway as perches for the birds.

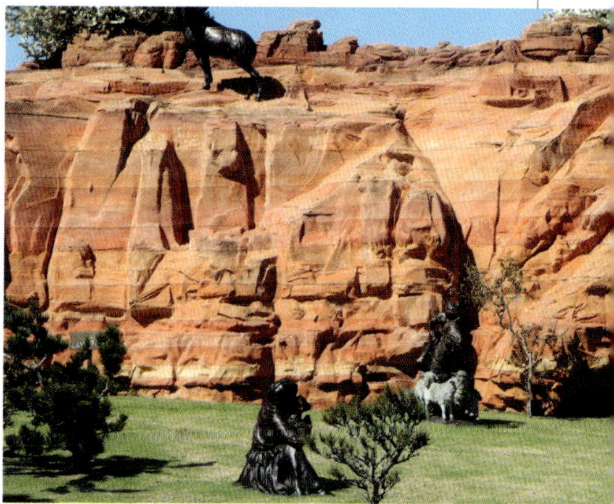

The Navajo Compound figures were created by Susan Kliewer in 2010.

This collection contains bronze figures of native persons and the faux backdrop is meant to evoke the sandstone cliffs of Arizona. Men are shown playing cards and giving directions. Women are depicted spinning yarn and weaving. Gatherers and sheep tenders are shown with their animals. Other bronze features include a covered wagon, bronze horse and mule pulling a covered wagon.

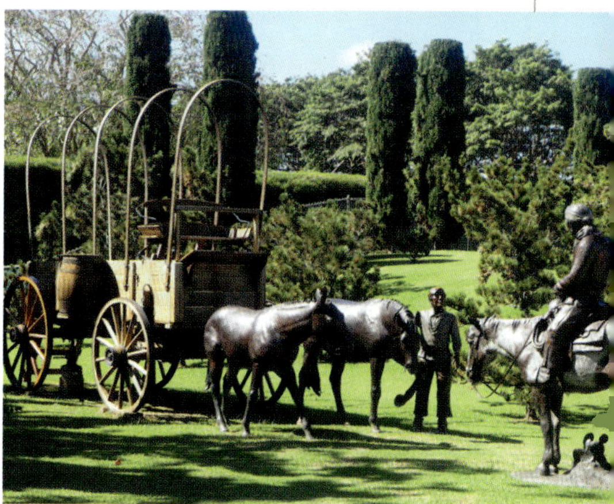

Both photos by Ray Soon

The third heritage section is the Alaskan Athabascan Village with a glacier backdrop.

It portrays the female chief of the tribe, Ganaadaii, sewing and

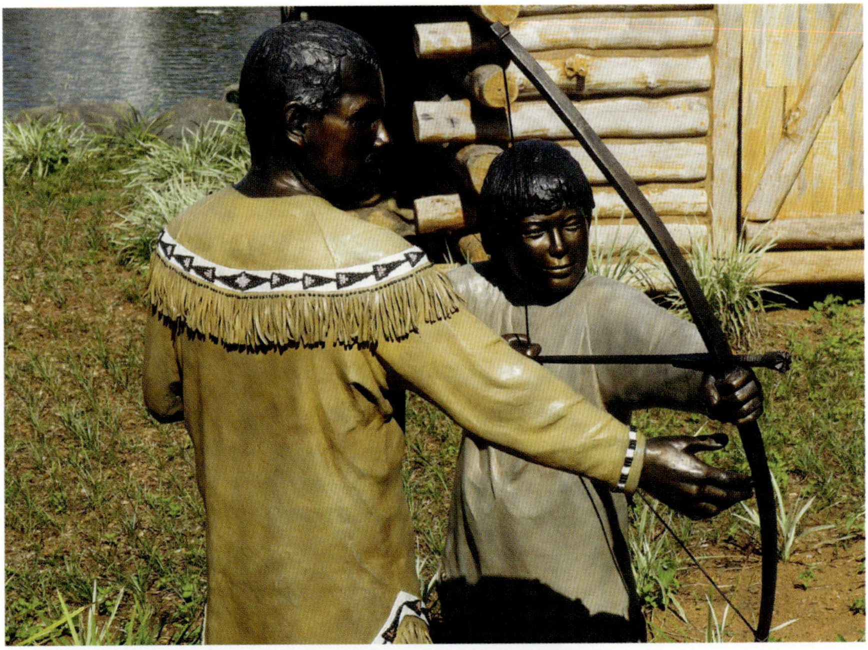

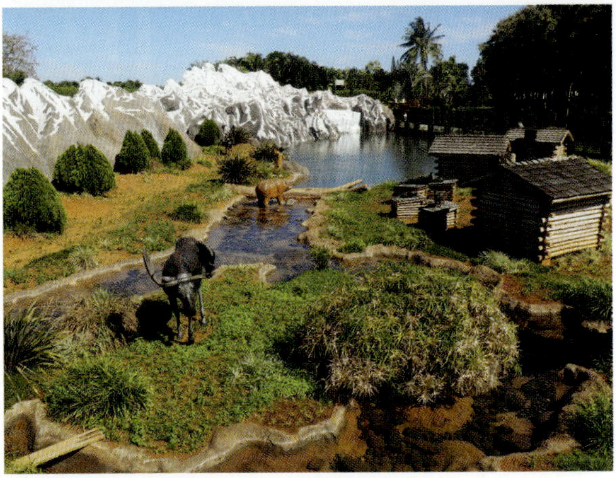

Both photos by Ray Soon

beading boots and another woman, Shin, is hanging fish to dry. This piece also features two men, Ch'akwaii, who is spearing fish, and Viti who is teaching his son Yinjii'ii how to use a bow. The backdrop shows a glacier and there is a considerable amount of wildlife including elk, wolves, moose, bald eagle family, and a bear. The figures are the creations of Holly Young including the fine painted beadwork and fringe. The animals were made by multiple artists including Randy Hand, Christine Knapp, Raymond Gibby, and Eva Stanley.

88 Buddhist Shrines

While conducting the research for this book, one of the delightful discoveries was the monuments created by Japanese immigrants to serve as miniature replicas of 88 shrines of the Shikoku pilgrimage. Pilgrimage is an important part of Shingon Mission practice.

Shikoku Pilgrimage

Shikoku Henro is a pilgrimage route where Buddhist priest Kukai (or, Kobo Daishi) is believed to have lived in the ninth century. The pilgrimage is a circular route 745 miles (1,200 kilometers) in length in a beautiful natural setting that passes eighty-eight temples and several sacred sites. Inside each temple is a different face of Buddha. The Shikoku 88 Temple Pilgrimage is circular and traditionally walked, taking about forty days, during which the pilgrim takes time to reflect, heal, and create life change.

The eighty-eight temples are believed to have been formed between the sixteenth and seventeenth centuries, although pilgrimages likely occurred for several centuries prior to that. When following the Shikoku routing, the walker will start at #1 Ryozenji in Tokushima prefecture and proceed clockwise to #88 Okuboji in Kagawa prefecture. Attired in white vest (hukui or hakue), sedge hat, (sugegasa) and carrying a staff (kongozue) and rosary (juzu), walkers are easily recognized and welcomed by the local community. The pilgrimage is registered as an important Japanese heritage site and unique cultural treasure.

88 Buddhist Replica Shrines

The Japanese who immigrated to Hawai'i (1868, People of the First Year) and the later immigrants (1885-1920), especially those who were Buddhist monks and religious figures, would have been familiar with the 88 shrines pilgrimage.

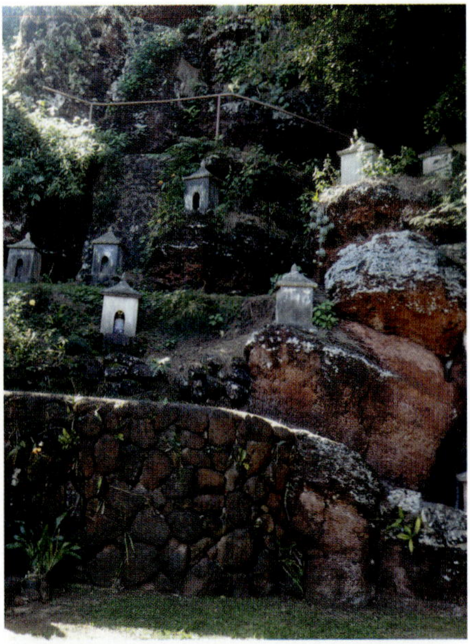

Photo by Ray Soon

Two sites on Kaua'i and one on Hawai'i contain replica 88 shrines, in memory of those in Shikoku, Japan. These are at Lawai International Center, site of an early Daishido (worship hall) established by Shingon pioneer Yujiri Jōgen in 1904 and recently restored by a non-denominational nonprofit; at the Waimea (Kaua'i) Shingon Mission, which was built in 1945 following World War II; and in Pa'auilo on Hawai'i Island.

A fourth site, in Hōlualoa, Hawai'i (near Kona), was destroyed in a landslide in the mid-1960s and deemed beyond repair. According to Bishop Kuki, a new temple, consolidating five smaller temples, was constructed in Hōlualoa and dedicated in 1972, but without the shrines.

With the demise of the sugar industry and scattering of the population, many of the Buddhist temples have fallen into disrepair, but there is affection for their symbolic meaning, and a desire to keep them for cultural reasons, several have been repaired and restored over the years. What is described below are those missions which house miniature 88 shrines pilgrimage sites.

Lawai International Center

Located near Kōloa town in Kaua'i, this site includes the Pavilion of Compassion and the 88 shrines pilgrimage walkway. The center owns thirty-two acres (comprising four moku) in Lāwa'i Valley (ahupua'a). The site has always been a place of refuge and healing. According to its website, it has been the site of a Hawaiian heiau, a Taoist temple, a Shinto Shrine, and a Shingon Buddhist temple. At one time the site was the location of the Filipino Camp for the McBryde sugar plantation. The shrines were originally built in 1904 by first generation immigrants and made of wood, When the local men were called to serve in World War II, they were each given a bag of dirt from around the temple so they could carry the land with them. They all came home. Gramma Nanoko kept the site up as much as possible, visiting regularly until the 1990s, but the land was becoming overgrown by then.

In 1990, under the leadership of Director Lynn Muramoto, the community dedicated itself to the site's restoration. The Pavilion, a replica of a twelfth century shrine, was shipped from Japan and assembled by volunteers in 2014-15.

The shrines were replaced with miniature cement shrines. The group conducted an international call for artists to create the mandalas that would be placed in each shrine. They exist along a winding path that turns six to seven times as it ascends the wall of the valley. Each one is numbered to correspond to the number of a shrine along the Shikoku pilgrimage route. Visitors frequently leave

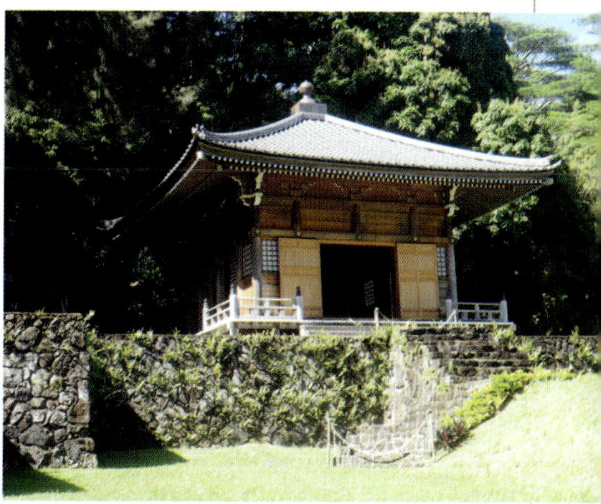

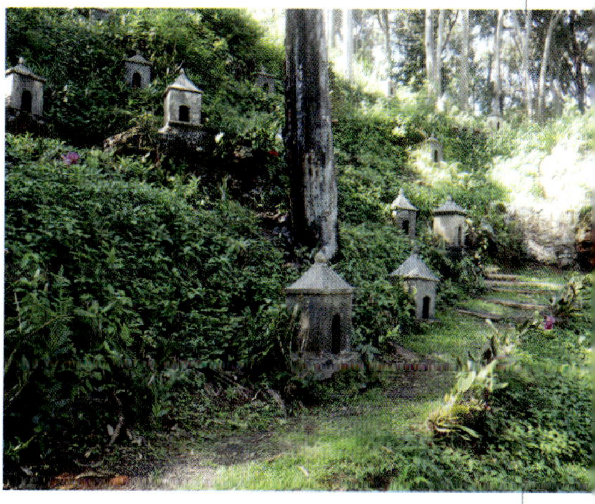

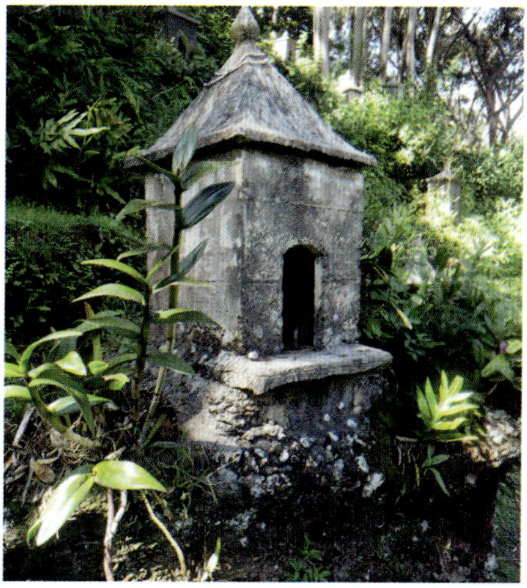

Photos by Ray Soon

small tokens such as polished rocks from the sea, coins or other mementos. The center is open once a month for volunteers to help with maintenance. The annual pilgrimage occurs in August of each year and is accompanied by playing of the bamboo flute (shakahastra).

The site also has a memorial to a priest who died in the 1960s and a peace pole written in four languages: Hawaiian, English, Chinese, and Japanese.

Waimea Shingon Mission

The original mission center, Waimea Daishido, was established in July 1908 by Rev. Jisen Omori. The temple lands were purchased and the

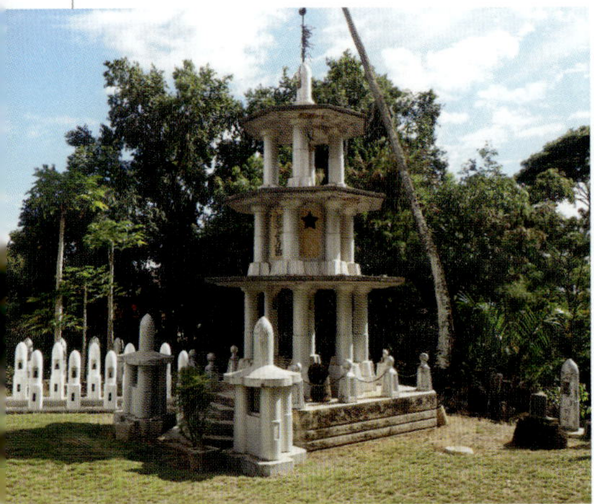

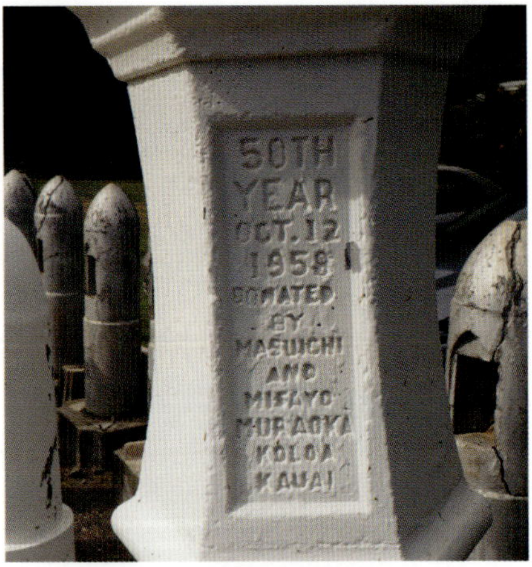

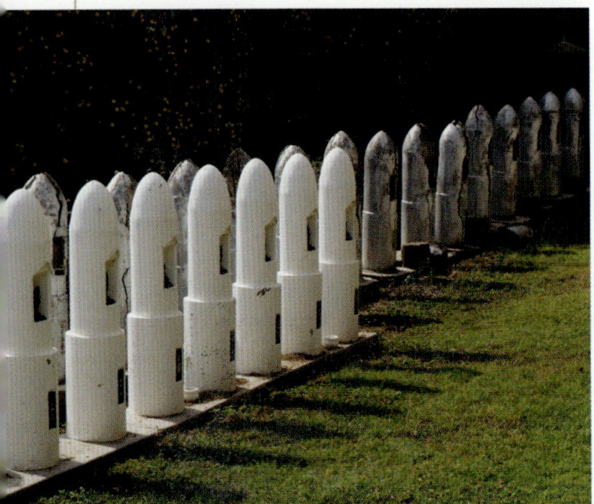

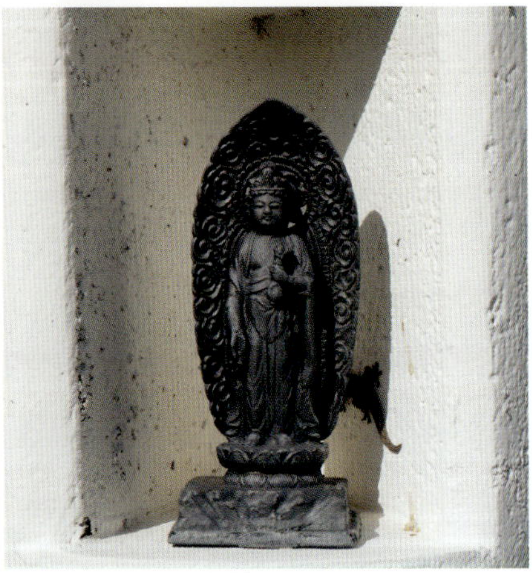

Photos by Ray Soon

mission was rebuilt in 1926. Two years later, the name was changed to Waimea Shingonji. The grounds are in the shadow of a large cliff sacred to Hawaiians.

The miniature "Shin Shikoku 88 Temple Pilgrimage" was built after World War II under the direction of Rev. Kakuho Asaoka. The memorial and Shikoku Buddha monuments were dedicated on December 21, 1946. The shrines are notable for their unusual artillery shell (some say bullet) shape, which is meant to represent "no more war." Black plates, written in Japanese, represent the number of the Buddhas. There are two rows of identically shaped shrines. At the back row are the original ones, built by members of the mission, many of whom had been placed in internment camps or who served during the war; still others were by family members of soldiers who died in the war. The concrete used for these is in various stages of deterioration, chunks have fallen, or rebar is showing. In the front row are the replicas created in 2008.

In 1976, a fire erupted in the Waimea Shingon Mission Temple and everything was reduced to ashes. It was rebuilt with a new minister's residence in 1979. This also marked the 75th anniversary of the mission. In August 2005 a project started to rebuild the damaged hachi kasho (88 Buddha monuments). The new ones were dedicated in May 2008 on the 100th anniversary of the mission. Today, there are two rows of the shell articles, the old crumbling ones in silver, and in front the new white ones.

There are multiple memorials celebrating anniversaries of the founding of this mission. The memorial bell tower was built on the 25th anniversary (1933). Inside the tower are the names of 90 persons who served in WW II. The matching pair of entry lanterns were built on the 50th anniversary (1958).

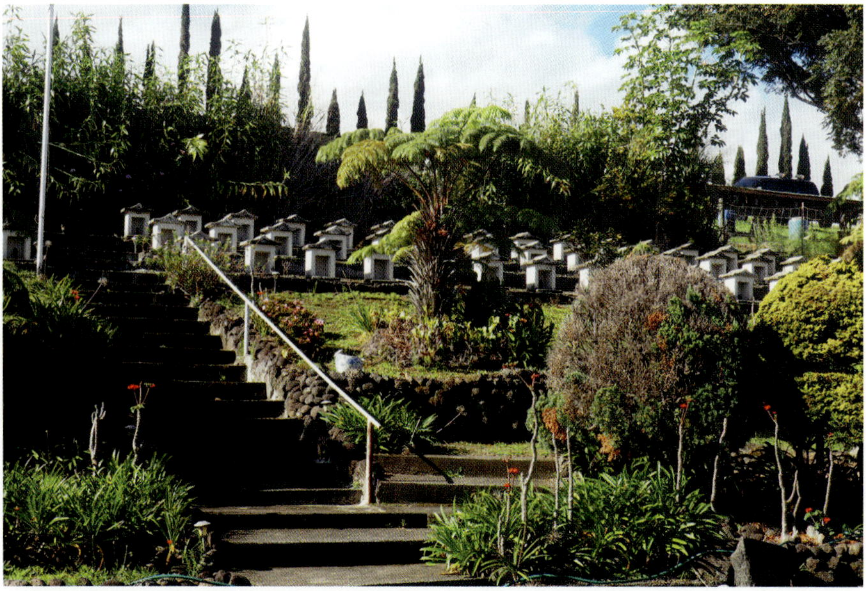

Photo by Ray Soon

Kongoji Mission 88 Miniature Shrines (Pa'auilo, Hawai'i Island)

This replica pilgrimage site at the Kongoji Mission was built near the temple by the Rev. Shugaku Koto. In 1938, Rev. Kakuo Shiba rebuilt the temple and expanded the minister's residence. The main temple was again renovated in 1966, and a judo hall added in 1970. High above the Pacific Ocean and an easy jog off the main circle island roadway, the site has a commanding view. It is in a residential area with a school behind it, with the sounds of dogs barking and roosters crowing nearby, adding to its ambiance.

The miniature pilgrimage sits on a hillside behind the temple and hall is accessed by climbing about twenty stairs to a sloping landing with three long rows of temples. Each temple is made of concrete in the shape of the box with a temple roof, about two feet high. Inside each box is a six-inch figure made of cut metal. These pieces are in fair condition: some boxes are missing a figure; and some are showing signs of concrete fatigue. The vegetation is tended for the safety of visitors.

REFLECTIONS

If you don't know history, then you don't know anything.
You are a leaf that doesn't know it is part of a tree.

— *Michael Crichton*

During the research phase for this book on the neighbor islands, it was quickly revealed that many important statues and markers exist there to identify and explore. I realized that some of these histories are in grave danger of being lost due to their age and stage of deterioration. The Lahaina fire of 2023 was another somber reminder of how historical landmarks and statues are subject to weather, natural disasters, and climate change. They are fragile.

This was confirmed when I spoke with Kim Moseley, a Maui artist who does statue (and glass window) restoration. She confirmed that records of dates, makers, and other relevant information were either never kept, or have been lost over the decades. As membership in churches and temples has declined over the last few decades, funds to upkeep cemeteries, churches and temples, and art works is increasingly not available. This book can help serve as a record of these cultural markers as of the early twenty-first century. In this chapter called "Reflections" four intertwined topics are addressed:

- What are the major historical themes about which statues and monuments are educating us? How does that vary from island to island?
- How do these statues and memorials create public spaces?
- Are statues and memorials still relevant today? What assists or impedes that relevance?
- How does the experience in Hawaiʻi compare to other places in the nation and the world?

What are the Historical Themes Used for Statues in Hawai'i Neighbor Islands?

The collective look at statues and memorials in Hawai'i, Kaua'i, and Maui delves into periods of Hawai'i's history, especially during the nineteenth and twentieth centuries and the lives people led. From the statues, one develops a deeper appreciation for a wide array of ali'i figures, paniolo and plantation workers, and the Catholic and Buddhist religious institutions that served the immigrant populations. More recently, one sees deep desire to honor war veterans and to promote peace. Understanding that most people forget stories after three generations, it can be conjectured that statues and markers are attempts to extend people's memories.

Theme 1: Earliest Pieces Copy European Models Favoring Explorers and Leaders

Though statues had been used to honor leaders and heroes in Europe for centuries, the custom was new to Hawai'i when it was introduced. In reflecting upon the earliest items, those installed between 1878 and 1928, it is notable how many were installed by persons not native to the islands. Only the Kamehameha statues and markers of the birthplaces of two ali'i had that honor of being erected by Hawaiians during that period.

The first item installed was the Cook obelisk in 1878, placed by the British government when similar items were being erected around the world to honor the 100th anniversary of Cook's expeditions. Statues and memorials to explorers is a theme here and elsewhere.

The second items erected were the two statues of Kamehameha installed in 1893 in Honolulu and in his birthplace Kapa'au, Hawai'i. King Kalākaua, who had been to Europe and seen statues firsthand, commissioned the Kamehameha statues. The reader will recall that his original intention was to coincide with the Cook anniversary celebrations around the world.

Both late-1800s pieces, the Cook Memorial installed by the British and the two Kamehameha statues installed by the Hawaiian Kingdom, are still standing on Hawai'i Island.

In 1928, a statue of Cook was installed in Waimea, Kaua'i. It is a replica of one in Scotland and is said to be the gift of the people of Kaua'i; it was erected at the location of Cook's "First Encounter" with Hawaiians. The statue came up on the 150th anniversary of his expeditions, when his achievements were again being honored worldwide.

Some luster has come off the Cook legacy and by the twenty-first century, his story is among those that native people no longer laud. As a result, his statues have suffered graffiti and sometimes calls for removal. The relation between Hawai'i and global explorers is as complicated here as it is around the world. The explorers introduced new ships, weaponry, food, and customs. But they also brought social disruption and disease. Captain James Cook's death occurred on February 14, 1779, at Kealakekua Bay, Hawai'i. The obelisk to Cook was placed in Kealakekua one hundred years later, in 1878 by his fellow countrymen, not by Hawaiians.

The next explorer chronologically was George Vancouver. While a crewman on Cook's second and third expeditions, Vancouver captained an expedition that arrived in March 1792, stopping for a break from the winter weather. Credited with introducing cattle to Hawai'i, the Vancouver Memorial was placed at Ma'alaea Harbor in Maui in 1969 by a hotelier from Canada. The dedication was attended by representatives of the Canadian government (Vancouver's adopted homeland after his finished voyaging) and from Maui County. Sadly, that memorial fell into disrepair. The story of the totem poles that once accompanied the Vancouver memorial is likely to become little more than a footnote in history.

Memorial pieces installed from 1900 to 1940 come in the forms of bronze medallions or plaques on large boulders. These are mostly on Kaua'i and honor members from sugar planter families upon their death. In two cases, these are credited to "grateful community friends." A similar bronze plaque placed on a large boulder is found on the slopes of Maunakea in Hāmākua, Hawai'i, erected in 1934. The plaque honors David Douglas, the famed botanist, who cataloged many of the species on

Hawai'i's volcanoes, and who tragically was caught in an animal trap. This memorial was installed by the Hilo Burns Club, a Scottish ethnic group.

Markers from this same period show the birthplaces of King Kamehameha III in Kealakekua Bay, Hawai'i (installed 1911) and the birthplace of Ka'ahumanu in Hāna, Maui (installed 1928). They are similar in style to the bronze plaques on the stone boulders, a popular type of monument among the sugar plantation families at the time.

The Rice Family (which includes the Isenberg and Cooke families) Memorial in Puhi Cemetery, on former Kaua'i Plantation lands, stands in contrast to the bronze on stone memorials of plantation owners due to its different look and materials. This elaborate carving of two mourning figures rising to the heavens, called "Beloved Dead," is set against a ten-foot-high relief wall.

Created by Stephen Sindring, it is an accomplished piece of art shown first in Paris, France, and Bremen, Germany, before it traveled around the horn from Europe to its intended place in Lihue Cemetery. These were families of wealth who had the knowledge, connections, and finances to commission the memorial. Its form and the quality of carved marble are later repeated in a white marble statue found at Holy Rosary Church in Pā'ia, Maui, another plantation-related area. The Pā'ia Damien statue was made in Italy using Italian white marble. It depicts Damien comforting a leprosy patient and was installed in 1976.

Theme 2: The Period Following World War II Brings War Memorials but also a Quest for Peace

World War II had a major impact on Hawai'i. It is clear that Hawaiian men enlisted as soldiers and their families took pride in assisting the United States' war effort, despite the discrimination and distrust shown toward them due to their Japanese ethnic background.

US involvement in the war started in Hawai'i with the bombing of Pearl Harbor. Many soldiers were trained in Hawai'i and sent directly from here to the Pacific Theatre. Placing markers was one of the ways that various survivors, such as veteran's groups, addressed their tragedy, loss, grief, and suffering, attempting to make sense of the difficult experience. Respect was shown both through large commissioned memorials to the war and through honor rolls remembering those soldiers from their towns and villages.

World War II memorials started appearing shortly after that war, around 1950. On Hawai'i Island, plaques that honor the veterans of World War II were erected at baseball fields on or near plantation camps. Most were expanded twenty to thirty years later to honor veterans of the Korean War and the Vietnam War. In Waimea, Hawai'i, a memorial honors the Tarawa Training Camp and in Ha'ikū, Maui, a memorial was placed at the training grounds of the 4th Marine Division. Both were World War II training sites.

As time has moved on, people's perspectives toward the creation of these memorials changed from honoring the dead, to a means of committing to the end of war, as a dedication to friendship, and toward world peace. On December 7, 2022, the 81st Annual Japan-US Joint Memorial Ceremony was held on Ford Island. Japanese Consul General Yataka Aoki was a featured speaker. He said, "We are here to honor those we lost. Let us always remember all that our two nations have built together, our friends after war, and make a commitment to doing our part to strengthen this friendship. May the world someday come to remember Pearl Harbor not just as a place where fierce war began, but as a powerful symbol of the later reconciliation and friendship which endured and the limitless potential they hold in our collective quest for peace."

The peace memorials started to appear a decade later than the war memorials, in the 1960s. Again, Hawai'i served as an important training ground, this time for volunteers in the Peace Corps. The Peace Corps Memorial was erected in 1963 as a memorial to John F. Kennedy (shortly after he died November 22, 1962). In 2011, the memorial was re-dedicated to Peace Corps volunteers from Hawai'i, and it was moved to the University of Hawai'i at Hilo campus.

Peace gardens became popular towards the end of the twentieth century. There are two on Kaua'i honoring Spark Matsunaga; one garden includes a statue of him. The Paleaku Gardens Peace Sanctuary in Captain Cook, Hawaiʻi, includes statues from various religions of the world. Busts to Dr. Martin Luther King, Jr. in Maui and the World Peace Kannon Statue in Hanapēpē, Kauaʻi, are also symbols of a quest for world peace. Today, the drive for peace is leading people to place peace poles around the islands.

Theme 3: Remembering and Honoring the Aliʻi Has Sustained

Royal subject statues were showcased in my previous book about statues on Oʻahu, *Reflections in Stone and Bronze: Exploring Hawaiʻi's History and Culture Through Sculpture* (Mutual Publishing, 2022). That book looked at fourteen royal figures made into statues. Honoring royal persons continues to be a theme on the neighbor islands. However, with the exception of Kamehameha, Kalākaua, and Liliʻuokalani, different royals are honored there.

The last decade of the 1900s and the first twenty years of the 2000s showed a renewed interest in statues and busts commemorating Hawaiian royalty. This came shortly after a modern-day cultural wave called the Hawaiian renaissance.

The first Hawaiian renaissance was in the 1870s. Hawaiʻi was still an independent nation seeking its own identity, versus one derived from either Great Britain or the United States. The second renaissance came one hundred years later, in the late 1960s and early 1970s. It was a cultural movement. The musical genre personified by the likes of Gabby Pahinui, Sons of Hawaiʻi; Keola and Kapono Beamer; the Kaʻapana Brothers; Olomana and others was one element. The interest in Hawaiian music was accompanied by renewed interest in the Hawaiian language, hula, traditional Hawaiian crafts, Hawaiian studies, paddling, and Polynesian voyaging (*Hōkūleʻa*). That cultural renaissance continued.

The 1978 Constitution Convention (ConCon) created the Office of Hawaiian Affairs and reclaimed the lands of Kahoʻolawe. Hawaiian became an official state language in 1978. Soon thereafter laws were passed requiring that new street names be in the Hawaiian language, a practice long in existence. Hotels built during this period often took the names of royals, especially when there was a strong place connection.

The commissioning of statues seemed to follow naturally. In Hilo, a statue on King Kalākaua was installed in 1988, made by Henry Bianchini. On Maui, Herb Kāne, noted for his extensive collection of drawings depicting famous events in early Hawaiian history, was commissioned to create Kamehameha I statue for the Grand Wailea Hotel on Maui (1990). A fifth Kamehameha statue intended for a hotel on Kaua'i (1965) was rejected by the local community, but installed instead in 1997 in Hilo, Hawai'i. A statue of Queen Ka'ahuamanu was created for a shopping center in Kahului by Tom Faught (1995). A statue of Queen Lili'uokalani by Dale Zarrella was added to the vast collection of the Fairmont Hotel (2018).

Around that same time, both the University of Hawai'i-Manoa and BYU-Hawai'i started degree programs in sculpture. Jan Gordan Fisher, artist of the Sesquicentennial Immigrant Monument (1965) in Kōloa, was the program director at BYU and later he became artist-in-residence at Grand Wailea in Maui. His apprentices went on to create many works in Hawai'i. Sean Browne taught at both UH-Manoa and Kapi'olani Community College. One of Browne's students, Kim Duffett, created the Spark Matsunaga statue in Hanapēpē and many pieces on O'ahu.

Other sculptors like Holly Young, Dale Zarrella, and Henry Bianchini came to Hawai'i and made it their home. This local talent pool showed serious respect for Hawaiian history and made statues more accessible to the public. Each of these Hawai'i-based sculptors has created one or more statues of a royal.

Queen Ka'ahumanu is a significant figure in Hawaiian history, deserving of more recognition than the single statue of her at a shopping center in Maui. It is fitting to have one on Maui, the island where she was born and raised and returned often. While Ka'ahumanu was one of Kamehameha's wives and a trusted advisor, her significance continued well after his death, when she co-led with the next generation of leaders (Kamehameha II and III), much of this time in Lahaina. Her birthplace had been noted with a plaque in Hāna, placed 140 years after her death.

People of Kauaʻi have long sought to place a statue honoring their last king, Kaumualiʻi. This was finally accomplished two hundred years after his death, with two versions. The first was placed at his homesite in Waimea in 2021, including renaming of the area back to its Hawaiian name and re-interpretation of the signage and history from a Hawaiian perspective. The second statue came just a year later in 2022 and depicts Kaumualiʻi with his wife Deborah Kapule in front of Kauaʻi Museum, a museum dedicated to his history. A statue of Kaumualiʻi's mother and aliʻi Chiefess Kamakahelei was placed at a school named for her in Puhi, Kauaʻi, in 2003, a little more than 200 years after her death.

The descriptions and dates just provided show that the royal statues well exceed the "third generation" of remembrance. They are closer to eight to ten generations. This proves their abiding significance in the culture through centuries.

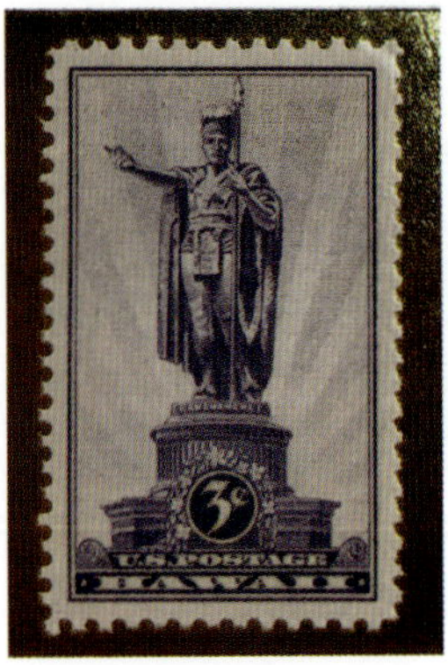

Photo by Cheryl Soon

The Kamehameha statue is so iconic that its form and gesture are used as the official marker of State of Hawaiʻi historic sites. The statue has been used on coins (the official Hawaiʻi coin in the US Mint's series on state coins) and on stamps (the 3 cent US Postage stamp issued in 1937).

Theme 4: Catholic Churches and Buddhist Temples are Important Sites for Statues

Religion has played a significant role in the cultural and political histories of the islands and church members continue to honor those contributions. Reflecting on the number of churches and temples that are the sites of statues, one realizes that this form of continuing a culture is just one of the many roles they play for the growing immigrant populations.

Catholic priests and Buddhist ministers came to Hawai'i in the middle of the nineteenth century, followed by one hundred years of building churches and temples, parish halls, and schools which are still an influence in the mid-twentieth century. They help immigrant populations both assimilate into a larger population and keep their roots and identities. The assimilation and identity roles continued along with the religious mission for over one hundred years and continues, albeit in altered forms to this day.

Among the oldest religious Catholic figure statues are those of Saint Anthony of Padua (1919) at the church named for him in Wailuku, Maui, and St. Benedict Church in Captain Cook, Hawai'i (statue date unknown). Early statues in marble or concrete were frequently sent from Italy. In the past twenty years, local artists have been making the Damien statues.

Baby boomers are the generation of people born from 1946-64—births that had been put off during the World War II and the Great Depression. Theirs was the largest generational group in US history. Through their careers and relative prosperity, they have had and continue to have a significant impact on the economy. They are the oldest of the current seven living generations. Those in the first wave are now in their seventies and at retirement age. The Japanese among them are typically *nisei,* or second generation and their children are *sansei.*

Boomers grew up in the 1950s and 1960s in a period of increasing opportunity. Two influences on youth at that time were the schools and social services provided by the established Catholic Churches and by Buddhist Societies. If you were Catholic (one-third of the population), you either attended one of the hundred Catholic schools or you attended Confraternity of Christian Doctrine (CCD) classes after school during the week. Catholic Social Services provided transitional shelters and housing assistance, outreach, medical, and vocational counseling to disadvantaged persons and families.

If you were Buddhist in the 1950s and 60s, you attended Japanese language school after English school ended. These schools were generally associated with one of the Missions. While the religion came to Hawai'i as early as 1850, it took several generations to assemble the donations to make possible donations for mission facilities and statues. Toward the middle of the twentieth century, many Hongwanji Missions started making purchases of bronze statues of Shinran Shonin, founder of the most popular sect of Buddhism in Hawai'i.

As far as one can tell without records, Shinran statues were generally purchased made to order from one of the copper foundries such as Kinjudo in Shiga Prefecture. Copper foundries date back to 500 A.D., but the works were mostly lost in World War II when they were melted down for their metal to make ammunition. The craft was renewed after the war. Copper alloy, also used in bells, has a distinct sound familiar to temple goers. Copper statues of Buddhist Shinran Shonin exist at Hongwanji Missions on all islands, including (among others) Waimea, Kaua'i, (1970) and the latest known in West Kaua'i (2022); Hilo Betsuin (1985) and Puna in Hawai'i island; and Lahaina, Kahului, and Wailuku on Maui.

Great respect and honor are accorded to Saint Damien and Saint Marianne Cope, who moved to the islands and each chose to serve the needs of patients with Hansen's Disease (leprosy). Damien lived from 1840 to 1889 and came to Hawai'i in 1864; Cope lived from 1838 to 1918 and came to Hawai'i in 1883. Hawai'i was in a crisis with leprosy and King Kalākaua sent out pleas for medical and financial assistance to deal with the effects. Catholic priest Damien and sister Cope, along with others, had overlapping years of influence that spanned five decades. Important memorials to them exist on Kalaupapa Peninsula, Moloka'i, at the location where patients were resettled by the government.

The Damien statue by Marisol Escobar was erected in 1969 at the Hawai'i State Capitol (with a duplicate in Washington DC following statehood). Its base words were altered when he became a saint. An equally impressive statue of Damien is the carved white marble of him comforting a leprosy patient on his knee, placed in 1976 at the Holy Rosary Church in Pā'ia, Maui. Many years later, a plaster statue of Damien was placed at Maria Lanakila Church in Lahaina, and a koa version at St. Theresa Church, in Ha'ikū, Maui. A cast bronze bust of Damien was created for placement at St. Benedict's (Painted Church) in Captain Cook, Hawai'i. Damien was canonized a saint in 2009. The busts and statues as well as stained glass windows, murals, and paintings are located at numerous places on Maui, Hawaiʻi, and Oʻahu—all places where he served prior to his final mission at Kalaupapa.

The first Cope statues came much later, with two erected in 2010 on Oʻahu sponsored by the Sisters of St. Francis. In 2022 a bronze statue of Cope was placed at the University of Hawaiʻi at Maui School of Nursing. Cope was the first nurse and opened the first hospital on Maui. The statue is a testimony to the reverence felt for Sister Marianne 100 years after her death. She had become a saint ten years earlier in 2012. Again, the connection is clear between place, statues, and points of reverence.

Theme 5: Interest in Statues and Memorials Honoring Immigrants and Workers

Immigrants played a major role in the evolution of Hawaiian history. This is more evident on the neighbor islands than on Oʻahu. Successive generations, proud of their contributions, believed it is important to honor their cultural roots. The immigrant workers who came between 1840 and 1920 are honored for their hard work and for the values which they passed on to next generations. Jan Gordon Fisher's sculpture piece that honors plantation workers (1965, Koloa, Kauaʻi) commissioned by the Hawaiian Sugar Planters Association is the best expression of the collective interest and respect.

Future generations of immigrants honored their ancestors and also their home country heroes, including Jose Rizal and Sun Yat-sen. The Jose Rizal (Filipino national hero) statue is found in Līhuʻe, Kauaʻi, and a bust at Kepaniwai Park on Maui. Sun Yat-sen statues on Maui are found at Kepaniwai Park and at Sun Yat-sen Park in Kula along with busts of him in Lahaina and at Kepaniwai. There is a statue of his brother Sun Mei, who lived for many years in Maui and helped fund Sun Yat-sen's revolutionary activities. Oʻahu has multiple statues and busts of Rizal and Sun Yat-sen.

Among the many unique memorial collections dating back several generations are three quite different miniature versions of the 88 Temples in Shikoku, a famous pilgrimage destination in Japan. The Shikoku temples are located around the island covering nearly 750 miles and offer pilgrimage of peace and reflection. Immigrants from Japan duplicated the concept in unique ways, covering no more than an acre on each site near a temple. In Lāwaʻi, individual miniature temples nestle along a winding footpath on a steep vegetated cliff. The version in Paʻauilo also shows individual temples, but they are aligned in straight rows, again on an embankment. The version in Waimea is much different. The 88 statues are contained within bullet-shaped encasements. The original set, much deteriorated, sits beside a newer version, both in straight lines.

Another unique setting for peace and reflection is at the Hindu Monastery in Kapaʻa, Kauaʻi. Covering 382 acres and anchored by the Kadavul and the San Marga Iraivan Temples, the Monastery welcomes visitors at limited time periods and to most parts of the grounds. Despite Hawaiʻi's relatively small Hindu population, the Monastery is home to Hindi pilgrims from around the world. A favorite place at the Academy is an assemblage of statues that honor the Shiva workers who toiled using traditional methods and tools to make the Temples.

Ranching and paniolo culture occur on all islands. The (2003) cowboy statue of Ikua Purdy in Waimea, Hawaiʻi, is probably the largest statuary piece in Hawaiʻi at 27 feet. It includes bronze plaques showing the cattle branding symbols and names of ranches from around the state. Many of the paniolo were Hawaiians or of Portuguese heritage.

Are Statues and Monuments Still Relevant?

The short answer to this question is yes. A public sculpture has many stories to tell. The first is the concept story it commemorates. Second is the story of how it is used for visits, gatherings, or celebrations. Finally, there is the story of how it is cared for or neglected. All are reflections of the community and how it changes over time.

Many of Hawai'i's statues are regular and ongoing sites for ceremonies and lei draping, and it is common to find statues with either a lei or a flower attached. Birthdays are celebrated, parades are staged, official song and dance programs held. Some figures are marked by state holidays (Kamehameha Day, Kūhiō Day). When events at memorials are repeated each year on special dates, these become social customs and traditions for those who gather. These ceremonies reinforce culture and history and indicate that, in Hawai'i, statues are still relevant.

Statues present opportunities for knowledge transfer and learning, both direct and indirect. When celebrations are held at statues, they become a "life experience" for a younger generation to learn from their elders. Speeches and rites are handed down from an authority who explains their interpretation and the lessons to be learned. Younger members can ask questions, compare themselves to others, and use their own reasoning to assess what is important and valued. It comes full circle when they become the elder generation and can decide what and how they will pass on lessons.

Further demonstration that statues are still relevant in Hawai'i is that they continue to be commissioned and installed. The desire to continue the tradition of erecting sculpture of local heroes is amply displayed in the late twentieth and early twenty-first century. There were more than a dozen statues made since 2000, most by local artists. Sculpture form has ignited the imagination of artists such as Sean Browne, Kim Duffett, Holly Young, Dale Zarrella, and Karen Lucas. These are serious and dedicated artists who studied local history and are willing to make their work affordable so it can be placed in the public domain. The State Foundation on Culture and the Arts not only contributes because it owns and maintains major statuary pieces through the Art in Public Places Program, but also through the Artist-In-Residence program.

Collectors have certainly added greatly to the tradition of sculpture, introducing local people to their beauty. Previously mentioned locations of major collections include King Kamehameha Golf Course on Maui, as well as Na 'Āina Kai and the Hindu Monastery on Kaua'i. School groups make regular visits to see their impressive collections and to learn more history. Other private collectors include churches and hotels. Some hotels have even created their own artist-in-residence programs.

Clearly, the sainthood of Damien and Marianne just after the turn of the century brought an interest in statues and memorials honoring them, especially on Maui. Moloka'i and Kalaupapa are a part of Maui, so this is expected. What is not expected is the variety of poses and materials used. The major Damien memorial is on Moloka'i at the Kalaupapa settlement and it can be expected that these memorials, and access to them, will be improved since it is now officially the Kalaupapa National Historical Park.

Impediments to having more statues and memorials include money and competition with other art forms for presenting stories. One such competitor is building murals, which in recent years have started depicting historical Hawai'i scenes and people. These are less in cost, perhaps reach the same number of people, but are less permanent, subject to demolition and peeling over time.

Many in younger generations prefer media presentation, videos and the like, and more contemporary subjects and figures. Statue controversy has led some to encourage theme-based sculpture over specific persons. But this only shifts the debate. The stories will continue for who gets to choose what is represented in the public realm, as well as what history is to be portrayed. We are all a part of that story.

How Statues Help Create a Sense of Place

Reflecting on the ways that statues and monuments have created a sense of place in communities around the islands, one sees several different presentations that help bond people to each other, their history, and place. As discussed previously in these pages, the landmarks can create gathering places where people celebrate not only the statuary figure, but its relationship to their community and its values. This happens in dozens of locations on each island.

Dominant Regional setting. These can be seen from a distance, with major entrances and signage. This description would apply to the Kamehameha statue in Hilo and to the Kaumualiʻi statue in Waimea, Kauaʻi. The spatial settings of these are state parks: Waiola Park in Hilo, and Pāʻulaʻula in Waimea. Here the parks have been upgraded to make them more special, using landscaping and providing suitable parking for persons to get out and explore.

Dominant Town setting. This is where the statue features are among the elements that define and describe that common history. Example of this is the paniolo statue and accompanying ranch branding symbols in the center of Waimea town, Hawaiʻi island.

Institutional and Building settings. This is where the statue reinforces that this is a special place. This can occur at government buildings such as with the Kamehameha statue at the (former) county courthouse in Kapaʻau and the Kaumualiʻi statue in front of Kauaʻi Museum in Līhue. It may occur in front of a school such as Kamakahelei in Puhi, Kauaʻi, and Kamehameha III in Lahaina, Maui. It may occur at religious sites such as the statues of Shinran Shonin at Buddhist Temples or the statues of saints and Damien at Catholic Churches. And it may occur at hotels or shopping centers such as the Kaʻahumanu in Kahului, the Kamehameha statue at Grand Wailea Hotel, and the Liliʻuokalani statue at Fairmont Hotel, all on Maui.

Small Urban Parks. Small parks have made excellent setting for status and memorials and help define such locales. Examples include the Captain James Cook statue at Hofgaard Park in Waimea, Kauaʻi; the Kalākaua statue at the park of the same name in Hilo; the Kūhiō Memorial in Kōloa; and the statues of the two brothers at Sun Yat-sen Park in Kula, Maui.

Stand-Alone Assemblages and Collections. These use statuary elements with landscape to create a unique environment for the pleasure of visitors. Two important collections and assemblages of statuary figures on Kauaʻi are at the Kauaʻi Himalayan Academy and Na ʻĀina Kai. Each has multiple pieces made by many artists. Both of these are private collections. Na ʻĀina Kai is open to visitors for a fee; the Himalayan Academy welcomes visitors to some portions of their vast property.

On Maui, the collection location is Kepaniwai Heritage Park in Wailuku. Kepaniwai presents a collection of ethnic villages including a Hawaiian hale (now dismantled), the home of a New England missionary; and sections for each major immigrant group that came to Kaua'i: Japanese contract laborers, Portuguese, Chinese, Filipino, Korean, plus the New England missionaries. The villages include representations of houses, gardens, some historical figure statues or busts, and explanatory bronze plaques. First established in 1952, the villages have had many additions, including markers of 50th, 75th, 100th anniversaries of that immigrant coming.

Community members help create and preserve their sense of place. Outdoor sculpture can be victim to pollution (acid rain), weather (storms and hurricanes), vandalism, and accidents. Statues and memorials must be maintained and when necessary, restored using proper conservation methods. In extreme cases, they may be forgotten, overgrown, and waiting to be rediscovered. Proper restorative care may involve cleaning, re-patination of the color, coating with protective wax, reapplying gold-leaf, and/or replacing missing parts. The State Foundation on Culture and the Arts has an ongoing program to inspect and maintain its statues.

In 1998, the King Kamehameha statue in Kapa'au received a Conservation Treatment Award with funding from the Heritage Preservation, Target, and the National Endowment of the Arts, one of 123 awarded nationally. Conservator Glenn Wharton led a community process that decided to keep the painted look of the statue; it was rededicated in June 2001.

Statues on the National Stage

In the wider world of sculpture, the period following the death of George Floyd (May 2020) precipitated not only the Black Lives Matters movement, but an active reckoning of its past and the removal of offensive statues (especially, but not only, Confederate-based) throughout the United States.

In December 2022, the City of Richmond, Virginia, the capital of the Confederacy during the Civil War, removed its last city-owned Confederate statue, the end of the removal process that lasted two years. Both the statue of Confederate General A.P. Hill and the base were removed by city crews. These statues were erected decades after the Civil War ended, in the "Lost Cause" movement that sought to (falsely) portray the southern cause as a noble rebellion to defend states' rights, rather than the battle over slavery that many believe it was.

The Southern Poverty Law Center tracks and produces an annual report on the status of nearly 800 confederate monuments. In 2020, there were 157 confederate memorials removed in the United States, and in 2021 another seventy-three. The US House of Representatives in 2021 voted to remove ten state statues from the National Statuary Hall collection. Florida has already removed the Edmund Kirby Smith statues and replaced it with black educator and civil rights activist Mary McLeod Bethune in July 2022; this is the first statue of a black leader in the Hall. Legislators in Louisiana, Mississippi, South Carolina, Georgia, Alabama, Arkansas, North Carolina, and West Virginia are passing legislation for their replacement choices.

Similar removal stories are happening in countries around the world in an effort to confront and reconcile colonialism, invasions, and other historic events imposed on native populations.

Hawai'i's reconciliation movement has called for the removal of two pieces: McKinley statue on O'ahu and the Cook obelisk on Hawai'i island. McKinley was US President at the time of annexation (1898) under the Newlands Resolution. Cook obelisk is at the site of his death where he had disrespected native people and customs. Neither movement has reached a critical point, but anticipate continued dialogue on each of these pieces.

Efforts to correct histories and tell it in Indigenous, non-Western, terms do exist in Hawai'i. Two examples make the point. First, the statues of Kaumuali'i. The people of Kaua'i have fought to honor their last king and to tell his story in their own terms, not through an O'ahu-centric lens. The name of the State Park has been changed from Russian Fort (or Fort Elizabeth) to Pā'ula'ula, its traditional name. New interpretive signage is being made to show this was the home and political base of Kaumuali'i.

Second example, the statue of Kamehameha made for a hotel on Kaua'i was refused by the people of Kaua'i in 1960s to acknowledge that the island was never conquered by him. The statue was stored for thirty years. It was moved to Hilo in 1997 upon request of Kamehameha Schools Alumni Group. It was warmly welcomed by the home island of Kamehameha.

Commentaries on current events and new interpretations of history can take many forms: street art and graffiti, murals on buildings, comedienne sketches, documentaries, traveling exhibits. In 2021, an outdoor public exhibit opened in New York Union Square. It showed busts of George Floyd, Breonna Taylor, and civil rights activist John Lewis who had died that year. The busts were made by Chris Carnabuci for Confront Arts exhibition called "Seeinjustice." The distinctive head pieces ranging in height from four to six feet, were made using computerized 3D models to create over 200 stacked layers, then painted with metallic bronze paint. The Taylor statue was later sold at a charity auction.

Around the world there are continual efforts to confront and reconcile difficult histories. My husband and I visited a museum in Budapest, Hungary, which is a repository of statues from their Soviet and Communist eras that had been removed. A similar museum of removed statues exists in Berlin, Germany. The People's Friendship Arch in Kyiv, Ukraine, overlooking the Dnieper River, opened in 1981 to commemorate USSR and Ukrainian ties. Under the arch is a statue of a Russian and a Ukrainian worker standing together. It was dismantled in April 2022 after the Russian invasion. The Kyiv Mayor said it had lost its ideological meaning. The arch will be renamed and become a new monument.

One of the counter arguments against removing statues is that this "erases history" or "tampers with history." This argument does not stand up to scrutiny. Removal actually raises awareness of history, broadens the interpretation of history from a singular expression of the statue to a wider one. At least this occurs during the time of and just prior to the removal. What comes next depends on a new generation of storytellers.

An example of confronting difficult history are the Legacy Museum and the National Museum for Peace and Justice, both erected in 2018 in Montgomery, Alabama. Montgomery was the birthplace of the confederacy and also the birthplace of the civil rights movement. The Legacy

Museum presents indoor exhibits and videos to show the story of the effects of slavery and mass incarceration. The National Museum for Peace and Justice is on six acres of outdoor sculpture, art, and design to contextualize racial terror. It presents 800 six-foot monuments with names and counties etched for the lynching victims in the United States. The museum is labeled "restorative truth-telling." The folks on Kauaʻi who are working with the State of Hawaiʻi Parks Division to rename and reinterpret Pāʻulaʻula are also engaged in restorative truth-telling.

Final Reflections

Everyone remembers where they were when…Kennedy was shot, or the twin towers fell, or when the world shut down because of COVID-19 virus pandemic. These were individual and collective experiences and memories. They were also life-changing. But these are experiences of our current generation where memory is fresh. Eventually, memory will fail us too. Which of our current experiences will eventually be remembered through statues or memorials?

Conducting the research for and writing this book, as well as my previous one about Oʻahu statues, has been an enjoyable journey of discovery, reflection, and expression. I hope that it is contagious, that book clubs, parents, teachers, and others will use these books as an opportunity for historic and cultural exploration. The books can be used as a starting point for historic exploration. My intent is to write a Teacher's Guide for using the book in classroom projects. When completed, the guide will be posted at my website, www.cherylsoon.com

MAKERS

Every piece of art in the world was once a blank space that someone chose to fill with inspiration, imagination, fear, obsession, logic, love, or passion.

— Stewart Stafford

The artist sculptors described here are all creative and interesting individuals who have unique histories. Some came up with the idea and donated their work, asking no payment. Others were contracted through a commission to create and oversee the artwork. The process may have involved multiple persons assisting with details or the casting process.

The information in this chapter for the artists no longer living comes from resource books and internet information about the artist. For those living artists, in-person interviews were conducted. The interviews provided great insight into their intentions, their lives as artists, and other prominent works they completed or that are in progress. Interviews were conducted in the end of 2022 and early 2023. The artists here are listed in alphabetical order by last name. Those with an asterisk were interviewed. Photos were provided by the artist or taken by the author.

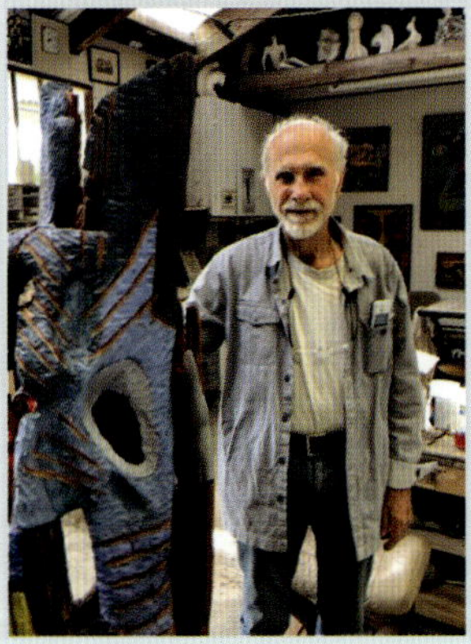

HENRY BIANCHINI* (1935-still living) created the sculpture of Kalākaua in Kalākaua Park, Hilo. Bianchini first sailed to Hawaiʻi in 1969 and upon approach saw an eruption of Maunaulu from 200 miles at sea. Shortly thereafter, he settled in Hawaiʻi. Bianchini has distinguished himself internationally as a carver, painter, and craftsman. He has earned several commissions from the State Foundation on Culture and the Arts, and received awards for his works. He works with bronze, stone, concrete, steel, ceramics, wood, clay and paper. He has installed works that are part of building and landscape designs including at the Hilo Library atrium and at the shoreline of Hilo Bay. He states, "Art is about breaking rules" which is why he loves modernism.

SEAN KEKAMAKUPAʻAIKAPONO KAʻONOHIOKALANI LEE LOY BROWNE* (1953-still living) is the creator of the Tony Kunimura Bust in Līhuʻe, and he assisted with completing the Damien statue at Painted Church in Kona. Also, on Hawaiʻi island, he created the sculptures the "Mahiole," the Helmet honoring Kamehameha at Keāhole/ Kona Airport and "Kahu o ka wai ola o Hilo," guardian of the life-giving waters of Hilo, at the Judiciary Building in Hilo. Browne created statues of Princess Pauahi, Prince Kūhiō, and King Kalākaua, all in Waikīkī.

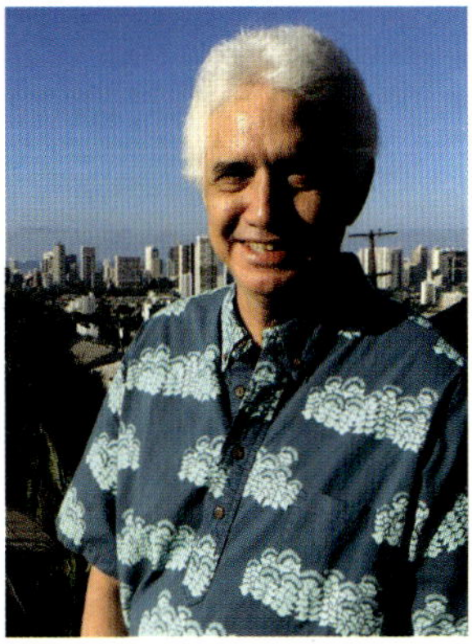

Browne was born in Hilo and attended Kamehameha Schools. He studied at the University of Redlands and then studied marble carving under Paoli Silverio in Italy. He returned to Hawaiʻi and earned an MFA in sculpture from University of Hawaiʻi. He was awarded a Fulbright Scholarship, which he used to study with Isamu Noguchi in Shikoku, Japan, who became his mentor.

Browne explains that all his work has a singular thread to Hawaiian history. As a graduate of Kamehameha, he had direct exposure to the gifts from the aliʻi, and wishes his work to honor them appropriately. His bronze, brass, granite, and marble monumental outdoor abstract sculptures can be found in public settings throughout Hawaiʻi.

SAIM CAGLAYAN* (still living) is the maker of the statue of Kaumualiʻi in Waimea. He has art galleries in California and in Kīlauea, Kauaʻi where he holds private classes and plein air painting. Born in Turkey, he came to

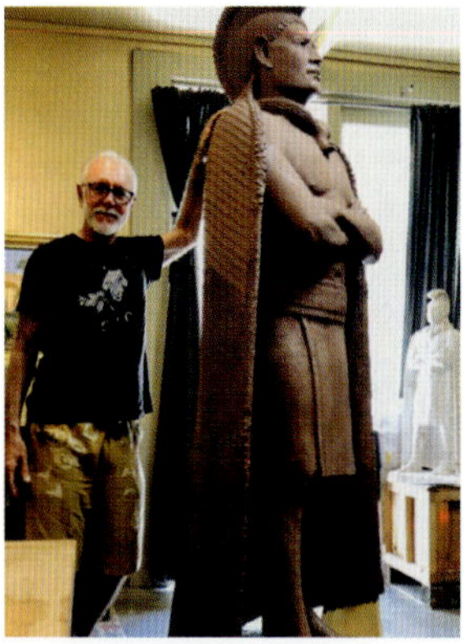

the United States in 1968. He studied Sculpture at California State, Long Beach. He has fulfilled many sculpture and painting commissions at hotels, corporate offices, hospitals.

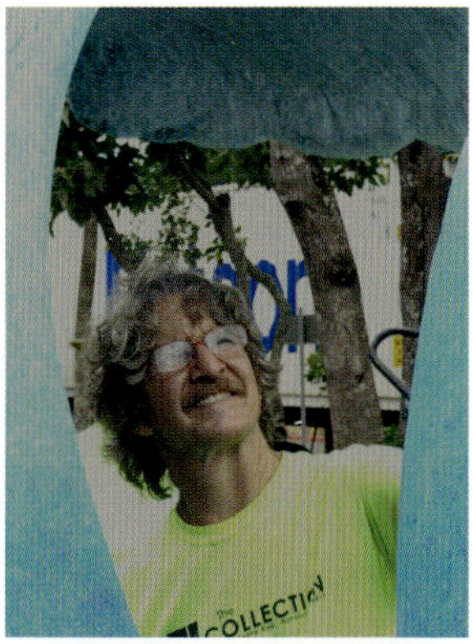

KIM DUFFETT* (1954- still living) is the creator of the Spark Matsunaga statue in Hanapēpē. He also made statues of Don Ho, Gabby "Pops" Pahinui, Alfred ʻĀpaka, and ʻIolani Luahine, all in Waikīkī and many other well-loved works such as the hula dancers at the entrance to Hilton Hawaiian Village. He also helped in several restorations, including that of Gandhi.

Duffett was born in Ohio and took to sculpting early in life by carving wooden birds. He had a formal art education and then traveled for several years in Europe before moving to Hawaiʻi in 1979. A three-year voyage through the South Pacific introduced him to carvers from that area of the world. He has been commissioned for both actual statue figures and abstract bronze cast figurines at luxury buildings, hotels, and public spaces.

The themes of his work and life beliefs are peace and ʻāina. Duffett is honored to be selected to show his work at the 2023 Biennale in Vienna. His six-foot-tall bronze is called Wahine Hapai, the Pregnant Woman.

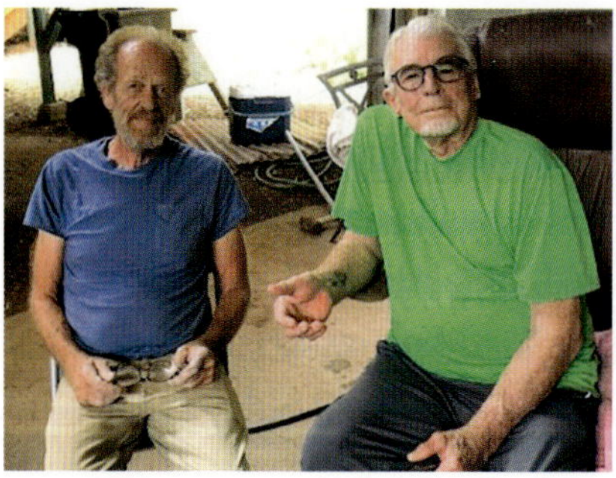

TOM FAUGHT* (1946-still living)—creator of the Kaʻahumanu statue in Kahului. He is a ceramist and sculptor living on Maui. He began his ceramics career when he was only eleven. In 1968 he established the Russian River Studio in

California and five years later in 1973 he created his studio and foundry in Maui.

His style is characterized as bold, daring, and pushing the leading edge in both design and materials (using a metalizing technique he developed). He considers making sculpture a "lesson in humility."

Faught (right in green shirt) worked on the Ka'ahumanu piece with Dan Skinner (left in blue shirt) to create the body form and face. Skinner is an accomplished artist in pottery and making lava eggs, among other pieces. Fast friends, they work together in their studio in Makawao.

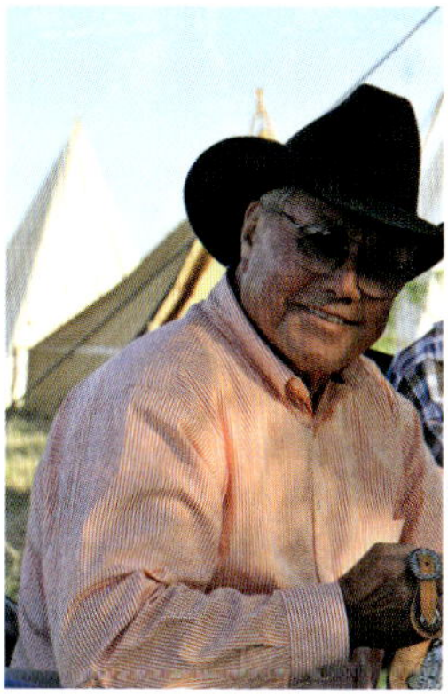

FRED FELLOWS* (1934-still living) created the statue honoring all Paniolo (featuring Ikua Purdy) in Waimea. Born in Oklahoma, he spent his early years exposed to the culture of the Otoe and Osage Native Americans. With his family, he joined the Okie exodus annually following the dust bowl trail to California. While in Oklahoma he was influenced by his grandfather who instilled an appreciate of art and museums. While in California, he learned how to handle horses, rope cattle, and build saddles. He honed his skills at Art Center in Los Angeles and worked as a commercial artist in the aircraft industry. He eventually lived in Montana for forty years. In 1969 he was invited to join the Cowboy Artists of America. His paintings, sculptures, and monuments are in permanent collections in several states Today, he lives in Arizona and visits Waimea whenever he can.

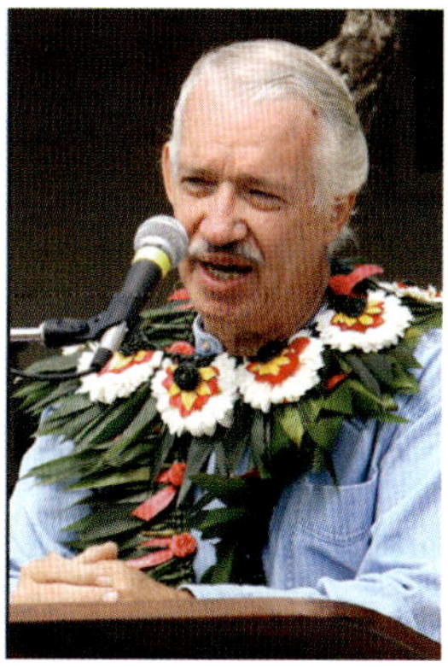

JAN GORDON FISHER (1938-2016) created the collection of figures honoring 300,000 immigrants in Kōloa. He also has statues throughout Hawai'i including Duke Kahanamoku, Princess Ka'iulani, Saint Louis IX, "Ma" Nā'oheakamalu Manuhi'i, and Robert Wilcox.

Jan Fisher was a native of California and attended Brigham Young University, graduating in 1965 with a degree in fine arts. He continued his education at Mills College in Oakland, where he studied under master Antonio Prieto. Fisher served his three years as a Mormon missionary in Sāmoa, where he first fell in love with the Polynesian people, moving to Hawaiʻi in 1970. This love continued as he served as an art professor at Brigham Young-Hawaiʻi.

Fisher was a member of the National Sculpture Society. His bronze sculpture of a Polynesian warrior ("Iosepa") is part of the monument honoring the Hawaiian community in the town of Iosepa, Utah. This warrior is meant to symbolize Joseph F. Smith, who served as a missionary in Hawaiʻi. "Iosepa" is the Hawaiian word for Joseph.

While serving as a professor at BYU-Hawaiʻi, Fisher translated his love for Polynesian people into art, often making them his subjects. He created multiple magnificent pieces for the Grand Wailea in Maui, including a spear fisherman, mermaid, and trios of male and female hula dancers. According to his obituary in *Ke Alakaʻi*, the BYU magazine, he mentored and befriended many students and left a legacy of pieces throughout Hawaiʻi. His mentee sculptor, Leroy Transfield, said upon his passing, "There was never a dull moment with the crazy guy. The longer I live, the more I understand and appreciate him, his contradictions, crazy experiences, and his unselfish generosity."

THOMAS RIDGEWAY GOULD (1818—1881) a Boston businessman who turned sculptor, created the statue of Kamehameha I. He did not become a neo-classical sculptor until reaching his fifties. He worked in Boston and Florence, Italy, making sculptures, portrait busts, medallions, and a bust of Emerson for Harvard University Library. His collection of seven marble, larger-than-life carvings were displayed at the 1876 Philadelphia Centennial Exposition to much acclaim.

Murry Gibson commissioned Gould for the sculpture of Kamehameha and the two work closely on the effort over several years. Gould was also commissioned to create the relief tablets on the base but died before they were finished. The work was completed by his son.

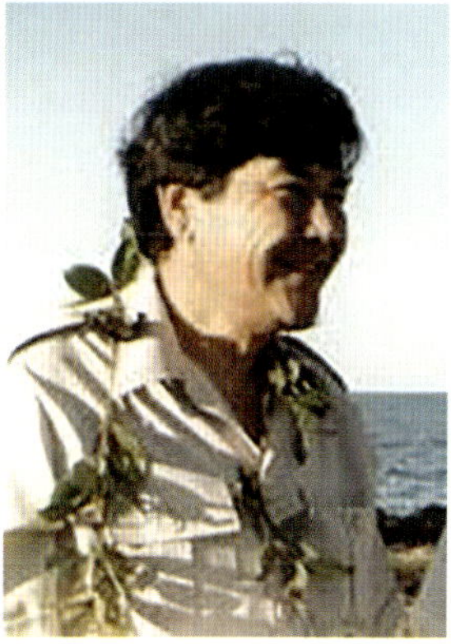

HERBERT KAWAINUI KĀNE (1928-2011), creator of the Kamehameha I statue in Wailea. Kāne, a celebrated and revered local figure is considered a principal in the renaissance of Hawaiian culture in the 1970s. He helped to found the Polynesian Voyaging Society and helped to design the voyaging canoe, *Hōkūle'a*, which he was the first captain in 1975. He is known for his Hawaiian historical and cultural paintings and writings.

Kāne studied at the School of the Art Institute in Chicago and at the University of Chicago. His career spanned advertising, publishing art, architectural design, painting, writing and sculpture. His work is in many private collections, the State Foundation on Culture and the Arts, National Park Service, National Geographic. He designed seven postage stamps for the US Postal Service. He resided for many years in rural South Kona. Kāne was named a Living Treasure of Hawai'i in 1987. He received many awards and honorary degrees during his lifetime.

KAREN LUCAS is the creator of the Kamakahelei statue in Puhi which was completed when she was artist-in-residence with the State Foundation on Culture and the Arts. Karen was born in Milwaukee, Wisconsin and arrived in Hawai'i in 1991. Her preferred mediums include figurative bronze casting, ceramic and glass mosaics, oil on canvas, ceramic and cast glass.

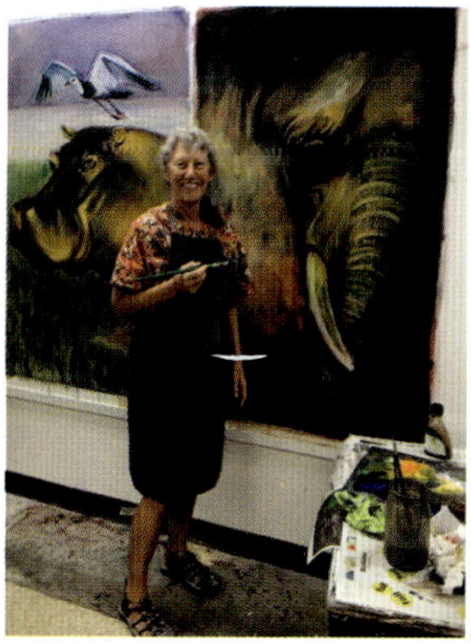

Karen served as an art therapist for Hospice Hawai'i. Until 2017, she was a lecturer at University of Hawai'i. Lucas holds a deep interest in Kalaupapa and has created many mosaics for churches in the islands.

She has had many other commissions for the State Foundation at public schools and private commissions with private schools and churches.

Her most recent piece is two glass tile mosaics commissioned from Honolulu Area Rapid Transit for the floor at the Hoʻopili Rail Station.

BOB PASHBY (1925-2005)—was a sculptor and mold-maker who worked on the Damien bust in Captain Cook, which was completed by Sean Browne. Pashby is best known for the popular sculpture, "Surfer in a wave" on the intersection of Kalākaua and Monsarrat near Queen's Surf Beach in Waikīkī beach (installed 2003). His memorial service was held there.

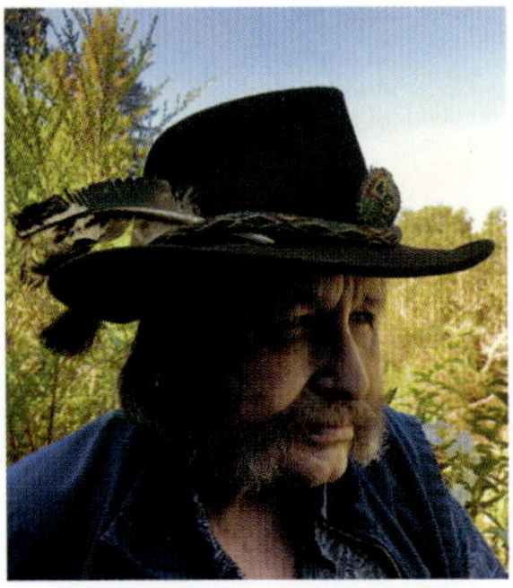

DON RICH (1941-2022) is responsible for the Richard Kawakami Bust. Don was born on an Indian reservation, where, at a young age, he was taught how to forge nails by his blacksmith father. His knowledge of metals grew. He moved to San Francisco area to study at the College of Arts and Crafts where he received a degree in sculpture. From there, he traveled to Pietrasanta, Italy to study the technique of Lost Wax Casting, a practice be brought back to the Bay Area. After returning to San Francisco, Rich opened the renowned Berkeley Art Foundry, where he cast the Kawakami bust. He worked with bronze and owned the Don Rick Studios until his death in 2022.

DR. FRED SORIANO (1945-2021) is the creator of the Sakada memorial to Filipino immigrants. Soriano was an artist/stone sculptor and an educator. He taught cultural anthropology at University of Hawaiʻi at Hilo.

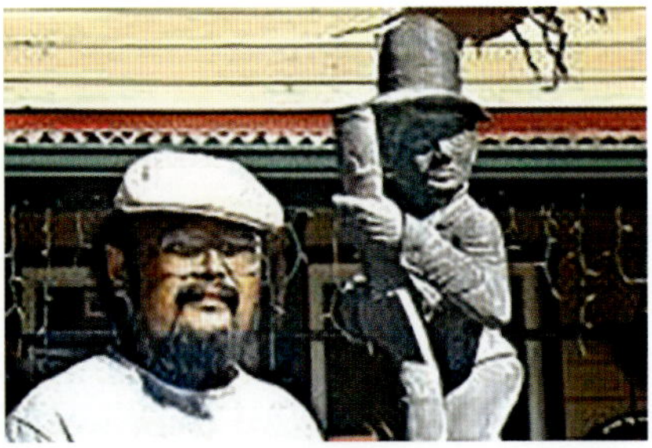

Born and raised in Pāhala, Soriano was the son of sugar immigrants from the Philippines. His research contributed to Hawaiʻi social issues of migration, immigration, and the end of the sugar era on Hawaiʻi Island.

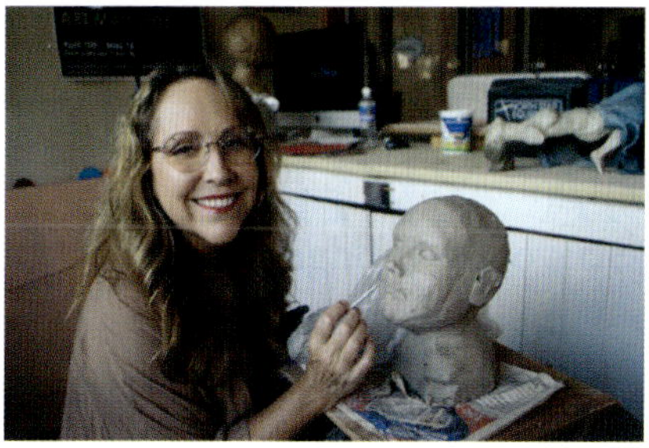

CHRISTINE TURNBULL* (still living) is the creator of the Kamehameha III bust at the school by the same name in Lahaina and the oldest elementary school west of the Mississippi. She considers this her most important piece to date and is proud to have her children and future family generations see this piece.

Surrounded and inspired by art her entire life, Christine moved to Maui with her husband, a fellow sculptor. They run their own gallery studio in Kahakuloa.

Christine began creating sculpture after the birth of her first son, twenty-four years ago. She has had several private commissions throughout the United States and her work has been shown at the Witte Museum and DoSeum Museum in San Antonio, TexasImua Family Services in Kahului, Maui and Charlie Naylor Recovery Center in Portland, Oregon, all display public works of life-size children.

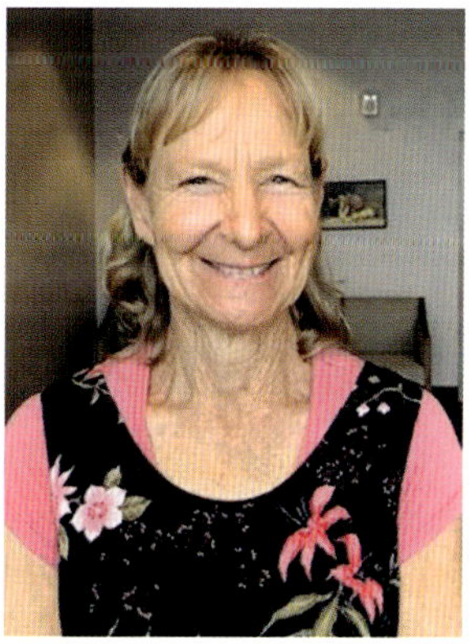

HOLLY YOUNG* (1957-still living) is the creator of the Craftsmen with Shiva. She also completed numerous other pieces at the Hindu Academy in Kapaʻa including the Hindu Hanuman monkey god statue, and other Hindu deities, the temple craftsmen, and other bronze works. She recently completed the series of 32 reliefs that line the perimeter of the temple there. Holly's work also figures prominently at Na ʻĀina Kai in Kīlauea where she is responsible for the statues of founders Ed and Joyce Doty. Holly completed figures for two of the cultural villages and other figures and birds in the sculpture garden.

Young's statue of Patsy Mink sits in front of the State Library and her statue of Queen Kapiʻolani is in Waikīkī.

Educated as a chemist, Holly consulted for a wide variety of industries such as writing recipes for commercial "green" (low solvent) paints and assisting the Bristol Museum with the preservation of nineteenth century paintings and cannon balls dredged from the English Channel. She moved to Colorado to follow a Hindu teacher, and while there, worked in a foundry, where she served as their resident artist. Becoming a sculptor was the next natural step for her when she moved to Hawai'i for religious and lifestyle reasons.

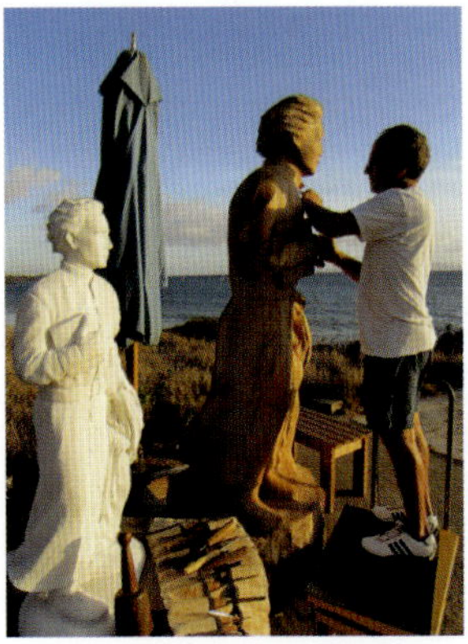

DALE ZARRELLA* (1961-still living) is the creator of the Queen Lili'uokalani (and other outdoor sculptures) at the Fairmont Hotel in Maui. He also has several carved koa pieces of royalty at the King Kamehameha Golf Course Clubhouse. Zarrella is well known for his statues of Saints Damien and Marianne including those at several churches and UH Maui College. One version of his Damien statue was given to Pope Benedict XVI after Damien was made a saint, with copies at the North American College in Rome and at St. John's Seminary in Camarillo, California.

Zarrella moved to Hawai'i at age 23 and after eight years conducting turtle research at Black Sand Beach in Hawai'i, he now resides on Maui. He is currently artist in residence at the Fairmont Kea Lani Hotel. His interest in Damien began with the urging of his father's first cousin, Fr. Alphonse Zarrella, Vice Rector of the oldest seminary in the world in Louvin, Belgium, where Damien was born and is buried.

GLOSSARY OF HAWAIIAN TERMS & PHRASES

ahupuaʻa	Land division typically extending from uplands to the sea
ʻahu ʻula	Feather cape
ʻai kapu	Forbidden eating practices
ʻāina	Land
aliʻi	Chief, Chiefess, noble, royalty
aliʻi nui	Ruling chief
aloha	Love, affection, compassion, mercy, sympathy, pity, kindness, sentiment, grace, charity; a greeting, salutation, regards
ʻamaʻama	A fish, also called mullet
hānai	Informal adoption arrangement of children in Hawaiian culture
heiau	Temple, ancient site for religious ceremony and prayer
hoʻokupu	Offering
kāʻei	Belt, sash, baldric; a baldric is usually used to hold a sword in place
kalo	Taro (*Colocasis esculento*) a staple food crop of Native Hawaiian people
kamaʻāina	One who has lived in Hawaiʻi for a long time
kanaka	Person of Hawaiian ancestry
kapu	Sacred injunctions that defined proper behavior. Kapu were in effect in the presence of aliʻi
kauhale	Home
keiki kapa moe	Baby blanket
kōkua	Help or helper; title given to family members who accompanied leprosy patients to Kalaupapa to care for them.
kuhina nui	Akin to regent or co-ruler. Political position that shared ruling powers. Position was eliminated in 1864.
Kumulipo	Origin; Name of a Hawaiian creation chant
kupuna	Elder/Elders
lei niho palaoa	Pendant often holding a hook shaped from ivory or coral and suspended by braided human hair. This was a Hawaiian neck ornament worn by chiefs of both sexes.
lua	Also spelled kuʻialua; ancient Hawaiian martial art based on bone breaking, joint locks, throws and other pressure strikes
luakini	Sacrificial heiau

luna	Bosses or supervisors on plantations
mahiole	Hawaiian feather helmet
Makahiki	Harvest festivities
malo	Loincloth
mele	Hawaiian song
mōʻī	Reigning sovereign, monarch, king or queen
moʻolelo	Story
nūpepa	Newspaper
paʻa kāhili	Kahili (feather standard) bearer
palaka	Literally, "frock." Connotes a popular cross striped pattern cloth worn by plantation workers and paniolo, initially in button-up long-sleeved shirts, but later in many types of clothing.
palaoa	Whale tooth neck pendant, usually hung by braided human hair
paniolo	Hawaiian Cowboy
pāʻū	Decorative clothing worn by female horsewomen, originally intended to protect under clothing. Made famous by Pāū riders in parades.
pū kaua	Leader, in particular a war general
Pāʻulaʻula	Red Enclosure. Name of the State Park in Waimea, Kauaʻi
tsunami	Series of extremely long waves caused by a large and sudden displacement on the ocean, usually the result of an earthquake.
ʻukulele	ʻUku (flea) + lele (jumping); Instrument adapted from Portuguese, widely used in and associated with Hawaiian music.
waʻa peleleu	Very large canoe
wahi pana	Sacred place
wahoo	A fish, also called ono
Waiomina	Hawaiian term for Wyoming
HAWAIIAN PHRASES	
Aloha ʻOe	Farewell to Thee. Song written by Liliʻuokalani in 1878
Kānāwai Mamalahoe	"Law of the Splintered Paddle"
Maʻi Hoʻokaʻawale ʻOhana	"Family Splitting Disease." Used to define leprosy patients (later named Hansen's Disease patients.
Maikaʻi no Kauaʻi hemolele i ka mālie	Beautiful Kauaʻi, so peaceful in the calm
Maui Nō Ka ʻOi	Maui is the Best, from an old Hawaiian bragging chant

Nā Lani ʻEhā	The Heavenly Four: Kalākaua, Liliʻuokalani Leleiōkoku and Likelike, royal siblings noted for their musical prowess.
Ola Nā Moku	The Islands Prosper; written on the seal of the County of Hawaiʻi
Ua Mau ke ea o ka ʻāina i ka Pono	"The Life of the Land is Perpetuated in Righteousness" or, "The Sovereignty of the Kingdom continues because we are righteous." First spoken by Kamehameha III (1843). Currently the State motto of Hawaiʻi.
OTHER LANGUAGE	
jizu	Japanese. Markers of dangerous places
Shingon	Japanese. A Buddhist sect spread by Kobo Daishi or Kukai that emphasizes esoteric teachings, or zen practice.
Jodo Shinsu	Japanese. A Buddhist sect founded by Honen and spread by Shinran Shonin.
Shikoku	Japanese. Location of a Buddhist pilgrimage route in Japan
Hachi kasho	Japanese. Individual Buddhist monuments in 88 shrine miniature displays
Issei, Nisei, Sensei	Japanese. First, second and third generations of Japanese immigrants
Gannenmono	Japanese. First Year People, people who came from Japan in 1868
Sakada	Philippine. First generation Filipino immigrants
Vaqueros	Mexican. Cowboys who came to Hawaiʻi to teach methods of ranchIng
Silpis	India. Traditional stone sculptors, originally from India, who use hand chisels.

Year	Subject	Type	Island
1878	Captain Cook	Obelisk	Hawai'i
1883	Kamehameha Great	Bronze	Hawai'i
1893	Damien Memorial	Rose granite	Moloka'i
	1900-1950		
1904	Paul Isenberg	Medallion on stone	Kaua'i
1907	Sacred Heart of Jesus	Bronze	Moloka'i
1911	Rice Family Memorial	Carved Stone	Kaua'i
1911	Kamehameha III Birthplace	Marker	Hawai'i
1915	Ishidoro Lantern	Stone Lantern	Kaua'i
1918	Christ with Saint Francis	White stone statue	Moloka'i
1919	Saint Anthony of Padua	White Stone	Maui
1925	William Hyde Rice	Medallion on stone	Kaua'i
1928	Ka'ahumanu Birthplace	Bronze plaque	Maui
1928	Captain James Cook— "First Encounter"	Fiberglass	Kaua'i
1930	Colonel Zephaniah Spalding	Medallion on stone	Kaua'i
1934	David Douglas Memorial	Bronze Plaque	Hawai'i
1947	Tsunami of 1946	Plaque on concrete	Kaua'i
	1950-2000		
1961	Japanese Immigration Commemoration	Pagoda and plaque	Kaua'i
1965	Sesquicentennial Sugar Plantation Immigrants	Bronze set	Kaua'i
1969	George Vancouver	Stone with plaques	Maui
1970	Shinran Shonin	Bronze	Kaua'i
1976	American Bicentennial	Bronze plaque on rock	Hawai'i
1976	Damien with Leper	White marble	Maui
1979	Damien	Bronze	Kamalō Moloka'i
1979	Jose Rizal	Bronze bust	Maui
1980	Damien	Bronze	Maui
1981	Chaminade	White stone	Maui

Location	Commission	Artist
Captain Cook-Ka‘awaloa	Gift of British	Unknown
Kapa‘au, Kohala	Kingdom of Hawai‘i	Thomas Gould
Kalaupapa	People of England (Edward III)	Edward Clifford
Rice Street	“Kaua‘i Friends”	Unknown
St. Francis Church	Unknown	Unknown
Kaua‘i Cemetery in Puhi	Families	Stephen Sindring
Kealakekua Bay Captain Cook-Ka‘awalo	Unknown	Unknown
Kapa‘a Park	2018 Restored by County of Kaua‘i	Unknown
Marianne Cope memorial & gravesite	Patients of Kalaupapa	Unknown
Wailuku St. Anthony Church	Church	Unknown
Kīpū	Private	Unknown
Hana Harbor	County Maui DPW	Unknown
Waimea	State Foundation Culture & Arts	Replica of Sir John Tweed
Upper Kapa‘a	Private	Unknown
Maunakea Slopes	Hilo Burns Club	Unknown
Laupāhoehoe Point	Community	Unknown
Civic Center	Gift of Japanese government	Unknown
Koloa	Sugar Planters Association	Jan Gordan Fisher
Ma‘alaea Harbor	County & Canadian Gov’t	Unknown
Waimea Honpa Hongwanji	Rev. & Mrs. Takanobu Koizumi	Unknown
Lili‘uokalani Gardens, Hilo	County of Hawai‘i	Unknown
Pā‘ia Holy Rosary Church	Church parish	Purchase
St. Joseph Church	Unknown	Unknown
Kepaniwai Park	AB & Frances Sevilla	Laoag, Philippines
St. Anthony Church, interior	Parishioners	Jean Charlot
St. Anthony School	Alumni	Unknown

Year	Subject	Type	Island	
1981	Scandinavian Monument	Bronze plaque on stone	Maui	
c1984	John Thomas Waterhouse	Bronze plaque on stone	Kaua'i	
1984 & 1998	Camp Tarawa	1984 Brass plaque 1998 Granite panels	Hawai'i	
1985	Shinran Shonin	Bronze	Hawai'i	
1988	King Kalākaua	Bronze	Hawai'i	
1988	Richard Kawakami Bust	Bronze	Kaua'i	
1988 & 1997	Jose Rizal	Bronze	Kaua'i	
Late 1980s	Father Damien	Bust	Hawai'i	
1990	King Kamehameha	Bronze	Maui	
1991	Plantation	Bell Tower & plaque	Hawai'i	
1992	Albert Lyman	Medallion cameo	Hawai'i	
1995	Queen Ka'ahumanu	Bronze	Maui	
1995	Damien	Bronze bust	Moloka'i	
1995	Tsunami of 1960	Clock & exhibits	Hawai'i	
1997	Kamehameha I	Bronze	Hawai'i	
1997	Jose Protacio Rizal*	Bronze	Kaua'i	
	2000-present			
2000	Tony Kunimura Bust	Bronze	Kaua'i	
2001	Prince Kūhiō	Bust	Kaua'i	
2003	Hawaiian Cowboy, Ikua Purdy	Bronze	Hawai'i	
2003	Chiefess Kamakahelei	Bronze	Kaua'i	
2004	High Chief & Chiefess of Maui	Koa	Maui	
c. 2004	Maryanne Kusaka	Plaque	Kaua'i	
2005	Sakada	Concrete statue	Kea'au Hawai'i	
2006	Craftsmen with Shiva Siddhaata	Bronze set	Kaua'i	
2007	Shugyo Daishi	Bronze	Hawai'i	
2008	Spark Matsunaga "Walking in the Garden"	Bronze statue pair	Kaua'i	
2010	Masaru "Purdy" Yokouchi	Cast Bronze	Maui	

Location	Commission	Artist
near McGregor Lighthouse	Scandinavian Centennial Committee	Unknown
Kīpū Kai	Private	Unknown
Parker Ranch Waimea	Community	Unknown
Hilo Betsuin	Betty, Harriet, Susan Takeda	Unknown
Hilo, Kalākaua Park	County of Hawai'i	Henry Bianchini
Līhu'e Airport Outside	State Foundation on Culture & Arts	Don Rich
Civic Grounds (replaced 1997)*	Kaua'i Filipino Community Assoc	Unknown
Captain Cook	St. Benedict (Painted Church)	B. Pashby & Sean Browne
Grand Wailea Hotel	Grand Wailea	Herb Kāne
Main Street, Hilo	Unknown	Unknown
Hilo Airport	State Foundation Culture & Arts	Unknown
Līhu'e	Queen Ka'ahumanu Shopping Center	Tom Faught
St. Philomena	Artist donation	Karen Lucas
Hilo	Community	Unknown
Hilo	Private	R. Sadrin
Līhu'e Civic	Private	Unknown
Līhu'e Civic Center	County of Kaua'i	Sean Browne
Kōloa	Royal Order of Kamehameha, Chapter III	Julius Rosenstein
Waimea	Paniolo Preservation Society	Fred Fellows
Middle School in Puhi	State Foundation Culture & Arts	Karen Lucas
Wailuku	Kamehameha Golf Course	Dale Zarrella
Līhu'e Civic	County of Kaua'i	Unknown
Kea'au Center	WH Shipman, LTD	Dr. Fred Soriano
Kapa'a	Kaua'i Hindu Monastery	Holly Young
Hilo	Hilo Hooganji Mission	Unknown
Hanapēpē	Storybook Theatre	Kim Duffett
Maui Arts and Culture Center	MACC	Sean Browne

Year	Subject	Type	Island	
2010 & 2019	Ed and Joyce Doty "The Founders"	Bronze set	Kaua'i	
2011	Sun Yat-sen	Bronze	Maui	
2011	Sun Yat-sen	Bronze	Maui	
2012	Sun Yat-sen	Bust	Maui	
2013	Sun Mei	Bronze	Maui	
2013	Brother Joseph Dutton	Marble	Moloka'i	
2013	Kamehameha III	Bust	Maui	
2015	Saint Damien	Plaster	Maui	
2016	Saint Damien	Koa wood	Maui	
2018	Queen Lili'uokalani	Bronze	Maui	
c2018	Saint Damien Saint Marianne Cope	Curly Koa Monkeypod	O'ahu	
2019	Chipper Wichman	Bronze bust	Kaua'i	
2021	Kaumuali'i	Bronze	Kaua'i	
2022	Ali'i A'imoku Kaumuali'i & Wahine Kekahakua	Fabricated	Kaua'i	
2022	Saint Marianne Cope	Bronze	Maui	
	DATES UNKNOWN			
	Shinran Shonin	Bronze	Hawai'i	
	Shinran Shonin	Bronze	Maui	
	Shinran Shonin	Bronze	Maui	
	Saint Benedict	White stone	Hawai'i	
	Kannon	Stone statue	Kaua'i	
	Saint Damien	Bronze	Moloka'i	

Location	Commission	Artist
Kīlauea	Na ʻĀina Kai Botanical Gardens & Sculpture Park	Holly Young
Kēōkea, Sun Yat-sen Park	Sun Yat-sen Foundation	China
Kepaniwai Park	Sun Yat-sen Foundation	China
Wo Hing Museum, Lahaina	Sun Yat-sen Foundation	China
Kēōkea, Sun Yat-sen Park	Sun Yat-sen Foundation	China
St. Joseph Church	John Perreira & Larry Helm	Carved in China
Kamehameha III School	School community	Christine Turnbull
Maria Lanakila Church, Lahaina	Church community	Unknown
Kīhei	St. Theresa Church	Dale Zarrella
Fairmont Kea Lani Wailea	Fairmont Hotel	Dale Zarrella
Education Center, Waikiki	Artist donation	Dale Zarrella
Nat. Tropical Botanical Garden	Thomas S. Kenan III	J. Brett Grill
Waimea	State Foundation Culture & Arts	Saim Caglayan
Līhuʻe	Kauaʻi Museum	White Clouds, Co
UH Maui College, School of Nursing	UH Maui	Dale Zarrella
Puna Hongwanji	Unknown	Unknown
Lahaina Hongwanji Mission	Unknown	Unknown
Wailuku Hongwanji Mission	Unknown	Unknown
Captain Cook	Unknown	Unknown
Hanapēpē	Kauaʻi Soto Zen	Unknown
Kaunakakai Settlement	Unknown	Unknown

REFERENCES

Adamski, Mary. "View from the Pew: Peace of Mind." *Star Bulletin*. September 20, 2008.

Azambuja, Leo, "Chiefess Kamakalelei, Alii Nui o Kauai. *For Kauai Online*. March 1, 2017.

Beers, Axel. "Honoring Sun Mei in Kēōkea." *Maui Time*. June 6, 2013.

Bergin, Billy. *Loyal to the Land: The Legendary Parker Ranch* (4 volumes). University of Hawai'i Press. 2003.

Boden, Sabrina. "Kealaula at Pua Loke continues transitional housing goals." *The Garden Island*. October 12, 2021.

Cascone, Sarah. "An Artist's Busts of George Floyd, Breonna Taylor, and John Lewis Go Up in New York's Time Square." *Art World*. October 1, 2021.

Ching, Jodie Chiemi. "Memorials—Monuments to Remember the Gannenmono." *Hawaii Herald*. June 15, 2018.

Clark, John R. K. *Guardian of the Sea: Jizo in Hawaii*. University of Hawai'i Press. 2007.

Cook, Chris. "Paul Isenberg remembered a 100 years later." *The Garden Island*. April 18, 2004.

Cooper, George and Gavan Daws. *Land and Power in Hawaii: The Democratic Years*. University of Hawai'i Press. 1990.

Croft, Lee. *Kaumualii and the Last of Hawaii's God Kings*.

Curammeng, Kahealani Martins. *They Came in Ships to Terra Nova: Portuguese Immigration to Hawaii, 1978-1913*. 2023.

Davis, Sarah. "Mystery of Deadly 1946 Tsunami Deepens." *Live Science*. December 05, 2004.

Douglas, Dr. Busha Yip. "The Life of Dr. Sun Yat-sen: His family and connection to Maui." Private paper provided by research coordinator, Wo Hing Society, Lahaina. Written c. 2012.

Daws, Gavan. *Holy Man: Father Damien of Molokai*. University of Hawai'i Press. 1973.

Dower, Lindsey. "Lawmakers want Russian Fort Elizabeth to have a new name." *Honolulu Star Advertiser*. March 29, 2022.

Downes, Patrick. "Our Lady of Peace: the patroness of the islands lives up to her name through the likeness of a unique and historic statue." *Hawaii Catholic Herald*. June 30, 2006.

Downes, Patrick. "Mary or Marianne? Hilo or Pahoa? The tale of the mysterious statue." *Hawaii Catholic Herald*. October 26, 2022.

Dr. Sun Yat-sen Hawaii Foundation Virtual Library. "How many Sun Yat-sen statues are there in Hawaii." January 25, 2019. Accessed September 21, 2022.

Durn, Sarah. "Excavating the Hawaiian History of Kaua'i's 'Russian Fort': A rich local history has long been overshadowed by a few months under a Russian flag." *Atlas Obscura*. November 30, 2021.

Egan-Elliott, Roxanne. "Capt. James Cook statue isn't returning to Inner Harbor, pedestal to be removed." *Time Colonist*. January 28, 2022.

Erickson, Gary G. "Hawaiian Norwegians honored by a nearly invisible memorial on Maui." The Norwegian American. May 3, 2012.

Evangelista, Alfredo G. "Bahay Kubo Renovations Complete." *Fil-Am Voice*. November 19, 2021.

Fasone, Cara. "Paniolo: The Hawaiian Cowboy." *Hawaiian Culture Stories*. Ocean Cloud Media. 2012.

Fernandez-Akamine, Puanani. "Honoring Kaua'i's Peaceful King: Kaumualii Valued the Lives of His Subjects More Than His Kingdom." *Ka Wai Ola*. Vol. 38, No. 05. May 2021.

Friends of King Kaumualii. "Honoring the Legacy of Kauai's Last King." 2020.

Fong, Mele. "Hawaiian Cowboy Culture and Ikua Purdy Lives on." Blog: Ukulele mele on Maui. January 29, 2018.

Freifels, Susan. "Monument honors issei who died with descendants." *Star Bulletin*. July 12, 1999.

Fujimoto, Dennis. "West Kauai Hongwanji Mission Celebrates 25 Years." *The Garden Island*. November 14, 2022.

Fullard-Leo, Betty. "The Woman Who Changed a Kingdom." *Coffee Times*. June, 1998.

Goodhue, Thomas W. *Queen Kaahumanu of Hawaii: A Biography*. McFarland & Company. 2022.

Greguras, Fred. "Camp Tarawa Today." *Historic Hawaii Foundation*. March 15, 2017.

Harrington, Kate. "Cowboys in the Tropics: A History of the Hawaiian Paniolo." *Folklife Magazine*. February 15, 2019.

Hibbard, Don. J. "Hāmākua Jodo Mission." Society of Architectural Historians. Archipedia.

Historic Hawai'i Foundation. "Hāmākua Jodo Mission: Past, Present, and Future." HHF Website Blog. October 22, 2021 and May 26, 2022.

Historical Marker Database. Scandinavian Migration to Hawaii. August 24, 2023. Revision by Larry Wilson.

Hitt, Christine. "Kauai Museum preserves the legacy of King Kaumualii, the island's last chief." *Hawaii Magazine*. January 17, 2018.

Hoff, Amy. "Scotland and Hawai'i in History. *Coffee Times/LBD Coffee*. Fall/Winter 2005-2006.

Hussey, John A. "Waimea beach (Cook Landing Site) Nomination Form." National Historic Landmark Program. May 24, 1962.

Kakesako, Gregg K. "The Little-Known Story of the Landmarks Left by World War II Italian Prisoners of War." *Hawaii Herald*. March 28, 2018.

Kealamakia, Spencer. "Remembering the Naha Stone." *Hawai'i Magazine*. November 7, 2017.

Kennicott, Philip. "A powerful memorial in Montgomery remembers the victims of lynching." *Washington Post*. April 24, 2018.

Klieger, P. Christiaan. *Kamehameha III: King of the Hawaiian Islands, 1824-1854*. Green Arrow Press. 2015.

Kona Historical Society. *A Guide to Old Kona*. Kalukalu, Kona. 1998.

Kyodo News. "Flame from Hiroshima A-bombed ruins to light Monument in Pearl Harbor. December 2, 2021.

Lahaina News. "Maria Lanakila Church celebrates its ties to Saint Damien." December 10, 2009.

Lahaina News. "The fascinating life of Queen Kaahumanu." March 3, 2016.

Lang, Leslie. *Exploring Historic Hilo: Small Town Series, Big Island*. Watermark Publishing. 2007.

Lavoie, Denise. "Richmond, Va., removes its last city-owned Confederate statue." *Honolulu Star-Advertiser*. December 13, 2022.

LeHoven, Tony and Susan Jane. *Na Aina Kai Botanical Gardens and Sculpture Park: A Collection of Beauty*. TV Juice Productions. 2011. Book and three-part DVD series.

Lin, Sara. "A History of Tsunamis in Hawaii. *Civil Beat*. March 11, 2011.

Lyte, Brittany. "Vandals Deface Sign at Kauai's Controversial Russian Fort." *Civil Beat*. March 17, 2022.

MacKenzie, Caroline L. "Time to update the Peace Corps Act." *Honolulu Star Advertiser*. September 18, 2022.

Martin, Lynn J., Editor and Project Director. *Nā Paniolo o Hawaiʻi*. State Foundation on Culture and the Arts and Honolulu Academy of Art. ND.

Marumoto, Masaji. "Vignette of Early Hawaii-Japan Relations: Highlights of King Kalakaua's Sojourn in Japan on His Trip around the World as Recorded in His Personal Diary." ND. https://evols.library.manoa.hawaii.edu/bitstream/10524/291/JL10060.pdf

Maui Now Staff. "Maui Honors Sun Mei with Statue in Kēōkea." *Maui Now*. June 4, 2013.

Meg. "Kalualauka [Doctor's Pit] Laupahoehoe, Hawaii." *Atlas Obscura*. Posted June 2, 2017.

Mills, Peter R. Hawai'i's Russian Adventure: A New Look at Old History. University of Hawai'i Press. 2002.

Mills, Peter R. "A New View of Kaua'i as 'The Separate Kingdom' after 1810." *The Hawaiian Journal of History 30*: 91-104. 1996.

Mills, Peter R. *Hawaii's Russian Adventure: A New Look at Old History*. University of Hawai'i Press. 2002.

Molodin, Alexander, and Peter R. Mills. "Addressing Tensions between Colonial and Post-Colonial Histories: Modeling Hawaiian Fort Paulaula/Russian Fort Elizabeth, Kauai Island, Hawaii." *Asian Perspectives 60 (1)*: 2-31. Project Muse, doi:10.1353/asi. 2020.

Moore, Susanna. *Paradise of the Pacific: Approaching Hawaii*. New York: Farrar, Strauss and Giroux. 2015.

Mossholder, Diane L. "Save Outdoor Sculpture: A Community-Based Conservation Program." *Getty Conservation Institute Newsletter*. Spring 2007.

Nakamura, Kelli. "Spark Matsunaga." *Densho Encyclopedia*. Last updated June 10, 2015.

National Park Service DataStore. Kalaupapa and Kalawao Settlements: Cultural Landscape Inventory Report, Kalaupapa National Historical Park. 2011. Accessed February 18, 2023.

Oaks, Robert F. *Hawaii: A History of the Big Island*. Arcadia Publishing. 2003.

Oaks, Robert F. "The and Now: The Mysterious Death of David Douglas." *KeOla Magazine*. Jan-Feb 2013.

Pactol, Catherine Cluett. "Brother Dutton Gifted to Molokai." The Moloka'i Dispatch. July 22, 2013.

Perlas, Marjorie. "The Untold Story of the Hawaiian Cowboy." Culture Trip. Com June 26, 2018.

Pignataro, Anthony. "Remembering Pundy." *MauiTime*. December 21, 2006.

Polynesian Voyaging Society. "Ku Holo La Komohana/Sail on the Western Sun: Celebrating over 125 years of Historical Connections and Intercultural exchanges between Hawai'i and Japan." 2007

Ponton, Evan A. and Philip H. Scharper Jr. *Catholic Churches of Hawai'i: A Shoal of Faith*. Mutual Publishing. 2018.

Price, John. "Where have all the Treasures Gone?" *Times Colonist*. March 26, 2017.

Proffitt, Aaron P. "Who Was Kobo Daishi?" *Tricycle, The Buddhist Review*. Summer 2018.

Rhoden, Giselle and Dailila Paul. "73 Confederate monuments were removed or renames last year, report finds." *CNN*. February 3, 2022.

Sabakibesm Rebecca. "Papa and Wakea: The Hawaiian Creation Story." *Ke Alaka'i*. November 15, 2013.

Seiden, Allan. *Hawai'i: The Royal Legacy*. Mutual Publishing. 1992.

Seiden, Allan. *Lili'uokalani: A Royal Album*. Mutual Publishing. 2017.

Shepard, F.P., G.A. Macdonald, and D.C. Cox. "The Tsunami of April 1, 1946." Scripps Institution of Oceanography *Bulletin*, UC San Diego. 1949.

Sigall, Bob. "Rear View Mirror." December 3, 2021. *Honolulu Star Advertiser*.

Soboleski,Hank. "Kauai's Spalding Monument." *The Garden Island*. April 29, 2018.

Sun, Dr. Lily Sui-fong, Editor. *An Album in Memory of Dr. Sun Yat-sen*. Private collection. Fourth Edition. 2018.

Sweeney, Catherine. "Grand Wailea Art: It's in Their DNA." *Traveling With Sweeney* Blog. May 3, 2013. Accessed September 28, 2022.

Takaki, Ronald. *Pau Hana: Plantation Life and Labor in Hawaii 1835-1920*. University of Hawai'i Press. 1983.

Tanabe, George J. and Willa Jane. *Japanese Buddhist Temples in Hawaii: An Illustrated Guide*. University of Hawai'i Press. 2013.

Thayer, Matthew. "Historic Pā'ia bell tower coming back to life." *The Maui News*. November 15, 2021.

Thayer, Matthew. "The Making of a Queen." *Supplement of the Maui News*. February 26, 1995.

The Herald Times. "Artist sculpts St. Damien statue for Pahoa Church." January 6, 2012.

Uechi, Colleen. “Queen Ka‘ahumanu at 250: March 17, 1768-June 5, 1832.” *The Maui News*. April 18, 2022.

US House of Representatives. History, Art & Archives. “Spark Masayuki Matsunaga.” ND. Accessed September 12, 2022.

Vorsino, Mary. “70 Years on, April Fools’ Day tsunami painful reminder of ocean’s destructive force.” Hawaii News Now. April 2, 2016.

Weaver, Anna. “St. Joseph, Kamalo, Molokai: one of several churches constructed by Father Damien.” *Hawaii Catholic Herald*. August 18, 2021.

Wharton, Glenn. *The Painted King: Art, Activism, and Authenticity in Hawai‘i*. University of Hawai‘i Press. 2012.

Wizinowich, Jan. “Shine On: The Peace Poles of Hawai‘i Island.” *Ke Ola*. Jan-Feb. 2022.

Wolforth, Tom. “King Kamehameha’s Conquest of Hawaii.” *Warfare History Network*. ND. Accessed September 28, 2022.

Wolman, David and Julian Smith. *Aloha Rodeo: Three Hawaiian Cowboys, The World’s Greatest Rodeo, and a Hidden History of the American West.* William Morrow (Harper Collins). 2019.

Wood, Paul. “The Hero Behind the Hero.” *Maui Nō Ka Oi Magazine*. ND. Accessed September 21, 2022.

Wood, Paul “The Other Maui Sun.” *Maui Nō Ka Oi Magazine*. ND. Accessed September 21, 2022.

Young, Peter T. “Catholicism in Hawai‘i.” *Ho‘okuleana* Blog. June 17, 2012.

Young, Peter T. “Kipu Kai.*” Images of Old Hawaii* Blog. March 11, 2020.

Young, Peter T. “Kapaa Japanese Stone Lantern (Ishdoro). *Images of Old Hawai‘i* Blog. March 18, 2020.

Young, Peter T. “Sun Mei.” *Ho‘okuleana* Blog. June 17, 2014. Accessed September 21, 2022.

Young, Peter T. “Marianne Cope.” *Images of Old Hawai‘i* Blog. February 27, 2022.

Young, Peter T. “Kapiolani House.” *Images of Old Hawai‘i* Blog. June 24, 2016.

Young, Peter T. “A Brief History of Whales in Hawaii.” *Ke Ola Magazine*. Jan-Feb 2013.

Young, Peter T. “Totem Poles.” *Images of Old Hawai‘i* Blog. April 28, 2020.

Young, Peter T. “Puerto Ricans.” *Images of Old Hawai‘i* Blog. November 22, 2015.

Zambucka. Kristin. *Kalākaua: Hawai‘i’s Last King*. Mutual Publishing. Original 1983. Reprint 2022.

Zarrella, Dale. *Portrait of an Artist*. Signature Book Printing. 2017.

Internet

www.lahainashingon.org

www.nps.gov/havo/learn/historyculture/paniolo.htm

https://paniolopreservation.org. “Monument Paniolo Pride.” July 27to, 2020.

https://ev.wikipedia.org/Kaumualii. Accessed February 28, 2022.

www.captaincooksociety.com/home/detail/statue-site-town-kaui-hawaiian-islands. Accessed March 3, 2022

https://en.wikipedia.org/org/wiki/James_Cook. Creative Commons Attribution—ShareAlike License 3.0 Accessed March 3, 2022.

www.nationalarchives.gov/uk/education/resources/captain-cook-in-hawaii. Accessed March 3, 2022.

www.history.com/this-day-in-history/cook-discovers-hawaii. Accessed March 3, 2022.

www.nps.gov/places/cook-landing-site.htm. Accessed March 3, 2022.

https://Nupepa Blog. March 23, 2014. Translation of "Monument to Kauikeaouli on his 100th birthday, 1914". *Nupepa Kuokoa*. 3/20/14

www.wikipedia.org/PaulIsenberg. Accessed April 3, 2022.

www.wikipedia.org/ZephaniahSwiftSpalding. Accessed April 3, 2022.

www.himalayanacademy.com accessed September 5, 2022.

www.wikipedia.org/SparkMatsunaga. Accessed September 12, 2022.

www.usip.org/spark-matsunaga-legacy. Accessed September 12, 2022.

www.peaceinstitute.manoa.hawaii.edu. Accessed September 12, 2022.

www.marialanakila.org. Accessed September 12, 2022.

www.kiheimemorial.org. Accessed September 19, 2022.

http://www.kinjudo.jp/index_e.html

www.verifythis.com. Jones, Erin. "Yes, there are Confederate Statues in the US Capitol's National Statuary Hall Collection." Accessed November 20, 2022.

www.hakusancreation.com/shugyo-daishi-and-the-pilgrim. William Ash by Hakusan Creation. Posted on August 22, 2014,

www.HiloHooganjiMission website. Mission History. Brief Timeline.

Hilodriving.com blog. October 2008.

National Park Service, Kalaupapa National Historical Park website.

www.damienchurch.org. Accessed February 18, 2023

www.sacredheartcatholicchurch.org. Accessed April 1, 2023.

HMdb.org. The Historical Marker Database. "Koloa, Birthplace of the Hawaiian Sugar Industry." Accessed April 11, 2023.

A

B

C

D

F

G

H

I

J

K

T

V

W

Y

Z